Routledge Revivals

New Methods in Reading Comprehension Research

Published in 1984, this volume presents methodologies for studying the ongoing psychological processes that occur as a person reads a text, as well as discussing the major findings that these methodologies have produced, to provide a handbook of reading comprehension research techniques.

Focusing on the comprehension processes that occur when a person is reading, rather than the representation that remains after the text has been read, the methodologies use measures such as reading times that reflect ongoing processes, rather than relying exclusively on conventional measures of memory performance such as recall. These methods make use of computer technology for rapid and flexible stimulus representation and data acquisition.

This book will allow researchers and students to select appropriate methodologies to investigate a range of fascinating questions about reading comprehension.

New Methods in Reading Comprehension Research

Edited by David E. Kieras and Marcel A. Just

First published in 1984
By Lawrence Erlbaum Associates, Inc.

This edition first published in 2018 by Routledge
2 Park Square, Milton Park, Abingdon, Oxon, OX14 4RN
and by Routledge
711 Third Avenue, New York, NY 10017

Routledge is an imprint of the Taylor & Francis Group, an informa business

© 1984 Lawrence Erlbaum Associates, Inc.

All rights reserved. No part of this book may be reprinted or reproduced or utilised in any form or by any electronic, mechanical, or other means, now known or hereafter invented, including photocopying and recording, or in any information storage or retrieval system, without permission in writing from the publishers.

Publisher's Note
The publisher has gone to great lengths to ensure the quality of this reprint but points out that some imperfections in the original copies may be apparent.

Disclaimer
The publisher has made every effort to trace copyright holders and welcomes correspondence from those they have been unable to contact.

A Library of Congress record exists under LCCN: 84001499

ISBN 13: 978-1-138-58525-6 (hbk)
ISBN 13: 978-0-429-50537-9 (ebk)
ISBN 13: 978-1-138-58527-0 (pbk)

NEW METHODS IN READING COMPREHENSION RESEARCH

Edited by:

David E. Kieras
University of Arizona

Marcel A. Just
Carnegie-Mellon University

LEA LAWRENCE ERLBAUM ASSOCIATES, PUBLISHERS
1984   Hillsdale, New Jersey   London

Copyright © 1984 by Lawrence Erlbaum Associates, Inc.
All rights reserved. No part of this book may be reproduced in
any form, by photostat, microform, retrieval system, or any other
means, without the prior written permission of the publisher.

Lawrence Erlbaum Associates, Inc., Publishers
365 Broadway
Hillsdale, New Jersey 07642

Library of Congress Cataloging in Publication Data
Main entry under title:

New methods in reading comprehension research.

Papers presented at a conference at the University
of Arizona, Dec. 10–11, 1981.
Bibliography: p.
Includes indexes.
1. Reading comprehension—Research—Congresses.
2. Reading—Research—Congresses. I. Kieras, David E.
II. Just, Marcel Adam.
LB1050.45.N49 1984   428.4'3'072   84-1499
ISBN 0-89859-364-6

Printed in the United States of America
10 9 8 7 6 5 4 3 2 1

To Our Children

No Our Children

CONTENTS

Preface   xiii

1. **The Influence of Methodologies on Psycholinguistic Research: A Regression to the Whorfian Hypothesis**   3
   Patricia A. Carpenter
   - Statistical Tools   4
   - Chronometric Paradigms   9
   - Summary   11

2. **A Survey of Some Important Techniques and Issues in Multiple Regression**   13
   George P. Knight
   - Overview of Multiple Regression   14
   - Collinearity   16
   - Measurement Error and Shrinkage   22
   - Repeated Measures Design   26
   - Other Least Square Linear Model Techniques   28

3. **The Word-by-Word Reading Paradigm: An Experimental and Theoretical Approach**   31
   Doris Aaronson and Steven Ferres
   - The Reading Procedure   32
   - The Experimental Variables   33

A Quality Research Tool 35
The Underlying Assumptions 39
Reading Units 42
Processing Load 45
Theoretical Development 47
Model Components 48
Reading Strategies in Children and Adults 50
The Time Course of Reading for Retention 58
Summary and Conclusions 63

4. **An Evaluation of Subject-Paced Reading Tasks and Other Methods for Investigating Immediate Processes in Reading**   69
D. C. Mitchell
Introduction 69
The Problem of Processing Spillover 71
The Subject-Paced Reading Task 73
The RSVP Task 76
Eye-Monitoring 79
Advantages and Disadvantages of
   Various Immediate Processing Methods 80
Substantive Findings Obtained with
   Our Techniques 82
Brief Conclusions 87

5. **Rapid Serial Visual Presentation (RSVP): A Method for Studying Language Processing**   91
Mary C. Potter
Introduction 91
Details of RSVP Methodology 92
Characteristics of RSVP Reading 97
RSVP Compared with Other Methods 98
Questions About RSVP as a Method 100
Research Using RSVP 110
Applied Questions About RSVP 114
Conclusions 115

6. **Priming and On-Line Text Comprehension**   119
Gail McKoon and Roger Ratcliff
Experiment 1: Activation of Concepts 120
Experiment 2: Organization of
   Information in Memory 121

Automatic and Strategic Processes in Priming 122
Priming Compared with Other On-Line Measures 125

7. **Eye Movements and Reading Comprehension** 129
   Keith Rayner and Patrick J. Carroll
   Issues and Problems in the Use of
      Eye Movement Data in Studying
      Reading Comprehension 130
   Eye Movements and Language Processing 134
   Summary 147

8. **Using Eye Fixations to Study Reading Comprehension** 151
   Marcel A. Just and Patricia A. Carpenter
   Methodological Issues 152
   Substantive Results 166
   Conclusion 179
   Appendix 181

9. **An Application of Multiple Regression Techniques to Sentence Reading Times** 183
   Arthur C. Graesser and James R. Riha
   Overview of Methodology 183
   Materials and Procedure 184
   Predictor Variables 186
   Problems and Issues in Applying
      Multiple Regression 193
   Results 200
   Summary 209
   Theoretical Conclusions and Issues 210
   Limitations of the Approach 214

10. **Components of Sentence and Word Reading Times** 219
    Karl Haberlandt
    General Assumptions of On-Line Methods 220
    Background for Research on
       Story Comprehension 222
    Reading Time Analysis by Multiple Regression 223
    Conclusion 244

11. **Thinking-Out-Loud as a Method for Studying Real-Time Comprehension Processes** 253
    Gary M. Olson, Susan A. Duffy, and Robert L. Mack
    The Use of Thinking-Out-Loud Protocols 254
    Types of Thinking-Out-Loud Tasks 257

Examples of Thinking-Out-Loud Data 261
Related Applications of TOL 279
Why Do TOL Data Produce Varying Results? 281
Summary and Conclusions 283

12. Coordinating Discovery and Verification Research 287
John B. Black, James A. Galambos, and Brian J. Reiser
Naturalistic Observation 288
Augmented Clustering 289
Systematic Questioning 292
Verbal Protocols 294
Conclusions 296

13. A Method for Comparing a Simulation to Reading Time Data 299
David E. Kieras
Simulation Models of Comprehension 300
The General Problem of
  Evaluating Simulations 301
The Method 306
Examples of Using the Method 310
Conclusion 323

14. Prose Comprehension and the Management of Working Memory 327
James R. Miller
Working Memory as
  Propositional Graph Structures 328
Working Memory as
  Integrated Text-Knowledge Structures 333
Syntactic Constraints on Conceptual Focus in
  Working Memory 337
Semantic Constraints on Conceptual Focus in
  Working Memory 340
Summary 344

15. Developing a Computer Model of Reading Times 349
Marcel A. Just and Robert H. Thibadeau
Constraints on the Model 350
Deciding to Use a
  Production System Architecture 350

Designing an Appropriate
   Production System Architecture   352
A Brief Overview of READER's Properties   354
The Mechanisms of Reading   355
The Use of Multiple Regression in
   This Approach   361
Summary   363

Author Index   **365**

Subject Index   **373**

PREFACE

The goal of this volume is to present some recently developed methodologies for studying the ongoing psychological processes that occur as a person reads a text, as well as presenting some of the major findings that these new methodologies have produced. The contributors were asked to provide a reasonably complete summary of the methodology they have developed, so that the various chapters together constitute a handbook of reading comprehension research techniques. They were also asked to provide a summary of their main results, so the chapters also provide an overview of the emerging characteristics of on-line comprehension processes. Those characteristics that repeatedly emerge in different chapters using different methodologies seem particularly worthy of attention. We hope that researchers and students will find the volume useful in selecting methodologies to investigate a range of fascinating questions about reading comprehension.

The methodologies described in the volume have all emerged since about 1975, perhaps because they have certain properties in common. First, they focus on the comprehension processes that are occurring as a person is reading, rather than on the representation that remains after the text has been read. Consequently, they use on-line measures such as reading times that reflect the ongoing processes, rather than relying exclusively on conventional measures of memory performance such as recall. These methods thus make use of recent computer technology for rapid and flexible stimulus presentation and data acquisition. Second, they tend to use regression analysis to provide some degree of statistical control over the variation in fairly naturalistic stimuli. Third, they tend to produce or be expressed in terms of fairly comprehensive theories of comprehension, which try to account for the many component processes of comprehension, and their interaction. Some of the more complex models are in the form of computer simulations.

The first major feature of the new method, an interest in the process, as opposed to the products, of comprehension, requires measures of various aspects of processing. One relatively direct measure is the amount of time taken to read a given portion of a text, such as a word or a sentence. The most popular way to collect this measure involves some type of self-paced paradigm, in which the subject controls the presentations of successive portions of the textual input. The use of eye-movement data is perhaps the most refined form of self-paced paradigm, in that it uses the subject's natural method of controlling the time course of the textual input. Another way to obtain information on comprehension as it is occurring is by collecting thinking-out-loud (TOL) protocols as a person reads a text. Several researchers have recently applied this technique to the process of prose comprehension, although its characteristics are rather different from the reading time approach. Finally, there are a set of indirect ways to investigate the comprehension process, which examine the products of comprehension, but using input manipulations and testing conditions that are closely related to the processing itself. Two such techniques are the Rapid Serial Visual Presentation (RSVP) technique and the priming technique.

The second major feature of the new methodologies is the use of multiple regression rather than analysis of variance. The reason for the use of multiple regression is that it easily deals with large amounts of data that reflect the influence of several continuous independent variables on a single dependent variable. Reading time experiments typically involve measuring or manipulating a large number of independent variables associated with each unit of text, and making one observation, the reading time, for every unit of the input. If the units are small, such as sentences or words, a large amount of data is obtained. Multiple regression thus is the natural statistical treatment of the data. This application has a few problems, but the results are generally very informative.

The third major feature of the new methods is that they are typically used in conjunction with complex and detailed models and theories of reading comprehension. In some ways this is only natural, in that the experimental paradigms and the statistical analysis involves working at a level of detail which is considerably beyond earlier work. Thus it is natural that the theoretical work would also be involved with much more detail. Several of the chapters in this volume make use of elaborate process models stated in the conventional verbal form, but some of them also make use of a more precise form of theoretical statement, namely that of computer simulation models. The use of such detailed theoretical models, together with data collection and analysis methods that involve a similar level of detail, allows the researcher to address comprehension processes at an unusually high level of precision. This commitment to a detailed analysis of comprehension is the key feature of the new methods.

OVERVIEW OF THE CHAPTERS

The first two papers, by Carpenter and Knight, present some very general methodological issues that span the rest of the papers in the volume. Carpenter's paper is on the influence of the new methods on psycholinguistic research. Drawing on the analogy of the influence of analysis of variance on experimental psychology, Carpenter points out some of the ways in which the growing reliance on multiple regression might influence the research on reading comprehension. She points out some of the important advantages, and especially the limitations, of multiple regression, with particular focus on the issue of the relative "importance" of independent variables, which reappears in many of the other chapters. Along with this, she points out an important issue about the nature of model fitting, that should act as a good antidote to the tendency to overuse overall goodness-of-fit measures. Finally, she points out some of the limitations of the current chronometric paradigms that are now so popular. This paper provides an excellent introduction to the entire volume, and may help temper some of the understandable enthusiasm that many of the contributors feel for these new methods.

Since multiple regression is used so frequently in these new methods, it was important to have a treatment of some central features of this statistical technique. Knight's contribution is especially useful in that it goes beyond a simple tutorial on standard features of the technique, which can be found in many textbooks, to present some of the more specialized, or little known, uses of multiple regression and some of the related techniques. For example, he summarizes the most efficient way to correctly analyze a within-subject design using multiple regression. Thus, Knight's chapter provides a good entry point into the multiple regression literature for those researchers who want to use this technique in its full range of abilities. Other introductory material on multiple regression can be found in many of the chapters, with Haberlandt's chapter especially recommended.

The remaining chapters in the book have been ordered roughly in an order of increasingly higher levels of processing. Thus, Aaronson and Ferres, Mitchell, Potter, and McKoon and Ratcliff deal mainly with time data gathered in single-word paradigms, Rayner and Carroll and Just and Carpenter use eye-movement data, and Haberlandt and Graesser and Riha deal primarily with reading times for entire sentences. The Olson, Duffy, and Mack and the Black, Galambos, and Reiser papers are on think-out-loud protocols. The final papers in the volume are based on the most elaborate available theories of reading, namely simulation models. These are the papers by Kieras, Miller, and Just and Thibadeau.

Aaronson's work on word-by-word reading times stands out as one of the earliest instances of these new methods. The Aaronson and Ferres chapter provides a thorough presentation of the methodological details of collecting word-by-word reading times, and an approach to developing mathematical models of these reading times, followed by some of the substantive results that have been obtained using this paradigm.

The paper by Mitchell provides a valuable service of evaluating three different major methodologies, namely the self-paced word-by-word procedure, the RSVP procedure, and priming tasks. Mitchell evaluates the advantages and limitations of each of these techniques, with special attention paid to the *spillover* question. The concern is whether the time spent on reading individual units of text accurately reflects the processing time on those units, or whether the processing of previously presented units could "spill over" into the processing of the current unit. This issue appears in some of the other papers, especially those by Aaronson and Ferres, Just and Carpenter, and Potter. Mitchell goes on to present a collection of substantive results obtained with these methods, which argue for a general conclusion that the role of top-down processing in comprehension is not as important as many have been led to believe.

Potter's paper on RSVP methodology provides an excellent presentation of this technique, along with many of the specific details involved in setting up an experiment. She also provides a helpful discussion of how RSVP methods compare to other comprehension methodologies. Most of the other methods presented in this book involve some kind of measure of reading time as the major dependent variable. But, the RSVP approach controls the reading time, and uses some post-reading measure, such as recall, as the major dependent variable. But, the primary concern is still on processing time, making the RSVP method a useful way to approach on-line processing. Potter's paper provides a broad summary of many substantive issues that can be addressed with the RSVP technique.

The chapter by McKoon and Ratcliff describes a technique that attempts to measure the strength of a given piece of the text representation. A probe stimulus is presented during or after the presentation of the text, and the subject's response time to the probe indicates whether a given concept had or had not been primed or activated by the text at the time when the probe was presented. By varying the point at which the probe is presented, one can examine the change in status of a given representation over time during the course of reading.

The papers by Rayner and Carroll and Just and Carpenter describe eye-movement methodologies, which provide the finest-grain performance measures. The Rayner and Carroll chapter provides an eloquent summary of the methodology along with a description of the major problems in applying the methodology. These problems are primarily concerned with the temporal relationship between the eye fixations and the cognitive processing involved. A strong form of this relationship, argued for by Just and Carpenter, is that the current cognitive processing is exactly reflected in what the eye is looking at. Various weaker forms, that the movement of the eye is not so closely linked to the on-going processing, would suggest that eye-movement data should not be interpreted so directly. However, Rayner and Carroll point out that despite this controversial issue regarding the interpretation of eye-movement data, much has been learned about reading using this technique.

The Just and Carpenter chapter describes the eye fixation methodology that they have developed over the last several years, specifying many of the methodological assumptions that underlie the data analysis and interpretation. It also provides a discussion of the major substantive results obtained with this paradigm.

The two papers by Graesser and Riha and Haberlandt represent the use of multiple regression analysis to account for the reading times on entire sentences as a function of empirically defined variables. The Graesser and Riha chapter presents a summary of the considerations that are important in doing such an analysis, using as an example a large and complex data set that provides information on the relationship of reading time to comprehension scores and individual differences between readers. This chapter has considerable practical detail on identifying and defining the many possible empirical variables. The Haberlandt chapter contains some excellent general material on the use of multiple regression in reading time analyses, with special attention paid to some of the assumptions of multiple regression. This chapter, like Haberlandt's earlier work, provides a good illustration of how multiple regression can be used with reading times in a complex theoretical analysis involving story schemas.

The chapters by Olson, Duffy, and Mack and by Black, Galambos, and Reiser concern the use of thinking-out-loud (TOL) data as a way to get at the cognitive processes going on during reading. The Olson, Duffy, and Mack chapter provides a comprehensive discussion of how this kind of work can best be done, as well as describing the unique results they have obtained with this method. The Black, Galambos, and Reiser chapter argues that the thinking-out-loud methodology is a valuable discovery procedure to produce initial hypotheses about comprehension processes. They point out that hypothesis discovery methods are little used and little understood, and provide a useful discussion of how this can be remedied.

The final three papers in the volume are distinguished by their reliance on an explicit computer simulation model of comprehension. The Kieras chapter presents a straightforward methodology that allows a complex computer simulation to be compared directly to reading time data. This can be used with any simulation model where it is reasonable to assume that the processes are additive with regard to processing time. The chapter by Miller takes a more general approach, and considers not only issues of data collection and analysis in the light of a simulation model, but also some of the important considerations in devising a simulation model for comprehension. The Just and Thibadeau paper is a compact description of the READER model, with a focus on how this model was compared to the eye fixation data obtained using the methods described in the Just and Carpenter chapter. This chapter provides a useful example of how an extremely complex simulation model can be compared to empirical data in various ways.

ACKNOWLEDGEMENT

The chapters in this volume were originally presented at a conference at the University of Arizona, December 10-11, 1981. Support for the conference and the preparation of this volume has been provided by the Office of Naval Research and the Army Research Institute for the Behavioral and Social Sciences, under Grant Number N00014-81-G-0107, NR 157-472. These agencies have shown a continuing commitment to sponsoring research on language comprehension that has contributed significantly to the progress in the field.

David E. Kieras
Marcel A. Just

NEW METHODS
IN READING
COMPREHENSION
RESEARCH

1 The Influence of Methodologies on Psycholinguistic Research: A Regression to the Whorfian Hypothesis[1]

Patricia A. Carpenter
Carnegie-Mellon University

Benjamin Whorf once proposed that the properties of a natural language influence the thought processes of the speakers of that language—that linguistic structures are the molds into which molten thoughts are poured, making some thoughts almost impossible and others almost inevitable. A frequent example concerns the Eskimo language, which is reported to have seven different words to describe various types of snow. The psychological question often asked is whether Eskimos perceive snow differently from those of us who have an impoverished lexicon with which to label the cold, white stuff. While the strong version of Whorf's hypothesis found little support, the weaker version continues to hold some intellectual attraction. But my main interest in this paper is not in either the strong or weak version of the Whorfian hypothesis. Instead, I would like to use the Whorfian hypothesis to make an analogy. In several important ways, the research methodologies used in a science are a large part of the language of the science. In this paper, I will discuss how methodologies influence the content and theories of any science, and consider the specific instance of the methodologies used in the study of comprehension.

The physical sciences provide striking case studies in which the methods and technology determined the theories, as much as the theory determined the development of new methods and tools. In biology, the quantum improvement on the microscope by Leewenhoek and those who followed him in the early 18th century led to the concept of the cell, and the rise of the theory that gave the cell

---

[1]The chapter was written while the author was a Fellow at the Netherlands Institute for Advanced Study.

prominence as the fundamental building block of biological structures. More recent technological advances, such as the electron microscope, have changed biology's focus from taxonomy and description to an emphasis on subcellular structure and function. In the social sciences, the tools are often less technological than the microscope or cyclotron, and tend to be conceptual tools instead. This dependence on conceptual tools coupled with the much shorter history of the social sciences makes it more difficult to point to methods that have clearly influenced the direction and content of these fields. Perhaps the best candidate for the role of major shaping force is the rise of quantitative analysis, particularly statistics.

The point of this exercise is not to determine whether methodologies or intrinsic scientific factors have more influence on the development of a science. The wise philosopher of science would immediately concede that both factors have an influence, and interact with each other. But the current discussion will be less responsible. I have decided to be one-sided and focus exclusively on the influence methodologies may have in channeling and shaping the current concepts in psychology, and in language research specifically. To echo Whorf's question, would we perceive our scientific world differently if we had a different methodological vocabulary?

STATISTICAL TOOLS

Statistical analysis is probably the most pervasive methodological tool in psychological research, often providing a common set of assumptions that span various sub-disciplines, such as personality, social, perception, and cognition. Just as technologies influence sciences, so do the conceptual tools inherent in the use of particular statistical techniques. To illustrate this point, it is easier to look at the issue historically, before considering the implications of the more recent innovations.

The Analysis of Variance

One common type of statistical analysis is the Analysis of Variance—the ANOVA. ANOVAs are so much a part of psychological research that it is difficult to find any general statistics book written for graduate psychology that omits the ANOVA. In spite of the current pervasiveness of the ANOVA, its rise and institutionalization in psychology occurred only in the last thirty years, as described by Rucci and Tweney (1980). The basic formulation of the ANOVA was presented by Fisher in the late 1920's. From the mid-1930's until the mid-1940's, a considerable number of expository articles appeared in the psychological literature describing the ANOVA as applied to psychology. In addition, there was a steady increase in the number of articles that used ANOVA as an analysis technique (except for a brief interruption caused by World War II). Also appearing in the 1940's were the first statistics textbooks designed especially for psychological research, which further disseminated the ANOVA. By the early 1950's, statistical methods became an intrinsic part of experimental psychology when graduate courses in statistics for psychology were established. By the 1980's, the assumption can be made that a psychologist from any research area at least understands the terms *F distribution, error term,* and *degrees of freedom.* So even though ANOVA sometimes seems like an inherent part of psychological research, it has not always been with us. The intriguing question, of course, is what its role and influence has been on the scientific development of psychology.

It might be too strong a statement to say that the institutionalization of the ANOVA caused a shift in thinking, but a shift seems to have occurred at about the same time ANOVA started to be used extensively. Rucci and Tweney note that the rise of the ANOVA was correlated with the demise of the single variable law in psychology. Coupled with the demise was shift to consideration of multiple, conjoint determinants of behavior. In part, this shift may have been due to the fact that the ANOVA facilitates thinking about the effects of several variables, that is, cross classification and the interaction among variables. One might also speculate about other, more recent influences of the ANOVA on the field. For instance, the availability of the ANOVA among experimental psychologists probably facilitated the dissemination and impact of Sternberg's additive factors methodology (Sternberg, 1969).

To push this methodological Whorfianism a little farther, we can consider how the "language" of the ANOVA shapes our conceptions of psychological issues. My hypothesis is that ANOVA permits and encourages issues to be framed and conceptualized in terms of nominal, or essentially qualitative, variables. Nominal variables, as introductory statistics books explain, are those without an underlying metric. Thus, it is possible to classify words as abstract or concrete, frequent or infrequent, pronounceable or unpronounceable and so on. These are examples of continuous quantitative variables that have been dichotomized or trichotomized, and each level treated as distinct from the others. The implicit assumption may be that there is no underlying metric. The consequences of having a method for showing that different levels of a factor affect behavior differently is that researchers are "encouraged" to search for differences, rather than the mechanisms that account for the differences.

Multiple Regression

The ANOVA is of course a special case of multiple regression. However, the conceptual difference between the two statistical tools may be larger than their formal mathematical relation would suggest. Regression techniques are convenient for exploring interval or ratio variables, those that have a continuous, or quantitative, underlying dimension. One of the important products of the regression analysis is the regression weight, which expresses how much the dependent variable (i.e. some aspect of the behavior) changes as a function of a unit of change in the independent variable (i.e. some aspect of the stimulus). Rather than simply determining whether long words take significantly longer to pronounce than short words, the regression model quantifies the amount of increase as a function of length. Such a mathematical result appears closer to the enterprise of model building than does the confirmation or disconfirmation of a difference among conditions. Obviously, not all interesting scientific issues involve quantitative stimulus dimensions. Even those that do might not involve a linear or continuous function to relate the independent and dependent variables. Nevertheless, it is interesting to speculate how current experimental psychology might be different if multiple regression had been the technique that was institutionalized in the discipline, with the ANOVA as a special case, rather than the reverse.

The Effect-Size Question. The few examples of regression analysis that already exist in the psycholinguistics literature suggest one way in which the tool has a subtle influence on its users. The R-squared measure in the regression analysis seems to lead researchers to ask about the importance of each variable in the regression equation. In the extreme, this becomes a step-wise regression in which variables are entered one at a time, and the computation of interest is the residual variance accounted for by each variable after the preceding variables have been entered. Of course, the analogous questions could be asked in ANOVA designs, but they seldom are, in spite of the suggestions of some authors (cf. Dwyer, 1974; Hays, 1963).

To ask about the importance of a particular effect, or more precisely, its underlying process, is a worthwhile concern. However, it is incorrect to assume that the R-squared measure provides the answer. The R-squared measure indicates the size of an effect in a given study, but not the importance of the process. The R-squared measure gives the variance accounted for by a given factor, but this estimate is not an inherent property of the factor. The estimate depends on the variation of that factor relative to the variation of other factors in the task. The implications of this become clearer if one considers a common example such as the variable of word length. In most reading experiments with natural text, word length accounts for a large proportion of the variation in gaze duration on a word. The unwary might be tempted to conclude that the process affected by word length is a particularly important one. But such a conclusion fails to consider that word length has such a large effect because it varies so widely, from words like *a, of, by* to *thermoluminescence,* and *microbiological.* Different variances and different R-squares would be obtained if the same readers were given texts in which the word lengths varied only a little (a restriction that occurs in many word perception experiments). This is just one reason why it is fallacious to equate the R-squared measure with the importance of an underlying process.

In order to assess the importance of a given subprocess in a task, the term *importance* must be specified more precisely than just the layman's sense. One possible specification is to consider practical importance, in the sense of determining performance in a "real-world" situation. In that case, the process should be evaluated in a context that approximates the situation to be explained. Both the size of the effect of the process, and the necessity or frequency of the process contribute to its practical importance. An alternative specification of importance can be in terms of theory development. Even a process that produces only a small effect or operates infrequently may be necessary to explain how a system works in particular contexts, and hence, may be theoretically important. Thus, the "importance" of a factor is a context-sensitive issue. The usefulness of evaluating importance is that it encourages researchers to explicitly consider the context of the process and model that is being evaluated.

It is difficult to assess more general effects that regression models might have in psychological research, since their use is too limited and recent. However, one way to indulge in such hypothetical reasoning, while minimizing its science-fiction character, is to examine a field in which this tool has been widely used. Then we can see whether there are lessons to be learned by example. Regression models lend themselves to this exercise quite easily, since they have been the workhorse of the sub-discipline of econometrics. We can see whether some of the successes and failures of this field hold any moral for psychology.

The Lessons of Econometrics. Part of economics cannot be an experimental science, since its domain includes large-scale economies. Economics requires tools for analyzing existing data on factors such as supply and demand, consumption, investment, and so on. This area embraced and developed regression techniques as a major analytic tool, and is called econometrics. This field has been so permeated by quantitative techniques, particularly regression models, that many textbooks on econometrics resemble advanced statistics books, with the content of specific economic theories relegated to appendices. While psychology and psycholinguistics differ from economics in that they are primarily experimental sciences, they too have a need for correlational techniques. Not every variable of interest can be controlled or systematically manipulated. Regression is useful when the uncontrolled variable is just a nuisance variable, so that the effects of the remaining variables can be examined after the effect of the nuisance variable has been partialled out. As in economics, regression also can be used to examine complex relations that cannot be manipulated experimentally. A good example is individual differences, which generally is not manipulated since we cannot experimentally create good and poor readers. Other manipulations require such large amounts of time or resources that they are not practical or feasible to manipulate, such as the effect of schooling or long-term training on the acquisition of language skills. As psycholinguistic research explores more complex situations, its methodological tools may increasingly resemble those that have been of use in other social sciences.

In spite of the differences between fields, we can examine econometrics for potential lessons concerning the role and limitations of regression analysis. One lesson that appears in this literature is that regression models are useful for identifying the variables that enter into a particular process. A weakness of the tool, however, is that the specific weights and exact parameters may easily be overinterpreted. Regression techniques do not discriminate very well between models with the same variables but with different functions, such as models that include vs. exclude interactions. Regression techniques may be most useful for establishing the variables and general aspects of their quantitative function, but then experimental tools are needed to explore processing details. A second lesson is that econometrics has sometimes degenerated into the rote application of statistical analyses without commensurate gains in the theory development. But this seems to be a danger with every new paradigm and methodology, and we can find instances within our own field without taking lessons from others. Beyond these general lessons, there are some technical issues that have been explored in considerable detail in the econometrics literature, including issues such as multi-collinearity, inferring causality, and so on, that may be of use to psychologists who are just beginning to use this tool.

The Purpose of Model Fitting

Now, I would like to go to a more abstract level and discuss the rationale for model fitting — assessing the fit between a model and some data. The argument I am going to expand upon is one that I encountered in a 1962 article by David Grant in which he talked about fitting models that were developed from mathematical learning theory. The models were probabilistic, but like some current modelling efforts, mathematical learning models made predictions about a number of aspects of the data — some with more success than others. Those researchers also faced the issue of fitting the predicted characteristics to the observed ones. One type of answer that was common then and is still used now is to compute an overall measure of fit. The model-fitting exercise was considered to be successful if the deviations were minor and non-significant. The ironic aspect of this approach, as Grant pointed out, was that the sloppier the data, the more likely one was to find non-significant differences between the predictions and the observations. The more careful the study, the more likely the researcher would have to contend with the sticky issue of significant discrepancies between the model's behavior and Mother Nature's. Grant suggested a particular statistical solution to the paradox, a solution that included two statistical tests: one for the goodness of fit and one for the non-randomness of the deviations. Of more interest than his particular statistical procedure, however, is the general rationale he gave for model fitting.

Grant argued that the statistical approach of testing the null hypothesis against the alternative hypothesis provides a misleading characterization of the scientific enterprise. Researchers are not in the position of accepting or rejecting hypotheses like a quality control supervisor on an assembly line. Our actual task is the long-range process of explaining phenomena. Hence, we should not test a model to determine if it is true (after all, no model can be proven true) or even to determine if it is false (in real life, we seldom deal with models that are truly useless). We should test a model to determine how it should be improved. This rationale has implications for how we evaluate the usefulness of a statistical method. An overall test of goodness of fit provides a ballpark estimate but in practice may not be very useful for improving the model. For that, we need a more detailed analysis of exactly where the model breaks down. In other words, a useful analysis is one that looks for systematic error variance in the data. In some sense, that is part of the technique of analyzing residuals that Karl Haberlandt described. Systematic deviations are much more useful and important for theory development than are general goodness of fit measures.

CHRONOMETRIC PARADIGMS

Statistical tools are only one component of research methodology. Another aspect includes the paradigms themselves. A central component of many of the chapters in this volume is a concern with the time course or chronometric aspects of comprehension. This is true of the papers that attempt to estimate the time course, either by measuring the reading time for single words using the button-pressing paradigm (Mitchell, Aaronson, Haberlandt), or eye fixations (Just and Carpenter, Rayner), or the time on clauses or sentences (Kieras, Olson). It is also true of those methodologies that attempt to control exposure time, such as the RSVP technique (Potter). Why is there such an interest in the temporal aspects of processing?

In some cases, the time course of a process has practical implications. For example, if there is some minimal time required for comprehension or some optimal time, then these parameters can be used in presenting the material in a more efficient manner. This is part of the idea behind RSVP or, for that matter, speedreading. But the major reason is that estimating a certain temporal parameter or even knowing how various linguistic and discourse structures increase comprehension time will help constrain the possible models and, in the appropriate circumstances, provide information concerning the sequence of processes.

The emphasis on chronometry may influence theory building or play a role in selecting which questions are explored. Does the fact that there are several sophisticated techniques for measuring and analyzing quantitative estimates of the time course of comprehension have such influences? My suggestion is that it may lead us to pursue quantitative differences to the exclusion of more qualitative ones. One area in which this argument can be made is that of individual differences. Many researchers have now shown that poorer readers take longer to access letter and word codes than good readers. But we shouldn't assume that this quantitative difference accounts for the qualitative differences we observe among people who read the same story or students who read the same text. The comprehension differences may be due partly to some process taking longer. It may also be due to qualitative differences in processing or knowledge that lead to the information being treated differently by different comprehenders. The chronometric approach may lead us to focus on quantitative differences to the exclusion of qualitative differences.

Another way that chronometric approaches may blind us to qualitative differences is by tempting investigators to examine only those types of tasks in which the strategic (and hence qualitative) differences are minimized. This may not be a bad research strategy, as long as we remember that many naturally occurring situations are superabundantly rich in the number of different strategies they can evoke. The qualitative measures like protocol analysis and question-answering and recall techniques (such as those described by Olson and Graesser) should be used to complement chronometric studies. These other methodologies allow inferences about the products of comprehension. They allow a researcher to explore miscomprehensions or idiosyncratic inferences that might be missed with techniques that depend entirely on averaging across instances or readers. Methodologies are tools that often produce firmer structures when they are used in combination with each other. Although it is current practice in journal articles to present several experiments that converge on a common hypothesis, the convergence is usually based on the effects of different kinds of manipulations (i.e. independent variables) rather than different methodologies. It would probably be at least as beneficial to use converging methodologies in the study of comprehension to link quantitative effects with qualitative measures of the products of comprehension.

Finally, a more subtle influence of these paradigms may be in restricting the range of questions that are explored. Many aspects of language comprehension and production do not fit easily into the chronometric mold. One of these aspects is the interactive nature of communication in spoken language. The study of text comprehension deals with text that is static and its properties specifiable using linguistic and discourse analysis. The reader cannot alter or affect the communication. Even listening comprehension, as it is usually studied, treats the text as a fixed quality. But this shouldn't blind us to the fact that language is a social tool for interaction and not only one-way channel. The comprehension process in a conversation may have significant components that are totally absent in reading comprehension experiments.

The second aspect of comprehension that is sometimes ignored within cognitive psychology is the affective side of reading. Outside of the laboratory, people read biographies that inspire them or engender warmth for the protagonist, they read thrillers that scare them or a Woody Allen essay that makes them laugh. But stimulus texts in comprehension experiments tend to be affectless. Even if we are primarily interested in research with potential pedagogical implications, the motivational components of reading — reading for the emotional satisfaction that accompanies the content — is an important educational consideration. We also know from studies on attitude change that the persuasiveness of an argument depends partially on how affect-laden the issue is. Cognition and comprehension in particular, do not occur in the absence of affect.

SUMMARY

My conclusion is that methodology and substance have a way of blending into each other, so that it is difficult to trace their separate contributions. Following the Whorfian analogy, I have tried to suggest ways in which our present theories and approaches to how people read, understand, and think may be influenced by the way we can measure and quantify their behavior. While we need statistical tools and paradigms, we need not use them without considering their usefulness and limitations. We should build and test our methodologies as carefully as we do our theories.

REFERENCES

Dwyer, J.H. Analysis of variance and the magnitude of effects: A general approach. *Psychological Bulletin*, 1974, *81*, 731-737.

Grant, D.A. Testing the null hypothesis and the strategy and tactics of investigating theoretical models. *Psychological Review*, 1962, *69*, 54-61.

Hays, W.L. *Statistics*. New York: Holt, Rinehart & Winston, 1963.

Rucci, A.J. & Tweney, R.D. Analysis of variance and the "second discipline" of scientific psychology: A historical account. *Psychological Bulletin*, 1980, *87*, 166-187.

Sternberg, S. The discovery of processing stages: Extensions of Donder's method. In W.G. Koster (Ed.), Attention and performance II. *Acta Psychologia*, 1969, *30*, 276-315.

2 A Survey of Some Important Techniques and Issues in Multiple Regression

George P. Knight
The University of Arizona

This chapter is designed to discuss some of the more specialized and lesser known aspects of the use of multiple regression analysis in reading research. I assume that the reader has some knowledge of advanced statistics and the basics of multiple regression and can thus appreciate this obviously brief discussion. For those who wish to become more familiar with multiple regression procedures, I suggest Cohen and Cohen (1975), Kerlinger and Pedhazur (1973), or Pedhazur (1982).

From the viewpoint of a methodologist, the methodologies described in this volume are impressive. Rather than employing artificially categorized and orthogonalized independent variables, this research involves studies of independent variables that are allowed to vary (more or less) within their natural continuous and covarying structures, and which rely upon both experimental and statistical control to rule out alternative explanations of the data. This research strategy is likely to produce findings more representative of "real world" situations and of greater external validity than those produced by the traditional designs involving artificially dichotomized and orthogonalized independent variables.

Although the use of less constrained independent variables in reading research may indeed produce more informative findings, such a research strategy also produces difficulties of analysis and interpretation. These difficulties are related to the use of nonorthogonal variables. However, the need to use continuous and nonorthogonal independent variables is in part the reason for the movement towards the use of multiple regression in reading research rather than the traditional analysis of variance, since a basic feature of multiple regression is that the independent variables may be categorical or continuous as well as orthogonal or nonorthogonal. The problems associated with the type of research strategies presented in this volume are problems inherent in understanding reality and are therefore not problems which will be solved by any data analytical technique. Nor will these problems invalidate any type of data analysis which is designed specifically to function with categorical or continuous and orthogonal or nonorthogonal independent variables. For example, the issue of collinearity among predictors is very important in several of the papers in this volume. Collinearity is a problem associated with the covariance between independent variables in the "real world," and no data analysis technique in and of itself can change the limitations set by the "real world."

OVERVIEW OF MULTIPLE REGRESSION

Multiple regression is a least square general linear model technique appropriate for the analysis of data sets containing a single dependent (criterion) variable and multiple categorical or continuous and orthogonal or non-orthogonal independent (predictor) variables. For those readers with expertise in analysis of variance, it may be helpful to consider analysis of variance as a special case of multiple regression in which the independent variables are categorical and usually orthogonal. For computation, SPSS (Nie, Hull, Jenkins, Steinbrenner, & Bent, 1975), BMDP (Dixon, Brown, Engleman, Frane, Hill, Jennrich, & Toporek, 1981), and most other statistical computer packages have subroutines for computing multiple regression analyses.

Although multiple regression is ideal for examining the relationship between independent and dependent variables that are interval level measures, this analysis technique can also be applied to situations in which the independent variable is qualitative in nature. A categorical independent variable can be represented in a multiple regression analysis by one or more dummy variables (see Cohen & Cohen, 1975; or Pedhazur, 1982), the exact number of dummy variables required being equal to the number of levels of the independent variable minus one. The dummy variables are created such that the first dummy variable assigns a score of "1" to the first level of the categorical independent variable and a score of "0" to all other levels. The second dummy variable assigns a score of "1" to the second level of the independent variable and a score of "0" to all other levels (including the first level). Dummy variables are repeatedly created until the last required dummy variable assigns a score of "1" to the next to the last level of the independent variable and a score of "0" to all other levels. Each level of the independent variable can then be identified by a set of scores ("0" and "1") across the k-1 (number of levels of the independent variable minus one) dummy variables. To examine the relationship of the categorical independent variable and the dependent variable, one simply sums the proportions of variance for all of the dummy variables to obtain the proportion of variance in the dependent variable associated with the categorical independent variable. Thus, a correlational procedure such as multiple regression can be used to examine the relationship between an interval level dependent variable and a nominal level independent variable. (Note that it is also possible to use a procedure similar to multiple regression to examine the relationship between nominal or ordinal level dependent variables and nominal or higher level independent variables. This statistical technique is called discriminant function analysis.)

In the course of the multiple regression analysis a number of useful pieces of information are generated. First, a prediction equation (or regression equation) is generated:

(1) $Y' = a_0 + b_1 X_1 + b_2 X_2 + \ldots + b_k X_k.$

In this prediction equation Y' refers to the predicted dependent measure score based upon some weighted linear combination of the independent (X) variables. The a_0 refers to the Y-axis intercept or the predicted dependent measure score (Y') when all independent variables have a value of zero. The b's in the regression equation represent the partial regression coefficients, each of which indicates the contribution of the associated independent variable when *all the other independent variables in the equation are held constant*. To some extent the partial regression coefficients indicate the relative importance of each independent variable in predicting the dependent variable. The partial regression coefficients are also sample statistics estimating the population parameters (β weights) in the general linear model for the population:

(2) $Y = \alpha + \beta_1 X_1 + \beta_2 X_2 + \ldots + \beta_k X_k + \epsilon.$

The specific values of the intercept and the partial regression coefficients are computed in such a manner as to minimize the sum of squared deviations of the predicted dependent scores from the true dependent scores $[\Sigma(Y - Y')^2]$, hence the name "least squares technique."

In addition to the regression equation the multiple regression analysis may produce a standardized regression equation:

(3) $Z_{y'} = A_0 + \beta_1 Z_{x1} + \beta_2 Z_{x2} + \ldots + \beta_k Z_{xk}.$

This standardized regression equation is computed in the same manner as the raw regression equation only using standardized independent and dependent variables. The purpose of such standardization is to equate the scales of measurement for each independent variable. Thus the standardized partial regression coefficients (β weights) indicate the relative importance of each independent variable after all other independent variables in the equation have been held constant and after all independent variables have been equated for scale of measurement.

The multiple regression analysis also produces a variety of estimates of the magnitude of the shared variance between the independent variables and the dependent variable. First the analysis produces the multiple correlation coefficient, $R_{y.12...k}$, which indicates the correlation between the true dependent scores and the predicted dependent scores, $r_{yy'}$. The squared multiple correlation, $R^2_{y.12...k}$, indicates the proportion of the variance in the dependent scores (Y) shared with the weighted linear combination of independent variable scores (X_1, X_2, through X_k). Further,

(4) $\quad R^2_{y.12...k} = r^2_{y1} + r^2_{y(2.1)} + \cdots + r^2_{y(k.12...k-1)}$

where r^2_{y1} is the squared correlation between Y and X_1, $r^2_{y(2.1)}$ is the squared semi-partial correlation (also called the part correlation) between Y and the residualized X_2 (i.e., X_2 after its shared variance with X_1 has been removed), $r^2_{y(k.12...k-1)}$ is the squared semi-partial correlation between Y and the residualized X_k (i.e., X_k after its shared variance with X_1 through X_{k-1} have been removed). Note that these correlations provide an estimate of the amount of variance in the dependent variable shared with each independent variable, except that *any covariance between two or more independent variables and the dependent variable cannot be accurately attributed to the effects of any one independent variable.* If two independent variables are orthogonal ($r^2_{12} = 0$) the squared semi-partial correlation $r^2_{y(2.1)}$ is equal to the squared zero order correlation between Y and X_2 (r^2_{y2}) because there is no shared variance between X_1 and X_2.

Of course, the multiple regression analysis also provides estimates of the reliability (significance) of the various statistics produced in the analysis. These reliability estimates are in the form of F values and the corresponding significance levels for the intercept (a_0), each partial regression coefficient (b), the squared multiple correlation ($R^2_{y.12...k}$), and each correlation or semi-partial correlation contributing to the squared multiple correlation (r^2_{y1}, $r^2_{y(2.1)}$, ..., $r^2_{y(k.12...k-1)}$).

COLLINEARITY

Collinearity refers to the situation in which the independent variables in the research design are correlated with one another. Multicollinearity refers to the situation in which one independent variable in the analysis is highly predictable from a linear combination of two or more of the other independent variables in the analysis. The problems created by collinearity among independent variables, and the alternative ways of dealing with these problems, have been discussed in more detail in Cohen and Cohen (1975), Darlington (1968), Gordon (1968), and Kerlinger and Pedhazur (1973). If two independent variables (X_1 and X_2) share common variance between themselves and with the dependent variable (Y), then it is not possible to unequivocally attribute that common variance to either X_1 or X_2. This situation may produce several problems, but as Huang (1970) points out, "the principles of least squares are not invalidated by the existence of multicollinearity; it is not least squares that is at fault. The fact is that the data will simply not allow any method to distinguish between the effects of collinear variables on the dependent variable."

The first step in dealing with collinearity or multicollinearity is to determine whether or not such a condition exists by looking at the intercorrelations among the independent variables. If the independent variables are correlated with each other, then the data demonstrates collinearity. However, you may also have correlations between the independent variables which are quite low and non-significant and still have a multicollinearity problem. The way to determine if multicollinearity exists is to use each independent variable as the criterion variable in a multiple regression analysis with all other independent variables as predictors. If any of the independent variables are highly predictable from a linear combination of the remaining independent variables, the researcher needs to consider the potential influence of the multicollinearity of the independent variables.

Clearly, it is not difficult to discover the degree of collinearity or multicollinearity among independent variables in a data set. The difficulty lies in judging whether or not the collinearity or multicollinearity causes any problems of computation or interpretation. Whether there are problems, with few exceptions, is dependent upon the researcher's purpose and situation. Although there have been several rules of thumb suggested (e.g., Klein, 1962), the adoption of a strategy for dealing with the problem created by such covariation depends greatly upon the researcher's intent and the specific aspect of the problem the researcher wishes to deal with. Once the researcher has decided that there is some interrelation among the independent variables, this collinearity or multicollinearity may produce several problems, which will now be described, along with some solutions to each one.

Extreme Covariation and Computational Problems

Very high covariation among the independent variables may produce computational problems because of the necessity to invert the correlation matrix. That is, when very high covariation exists among the independent variables, the correlation matrix approaches singularity and the computer cannot perform the required matrix algebra. However, most modern computers have sufficient computational accuracy to deal (mathematically) with all but the most extreme covariation ($r = .80$ or greater). When two or more independent variables do exhibit this extreme covariation, the researcher must question the identity of those variables. It may be that the highly interrelated assessments are really separate measures of the same underlying construct, in which case they may be combined to form a composite score. This composite score may be computed by using either unit weightings or weightings derived through principal components or factor analysis. The composite score can then be used in the multiple regression analysis to eliminate the extreme covariation. Alternately, it may be that there exists some causal relationship between these independent variables and that the researcher can eliminate all but the most important of these variables from the analysis. Of course, the decision as to which variables to eliminate is based upon theoretical grounds *prior* to inspecting the predictive utility of the independent variables. In either case, whether the variables are combined or some are eliminated, the computational problem is solved.

Reliability of Partial Regression Coefficients

Another problem associated with the use of non-orthogonal independent variables is the potential for producing unstable partial regression coefficients for all of the interrelated independent variables. Remember that the partial regression coefficients represent the relationship between the particular independent variable and the dependent variable while all other independent variables are held constant. If two independent variables are highly interrelated, both may have insignificant partial regression coefficients even though they share a substantial portion of common variance with the dependent variable. Further, the standard error of the partial regression coefficient is large, thereby reducing the likelihood of obtaining statistical significance. There are several ways of dealing with this problem. First, a stepwise regression and cross-validation may be performed. The stepwise regression procedure allows the researcher to determine which of the interrelated independent variables shares the greatest amount of variance with the dependent variable and the cross-validation consists of applying the regression equation developed from one sample to a second sample, and thus provides information regarding the reliability of the partial regression coefficients. Second, increasing the sample size may help in the significance testing since this decreases the standard error of the partial regression coefficient. Third, the combination or elimination of variables as described above will also solve this problem. However, it is important to remember that the elimination of variables should be based upon theoretical grounds and prior to any knowledge of the predictive utility of each independent variable.

Interpretational Difficulties

Perhaps the most important problem associated with the use of interrelated independent variables, and a problem associated with the computational and reliability problems discussed above, is the difficulty of interpreting the partial regression coefficients and the proportion of variance attributed to each independent variable. As with the other problems produced by the interrelated independent variables, there are several ways of handling the interpretational problems. However, it should be noted that none of these strategies is totally satisfactory in all situations nor do any of them eliminate all of the problems of interpretation.

Specification of Entry Order. If the research area is sufficiently mature the researcher may *a priori*, on the basis of theory or previous findings, order the entry of variables into the regression equation. This procedure, however, like many of the other potential solutions, requires a great deal of knowledge of the research area. In particular this strategy requires either previous information or theory specifying that some of the independent variables are of lower causal priority. The higher causal priority independent variables can then be forced into the regression equation before the lower causal priority independent variables are entered.

Several Regression Equations. Another strategy for assisting interpretation may be to develop several regression equations, differing in the order of entry of the interrelated independent variables. Although this does not eliminate the interpretational problem, it does allow the researcher to consider several plausible alternative explanations. In addition, it may be that all of these alternatives are equally valuable in supporting the hypotheses. For example, the hypothesis may indicate that familiarity influences comprehension. The researcher may collect a set of data and find considerable covariation between two measures of familiarity: the subject's rating of the familiarity of the material, and a prior knowledge test given to the subject just before reading a series of passages. The researcher may then generate two regression equations each of which includes one of the indices of familiarity. If each of the regression equations indicates that the indices of familiarity are related to comprehension in the same manner, then the researcher has provided considerable support for this hypothesis. This may even be the case if the two measures of familiarity have considerable error variance and do not correlate extremely highly with one another.

Follow-up Studies. A follow-up study can be conducted to examine how the interrelated independent variables are related to the dependent variable in the special case in which the independent variables have been orthogonalized by the research design. This may allow the researcher to specify the order of entry into the original regression equation.

Eliminating Variables. The researcher may elect to eliminate some of the interrelated independent variables from consideration. However, this procedure amounts to setting the partial regression coefficients for these independent variables to zero; and, as an aid to interpreting the data, this strategy should be used with caution. The researcher must have had some reason for collecting the data on all of the independent variables to begin with. If the reason was based upon a theoretical position, it is difficult to simply eliminate variables. On the other hand, if some of the interrelated independent variables are clearly of lower causal priority, then elimination of variables may be a viable means of dealing with the interpretational problem associated with the collinearity or multicollinearity.

Commonality Analysis. Another strategy which may assist in interpretation is commonality analysis. This procedure is designed to divide the shared variance between the dependent variable and two or more independent variables into the *unique* (U) contribution of each independent variable and the *common* (C) contribution of each independent variable in conjunction with other independent variables (Mood, 1971). The *unique* contribution of an independent variable is the proportion of variance attributed to that independent variable when it is the last variable entered into the regression equation. Therefore, the value of the unique contribution is the squared semi-partial correlation between the residualized dependent variable and the independent variable after all of the shared variance between the dependent variable and all other independent variables has been removed. The *common* contribution of the independent variable is the proportion of shared variance between the dependent variable and the independent variables after the *unique* contributions of each independent variable have been removed. For example, in the two independent variable case:

(5) $U(X_1) = R^2_{y.21} - R^2_{y.2}$

(6) $U(X_2) = R^2_{y.12} - R^2_{y.1}$

(7) $C(X_1 X_2) = R^2_{y.12} - U(X_1) - U(X_2)$.

Also, it is possible to express any degree of association between the dependent variable and any independent variable as a composite of the *unique* contribution and the *common* contribution. In our example with two independent variables:

(8) $R^2_{y.1} = U(X_1) + C(X_1 X_2)$

(9) $R^2_{y.2} = U(X_2) + C(X_1 X_2)$.

Thus, commonality analysis allows the researcher to separate the components of variance in a manner that may sometimes aid in interpretation. In particular, this is the case if some of the commonalities make theoretical sense. Kerlinger and Pedhazur (1973) provide a thorough description of this technique and some of the hazards of using it.

Path Analysis. A final procedure which may help in interpretation when the data set contains interrelated independent variables is path analysis (Wright, 1960; Li, 1975). Path analysis is a procedure designed to assess the direct and indirect effect of an independent variable on a dependent variable by testing theoretically derived causal models. That is, path analysis is designed to test the tenability of a set of causal hypotheses based upon the theoretical framework specified by the researcher. In essence, path analysis consists of conducting a set of specific multiple regression analyses and using the standardized partial regression coefficients (B's) in a path model.

The theoretical model specified in Figure 1 suggests that X_1 causes X_2 and Y, and X_2 causes Y. The path coefficients in this model (B_{21}, $B_{y2 \cdot 1}$, & $B_{y1 \cdot 2}$) represent the degree of causation associated with each independent variable. Each path coefficient is the standardized partial regression coefficient between the affected variable (Y) and the causal variable (X) when all independent variables which have any causal relation with X are included in the regression equation. This path model requires the standardized partial regression coefficient from two regression equations: X_1 predicting X_2, as well as X_1 and X_2 predicting Y.

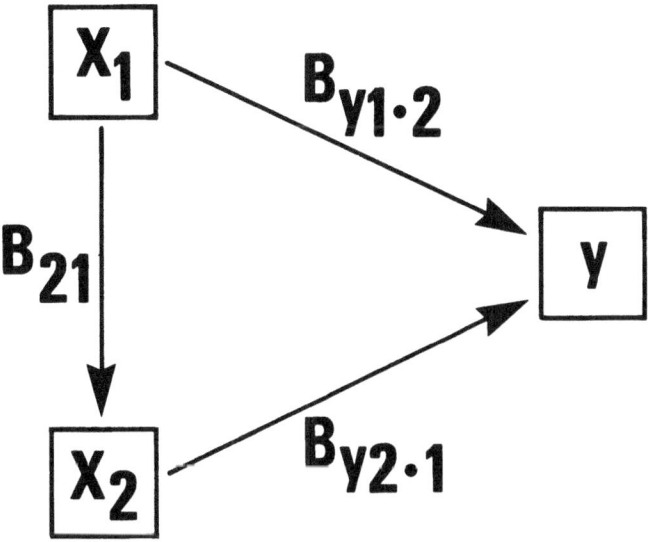

FIG. 1. A simple path model with standardized partial regression coefficients for path coefficients.

This path analysis allows the researcher to generate several types of information that may be helpful in interpreting a data set which contains interrelated independent variables. First it is possible to break the correlation between the dependent variable and an independent variable into a direct and an indirect component. In our example, we could determine the proportion of variance in Y caused directly by X_1, the proportion of variance in Y caused directly by X_2, and the proportion of variance in Y caused indirectly by X_1 through its association with X_2. Expressed mathematically,

(10) $\quad r^2_{y1} = B^2_{y1.2} + B^2_{y2.1} B^2_{21}$

(11) $\quad r^2_{y2} = B^2_{y2.1}$

where $B^2_{y1.2}$ indicates the direct relationship between Y and X_1, $B^2_{y2.1}$ indicates the direct relationship between Y and X_2, and $B^2_{y2.1} B^2_{21}$ indicates the relationship between Y and X_1 through X_2.

Second, path analysis can be used to test the components of the path model. That is, using the path coefficients it is possible to reproduce the correlation matrix for all of the variables in the path model. The researcher could then set specific path coefficients in the model to zero and determine if the original correlation matrix, or a very close approximation, is reproduced. If so, the path set to zero is not needed and a more parsimonious model results. Thus, this procedure allows the researcher to find a good causal model.

For example, variable X_1 could be the number of words in a passage; variable X_2 could be the amount of parsing effort required by the passage according to some theory; and Y could be the amount of time required to read the passage. Further, the researcher may wish to test the plausibility of two causal models: (1) the model presented in Figure 1 which suggests that both the number of words and the amount of parsing directly influence reading time, and the number of words in the passage also indirectly influences reading time by influencing the amount of parsing required; and (2) a model suggesting that parsing directly influences reading time while the number of words in the passage indirectly influences reading time by influencing the amount of parsing required. The researcher would reject model 1 in favor of model 2 above if the following were true: (a) $B_{y1.2}$, the standardized partial regression coefficient for the number of words predicting reading time with the amount of required parsing included in the regression equation, is not significantly different from zero; (b) the other standardized partial regression coefficients in the model (B_{21} and $B_{y2.1}$) are both significantly different from zero and have the correct sign; and (c) the correlation matrix between the number of words, amount of required parsing, and reading time can be reproduced with reasonable accuracy when assuming that $B_{y1.2} = 0$.

MEASUREMENT ERROR AND SHRINKAGE

Some of the recent research on reading has been distinctly quasi-experimental in nature. That is, some of the independent variables have been precisely manipulated while other independent variables have been measured or assessed variables. For example, the researcher may be interested in the influence of variables such as prior knowledge (assessed independent variable) and passage length (manipulated independent variable) on reading performance (assessed dependent variable). Since the dependent variables and some of the independent variables of interest have often been assessed variables, the errors of measurement associated with such asssessments may become an important consideration. The measurement error and lack of perfect reliability of the assessments places certain constraints upon the relationships among the variables and in turn influences the result of the multiple regression analyses. This issue has received little or no attention in reading research using multiple regresssion.

Attentuation

In the simple case of one independent and one dependent variable, measurement error attenuates the correlation between the two variables and thereby makes the correlation smaller than it would be if there were no measurement error (cf., Cohen & Cohen, 1975; Nunnally, 1967). Further, it is possible, based upon measurement theory, to estimate what the correlation between the two variables would be if there were no measurement error. This estimate is computed using the following formula:

$$(12) \quad \hat{r}_{yx} = \frac{r_{yx}}{\sqrt{r_{yy}} \sqrt{r_{xx}}}$$

where $\hat{r}_{yx}$ is the estimated correlation, r_{yx} is the correlation between the fallible measures of Y and X, r_{yy} is the reliability of the measure of Y, and r_{xx} is the reliability of the measure of X.

In addition, measurement theory provides a means for estimating the maximum possible correlation between less than perfectly reliably measured variables. For example, in Eq. (12) the theoretical maximum possible value of r_{yx} is 1.00. Therefore:

$$(13) \quad \max r_{yx} = \sqrt{r_{yy}} \sqrt{r_{xx}}.$$

If the reliability coefficients of both Y and X were only .7, then the maximum possible value of r_{yx} is .7 and the maximum proportion of the variance in Y associated with X is $.7^2$ or .49. Clearly, in this simple case, accounting for a small proportion of the variance is not all that unimpressive given this low maximum value.

The situation is somewhat different if multiple independent variables are involved in that measurement error can easily lead to an overestimate of the population multiple correlation. This is in contrast to the attenuation effect producing an underestimate of the correlation between a single independent variable and a dependent variable. As Cohen and Cohen (1975) point out, measurement error may cause either an underestimate, or overestimate, of the partial regression coefficients, the partial correlations, and the semi-partial correlations. In the stepwise regression procedure, the formula for computing the semi-partial correlation is as follows:

$$(14) \quad r_{y(2.1)} = \frac{r_{y2} - r_{y1} r_{12}}{1 - r_{12}^2}$$

An estimate of the semi-partial correlation if there were no measurement error can be obtained by modifying Eq. (14) to correct for the degree of measurement error. The corrected formula is as follows:

$$(15) \quad \hat{r}_{y(2.1)} = \frac{r_{11}r_{y2} - r_{y1}r_{12}}{r_{11}r_{22} - r_{12}^2}$$

Note that both the numerator and denominator are different in Eq. (15) compared to Eq. (14), and that it is difficult to determine if the uncorrected semi-partial correlation is an underestimate or overestimate of the corrected semi-partial correlation. Further, in the stepwise entry procedure overestimated semi-partials are at an advantage since the selection of variables for entry after the first step is based upon the largest semi-partial correlation controlling for all other variables already in the equation. Thus, an overestimated R^2 is likely.

Clearly, the problems associated with errors of measurement are not easy to deal with. Perhaps the easiest solution is to ensure that the assessment of variables is as error free as possible. If the variables of interest and the assessment devices are carefully defined and constructed, and if the resulting reliabilities are quite high, the researcher need not be concerned with the effects of measurement errors upon the regression analysis. Alternately, if the reliabilities are high and if the researcher assumes that the measurement errors are random, the researcher may wish to use corrections for attenuation (see Nunnally, 1967; Pedhazur, 1982). However, this approach results in additional problems associated with significance testing and interpretation (Pedhazur, 1982). The reader may wish to consult Pedhazur (1982); Blalock, Wells, & Carter (1970); and Zeller & Carmines (1980) for additional suggestions.

Shrinkage

A related issue which those conducting reading research may wish to consider is the problem of shrinkage in least square linear model techniques. In multiple regression, the partial regression coefficients are computed such that the sum of squared deviations of Y' from Y is the minimum possible value given the data set. This in effect is treating the correlations between all variables as though they were perfectly accurate and subject to none of the errors generated by less than perfect reliability of measurement and chance covariability. Thus, the multiple regression analysis computes the highest possible multiple correlation in the data set and, by capitalizing upon chance, overestimates the true population multiple correlation. In turn, if one were to apply the original regression equation to a second sample or to the population, the second sample or population multiple correlation would nearly always be smaller than the original multiple correlation. This decrease of the multiple correlation from the original sample to a second sample or the population is known as "shrinkage."

The degree of overestimation of the multiple correlation, and hence the expected shrinkage, is dependent in part upon the ratio of the number of cases to the number of available independent variables. Note that this is the ratio of the number of cases to the number of independent variables being considered by the regression procedure, not just the number of independent variables which end up being entered into the regression equation. The smaller this ratio, the greater the degree of overestimation; and for a relatively low ratio the overestimation can be very substantial. For example, Carter (1979) has demonstrated that with 10 cases and 5 independent variables a population R^2 of .2 can produce a sample R^2 of nearly .6; with 10 cases and 15 independent variables a population R^2 of .2 can produce a sample R^2 of nearly .75.

Some of the studies presented in this volume rely upon a relatively low ratio of cases to independent variables. This was particularly true when the researchers employed certain strategies such as using small sample sizes because of the expense of collecting larger data sets, or artificially reducing the sample size by collapsing across subjects and considering passages or sentences as cases. The general solution to this problem is to use large samples. Kerlinger and Pedhazur (1973) indicate that some authors suggest rules of thumb such as 30 subjects per independent variable or at least 400 subjects. Clearly, however, these rules are very conservative and rarely feasible in cognition research.

An alternative to having very large samples is to estimate the degree of overestimation of the multiple correlation. Several correction formulas have been proposed, and Carter (1979) has provided an empirical comparison of these formulas using Monte Carlo techniques to generate data sets with known characteristics. Carter's recommendation is to use the formula for the adjusted squared multiple correlation coefficient ($\hat{R}^2$) developed by Olkin and Pratt (1958) and Harris (1975):

$$(16) \quad \hat{R}^2 = 1 - \left(\frac{N-3}{N-k-1}\right)\left[(1-R^2) + \left(\frac{2}{N-k-1}\right)(1-R^2)^2\right]$$

where R^2 is the squared sample multiple correlation, N is the number of cases, and k is the number of independent variables.

Carter (1979) suggests that if the $\hat{R}^2$ as calculated by the above formula is less than .6, then a better adjusted value is provided by the following formula, developed by Wherry (1940):

$$(17) \quad \hat{R}^2 = 1 - (1-R^2)\left(\frac{N-1}{N-k-1}\right)$$

However, Carter's empirical comparison of the alternative formulas for calculating shrinkage estimates investigated only a few of the possible values of R^2, sample sizes, and numbers of independent variables. Thus, the accuracy of these formulas is not yet fully known, and researchers should use them with caution.

Perhaps a better approach to dealing with shrinkage at the present time is to cross-validate or double cross-validate the regression equation. Cross-validation refers to the process of applying the regression equation from the original sample to a second sample and examining the difference between the original and second multiple correlation. If this difference is small, the researcher may conclude that the overestimation is not serious and re-compute the regression equation based upon the combined samples. Double cross-validation refers to the process of applying the regression equations from each of two samples to the other sample. The researcher can then examine the difference between the two original multiple correlations, the difference between the two original and the two alternate sample multiple correlations, and the difference between the two regression equations. Again, if these differences are small, the researcher may conclude that the overestimation is small and re-compute the regression equation for the combined samples.

REPEATED MEASURES DESIGNS

Many experiments in reading research use repeated measures or within-subjects designs. However, most uses of multiple regression in reading research ignore this fact. Many researchers collapse their data across subjects in order to investigate the effects of various conditions such as passages or text types. Such a procedure unnecessarily discards much of the information available in the data sets and is likely to produce conservative significance tests. This is because the procedure does not remove subject variance from the error term. It is quite possible to conduct multiple regression analyses on such designs without the loss of information associated with collapsing across subjects (Pedhazur, 1977, 1982).

The most straight-forward way of using multiple regression to analyze data from a repeated measures design is to generate a series of dummy variables to represent the subjects effect. In a repeated measures design having N_s subjects, $N_s - 1$ dummy variables (as described earlier) could be entered into the multiple regression equation in order to identify the proportion of variance in the dependent variable associated with the subjects factor. This procedure can be difficult, especially as the number of subjects increases and the number of dummy variables needed to conduct the analyses becomes very large. Pedhazur (1977, 1982), however, has developed a "Criterion Scaling" procedure to allow a simpler means of analyzing repeated measures data by multiple regression. The procedure requires using an independent variable representing the individual subject's performance, such as the total (or mean) of each subject's dependent variable scores across all conditions. A multiple regression analysis could then be conducted in which the subject variable is entered into the regression equation in addition to the other variables. This procedure allows the researcher to estimate the variance in the dependent variable attributable to subject variance, as well as the condition variance. This analysis provides the correct estimates of the proportions of variance and the respective sums of squares, but requires minor adjustments to the corresponding F values. These adjustments to the F values are the result of representing the subject variable as having only one degree of freedom, when in fact it has $N_s - 1$ degrees of freedom. Thus, the corrections required are designed to enter the appropriate number of degrees of freedom in the numerator and denominator of the F test.

For example, suppose the repeated measures study consisted of having 20 subjects read each of four passage types and then complete a test of the proportion of the material recalled after reading each passage (of course with different content material in each passage type). The passage type factor would be represented by three dummy variables (X_1, X_2, and X_3). The X_1 dummy variable would code a "1" for the first passage type and a "0" for each of the other three passage types. The X_2 dummy variable would code a "1" for the second passage type and a "0" for each of the other three passage types. The X_3 dummy variable would code a "1" for the third passage type and a "0" for each of the other three passage types. Thus each passage type can be differentiated by the pattern of codes across the three dummy variables (1,0,0; 0,1,0; 0,0,1; and 0,0,0). The subject factor would be represented by a variable (X_4) consisting of the total recall score for each subject across all four passage types. These four variables would be entered into a multiple regression analysis using the recall scores as the dependent variable (Y). The regression analysis will indicate the proportion of variance in recall scores associated with the passage type factor ($R^2_{y.123}$) and the proportion of variance in recall scores associated with the subjects factor ($R^2_{y.4}$). The F tests on the proportion of variance associated with the passage type (pt) and subjects (s) factors provided by the usual analysis would use the following formulas, which are actually incorrect in this case:

(18) $\quad F_{pt} = \dfrac{R^2_{y.123}/k_{pt}}{(1 - R^2_{y.1234})/N_s k_{pt} - k_{pt} - k_s - 1}$

(19) $\quad F_s = \dfrac{R^2_{y.4}/k_s}{(1 - R^2_{y.1234})/N_s k_{pt} - k_{pt} - k_s - 1}$

where $k_{pt} = 3$ corresponds to the number of dummy variables representing the passage type factor, $k_s = 1$ corresponds to the number of variables representing the subjects factor, and $N_s = 20$ corresponds to the number of subjects in the study. Note that these degrees of freedom (k_{pt}, $N_s - k_{pt} - k_s - 1$; and k_s, $N_s - k_{pt} - k_s - 1$) are incorrect. In a repeated measures analysis the numerator of the F ratio for the subjects factor has $N_s - 1$ degrees of freedom, which is the number of subject dummy variables that would be required. But in Eq. 18 and Eq. 19 the subjects factor is credited with only one degree of freedom. Therefore, the formulas for calculating the F statistics need to be adjusted. The correct formulas are as follows:

$$(20) \quad \hat{F}_{pt} = \frac{R^2_{y.123}/k_{pt}}{(1 - R^2_{y.1234}) / N_s k_{pt} - N_s - k_{pt} - 1}$$

$$(21) \quad \hat{F}_s = \frac{R^2_{y.4} / N_s - 1}{(1 - R^2_{y.1234}) / N_s k_{pt} - N_s - k_{pt} - 1}$$

An interesting possibility related to the above approach is an analysis strategy occasionally used in human judgment research (Hammond, Stewart, Brehmer, & Steinmann, 1975). This technique involves developing a multiple regression equation for each subject and using cluster analysis to group subjects into like categories based upon the regression equations. This technique requires that the number of observations on each subject be relatively large. Once the regression equation is computed for each subject, the intercept and partial regression coefficients become the new data set. This new data set is then clustered to produce groups of subjects for whom performance is related to the independent variables in different ways. These groupings can then be used in a discriminant function analysis to determine how the groupings are related to subject characteristics. In other words, subject characteristics can be used to predict the group membership which defines the pattern of interrelations between the dependent variable and the independent variables.

OTHER LEAST SQUARE LINEAR MODEL TECHNIQUES

Finally, those conducting research on reading processes may wish to investigate other least square linear model techniques besides analysis of variance and multiple regression. Many reading experiments produce data sets that actually contain multiple *dependent* variables. For example, reading performance may be characterized by both recall accuracy and speed. The appropriate least square linear model technique for a data set having multiple independent variables and multiple (continuous) dependent variables is canonical correlation. In canonical correlation, a least square analysis is conducted to produce the maximum correlation between some linear combination of the independent variables and some linear combination of dependent variables. Thus the canonical correlation analysis produces a set of coefficients similar to partial regression coefficients for the independent variables and a corresponding set of coefficients for the dependent variables. Multiple regression is simply a special case of canonical correlation. But unlike multiple regression, canonical correlation analysis can produce more than one equation. The available programs first select the set of regression-like weights for the independent and dependent variables based upon the largest source of shared variance. Then the procedure selects the second set of regression coefficients which is orthogonal to the first and based upon the largest source of shared variance left in the data. Thus, the canonical correlation analysis has the potential for revealing several relationships between the independent and dependent variables within one data set, and may lead the researcher to consider effects that may not have been considered before.

In conclusion I would like to reiterate the importance of using complex research designs and sophisticated data analyses to investigate complex behaviors such as reading. In doing so, however, there will inevitably be difficulties associated with the data analyses and interpretation, many of which have been addressed by those contributing to this volume. I hope this chapter will encourage reading researchers to address some new and important issues in the future.

REFERENCES

Blalock, H.M., Wells, C.S., and Carter, L.F. Statistical estimation with random measurement error. In E.F. Borgatta & G.W. Bohrnstedt (Eds.), *Sociological methodology 1970*. San Francisco: Jossey-Bass, 1970.

Carter, D.S. Comparison of different shrinkage formulas in estimating population multiple correlation coefficients. *Educational and Psychological Measurement*, 1979, *39*, 261-266.

Cohen, J. and Cohen, P. *Applied multiple regression/correlation analysis for the behavioral sciences*. Hillsdale, New Jersey: Lawrence Erlbaum Associates, 1975.

Darlington, R.B. Multiple regression in psychological research and practice. *Psychological Bulletin*, 1968, *69*, 161-182.

Dixon, W.J., Brown, M.B., Engelman, L., Frane, J.W., Hill, M.A., Jennrich, R.I. and Toporek, J.D. *Biomedical computer programs: P-series*. Los Angeles: University of California Press, 1981.

Gordon, R.A. Issues in multiple regression. *American Journal of Sociology*, 1968, *73*, 592-616.

Hammond, K.R., Stewart, T.R., Brehmer, B., and Steinmann, D.O. Social judgment theory. In M.F. Kaplan and S. Schwartz (Eds.): *Human judgment and decision processes*. New York: Academic Press, Inc., 1975.

Harris, R.J. *A primer of multivariate statistics*. New York: Academic Press, Inc., 1975.

Huang, D.S. *Regression and econometric methods*. New York: John Wiley & Sons, Inc., 1970.

Kerlinger, F.N. and Pedhazur, E.J. *Multiple regression in behavioral research*. New York: Holt, Rinehart & Winston, 1973.

Klein, L.R. *An introduction to econometrics*. Englewood Cliffs: Prentice-Hall, 1962.

Li, C.C. *Path analysis. A primer*. Pacific Grove, CA: The Boxwood Press, 1975

Mood, A.M. Partitioning variance in multiple regression analyses as a tool for developing learning models. *American Educational Research Journal*, 1971, *8*, 191-202.

Nie, N.H., Hull, C.H., Jenkins, J.G., Steinbrenner, K., and Bent, D.H. *Statistical package for the social sciences (2nd ed.)* New York: McGraw-Hill Book Company, 1975.

Nunnally, J.C. *Psychometric theory*. New York: McGraw-Hill Book Company, 1967.

Olkin, I. and Pratt, J.W. Unbiased estimation of certain correlation coefficients. *Annals of Mathematical Statistics*, 1958, *29*, 201-211.

Pedhazur, E.J. Coding subjects in repeated measures designs. *Psychological Bulletin*, 1977, *84*, 298-305.

Pedhazur, E.J. *Multiple regression in behavioral research*. (2nd. Ed.). New York: Holt, Rinehart & Winston, 1982.

Wherry, R.J. Appendix A. In Stead, W.H. and Sharyle, C.P. *Occupational Counseling Techniques*, 1940.

Wright, S. Path coefficients and path regressions: Alternative or complementary concepts. *Biometrics*, 1960, *16*, 189-202.

Zeller, R.A., and Carmines, E.G. *Measurement in the social sciences*. New York: Cambridge University Press, 1980.

3
The Word-by-Word Reading Paradigm: An Experimental and Theoretical Approach[1]

Doris Aaronson and Steven Ferres
New York University

When people read, at least three aspects of the situation are important: the linguistic attributes of the text, the cognitive demands of the performance task, and the individual reader's abilities. This paper is concerned with an experimental procedure that permits variation on all three dimensions, and with theoretical methods to interpret the reading time data acquired with that procedure.

In the basic procedure, subjects press a button to display one word at a time in the center of a screen. When the computer displays each word, it extinguishes the preceding word and records its reading time (RT). To study the effects of linguistic attributes, these subject-paced word-by-word RTs were analyzed for sentences that varied in lexical, syntactic and semantic properties. To study performance task differences, the same sentences were read by subjects either for immediate comprehension of gist or for complete retention of the sentences. To study reading abilities, the data were compared for fast and slow readers in fifth grade and college populations.

The theoretical approach used to interpret the RT data involves developing quantitative models with additive time components for processing lexical (L), structural (S) and meaning (M) attributes of sentences: $RT = f(L) + g(S) + h(M)$. These models provide a methodological tool to examine reading "strategies" for different subject populations engaged in different reading tasks. In the models, a strategy is defined in terms of the particular linguistic processors that are used, and

---

[1]This research was supported in part by Grant MH16,496 from NIMH to New York University. We thank Stanley Goldstein, Superintendent, and Goldie Brown, Reading Specialist, of Manhattan Public School District No. 1 for their help in obtaining experimental subjects. We thank Don Mitchell and Robert Sherak for helpful comments on a prior draft.

the amount of time they are used during reading. The models and data provide evidence for a structurally-oriented strategy when reading for retention, and a meaning-based strategy when reading for comprehension.

This paper is divided into two main sections. The first section deals with the experimental paradigm, and focuses on the procedural details, the situational and linguistic variables, the rationale for using the paradigm as a research tool, and the assumptions underlying its use. The second section deals with methods of constructing and testing theories of the reading process. A general class of information-processing models is described. Then specific equations are developed and tested against the RT data from two different experiments that used the word-by-word paradigm.

THE READING PROCEDURE

Subjects view sentences displayed on a computer screen one word at a time in a self-paced silent reading task. The time-course of events on a trial is illustrated in Figure 1. Preceding each trial the word READY appears. When the subjects want to start a trial, and *each time* they want to read another word, they press a response button with their dominant index finger. This button press extinguishes the previous word and displays the next word on a video monitor in the center of the screen. When the computer displays each successive word, it records the reading time in milliseconds for the previous word. The letters are all capitals, about ¼ inch tall, ⅙ inch wide, easy to read, and displayed at a comfortable reading

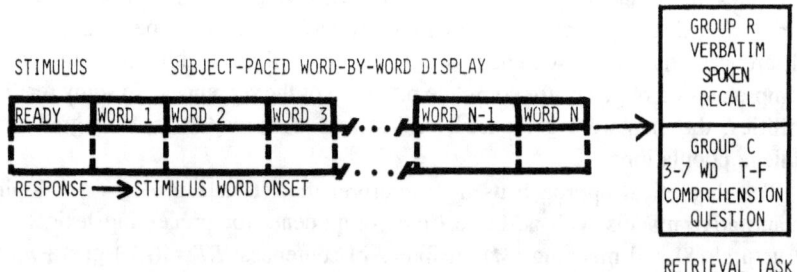

FIG. 1. The time course of events on a trial.

illumination. A different sentence is presented on each trial. The semidark-adapted subject sits about 1.5 feet from the screen, in low illumination.

In each age group, subjects are equally divided into two post-sentence task groups: recall and comprehension. Immediately after the last word in each sentence is extinguished, subjects in the RECALL group see the word RECALL displayed with dashes on each side. In some experiments the subjects are instructed to speak their verbatim recall aloud into a microphone connected to a tape recorder. In other experiments, subjects write their recall on a prepared answer sheet. For subjects in the COMPREHENSION group, a 3-7 word true-false statement about the sentence content is displayed immediately after the last word in each sentence is extinguished. The subjects respond by pressing one of two keys labeled "T" or "F". Instructions for each group stress speed and accuracy on the post-sentence response task. Subjects have 6-8 practice sentences and 80-90 test sentences in experiments that last about 1 hour, with a brief half-time break.

THE EXPERIMENTAL VARIABLES

The same basic procedure permits us to collect data using many different experimental variables that focus on either the reading situation or the text structure. Table 1 shows some of the variables we have used in previous research.

Situational Variables

Four situational variables are listed in the top of Table 1, and described below.

Task. The two different reading tasks are used because natural reading situations vary in their memory and comprehension demands (Aaronson, 1976). We selected two extremes on the "memory-comprehension" continuum to illustrate the wide range of reading strategies that are used by subjects in different performance tasks. In many natural reading tasks, components of these strategies are often mixed. Other post-sentence response tasks could easily be used to set "reading goals" and "cognitive demands" for the subject. For example, these might include recognition memory, sentence paraphrasing, or adding a continuation sentence.

Age. We have used two age groups: 9-11 year old fifth graders (reflecting the broad socio-economic range of the Manhattan public schools), and college-age adults. Fifth graders were selected because they read reasonably smoothly in units larger than individual words, but they are not yet fully mature and skilled readers. Thus, the children should approximate task-related adult reading strategies in many respects, but should also show mixtures of adult strategies for two reasons. First, at this stage of acquisition, children should have learned many strategy components, but they may not yet have combined them optimally. Second, their

TABLE 1
Experimental Variables

Situational Variables	
TASK:	Recall; Comprehension
AGE:	5th Grade; College
SPEED:	Slow & Fast Readers
PRACTICE:	Two Half-hour sessions or 10 Balanced Blocks
Linguistic Variables	
LEXICAL:	Number of Letters; Number of Syllables; Lexical Category; Word Frequency
SYNTACTIC:	Number of Phrases; Phrase Length; Phrase Position; Word Location in Phrase; Verb Type; Embedded Clauses; Sentence Structure
SEMANTIC:	Semantic Facilitation: Redundancy; Semantic Integration with Prior Context; Rated "Importance" of Words in Sentence; Verb Attributes (Static/Dynamic; Active/Passive); Causal/Descriptive Sentences; Anaphoric Relationships (Noun/Pronoun)

daily reading tasks or goals, e.g., school related and leisure reading, are not as clearly or as frequently differentiated as those of adults. Such reading "strategies" are generally not explicitly taught in the schools. Thus, changes in reading time (RT) patterns with age may have implications for reading instruction in general and also for remediation.

Speed. Reading time patterns over the sentence, and the associated reading strategies, vary with the capabilities of the individual reader. To shed light on such variations, the RT data were analyzed separately for slow and fast readers. The division was based on median splits of the data for each age and task group.

Practice. The RT data were analyzed separately in two half-hour sessions, and in some cases in 10 blocks of sentences balanced for various linguistic variables. These practice data permit us to determine which aspects of reading strategies are stable and replicate over time, and which aspects are flexible and change with increasing exposure to a particular set of task demands.

Linguistic Variables

Three classes of linguistic variables are listed at the bottom of Table 1: lexical, syntactic and semantic attributes of text. In terms of psychological and linguistic criteria, these classes are not mutually exclusive. But, we have varied selected stimulus properties that emphasize predominantly one or another class.

Lexical Attributes. Individual words were varied in the number of letters or syllables, and in their lexical category (e.g., noun, verb, pronoun, article, etc.). Depending on the stimulus set, word frequency was based on either adult norms (Kucera & Francis, 1967) or norms for children's readers (Carroll, Davies, & Richman, 1971).

Syntactic Attributes. Although the displays contained individual words, the sentences were systematically varied based on several syntactic attributes. As indicated in Table 1, these attributes primarily concern the number, types, and locations of phrases and clauses in the sentences.

Semantic Attributes. The semantic variables in Table 1 focus on meaning relations among the words in context, rather than on individual word properties. The data analyses are based on RT differences between words that are or are not predictable from prior sentence context, and on RT correlations between word pairs that share semantic content, such as nouns and their anaphoric pronouns.

A QUALITY RESEARCH TOOL

The word-by-word reading procedure was developed as a laboratory research tool for the five reasons listed in Table 2 and discussed below. To highlight properties of

TABLE 2
Rationale for the Word-by-Word Paradigm

A QUALITY RESEARCH TOOL
1. On-line measurement
2. Flexibility in linguistic & task variables
3. Sensitivity to individual subjects on individual sentences
4. Reliability over subjects and sentences
5. Easy & cheap

FEW ASSUMPTIONS & THEY ARE TESTABLE
1. The procedure is "natural"
   A. Subject paced, not experimenter paced
   B. Reflects cognitive processing
   C. Reveals natural task-linked strategies
   D. Reflects prior reading habits
2. Words are an important reading unit
   A. RTs reflect processing of words
   B. RTs reflect processing of smaller & larger units
3. Processing load assumption
   A. RTs reflect the momentary processing load
   B. "Immediacy" assumption not needed
   C. "Eye-mind" assumption not needed

---

the procedure, its underlying assumptions and theoretical implications, illustrative data are drawn from several different studies. These studies all used the same basic procedure (Figure 1), but differed in the linguistic and situational variables described in Table 2.

On-Line Measurement

The word-by-word paradigm is an "on-line" procedure for indexing perceptual encoding during reading. That is, the RT duration data are obtained *while* the subject is perceiving each individual word. With most other procedures, indirect inferences about perception are made based on subsequent memory and comprehension responses obtained at time delays after the sentence is read. Further, procedures that collect a single RT after an entire phrase, sentence or paragraph is read do not permit the fine grain data analyses possible with single word RTs.

Flexibility

The procedure's flexibility makes it easy to vary both the *linguistic attributes* of the stimuli and the *cognitive demands* of the performance task. The averaged adult data for the sentences in Figure 2 illustrate results from both of these types of

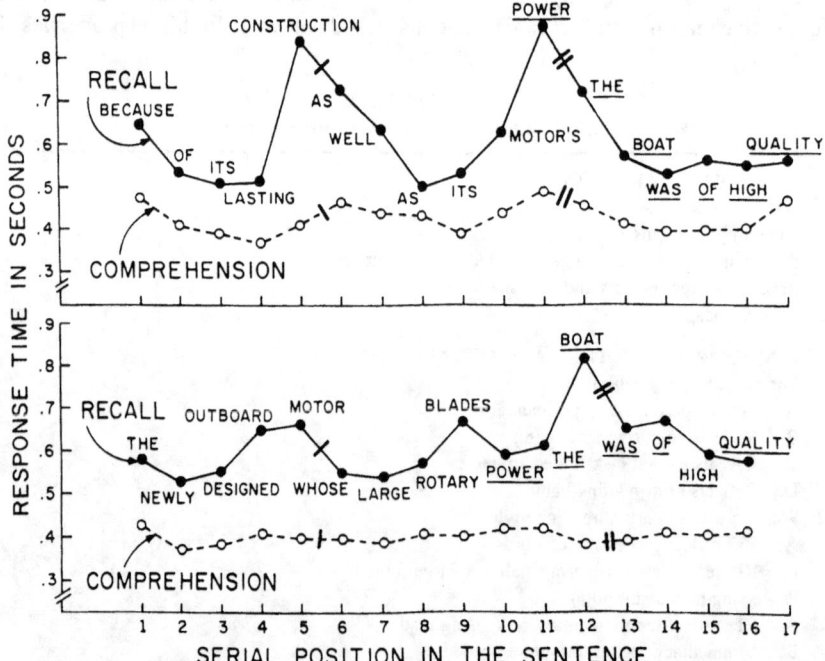

FIG. 2. Mean RTs over sentence positions for adults in the recall and comprehension task.

variations. The solid and dashed RT curves are for recall and comprehension subjects respectively. Sentences in the two panels have identical words in their second halves, but the first halves impose different grammatical structures on the later words. The use of sentence pairs such as these provides a method for separating the role of lexical and syntactic variables in reading. In comparing the identically worded second halves of the two sentences, we see that recall subjects have prolonged RT peaks at phrase boundary words, marked by short lines, regardless of the individual words. In the top panel "power" is at an RT peak and "boat" is in a trough, but in the bottom panel, the RT relation is reversed. The RT profiles for comprehension subjects contrast sharply with those for recall subjects. The data are about 200 msec per word faster and the RT patterns from one word to the next are much smoother. Other data analyses show that comprehension RTs primarily reflect the semantic rather than the syntactic structure of the sentence.

Sensitivity

The procedure is an exceedingly sensitive tool. It can be used to measure reading times for *individual subjects* reading individual sentences. One doesn't have to rely on group averaging that eliminates "noise" in order to see many of the important trends. Figure 3 shows data for six individual adult recall subjects for the two sentences in Figure 2. All six subjects reflect the main group trends illustrated in the previous figure: prolonged RTs at phrase breaks and RT scallops within phrases. The three subjects in the top panel differ in mean reading speed. The three subjects in the bottom panel differ in RT slope over serial positions, perhaps indicating differing rates of integrating information over the sentence.

Reliability

The word-by-word RT procedure yields very reliable data. In comparison to other experimental procedures used to study reading, the variability is quite low. For example, the replication of phrase-based trends from one subject to another in Figure 3 illustrates the "between-subjects" reliability. Also, the major linguistic trends for variables in Table 2 are reliable over sentences, with an average standard error of 16 msec. The low variance may be due in part to "naturalness" and motivational aspects of the procedure. Subjects report that they have no difficulty with the procedure and that they enjoy the experiments.

Easy and Cheap

The word-by-word procedure is both easier to run and less expensive than other procedures that obtain an equivalent amount, reliability and validity of data. For example, eye-movement procedures require expensive recording equipment and a fair amount of expertise in using the equipment and in interpreting the data. Those

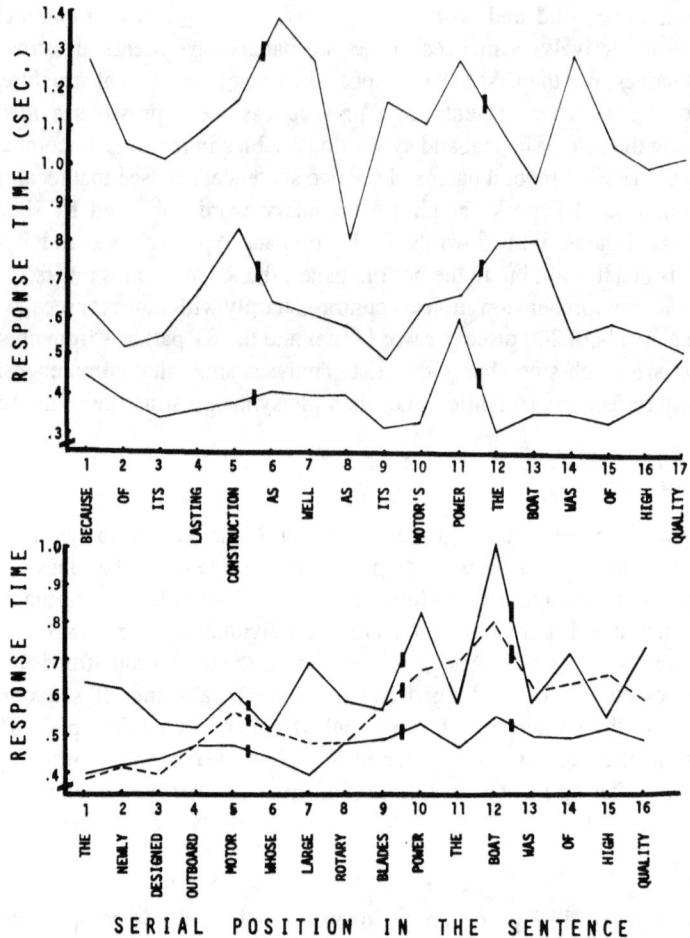

FIG. 3. RTs over sentence positions for 6 adults in the recall task.

procedures also require frequent "calibration" tests throughout the session to check whether the equipment and the subject are correctly aligned. There is a large cost in preprocessing the continuous wave-forms before even the most basic statistical analyses can be done. During the past two years, Carpenter and Just have shifted portions of their research from the eye-movement recording procedure to the word-by-word procedure because of the reductions in time, cost and technical complications (Just & Carpenter, this volume).

The word-by-word reading procedure is easy to set up and has now been used on (at least) five different computers with five different programming languages. Our first experiments used the Harvard PDP-4 programmed with a language called Lexigraph, developed by Dan Forsyth. Later experiments used the N. Y. U. PDP-8I with the programming language SIMPLE (Aaronson & Brauth, 1972). We are now setting up research on the PDP-11/34 Unix System with an expanded version of SIMPLE programmed in "C" primarily by Robert Sherak. Don Mitchell has a version of the word-by-word paradigm running in England on a PET microcomputer (Mitchell, this volume), and Just and Carpenter have another version running at Carnegie-Mellon on a PDP-11/34 RSX-11M system (Just, Carpenter, & Woolley, 1982). Hence, the word-by-word procedure is highly transportable among research laboratories, permitting researchers to replicate each other's experiments and to have a common methodological framework in which to compare results.

THE UNDERLYING ASSUMPTIONS

The use of the word-by-word procedure to study reading is based on the three assumptions outlined in the bottom of Table 2. (a) The procedure incorporates many features of "natural" reading. (b) Single words are an important reading unit. (c) The RTs reflect the momentary cognitive processing load. These assumptions are considered in detail below.

Naturalness

The word-by-word procedure resembles "natural" reading in at least four important ways.

RTs are Subject Paced. The reading times for each word are paced by the subject rather than the experimenter. Individual subjects have natural differences in their overall reading rates and in their RT patterns over a sentence. Experimenter-paced procedures that are the same for all subjects restrict the range of strategies that can be used and may force subjects into a common rate or reading strategy.

RTs Reflect Cognitive Processing. The RTs are not limited by motor response times. The word-by-word RTs are slower than motor RTs of about 75 msec/word for two adult control subjects who pressed the button to advance the displays but did not read the words. This provides evidence that there is no "floor" effect contaminating the data. Rather, the cognitive processing of linguistic information limits the RTs. The data include word strings with reading rates of 300-600 wpm, as fast as moderately rapid natural reading rates. But subjects selectively respond more slowly at key content words, phrase boundaries, and other important points. That is, they do not respond in an even rhythm or out of phase from important linguistic features in the sentence.

RTs Reveal Natural Strategies. The data provide evidence that the word-by-word procedure encourages task-linked reading strategies similar to those that occur naturally in our daily reading tasks. For example, memory demands are high when students study for exams, when lawyers read witness testimony in preparation for a trial, or when clergy read Biblical passages in developing a sermon. Reading for immediate comprehension occurs when we read newspapers, magazines or novels simply to get the main points, characters, actions and themes.

As suggested earlier and discussed in more detail later, the word-by-word RTs reveal a structure-oriented strategy (e.g., Figure 2) when reading for retention, but a meaning-oriented strategy when reading for comprehension. As a partial validity check on the method, the task-linked RT strategies can be compared to data obtained with other methods in past research. Accordingly, past research has provided evidence that a phrase-structure "chunking" strategy can decrease perceptual decision time (Miller, 1962), optimize memory capacity during retention (Miller, 1956; Tulving & Patkau, 1962; Anglin & Miller, 1968; Glanzer & Razel, 1974) and provide address nodes during retrieval (Wilkes & Kennedy, 1969, 1970; Tulving, 1968) when verbal information must be stored in memory. In contrast, a comprehension strategy preserves information on meaning, often destroying much of the original lexical and structural information in the process. Readers recode the original ordered string to determine propositions and deep structure relationships among sentence components (Miller & McKeen, 1964); they abstract key concepts and discard minor details (Haberlandt et al., 1980; Bartlett, 1932); and they recode verbal information into visual images that idealize the original meaning or that contain features never presented (Begg & Paivio, 1969) to provide an emphasis or to obtain compatibility with a previously established semantic framework (Miller & Johnson-Laird, 1976).

To provide further validity for the naturalness of the word-by-word procedure, the data can be compared to those obtained from eye-movement procedures. Just and Carpenter have compared RT patterns between our methods and their eye-movement recording procedures, and they found similar RT patterns (Just, Carpenter, & Wooley, 1982; Just & Carpenter, this volume). Further, Ferres and Aaronson (1981) replicated many of the results obtained in Just and Carpenter's 1980 *Psychological Review* paper. That is, RTs for words could be accounted for well in terms of linear functions of their linguistic attributes, such as number of syllables, word frequency rank, and word occurrence at phrase breaks. For the particular attributes that are comparable, our coefficients on individual terms were even in the same numerical ball park as Just and Carpenter's. It increases scientific validity when different procedures from different labs replicate each other.

RTs Reflect Prior Reading Habits. Finally, practice effects in the data suggest that subjects are employing strategies based on prior reading habits. With increased practice, for fast adult readers there is little or no change in RT *patterns* that reflect syntactic and semantic coding. But RT patterns for child subjects and slow adult readers become smoother as the session progresses. These practice effects are what one would expect if the laboratory task were tapping into natural reading strategies.

The data in Figure 4 for adult recall subjects provide a quantitative illustration of practice effects by comparing changes in RT slopes and RT intercepts over two

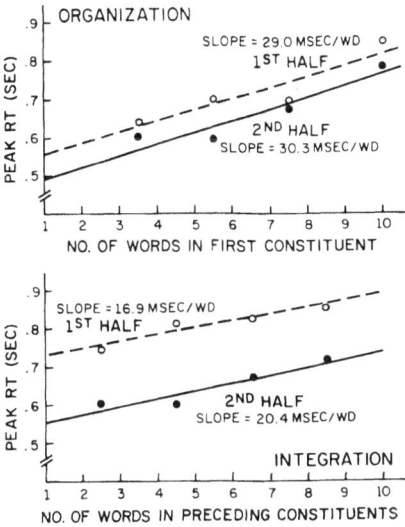

FIG. 4. Effects of practice on phrase peak RTs for adult recall subjects.

half-sessions. These data are the *peak* RTs at phrase break words, graphed separately for each half-session of practice. The top panel shows that phrase peak RTs increase linearly with the number of words to be "organized" from the current phrase, ending at the given peak. The bottom panel shows that phrase peak RTs also increase with the number of words to be "integrated" from all previous constituents. Thus, the RT *slopes* reflect the rate of contextual processing for units larger than a single word. In contrast, the intercepts are determined by factors associated with individual displays, regardless of the amount of prior linguistic context — such as the mean time to decode novel characters on the computer displays and to press the button to get each display. The dashed and solid lines on each panel are fit respectively to data from the first and second half-sessions. The parallelness of those lines provides evidence that the rate of "higher-level" cognitive processing does *not* change from the first to the second half-session of practice. Practice only affects individual display factors, such as getting used to the novel type font and to pressing the button. Indeed these differences in practice effects are expected if the cognitive processing in the lab is similar to that done during years of natural reading outside of the lab.

Comparison to Other Methods. The button-pressing feature of the word-by-word procedure may be criticized as "unnatural". But all other methods of studying reading also have some problems regarding "naturalness". Tools for laboratory research are, for good reasons, often not completely "natural". In many research procedures subjects are required to press a button to display one sentence at a time (e.g., see chapters in this volume by Kieras, Graesser, Haberlandt). That is not "natural" either. However, an advantage of the single word paradigm is that it is possible to evaluate the extra time involved in the "unnatural" button pressing separately from the more natural higher-level coding processes. The analysis in Figure 4 that separately examines the effects of experimental factors on RT slopes and intercepts is one such method of evaluation.

Many eye-movement procedures are not "natural" in ways different from the word-by-word procedure: they use bite boards, head clamps, contact lenses, and may restrict foveal or peripheral vision (e.g. see chapters in this volume by Rayner and by Just and Carpenter). But these eye-movement procedures have advantages as research tools that our procedure doesn't have.

It is important in research to have various techniques that complement and corroborate each other. The collection of chapters in this volume suggests that this is happening. For example, both Graesser's research and ours find that the RT for single sentence displays is a linear function of the number of syllables read. Haberlandt's sentence displays yield effects of syntactic and semantic variables that agree with our results. In Mitchell's procedure (this volume; Mitchell & Green, 1978), subjects pressed a button to obtain three-word displays. Both his results and ours (Ferres, 1981; Ferres & Aaronson, 1981) show RTs to increase with the number of letters and syllables read, and to decrease with word frequency. Further, in a comprehension task, RTs for three-word groups showed effects of semantic but not syntactic variables (Mitchell & Green, 1978) in agreement with Aaronson and Scarborough (1976). As mentioned earlier, replications in terms of both empirical trends and theoretical ideas have occurred between our lab and Just and Carpenter's lab (this volume). The analysis of mental events in the brain in terms of data from behavioral responses involves very indirect measurement and inference processes, regardless of the method. Thus, the fact that several different experimental and analytical methods can be compared provides some safeguards for the entire community of researchers studying reading.

READING UNITS

Word Units

Our procedure assumes that words are important reading units in terms of cognitive and linguistic criteria, and that the word-by-word RTs reflect the processing of individual words. Many aspects of the RT data provide evidence to support these notions. For example, an important property of words is their lexical category, and RTs for such categories vary in theoretically meaningful ways. Figure 5 shows the "relative" reading times (i.e. the difference between the RT for the given word and the mean RT for the words in its sentence) for words in 18 lexical categories for adults in the two tasks groups (from Aaronson and Ferres, 1983b). Positive Y-values for "relative" reading times correspond to RTs that are longer than the average for their sentence; negative values to RTs shorter than average. The top right graph shows RTs for content words. The data show that lexical verbs, auxiliary verbs, adverbs for those verbs, and nouns, are generally read slower than average while adjectives and their adverbs are generally read faster. The bottom

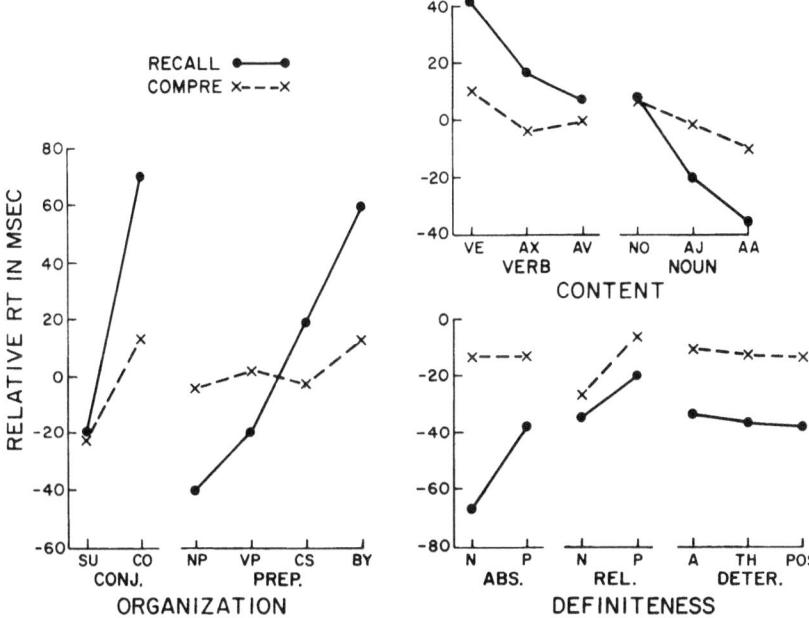

FIG. 5. Relative RTs for 18 lexical categories for two task groups.

right panel shows that "definiteness" function words have shorter RTs than average, including "absolute" (e.g., he, his) and relative (e.g., who, whose) nominal and possessive pronouns, and the determiners "a" and "the". On the left, RTs for "organization" function words, such as (subordinate and coordinate) conjunctions and prepositions, depend on their role in the sentence context.

Figure 5 highlights some important aspects of reading individual words that are in accord with the hypothesis of task-linked reading strategies. *Within* each major word class, RTs for the recall subjects are generally longer for categories relatively more important to structure. For example, within the content words, recall subjects' RTs are longer for the verb set that links the sentential subject and predicate, than for the noun set. Within the function words, the RTs are longer for the organizational words that initiate clauses and phrases, than for the definiteness words that delimit or substitute for nouns. But, the RTs suggest that comprehension subjects spend more of their time processing meaning and less of their time processing structure, in comparison to recall subjects. Within the content words, comprehension subjects spend less of their time on the verb set and more of their time on the noun set than do recall subjects. Within the function words, comprehension subjects spend less of their time on the organization words and more of their time on the definiteness words than do recall subjects. The results graphed in Figure 5 were all replicated using ratios of words to their sentence means, consistent with proportional as well as additive theories of processing time. These data are reported fully elsewhere (Aaronson & Ferres, 1983a, b, c).

Other Units

Although our procedure assumes that words are an important reading unit, this procedure also provides data on the role of units both smaller and larger than the word. For example, Figure 6 shows RT difference scores for three levels[2] of reading units. The left-most panel shows the effects of units smaller than a word: the RT difference between one and two syllable words. We see that syllable effects are larger for fifth grade children than for college age adults. The middle panel shows some word level effects: the RT difference between prepositions of high and low frequency *rank*, i.e., between rare and common words in the vocabulary (Kucera & Francis, 1967). Again, the children show larger word-level effects than the adults. Data for other word classes show similar effects of word frequency on RT. The right-most panel shows phrase-unit effects: RT differences between verbs at phrase breaks and matched verbs not at phrase breaks. Here, the age effect is reversed: adults show larger phrase unit effects than children, as one might expect based on other language development research (e.g., the syntagmatic/paradigmatic shift).

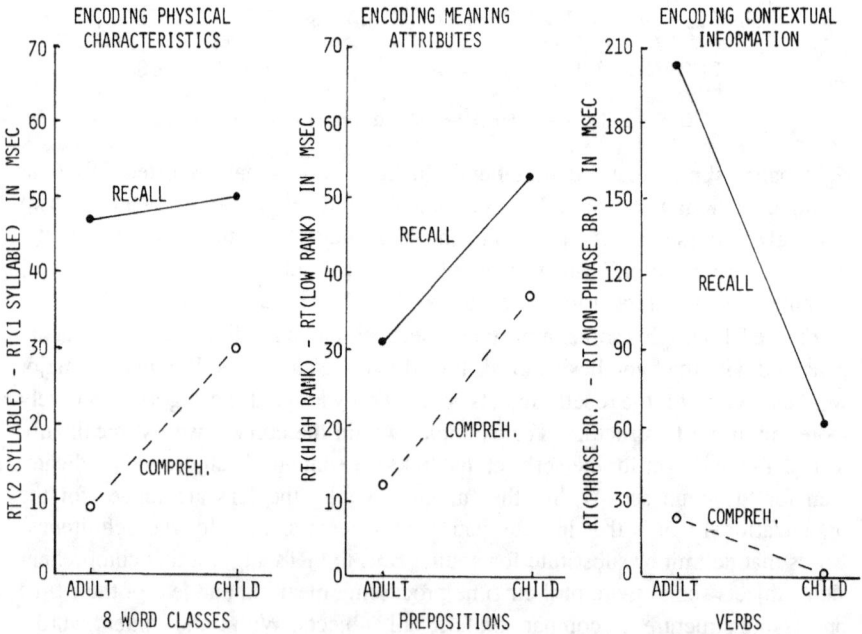

FIG. 6.   RT difference scores for three levels of reading units.

---

[2]Because there are moderate correlation values between lexical, meaning and structural attributes of the stimuli, the graphs in Figure 6 are subsets of the data selected to hold fixed the attributes other than the one being considered. Trends in the data for other word classes in general agree with those in Figure 6.

In sum, the RTs from our procedure show that words are an important processing unit in reading. But, the word-by-word displays can also provide data concerning the processing of units both smaller and larger than the word. There is no need to assume that the "fundamental" unit of reading is the word or that the procedure taps into processing only at the word level.

PROCESSING LOAD

Momentary Processing Load Assumption

The use of the word-by-word procedure requires a "processing load" assumption: *the RTs for individual words reflect the time subjects spend processing information related to those particular words.* For some words the RT probably does *not* include the entire amount of time needed to process the given word; some small amount of processing may be deferred. Also, for some words the RT probably does include additional time to process prior context that is related to the given word. The RT data for pronouns in Figure 7 (from Aaronson & Ferres, 1983b) illustrate these points. The data on the left are for "absolute" (as opposed to relative) pronouns involved in forward and backward anaphoric referencing. Backward referencing is when the noun comes first, and then the pronoun refers back to it: e.g., "when *Bill* ate, *he* spilled food in *his* lap". In forward referencing, the pronoun precedes the noun: e.g., "After *she* did *her* work, *Mary* watched TV". The X-axis includes points for nominal (e.g., she) and possessive (e.g., her) pronouns for both adult task groups. On the Y-axis all "relative" RTs are negative, because pronouns have shorter RTs than average. The data show that RTs are longer for backward than forward referencing pronouns for both task groups. When backward referencing pronouns are encountered, the subject reprocesses prior context to form the semantic relationship between the noun and its pronominal referent (Lesgold, 1972; Clark & Clark, 1977). In contrast, when forward referencing pronouns are encountered, their RTs are shorter, providing evidence that some of their processing is postponed until the associated noun can more fully define the pronoun's meaning in its sentence context (consistent with Miller, 1962).

Although RTs for individual words do not include all or only the processing time for the given word, we preferred the word-by-word procedure to eye-movement recording procedures because it provides tighter control in terms of the "processing load" assumption. With the usual eye-movement techniques the experimenter has even less control over the relation between the displayed text and the cognitive processing because multiword viewing, peripheral preview (forward and backward) and regressive eye movements are permitted. For example, recent research indicates that the eyes can and do pick up useful information over a "perceptual span" up to 18 letters to the right of fixation, and somewhat less to the left of fixation (McConkie & Rayner, 1975, 1976; Rayner, 1975; Hochberg, 1976).

Thus, the subject may actually be viewing text one to three words away from the word being scored as fixated in standard eye-movement procedures. Further, in those procedures, saccades between words and between lines consume time during which cognitive processing of the text may occur, and it is not clear how to allocate that time theoretically. Researchers generally delete saccade times, about 10% – 15% of the total, from data analyses (Just & Carpenter, 1980; Hogaboam & McConkie, 1981). Past eye movement research provides evidence that, on the average, the eyes in fact fixate about once per word, i.e., per 8 letters (Rayner & McConkie, 1976; Just & Carpenter, 1980). Thus, the single-word displays ensure that the subject is not viewing previous or subsequent words, and the single-word display size reflects the mean and the mode of what occurs in natural reading.

The Immediacy Assumption

Just and Carpenter (1980) state that the link between their eye fixation data and theory assumes "that a reader tries to interpret each content word of a text as it is encountered... Interpretation refers to processing at several levels such as encoding the word, choosing one meaning of it, assigning it to its referent, and determining its status in the sentence and in the discourse... that the interpretations at all levels of processing are not deferred..."

In contrast, Mitchell's recent work (this volume) suggests that some processing of words is deferred; i.e., there is "processing spillover" during the fixation of subsequent words. Reading times for words are affected by the size of previous displays and whether or not they contain anomalous material. Eye-voice span data suggest that a second or more may elapse between a word's initial perception and completion of its full processing (Gibson & Levin, 1975; McConkie et al., 1979). The data on forward referencing pronouns in Figure 7 provides evidence that the "Immediacy Assumption" is not completely true for our procedure. Most probably it is also not completely true for the eye movement paradigms either

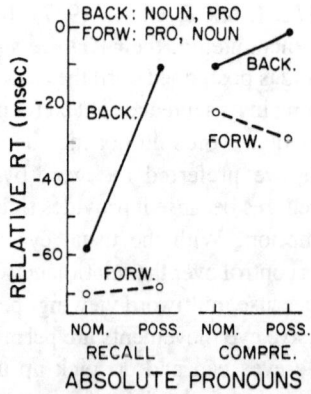

FIG. 7. Relative RTs for forward and backward referencing pronouns.

(Hogaboam & McConkie, 1981). But, the strong form of this assumption is not needed for most of the theoretical interpretations of the RT data obtained with either button-pressing or eye-movement procedures. The important problem is to account for the amount and location of deferred processing. Mitchell's procedures that vary the size of the stimulus display and the nature of the displayed material are a start in this direction. Mathematical models that include terms for current and deferred processing provide a second type of research tool to account for the time course of cognitive processing during reading.

The Eye-Mind Assumption

Just and Carpenter also assume that "the eye remains fixated on a word as long as the word is being processed ... " in contrast to an alternative view "that data acquired from several eye fixations are internally buffered before being semantically processed" (e.g., Bouma & deVoogd, 1974; Mitchell, this volume). Essentially this assumption has been discussed by others under the name "Eye-Mind Lag" assumption (Hogaboam & McConkie, 1981; McConkie, et al., 1979). A review of recent literature provides evidence both for and against this assumption. But, far more work is needed in order to determine the details of when and how much verbal material is "buffered", and when and how much prior context is processed when viewing subsequent words. The backward referencing pronoun data in Figure 7 suggest that prior context (perhaps the related noun) is processed while the pronoun is viewed, increasing its RT. Further, the prolonged RTs at phrase boundary words, obtained by Just and Carpenter and by us (see Figures 2, 3, 4), probably reflect both "immediate processing" of the given word and "delayed processing" of prior phrase context held in an internal buffer. Again, the strong version of the Eye-Mind Assumption is probably not needed to interpret the RT data. It is sufficient to assume that the RT for a given word reflects the momentary processing load while viewing the given word, i.e., information directly related to the given word, and also contextual information cued by the given word.

THEORETICAL DEVELOPMENT

The second part of this paper is concerned with theoretical procedures to interpret the word-by-word RTs. Our approach is to develop linear equations, based on cognitive processing assumptions, to predict various aspects of the RT data. The models for several experiments, two of which will be considered here, have commonalities and are all consistent with a general class of information processing models. The models are tested in two different ways: by the usual quantitative goodness-of-fit statistics and by trends in the RT data relevant to the qualitative nature of processing assumed for each reading time component in the models.

MODEL COMPONENTS

Figure 8 is a flow chart for the class of models to be considered. It is assumed that all words first undergo orthographic and lexical coding, regardless of the subsequent performance task. As the models do not separate orthographic and lexical coding, we refer loosely to this early processor as lexical for ease of discussion. Coding at this level includes translations of visual input to letter, syllable, or spelling pattern units, and then into word units that can be accessed in a mental lexicon. The lexical entry includes information on pronunciation, grammatical categories, and word meanings. Preliminary processing is begun on these attributes at this early stage. But information about the word's semantic and syntactic role in the particular sentence being read is handled at later stages.

After lexical access, the nature and time-course of the coding depend on task and subject factors. Based on the results of the parameter estimation programs, more of the higher-level coding occurs in the "structural processor" on the left for the memory task, and for the slow readers. We assume that the structural processing includes covert pronunciation of the word in relation to the intonation contour of the sentence. Covert pronunciation (subvocalization or auditory recoding) is located in the structural rather than the lexical processor for two reasons. First, recent research on lexical access provides evidence that knowledge of a word's pronunciation is optional and follows lexical access (Shulman, et al., 1978;

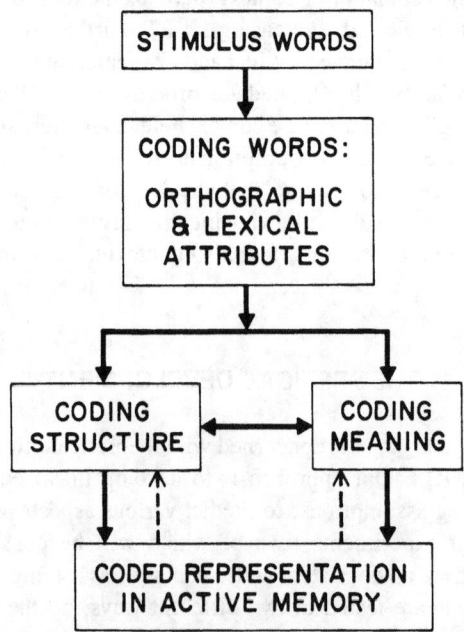

FIG. 8. Flow chart for a class of reading models.

Frederiksen & Kroll, 1976; Spoehr, 1978; Taft, 1979). Second, in English (and other languages) the "auditory" intonation contour is closely related to the surface parsing determined by the syntactic structure of the sentence. Accordingly, recent literature provides evidence that auditory recoding and syntactic coding are correlated. For example, both types of coding are done in memory tasks, but not in comprehension tasks (Kleiman, 1975; Levy, 1975; Baron, 1973, 1977; Baron & McKillop, 1975).

The processor on the right provides a fuller coding of meaning. Based on model testing and parameter estimation, this processor is used more extensively for the comprehension task, and by children. In the meaning processor, words and phrases are integrated with their context and relationships are formed among words and propositions. Individual words, initially decoded during lexical processing, are interpreted based on context.

The work of others, as well as our own research, provides both psychological and linguistic reasons to incorporate in the model separate processors for structure and meaning. But, the psychological properties of structure and meaning probably do not have strict one-to-one mappings with the linguistic attributes of syntax and semantics. Because of natural correlations between syntax and semantics, the structure processor may simultaneously gain some semantic information, and the meaning processor may simultaneously gain some syntax. For example, semantic cases, such as agent and patient, are moderately correlated with the syntactic roles of subject and object. Sapir (1921) pointed out the parallels between the semantic categories of "reference" and "predication" and their syntactic counterparts, "noun" and "verb". Semantic propositions and syntactic constituents are moderately correlated in terms of both the individual words comprising units and the order of those words. The language user makes use of such correlations and redundancies. Thus, when comprehension of gist is required for relatively simple text, the meaning processor alone can often do the job (Clark & Clark, 1977). Along these lines, some of our pilot work shows moderate agreement between subject ratings of "phrase" units and "idea" units in sentences. In sum, although some correlations may exist the present model has two "higher level" processors, with the structural processor focusing primarily on syntactic attributes and the meaning processor focusing primarily on semantic attributes.

After structure and meaning are processed, the coded representation goes into active memory for later use, as indicated at the bottom of Figure 8. Estimation procedures for the algebraic models assign coding times to the lexical (L), structure (S), and meaning (M) processors in this flow chart. Then, the RT predictions are based on an additive function of those processing times: $RT = f(L) + g(S) + h(M)$. For conceptual simplicity additive equations are often interpreted as serial processes. But, this is only one possible representation for additive time components. In general, RT data cannot distinguish serial representations from parallel-processing, time-sharing, or interactive representations (Snodgrass & Townsend, 1980; Townsend, 1971, 1972) which are more likely the case in reading tasks (Smith,

1979). Hence, readers should feel free to choose whichever representation of additivity is most compatible with their own theoretical ideas.

READING STRATEGIES IN CHILDREN AND ADULTS

To provide a test of the three-stage theory of reading, we present the highlights of an experiment that compared reading strategies for the recall and comprehension tasks in children and adults. The complete study is reported elsewhere by Aaronson and Ferres (1983d, submitted). In this experiment, sentences were kept at the third or fourth grade level, to provide text which could be read easily by both fifth grade children and college students. All subjects read 80 sentences with the word-by-word procedure. Immediately after each sentence, recall subjects spoke the sentence aloud into a microphone, while comprehension subjects pressed keys labeled "true" and "false" in response to 4-7 word statements about the sentence. The model predicts the mean RTs when these two different task groups read the same sentences.

The Model Equations

Table 3 has the linear RT equations to predict the mean word-by-word RTs for this experiment. These equations are a particular realization of the general model in Figure 8, including time components for coding lexical, structural and meaning information from the text. The ordered codes on the left are abbreviations for the 16 conditions: two ages, adult (A) and 5th grade children (C); two tasks, recall (R) and comprehension (C); two reading speeds, fast (F) and slow (S) readers based on a median-split; and two half-sessions of practice, labeled 1 and 2.

As the model flow chart in Figure 8 indicates, all groups in Table 3 have lexical coding times, and those are listed as the first term. The chi-square estimation program (Stepit, Chandler, 1965) yielded a lexical coding time of $L = 141$ msec for all conditions (see parameter values in Table 4). In addition to time for decoding the words, this lexical time also includes the motor time for button pressing to display the given words, perhaps partially in parallel with the decoding. Linear regression models based on eye-movement data also include a motor time in the base term, for the saccade needed to get each word (Just & Carpenter, 1980). Slow individuals in both task groups have an additional lexical time of $I = 196$ msec. Further, lexical times have been increased during the first half-session of practice by a constant, $P = 156$ msec. As the top and bottom halves of Table 3 are identical except for "P", the discussion which focuses on the top can easily be extended to the bottom. Finally, lexical times are longer for children than adults by an age constant, $A = 235$ msec.

Next, consider the terms on the right of Table 3. The task-linked reading strategies differ in the amount of time spent coding structure or meaning. First

3. WORD-BY-WORD READING   51

TABLE 3
Model Equations

Condition	Orthographic & Lexical Times				Meaning & Structure Times		
ARF2	L				βM	+	βS
ARS2	L	+ I			βM	+	S
ACF2	L				M		
ACS2	L	+ I			M		
CRF2	L		+ A		M	+	βS
CRS2	L	+ I	+ A		M	+	S
CCF2	L		+ A		βM		
CCS2	L	+ I	+ A		M	+	βS
ARF1	L			+ P	βM	+	βS
ARS1	L	+ I		+ P	βM	+	S
ACF1	L			+ P	M		
ACS1	L	+ I		+ P	M		
CRF1	L		+ A	+ P	M	+	βS
CRS1	L	+ I	+ A	+ P	M	+	S
CCF1	L		+ A	+ P	βM		
CCS1	L	+ I	+ A	+ P	M	+	βS

consider the top four equations for adult RTs. The fast and slow adult recall subjects have additive times for coding meaning, M, and structure, S. M and S are the maximum amount of time that can be allocated to coding, and the estimated values were 102 and 401 msec respectively. In addition to full or no coding, the β-multipliers permit partial coding. For all conditions β was estimated at the same value, about ⅓. When estimated times are filled in, the equations show that adult recall subjects spend most of their time coding structure, rather than meaning. Further, structural coding time is greater for slow than fast recall subjects. In contrast, the next two equations hypothesize that adult comprehension subjects code only meaning.

Next, consider the four equations for fifth grade children. The higher-level coding for children is assumed to be a mixture of the adult components as follows: (a) Recall children spend more time coding meaning than recall adults. This is in line with the developmental literature on syntagmatic and paradigmatic coding. Those studies show that children often use semantic information to do their syntactic coding. For example, children misinterpret passive noun-verb-noun strings as actor-action-object (Bever, 1970; Gowie & Powers, 1978), and they misinterpret pronouns by substituting the semantic attribute of sex for the syntactic attribute of gender (Graesser & Mandler, 1975). (b) The equations show that comprehension children spend more time coding structure and less time coding meaning than comprehension adults. In Table 3, the extra structural coding time for slow comprehension children is in line with literature suggesting that children subvocalize a lot during reading (Gibson & Levine, 1975). Remember that auditory recoding or subvocalization was located in the structural processor, in Figure 8. Such subvocalization probably contributes to the increased structural coding time for children, slow readers, and recall subjects, in line with past research (Huey, 1908).

Thus, the equations show task-linked strategies for the adults with recall subjects oriented toward structure and comprehension toward meaning. The children's strategies basically approximate those of the adults, but both groups of children mix the adult strategies. Recall children code more meaning than recall adults; comprehension children code more structure and less meaning than comprehension adults.

Tests of the Model's Overall Fit

Figure 9 and Table 4 contain data that test the model: the observed and predicted mean RTs for all 16 conditions. The top two curves in Figure 9 are respectively for the first and second half sessions of practice. The model fits the data well, with a Pearson correlation between the model and the data of $r = .99 (p < .01)$. As the various lexical coding components comprise a substantial percentage of the total RT (44% to 94%), one might be concerned that the model fit could be attributed

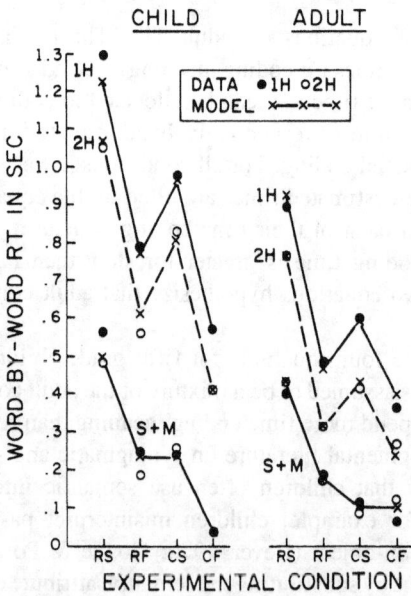

FIG. 9. Predicted and observed data for the 3 component reading model.

TABLE 4
Model Predictions, Observed
Data & Parameter Estimates

Cond	Model Msec	Data Msec	Cond	Model Msec	Data Msec	Parameters	
ARF1	470	484	ARF2	314	315	L = 141	msec
ARS1	929	898	ARS2	773	773	I = 196	msec
ACF1	398	362	ACF2	243	269	A = 235	msec
ACS1	595	598	ACS2	439	424	P = 156	msec
CRF1	771	790	CRF2	615	561	M = 102	msec
CRS1	1230	1295	CRS2	1074	1052	S = 401	msec
CCF1	566	567	CCF2	411	410	β = .345	
CCS1	968	973	CCS2	811	829		

primarily to lexical rather than structure or meaning components. A test of the fit with those lexical times subtracted out, provides evidence that this is not the case. With the lexical component removed, the correlation between model and data is $r = .98 (p < .01)$.

A second statistical test can also be done on the variances. Additive processing with more coding stages should have larger RT variances (Sternberg, 1969). For example, ACF2 had 2 coding times comprising their total RT, while CCS1 had 6. Accordingly, a Spearman correlation coefficient between the number of coding stages and the variances of each of the 16 conditions had a value of $rho = .822 (p < .02)$.

Tests of the Model's Processing Components

Next, consider tests of the qualitative nature of coding for each group of readers. Do the additive time components really reflect the structure and meaning processors hypothesized in the Figure 8 flow chart? To provide evidence on the qualitative nature of processing, the RT data were examined for some of the syntactic and semantic variables shown in Table 1.

Figure 10 shows three types of structural indices for the eight groups of subjects. These data are averaged over both half-sessions of practice, as equations for the two halves make identical predictions for coding structure and meaning. The data are labeled AR, AC, CR, and CC respectively for adult recall, adult comprehension, child recall, and child comprehension. The data in all three panels are RT difference scores. The left-most panel shows the RT differences between words at phrase breaks and words at phrase intermediate positions. The middle shows RT differences between lexical and copular "being" verbs. The lexical verbs signal a more complex sentence structure than do the copulas. These lexical verbs are transitive and their sentences have three major constituents: subject, verb, and object. The copulas are intransitive and their sentences have two constituents that

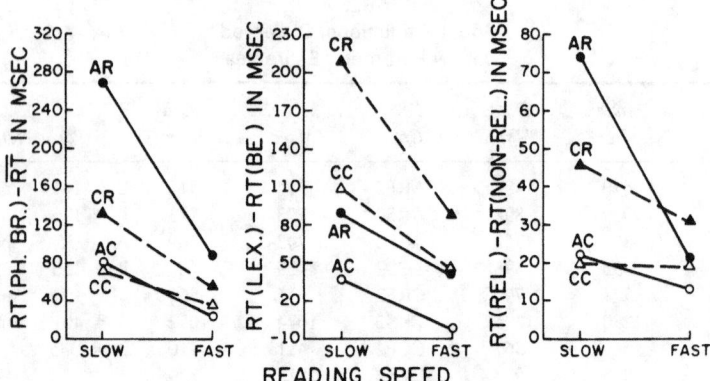

FIG. 10. Structural indices for 8 groups of subjects.

are closely related: a subject with a predicate nominative or a predicate adjective that refers back to the subject. The right-most panel shows the RT differences between sentences of differing syntactic complexity: those with embedded relative clauses and those without. Subjects who should devote more time to coding structure should have higher values on these three empirical indices. Although these indices obviously do not tap structural coding exclusive of all lexical and meaning processes, they do *emphasize* syntactic aspects of the stimuli.

Four comparisons in this figure are of interest based on the model equations in Table 3. First, compare the two adult task groups with the solid lines connecting circles. All three structural indices are higher for recall than comprehension readers, as predicted by the model. Second, compare the two child task groups with dashed lines connecting triangles. Again, all three structural indices are higher for recall than comprehension, as expected. Third, the model predicts equal structural coding for the child and adult recall subjects. Accordingly, child recall scores are lower than adults' in the first panel, higher in the second and about equal in the third. Finally, the model predicts slightly more structural coding for children than adults in the comprehension task, perhaps because of extra subvocalization. The combined data for the three indices bear this out. Thus, these three empirical indices provide support for the qualitative differences in structural coding hypothesized by the model.

Next, consider the three indices for coding meaning in Figure 11. All three indices emphasize semantic *relations* between words and their prior context, as opposed to semantic attributes of individual words. Semantic integration, in the left panel, is indexed by a Pearson correlation coefficient between prepositions and their *prior* associated content words. Prepositions closely follow a content word and signal the reader to prepare for a semantic relationship: the object of the preposition will modify the meaning of the prior content word (for example, in "swam with great speed"). There should be a positive correlation between the RT for a preposition and its prior content word. Content words that contribute greater

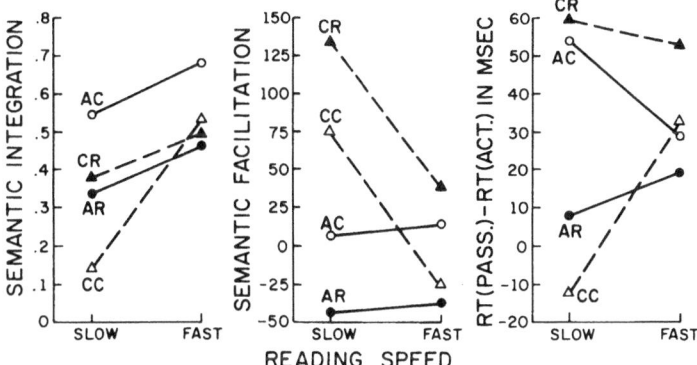

FIG. 11. Meaning indices for 8 groups of subjects.

semantic importance to the sentence as evidenced by larger RTs (Ferres, 1981) should have associated prepositional modifiers that incorporate some of their importance, and thus also have larger RTs. The middle panel, labeled "Semantic Facilitation", has RT differences between nouns that are rather unpredictable from context and those that are very predictable. Predictability was determined by an independent experiment. The right panel contains RT differences between passive and active verbs. Passives are considered to be semantically more complex than actives, based on propositional theories (Anderson & Bower, 1973), information theory (Clark, 1965), theories of semantic marking (Anisfeld & Klenbort, 1973) and semantic expectancy (Bever, 1970). For all three empirical indices in this figure, subjects who do more semantic coding, according to the model, should have higher values, as discussed in detail below. Again, these indices primarily *emphasize* semantic coding, although they may also tap other linguistic attributes.

Four comparisons in Figure 11 are of interest in testing the model in Table 3. First, when comparing the adult task groups, we expect higher meaning values for comprehension subjects, with their meaning-oriented strategy, than for recall subjects. In comparing the solid lines, this is true in all three panels of Figure 11. As a concrete example, Figure 12 shows some semantic facilitation data for the adult task groups for two sentences. In the top sentence "suit" was highly predictable from context, and in the bottom sentence "years" was highly predictable. Accordingly, comprehension RTs are decreased at these points. But the recall RTs are what one would expect based on other linguistic attributes. "Suit" is at a phrase boundary in the top sentence, and is thus elevated for recall subjects. "Years" is in the middle of a phrase and thus is in an RT trough for recall subjects.

For the meaning indices in Figure 11, the model makes a task prediction for children that is opposite to that for adults: recall children should code both more meaning and more structure than comprehension children. Accordingly, the dashed lines in all three panels show child recall higher than child comprehension. Third, these recall children, who may use semantic information to interpret both

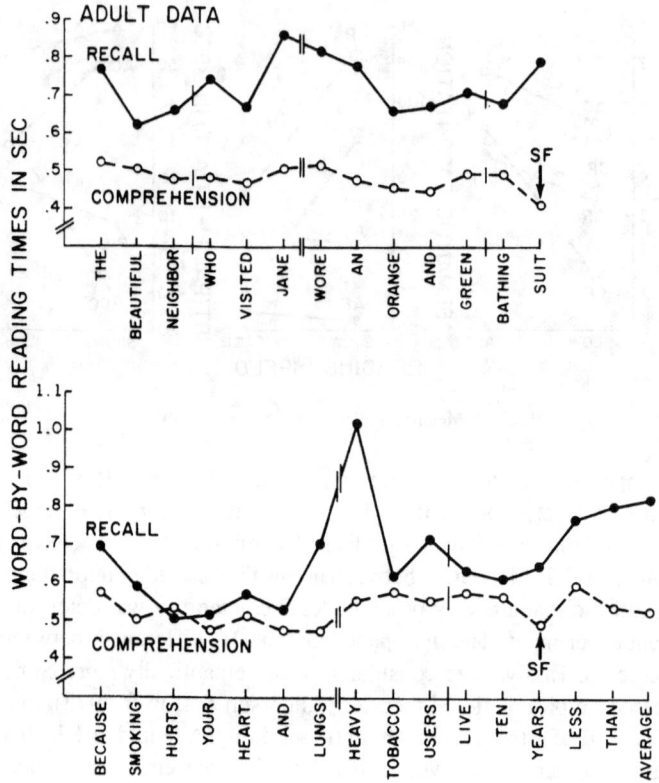

FIG. 12. Examples of semantic facilitation in RTs for comprehension subjects.

meaning and structure, should spend more time coding meaning than recall adults. Accordingly, this is true in all three panels. Finally, child comprehension subjects should code slightly less meaning than adult comprehension, and the combined data for the three panels bear this out. Thus, these three indices provide support for the qualitative differences in coding meaning hypothesized by the model.

Mixture Strategies for Child Readers

To review, the model predicts strongly task-linked reading strategies for adults: a structure oriented strategy for recall, and a meaning oriented strategy for comprehension subjects. Reading strategies for children approximate their adult counterparts. But children also show mixtures of the adult processing components. This is reasonable in light of the child development literature. However, reading development is a dynamic process, and these averaged data tap into the age scale at only two points. But the profiles for individual subjects reading individual sentences provide further information.

Although there were no clear dichotomies, we observed (at least) three types of RT profiles suggesting a developmental sequence in children. These profiles or patterns varied somewhat systematically with overall reading speed. (a) Some of the slowest readers showed profiles with very high variance, and little resemblance to either adult pattern. There were often three or four prolonged RT peaks per sentence, generally at content words, with time values exceeding two seconds. Although these peaks might indicate points for grouping information into units larger than a word, they might also indicate hesitations at trouble spots. (b) A fair number of children have RTs averaging about one second per word. The subvocalizations of some of these children became quite vocal during practice trials as they moved their lips, whispered, or read audibly. Many of these subjects often mixed the two adult strategies within single sentences. Figure 13 shows sentence profiles from two such children. In the top graph, the first half of the sentence has phrase-based scallops typical of the recall strategy and the second half has a smoother pattern with minor variations at "semantically appropriate" points, characteristic of the comprehension strategy. A profile with these components in the reverse order is on the bottom. (c) Many of the fastest children showed sentence profiles indistinguishable from the adults, with fairly consistent recall or comprehension features. However, some of these children alternated between the two strategies from one trial to the next. Figure 14 illustrates data from one such child.

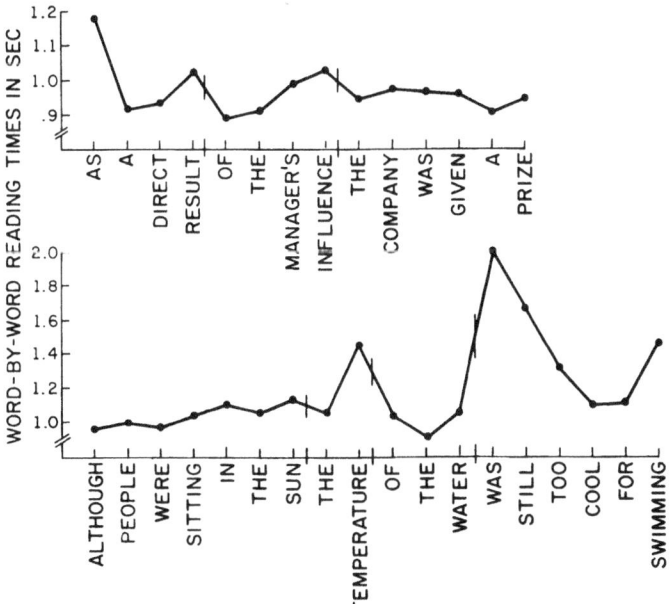

FIG. 13. RT profiles for two children who mix the recall and comprehension strategies within a sentence.

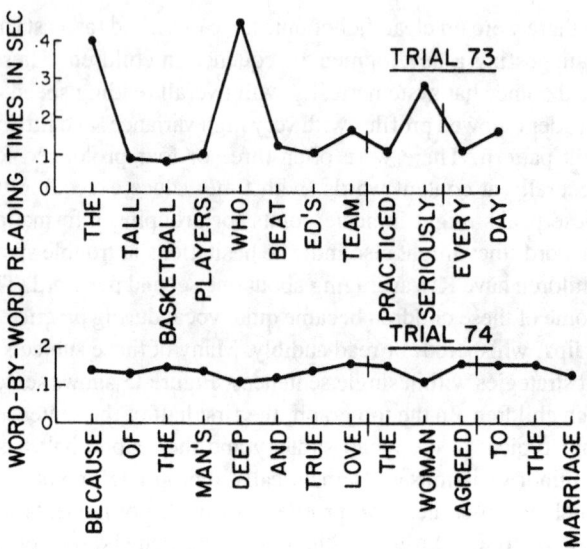

FIG. 14. RT profiles for a child who mixes the recall and comprehension strategies from one sentence to another.

Thus, the "mixture" strategies for child readers include at least three different types of mixtures that are roughly correlated with overall reading speed. The developmental process may progress from a rather undifferentiated and noisy profile, to a mixing of adult components within a sentence, to an alternation of strategies from one sentence to another, to fully developed adult strategies. Note also that most adults did not show clear examples of the "appropriate" strategy on every trial. However, most of the adults showed the task-related RT patterns on most of their trials.

THE TIME COURSE OF READING FOR RETENTION

A different approach towards the development of linear models was provided by a detailed examination of the phrase break RTs when adults read for retention (Aaronson & Scarborough, 1976, 1977). In the previous study on children and adults, phrase break RTs were used as a structural index, because phrase boundary words are particularly important cues for parsing the surface structure syntax. But, the inordinately long RTs at phrase breaks for recall adults (e.g., figures 2, 3, 6C, 10A, 12) suggest that much more than single words are processed at those points. At phrase breaks, subjects may also do higher level contextual processing of the entire phrase, or of the prior sentence context, in terms of both structural and meaning attributes.

A three-component linear model is again used to account for the RT patterns, this time only for the phrase peak RTs, rather than the mean RT for all words. First, we briefly consider the model equation, and point out some relationships it has to the previous model for child and adult RTs. Then we consider more detailed tests of the phrase peak model in relation to the reading time data. In this experiment adults read 90 sentences of average difficulty, i.e., based on newspaper and magazine text. Their post-sentence recall was written on a prepared response sheet, rather than spoken as in the previous study.

The Model Equation

Figure 15 shows the additive equation that quantifies the processing at phrase breaks. On the left, R includes the time for reading the particular phrase boundary word, along with the motor time to get the stimulus display. The second time component is for *organization* of the current phrase or constituent. Wc is the number of words in that *current* phrase, and θ is the amount of time per word used in organization. The third time component is for *integration* of prior context with the current phrase. Wp is the number of words in all *preceding* context, and I is the amount of time per word used in integration. For the example sentence in the top panel of Figure 2, if the model is predicting the RT for the phrase peak at the word "power", then $Wc = 6$ ("as well as its motor's power") and $Wp = 5$ ("because of its lasting construction").

Although the child-adult model concerned RTs for individual words and the phrase peak model concerns higher-level contextual processing, a comparison of results from the two studies suggests processing analogies or equivalencies between the two models for the three additive time components. First, the *lexical* terms of the child-adult model and the *reading* term, R, for the phrase peak model both represent the earliest stage of the three processors and a stage that is common to all subject groups. The data from both studies show a substantial time difference (over 150 msec) at this stage between slow and fast readers (see Figure 16A).

TOTAL RT AT CONSTITUENT BREAK

| READING AND MOTOR TIME FOR THE CURRENT WORD $R = 512$ MSEC | + | ORGANIZATION TIME FOR THE CURRENT CONSTITUENT $\theta = 30.5$ MSEC/WD | + | INTEGRATION TIME FOR PRECEDING CONSTITUENTS $I = 17.6$ MSEC/WD |

$$RT = R + \theta(W_C) + I(W_P)$$
$$RT = 512 + 30.5 W_C + 17.6 W_P$$

FIG. 15. An additive model for phrase peak RT's.

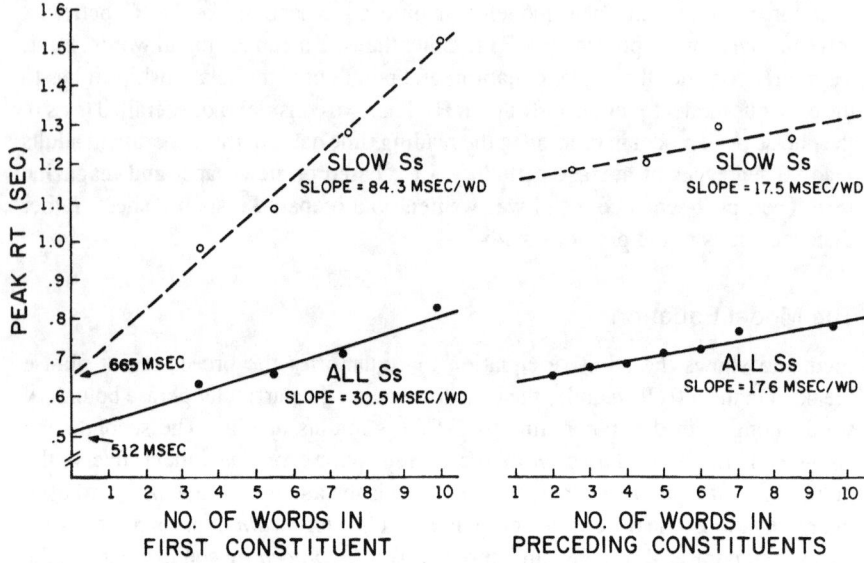

FIG. 16. Peak RTs used to estimate organization (left) and integration (right) parameters.

Next, consider analogies between the structure and meaning terms for the child-adult model, and the organization and integration terms for the phrase peak model. *Organizing*, chunking, or forming a larger unit from the individual words, one phrase at a time, is a central aspect of providing *structure* for the sentence as a whole. *Integrating* all prior context with the current phrase is a central aspect of forming *meaningful* relations among propositions throughout the sentence. A comparison of the results for the two studies shows five parallels between these component pairs, suggesting that they may represent the same processors. These parallels are listed here, to provide an overview for the reader, and they are discussed in more detail below. (a) Recall subjects in the child-adult study code both structure and meaning for individual words, and recall subjects in the phrase peak study code both "structure" (i.e., organization) and "meaning" (i.e., integration) for larger contextual units in the sentence (see Figure 16, as discussed below). (b) In the child-adult study, adult recall subjects spent more time coding structure than meaning, and in the phrase peak study adult recall subjects spent more time organizing phrase units than integrating prior context (as can be seen from comparisons of RT slopes in Figure 16A and 16B). (c) In both studies, more time is spent on "structural" (organizational) coding by slow than fast subjects (Figure 16A slopes). (d) But slow and fast adult readers spend the same amount of time coding "meaning" (integrating semantic information) in both studies (Figure 16B slopes). (e) For both studies, practice affects only the earliest stage of processing, and not higher level terms for coding "structure" and "meaning" (Figure 17, intercepts and slopes). This is expected if L and R times include button pressing and reading novel computer characters, but the other terms represent processes used regularly during a decade or so of daily reading.

In sum, the child-adult model focused on linguistic coding at the word level, while the phrase-peak model focuses on linguistic coding of higher-level units in the sentence. As close parallels exist between coding the "structure" and "meaning" of words and of phrase units, we will continue to use the same terminology in order to highlight the parallels. In essence, we hypothesize (a) that readers process the structure and meaning of text for each of several levels or unit sizes, such as the word, the phrase or clause, the sentence, the paragraph and the chapter or story, and (b) that there are strong commonalities or analogies in the processing among levels. The hypotheses of separate processors for "structural organization" and "semantic integration" at the phrase and sentence levels do not deny that subjects process meaning and structure when they initially read the individual words. Further, the higher level or "macro" processes of organizing a phrase into a structural unit and of integrating the meaning of prior context with the current phrase may actively involve both semantic and syntactic attributes of the individual words.

Parameter Estimates and Test of Linearity Within Components

Figure 16 shows some of the data used to test the model and to estimate the parameters. The Y-axes are for *only* the RT peaks at phrase break words. The two X-axes are respectively, the number of words in the current (most recent) phrase, and in phrases preceding the current one (i.e., in all prior context). Thus, in terms of the phrase peak model, the left panel contains the organizational or structural coding times, and the right panel contains the integration or meaning times. The organization parameter Θ on the left, is the slope of the best fitting least-squares line for the peak RT at the phrase breaks, when the number of words in the associated *current* phrase is varied. The integration parameter (I) on the right, is the slope of the least-squares line for the peak RT at phrase breaks, when the number of words in *prior* context is varied. (The stimuli were designed so that current and prior phrase lengths were independent). The solid bottom lines are the best fit regression lines for all subjects and the top dashed lines are the fit for the 25% slowest readers.

There are three important points about these graphs. (a) The data are fit well by straight lines, suggesting that the processing *within* each component is an additive function of th number of words to be processed. (b) The slopes are steeper in the left than the right panel, suggesting that adult recall subjects spend more time per word coding structure than coding meaning. (c) Slow recall subjects are *not* uniformly slow in their reading processes. They are slower in lexical coding, included in the Y-intercepts. And, they are almost three times slower than average in organizational or structural coding, as indicated by the slopes on the left. But, the time slopes to integrate meaning are equal for slow and fast recall subjects, as illustrated on the right. Note that these points are also expressed by the equations in Table 3 for the adult recall subjects in the other experiment.

Tests of Additivity Between Component Means

Figure 17 provides data to test the additivity between the model components for organizing structure and integrating meaning. These data are a breakdown of data in Figure 4 showing that practice does not affect the higher-level processing rates during reading. Within each panel the data have been split in order to determine the best fit line for a given processor, when there is either a light or a heavy load on the other processor. For example, consider the upper left panel. This graph contains lines for structural organization of the current phrase, when there is either a light or a heavy load to be integrated from prior context by the meaning processor. The bottom solid line is fit to the peak RTs for the current phrase, when there is a very light load to be integrated; in fact zero words in preceding phrases. The dashed line is fit to the peak RTs for the current phrase when there is a heavier load to be integrated from preceding phrases, a mean of 5.4 words.

Analogously, the upper right panel contains lines for integrating meaning, when there is either a light or a heavy load to be organized by the structural processor. The bottom solid line for integration is fit to the peak RTs when short current phrases are organized, i.e., 2–3 words. The top dashed line is fit to peak RTs when long current phrases are organized, i.e., 4–7 words.

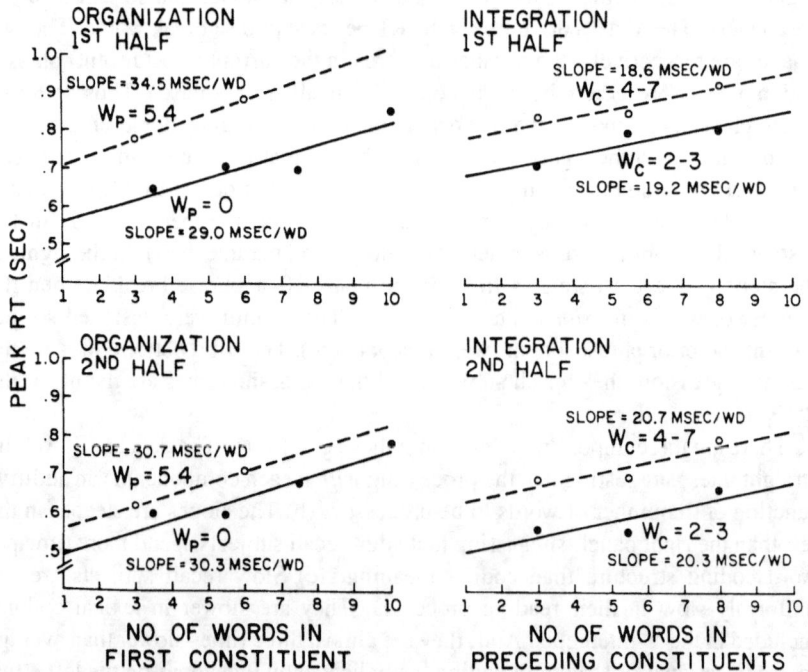

FIG. 17. Peak RTs showing additivity between model components for organizing structure and integrating meaning.

The main point about this figure is that structural organization and semantic integration do not interact. The pairs of lines in each panel are roughly parallel or additive. The organization rate is not slowed down by a heavy integration load; and the integration rate is not slowed down by a heavy organization load. Hence, the assumption of additivity of processing times during reading for these two components is justified.

Test of Component Independence

Figure 18 shows some unexpected information about the structure and meaning processors: these times are not only additive, but also stochastically independent. Additivity does not necessarily imply independence. For example, two correlated processors might have additive times which both slow down or speed up together, depending on the subject's attention or arousal level. For stochastically independent processors, the variances should be additive. The data in Figure 18 are RT variances for organization time with a light or heavy load on integration, and for integration time with a light or heavy load on organization. The graph shows roughly parallel lines for these variances, providing evidence that the coding times for structure and meaning are stochastically independent.

In sum, the peak RT data for recall subjects provide evidence for additive and independent processors to code lexical, structure and meaning information at phrase boundaries. Further, the additive relations among these three types of processors show parallels to the processing model hypothesized for word RTs in Table 3.

SUMMARY AND CONCLUSIONS

The word-by-word reading procedure has proven to be a useful research tool. It provides "on-line" measurement of reading times in a paradigm that permits wide variation in linguistic and task variables. It is sensitive enough to examine the RT patterns for individual subjects on individual trials, and it yields data that have high reliability over both subjects and sentences. Using the procedure to study reading requires only three relatively weak assumptions that are testable by the RT data: (a) the reading procedure is natural; (b) words are an important reading unit; and (c) the RTs reflect the momentary processing load.

The paradigm has generated a wealth of detailed data that can be used to test models of the reading process. The models we have investigated predict RTs in terms of additive equations with components for coding lexical, structural and meaning information. Both the quantitative predictions and the underlying qualitative assumptions of the models are well supported by the RT data.

Mathematical models in psychology can be classified into three broad categories: stimulus-response models, response-response models, and hypothetical con-

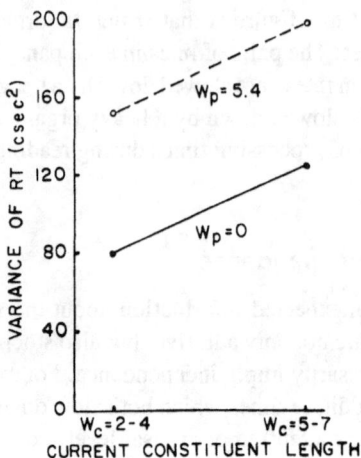

FIG. 18. Peak RT variance supporting independence between model components for organizing structure and integrating meaning.

struct-response models. (See Bush, Galanter & Luce, 1963 for a similar classification). We have been able to develop all three types of models within the framework of additive linear equations, as summarized below.

Stimulus – Response Models

This class of models predicts the reading time data from stimulus attributes of the text. The phrase peak RT model is of this type. Phrase break RTs are predicted in terms of the number of words in the "current" and "preceding" phrases of the sentence. The model for one of our recent projects is also of the stimulus-response type (Ferres, 1981; Ferres & Aaronson, 1981). For that research, RTs are predicted for four categories of content words (nouns, verbs, adjectives, adverbs) and four of function words (conjunctions, prepositions, pronouns, articles), for child and adult readers in the recall and comprehension tasks. All three processing components in those RT equations are functions of stimulus attributes: the lexical component is based on the mean number of syllables in each category of words; the structural component is based on the proportion of words in each category that occur at phrase boundaries, and (c) the meaning component is based on the average word frequency rank for the category.

Response – Response Models

This type of model would predict the reading time data in one experiment from subject responses in an independent psycholinguistic task. The model to account for the lexical category RTs in Figure 5 is of this type (see Aaronson & Ferres, 1983a, b, c). For that project one group of subjects gave 5-point ratings for the contributions of the words to the structure and meaning of their sentence. These ratings were then used to predict the RTs for other subjects. An additional type of response-response model would predict one type of data (e.g., the recall or comprehension accuracy) from another type of data (e.g., reading times) within the same experiment.

Hypothetical Construct – Response Models

This type of model accounts for the RTs solely in terms of underlying hypothetical constructs or assumptions about the reading process. No external information is involved, such as the stimulus attributes or subjective ratings in the other two classes of models. The model for the child and adult reading data in Table 3 and Figure 9 is of this type. Here, processing time parameters for lexical, structural, and meaning information are determined only by the RT data. Although it is not necessary for this type of model, other independent aspects of the data were used to provide evidence on the qualitative nature of the hypothesized processors.

Converging Techniques

All three of the above approaches to model building have been taken in a series of experiments with the word-by-word reading paradigm, and they corroborate each other on important theoretical points. For all of the studies, more time is spent on linguistic coding when subjects read for complete retention of the text than for immediate comprehension of gist. Further, the nature of the coding strategy differs with the performance task demands. Subjects reading for retention spend more of their time coding structure and less of their time coding meaning, in relation to subjects reading for comprehension. Finally, slow readers are not uniformly slow. They are selectively slow in coding lexical and structural attributes, but not in coding meaning. This finding suggests some speculations about the similarities and differences between reading and listening. *Coding linguistic information from these two modalities may be similar for meaning attributes, but different for lexical and structural attributes.* For the listener, the sentence is received in an acoustic intonation contour that has already organized letters into word-units, and words into phrase-units. But, when faced with printed text, the reader must do these two types of coding himself. The slow reader may be slow because of the lexical and structural processing unique to reading, not the meaning processing that is common to both reading and listening.

In sum, the word-by-word paradigm, in conjunction with the development of additive models, has provided an understanding of the reading process in a more detailed way than is possible with most other research approaches.

REFERENCES

Aaronson, D. Performance theories for sentence coding: Some qualitative observations. *Journal of Experimental Psychology: Human Perception and Performance*, 1976, *2*, 42-55.

Aaronson, D., & Brauth, S. SIMPLE guidelines for developing a computer-based laboratory. *Behavior Research Methods and Instrumentation*, 1972, *4*, 257-264.

Aaronson, D., & Ferres, S. A structure and meaning based classification of lexical categories. In S. White, B. Kachuk & F. Podwall (Eds.) *Reading and reading disability: Scanning the 80's*. New York: The New York Academy of Sciences, 1983. (a)

Aaronson, D., & Ferres, S. Lexical categories and reading tasks. *Journal of Experimental Psychology: Human Perception and Performance*, 1983, *9*, 675-699. (b)

Aaronson, D., & Ferres, S. A quantitative model for coding lexical categories. *Journal of Experimental Psychology: Human Perception and Performance*, 1983c, *9*, 700-725.

Aaronson, D., & Ferres, S. Reading strategies for children and adults: Some empirical evidence. *Journal of Verbal Learning and Verbal Behavior*, 1983. (d)

Aaronson, D., & Ferres, S. Reading strategies for children and adults: A quantitative model. Submitted for publication.

Aaronson, D., & Scarborough, H. S. Performance theories for sentence coding: Some quantitative evidence. *Journal of Experimental Psychology: Human Perception and Performance*, 1976, *2*, 56-70.

Aaronson, D., & Scarborough, H. S. Performance theories for sentence coding: Some quantitative models. *Journal of Verbal Learning and Verbal Behavior*, 1977, *16*, 277-303.

Anderson, J. R., & Bower, G. H. *Human associative memory*. Washington, D. C.: Winston & Sons, 1973.

Anglin, J. M., & Miller, G. A. The role of phrase structure in the recall of meaningful verbal material. *Psychonomic Science*, 1968, *10*, 343-344.

Anisfeld, M., & Klenbort, I. On the functions of structural paraphrases: The view from the passive voice. *Psychological Bulletin*, 1973, *79*, 117-126.

Barlett, F. C. *Remembering: A study in experimental and social psychology*. Cambridge, England: Cambridge University Press, 1932.

Baron, J. Phonemic stage not necessary for reading. *Quarterly Journal of Experimental Psychology*, 1973, *25*, 241-246.

Baron, J. Mechanisms for pronouncing printed words: Use and acquisition. In D. LaBerge & S. J. Samuels (Eds.), *Basic processes in reading: Perception and communication*. Hillsdale, N. J.: Lawrence Erlbaum Associates, 1977.

Baron, J., & McKillop, B. J. Individual differences in speed of phonemic analysis, visual analysis and reading. *Acta Psychologica*, 1975, *39*, 91-96.

Begg, I., & Paivio, A. Concreteness and imagery in sentence meaning. *Journal of Verbal Learning and Verbal Behavior*, 1969, *8*, 821-827.

Bever, T. G. The cognitive basis for linguistic structure. In J. R. Hayes (Ed.), *Cognition and the development of language*. New York: John Wiley & Sons, 1970.

Bouma, H., & deVoogd, A. H. On the control of eye saccades in reading. *Vision Research*, 1974, *14*, 273-284.

Bush, R. R., Galanter, E., & Luce, R. D. Characterization and classification of choice experiments. In R. D. Luce, R. R. Bush, & E. Galanter (Eds.), *Handbook of mathematical psychology*. New York: Wiley, 1963.

Carroll, J., Davies, P., & Richman, B., (Eds.) *American heritage word frequency book*. New York: Houghton-Mifflin, 1971.

Chandler, J. P. Subroutine stepit. *Quantum Chemistry Program Exchange*, Department of Chemistry, Indiana University, Bloomington, IN, 1965.

Clark, H. H. Some structural properties of simple active and passive sentences. *Journal of Verbal Learning and Verbal Behavior*, 1965, *4*, 365-370.

Clark, H. H., & Clark, E. V. *Psychology and language*. New York: Harcourt Brace Jovanovich, Inc., 1977.

Ferres, S. *A word class encoding model for adults and children in comprehension and recall tasks*. Ph. D. dissertation, New York University, 1981.

Ferres, S., & Aaronson, D. A word class encoding model for reading units. The Psychonomic Society, Philadelphia, PA., 1981.

Frederiksen, J. R., & Kroll, J. F. Spelling and sound: Approaches to the internal lexicon. *Journal of Experimental Psychology: Human Perception and Performance*, 1976, *2*, 361-379.

Gibson, E. J., & Levin, H. *The psychology of reading*. Cambridge, MA: The MIT Press, 1975.

Glanzer, M., & Razel, M. The size of the unit in short-term storage. *Journal of Verbal Learning and Verbal Behavior*, 1974, *13*, 114-131.

Gowie, C. J., & Powers, J. W. Children's use of expectations as a source of information in language comprehension. *Journal of Experimental Child Psychology*, 1978, *26*, 472-488.

Graesser, A., & Mandler, G. Recognition memory for the meaning and surface structure of sentences. *Journal of Experimental Psychology: Human Learning & Memory*, 1975, *104*, 238-248.

Haberlandt, K., Berian, C., & Sandson, J. The episode schema in story processing. *Journal of Verbal Learning and Verbal Behavior*, 1980, *19*, 635-650.

Hochberg, J. Towards a speech-plan eye-movement model of reading. In R. A. Monty & J. W. Senders (Eds.). *Eye movements and psychological processes*. Hillsdale, N. J.: Lawrence Erlbaum Associates, 1976.

Hogaboam, T. W. & McConkie, G. W. The rocky road from eye fixations to comprehension. Technical Report No. 207. University of Illinois Center for the Study of Reading, May 1981.

Huey, E. B. *The psychology and pedagogy of reading*. New York: MacMillan, 1908.

Just, M. A., & Carpenter, P. A. A theory of reading: From eye fixations to comprehension. *Psychological Review*, 1980, *87*, 329-354.

Just, M. A., Carpenter, P. A., & Woolley, J. Paradigms and processes in reading comprehension. *Journal of Experimental Psychology: General*, 1982, *111*, 228-238.

Kleiman, G. M. Speech recoding in reading. *Journal of Verbal Learning and Verbal Behavior*, 1975, *14*, 323-339.

Kucera, H., & Francis, W. N. *Computational analysis of present-day American English*. Providence, R.I.: Brown University Press, 1967.

Lesgold, A. M. Pronominalization: A device for unifying sentences in memory. *Journal of Verbal Learning and Verbal Behavior*, 1972, *11*, 316-323.

Levy, B. A. Vocalization and suppression effects in sentence memory. *Journal of Verbal Learning and Verbal Behavior*, 1975, *14*, 304-316.

McConkie, G. W., Hogaboam, T. W., Wolverton, G. S., Zola, D. & Lucas, P. A. Toward the use of eye movements in the study of language processing. Technical Report No. 134, University of Illinois, Center for the Study of Reading, August, 1979.

McConkie, G. W., & Rayner, K. The span of effective stimulus during a fixation in reading. *Perception and Psychophysics*, 1975, *17*, 578-586.

McConkie, G. W., & Rayner, K. Asymmetry of the perceptual span in reading. *Bulletin of the Psychonomics Society*, 1976, *8*, 365-368.

Miller, G. A. The magic number seven plus or minus two. *Psychological Review*, 1956, *63*, 81-97.

Miller, G. A. Decision units in the perception of speech. *IRE Transactions*, 1962, *IT-8*, 81-83.

Miller, G. A., & Johnson-Laird, P. N. *Language and perception*. Cambridge, MA: Harvard University Press, 1976.

Miller, G. A., & McKeen, O. K. A chronometric study of some relations between sentences. *Quarterly Journal of Experimental Psychology*, 1964, *16*, 297-308.

Mitchell, D. C., & Green, D. W. The effects of context on immediate processing in reading. *Quarterly Journal of Experimental Psychology*, 1978, *30*, 609-636.

Rayner, K. The perceptual span and peripheral cues in reading. *Cognitive Psychology*, 1975, *7*, 65-81.

Rayner, K., & McConkie, G. W. What guides a reader's eye movements? *Vision Research*, 1976, *16*, 829-837.

Sapir, E. *Language*. New York: Harcourt, Brace & World, 1921.

Shulman, H. G., Hornak, R., & Sanders, E. The effects of graphemic, phonetic, and semantic relationships on access to lexical structure. *Memory and Cognition*, 1978, *6*, 115-123.

Smith, F. Conflicting approaches to reading research and instruction. In L. B. Resnick & P. A. Weaver (Eds.), *Theory and practice of early reading*. (Vol. 2). Hillsdale, N. J.: Lawrence Erlbaum Associates, 1979.

Snodgrass, G. S., & Townsend, J. T. Comparing parallel and serial models: Theory and implementation. *Journal of Experimental Psychology: Human Perception &Performance*, 1980, *6*, 330-354.

Spoehr, K. T. Phonological encoding in visual word recognition. *Journal of Verbal Learning and Verbal Behavior*, 1978, *17*, 127-141.

Sternberg, S. The discovery of processing stages: Extensions of Donder's method. In W. G. Koster (Ed.), *Acta Psychological: Attention and performance II*. Amsterdam: North Holland, 1969.

Taft, M. Lexical access via an orthographic code: The basic orthographic syllabic structure (BOSS). *Journal of Verbal Learning and Verbal Behavior*, 1979, *18*, 21-39.

Townsend, J. T. A note on the identifiability of parallel and serial processes. *Perception & Psychophysics*, 1971, *10*, 161-163.

Townsend, J. T. Some results on the identifiability of parallel and serial processes. *British Journal of Mathematical and Statistical Psychology*, 1972, *25*, 168-199.

Tulving, E. Theoretical issues in free recall. In T. R. Dixon & D. L. Horton (Eds.), *Verbal behavior and general behavior theory*. Englewood Cliffs, N. J.: Prentice-Hall, 1968.

Tulving, E., & Patkau, J. E. Concurrent effects of contextual constraint and word frequency on immediate recall and learning of verbal material. *Canadian Journal of Psychology*, 1962, *16*, 83-95.

Wilkes, A. L., & Kennedy, R. A. Relationship between pausing and retrieval latency in sentences of varying grammatical form. *Journal of Experimental Psychology*, 1969, *79*, 241-245.

Wilkes, A. L., & Kennedy, R. A. Response retrieval in active and passive sentences. *Quarterly Journal of Experimental Psychology*, 1970, *22*, 1-8.

4

An Evaluation of Subject-Paced Reading Tasks and Other Methods for Investigating Immediate Processes in Reading[1]

D. C. Mitchell
Exeter University, England

INTRODUCTION

Over the last 5-6 years my colleagues and I have made use of three main experimental techniques for investigating immediate processing. In chronological order these were the Rapid Sequential Visual Presentation (RSVP) task, the Subject-Paced Reading Task and various types of priming tasks.

I shall describe each of these techniques briefly and then go on, first, to consider some important methodological problems associated with immediate processing measures and then to weigh up the strengths and weaknesses of the main techniques. Finally, I shall describe some of the theoretical and experimental issues we have tackled using our techniques.

The RSVP Task

The version of this task that I have used (e.g. in Mitchell, 1979) is a straightforward adaptation of the technique developed by Forster (1970). The successive words of a sentence are presented individually in a rapid sequence at a fixed point on a CRT screen, and at the end of the presentation the subject is required to report as much

---

[1] Much of the work reported in this chapter was supported by Grant No. HR3056 from the British S. S. R. C. to David Green and myself. The work was carried out in collaboration with Dr. Green and I gratefully acknowledge his contribution to all phases of the investigation. Thanks are also due to Vanessa Parffrey, Dennis Norris and Joan Harris for providing research assistance, to Doris Aaronson, Andrew Monk and Rosemary Stevenson for commenting on an earlier draft of the chapter and to Alec Willcox for drawing the diagram of the "Recognizer".

of the material as he can recall. It is sometimes claimed (e.g. Forster, 1980, and by Potter, Kroll and Harris, 1980) that performance in this and other versions of the RSVP task reflects the ease with which the subject is able to process each word as it arrives. However, I shall argue later that this is not the only influence and perhaps not even the most important influence on performance. For this reason I think the task is of limited value as a technique for investigating immediate processes in reading.

Subject-Paced Reading Tasks

David Green and I have used a variety of tasks in which subjects press a button to control the presentation of successive segments of text. In all of our experiments the first word of each new display appears at a fixed point on the screen and the stimulus material remains in place until the subject presses an "advance" button. When this happens the display is immediately replaced by the next portion of the text and the process continues until the subject reaches the end of the paragraph or passage. The main experimental measure we have used is the interval between successive button presses (i.e. the viewing time for any given display) and the assumption is that this measure reflects the time taken to execute at least some of the major processes associated with analysing the material in the display. In the course of conducting experiments using this technique we have segmented texts in a variety of different ways ranging from one word at-a-time, through three words at-a-time to displays varying unsystematically between one and twenty or more words in each segment. In almost every case the texts used were coherent passages of prose based on the writings of well-known authors and in most experiments the passages were at least 1000 words long. In every case the passages were followed by extremely simple comprehension questions which were intended to encourage the subjects to read for meaning. We have avoided using isolated sentences because this is obviously not the kind of material that people read in normal circumstances and it is not certain what it means to "comprehend" a sentence when it is presented by itself. Our commitment to investigating comprehension in *texts* as opposed to *sentences* has sometimes led us to embed as few as 20 or 30 critical displays in a long text and analyse the viewing times for these displays alone, throwing away 95 of the data collected. This is quite expensive in terms of data collection, but it does mean that the form of processing is determined by the character of the passage as a whole and not by local and possibly artificial strategies that the subject might invent to handle the experimental materials.

Priming Tasks

Here a portion of text ranging in size from an incomplete sentence to a short paragraph is followed at some point by a test stimulus consisting of a string of letters. The subject is required to indicate as quickly as possible whether or not this string is an English word. The rationale of the technique is that the time required to make this decision should be influenced by the results of processing the contextual material. If this is true, the lexical decision task can be used to probe the status of various processes at given points in the text. We first used the technique (rather unsuccessfully) in 1974 and 1975 (cf. Mitchell & Green, 1975), but recently Noel Sharkey and I have been able to find more fruitful applications (Sharkey & Mitchell, 1981a, b). I'll return to these experiments in more detail later.

THE PROBLEM OF PROCESSING SPILLOVER

Presumably the aim of any immediate processing task is to provide a series of detailed experimental measures to reflect the processing demands associated with small portions of text at specified points in the passage. Measures of this kind could potentially be very informative in the investigation of questions concerning on-line processing in reading. Ideally, such a measure should reflect the processing associated with a single, clearly-specified portion of text (i.e. it shouldn't be influenced by the analysis devoted to other materials, such as the words or phrases that precede or follow the current segment of text). A measure that failed to meet this condition would be less useful for most theoretical purposes, because it would be difficult to disentangle the effects associated with the alternative portions of text and this would make the measure almost impossible to interpret.

If the measure is to provide an accurate reflection of the processes associated with a given segment of text, then it must take in the *full* analysis of the current material and it must *not* be influenced in any way by the processing associated with earlier displays. In the following discussion, response measures of this kind will be referred to as being under the *Direct Control* of the processing for a given portion of the text. This corresponds to Just and Carpenter's (1980) *eye-mind assumption* which states that "the eye remains fixated on a word as long as the word is being processed" (p. 330). However, their term will not be used here because it doesn't generalize easily to tasks that are not based on eye-monitoring. The alternatives to *Direct Control* are that the response measure either fails to take in all of the relevant processing or that it fails to exclude extraneous processing. In most immediate processing tasks the end of one response measure is immediately followed by the beginning of another, together with a new portion of text. In this situation any uncompleted processing will spill over from one response measure to the next. In other words, certain aspects of processing will be postponed and join a queue or buffer so that they can be dealt with later (cf. Bouma & de Voogd, 1974). Here the response measure will be influenced not only by the problems in the current display but also by any *backlog* or processing that may have built up in the buffer. I'll refer to this as the *Buffer Control* hypothesis.

In a moment I'll consider which of the two models provides a more accurate characterization of the processes in various immediate processing tasks. However, before doing this it might be useful to spell out the pattern of behavior which might be expected on the two models. The first point is that on *both* models it is possible for a textual problem introduced during the current display to be reflected immediately in the current response measure. On the *Direct Control* hypothesis this would occur simply because the response would be delayed while any necessary processing was completed, while on the *Buffer Control* model extra processing might occur because the linguistic operations associated with the current display are added to the buffer and then immediately exercise an influence on the response measure in their capacity *as part of this governing buffer*. Clearly this means that there is no way of distinguishing between the models on the basis of the reader's response to the *current* display. However, the situation is different when it comes to a consideration of any *later* reactions to the material. On the *Direct Control* hypothesis such reactions simply shouldn't occur. If the work is completed during the initial response to the display and there is no processing spillover then none of the subsequent measures should be affected in any way by the initial processing difficulties. However, delayed effects of this kind could easily occur on the *Buffer Control* hypothesis because the tasks may be added to the buffer too late for them to have any effect on the current measure or alternatively they may only reach the head of the processing queue after one or two measures. This means that the most direct way of distinguishing between the hypotheses is to examine the data to see whether there are any effects of processing difficulty on response measures other than the most immediate one.

In the next section I'll apply this test to each of the immediate processing measures I mentioned earlier, but before doing this it may be useful to comment briefly in certain value judgements that are sometimes associated with the two types of control.

From a purely methodological point of view processing spillover of the kind discussed above may be viewed as a strictly *negative* feature of an experimental task (on the grounds that it tends to complicate the interpretation of the putative immediate processing data generated by the technique). Such an orientation will be evident in much of the discussion below. However, there are circumstances in which evidence of spillover might be considered an *advantage* rather than a *disadvantage* of the task. In particular, it is conceivable that parallel processing (and therefore spillover) is a normal feature of "natural" reading. If it is, then it could be argued that any task that minimizes spillover only does so by *distorting* the normal reading process, in which case the task may merely buy experimental convenience at the cost of ecological validity. At present the evidence for overlapping processes in "natural" reading is rather limited, and, in any case, its status is somewhat uncertain since it is based on the kind of experimental techniques that are themselves the subject of examination in the present volume.

For this reason in the methodological discussions to follow evidence of processing spillover will be treated primarily as an undesirable defect of a technique and one that should be eliminated if this is in any way possible.

THE SUBJECT-PACED READING TASK

Single Word Version

In order to get an impression of the kind of control that operates in this task I have carried out a fairly detailed analysis of one of the experiments conducted by Dave Green and myself (cf. Mitchell and Green, 1977).

First I carried out a series of regression analyses similar to those reported in an earlier paper (Mitchell and Green, 1978). In the present series of tests the independent variables were the reading times for 101 words towards the end of a 250 word passage. The data from the first and last word of each sentence within this segment of the text were excluded from the analysis. The independent variables were (1) the ordinal position of the word in the passage as a whole; (2) its position in the current sentence; (3) the number of letters in the words; (4) the number of syllables in the word; (5) the logarithm (base 10) of its frequency and, finally, three measures that referred to the properties of the immediately *preceding* word in the passage; (6) the number of letters in this last word; (7) its number of syllables and (8) the logarithm (base 10) of its frequency. A separate regression analysis was run for each of the twelve subjects and the regression coefficients were submitted to t-tests to determine whether they differed significantly from zero. The only effect to reach significance was the frequency of the *current* word (mean value: -46.6 ms/log frequency; $t(11) = p < 0.005$). The fact that the response times were not reliably affected by the properties of the preceding word appears to provide some support for the view that reading time in this task is governed in the manner suggested by the *Direct Control* hypothesis. However, we were uneasy about drawing this conclusion because it depends on accepting the null hypothesis, because the data base (reading times for 101 words and 12 subjects) was much smaller than the base we had used for previous tests, and lastly because there was at least some suggestion that the frequency of the previous word might be producing a spillover effect (the mean size of the carry-over effect was -12.4 ms/log frequency; $t(11) = 1.39$).

To conduct a more stringent test of the *Direct Control* hypothesis we replaced one of the words near the end of the passage with a word that was semantically anomalous in that position. On the *Direct Control* hypothesis this change should produce an immediate and substantial increase in reading time, but this is not what happened. Although the mean viewing time for the changed word was longer than the mean reading time for the preceding 40 words that were not ends of sentences (823.7 ms vs 719.2 ms) the effect was only shown by a few of the subjects and it failed to reach significance ($t(11) = 1.22$). Most of the subjects apparently failed to relate the current word to the prior context before they initiated their response to the word. The data suggested that most readers postponed this operation until the next frame or even later. In order to determine the point at which this additional processing occurred, we tried to identify frames on which the subject paused slightly longer than usual. (To do this we used a relatively weak criterion - a viewing time that was 1.0 or more standard deviations above the mean of the subject's response time to the 40 preceding words). It transpired that only 4 of the 12 subjects paused as soon as they read the changed word, none paused on the next display, two on the third display and the rest showed no sign of pausing at all. These results suggest that some of the subjects were allowing certain aspects of processing to spillover into later response intervals (as expected on the *Buffer Control* hypothesis) while others were processing the material so superficially that they failed to notice the anomaly at all. Comments by subjects after the end of the experiment suggested that they tended to drift into a strategy of responding before completing their analysis of the word because they felt uncomfortable reading at the slow rate imposed by the *Direct Control* strategy. Further evidence that there is spillover for certain aspects of processing in the single-word task has been reported by Aaronson and Ferres (this volume).

Three Word Version

The subject's failure to react immediately to anomalous material prompted us to refine the subject-paced reading task in a fairly simply way - by presenting the words in groups of three rather than one at a time. This produced marked improvements in the task. To illustrate this I shall describe some analyses that I have recently carried out on the data from a previously published experiment (Experiment IV from Mitchell and Green, 1978). First I carried out a regression analysis similar to the one I've just described except that the data base was considerably larger (219 viewing times—i.e. reading time for 657 words, for each of 24 subjects). The independent variables and results are shown in Table 1. As you can see the properties of the current display influence reading times in ways that are by now quite well established. However, I was mainly interested in the effects of the properties of the previous display. In this experiment there was little reason to suspect that the word frequency effect was carrying over from one display to the next. The main effect was somewhat smaller than that in the single word study (-3.23 ms/log frequency) and it did not approach significance for any of the three words. Unfortunately, however, there *was* clear evidence that reading time was affected by the *size* of the preceding display.

In addition to these tests I looked at subjects' reactions to anomalous material as in the last experiment. In this case the anomaly was created by removing a few words from the text presented to half of the subjects in another experiment in the same series (Experiment III, Mitchell and Green, 1978). (For the other half the words were left in and in this case the material was perfectly sensible). In contrast with the corresponding test in the single word task this test yielded clear evidence that the subjects reacted to the anomaly immediately. The mean reading time for the critical material was considerably longer for the group in which it was anomalous (2825.8 ms) than when it was sensible (1589.9 ms) and this effect was

TABLE 1
The Results of a Regression Analysis to Assess the Importance of
Spillover Effects on Prefinal Viewing Times for Experiment IV
(Mitchell & Green, 1978).

Independent variable	Mean raw coefficient	t-value ($df=23$)	level of significance
Properties of current display			
Size	19.3 ms/character	5.09	$p<0.001$
Log (frequency of word 1)	-41.71 ms/log freq.	5.71	$p<0.001$
Log (frequency of word 2)	-20.00 ms/log freq.	3.46	$p<0.01$
Log (frequency of word 3)	-41.31 ms/log freq.	5.25	$p<0.001$
Rated difficulty	40 ms/rating unit	4.38	$p<0.001$
Position in sentence	9.03 ms/display	2.67	$p<0.05$
Position in passage	-0.41 ms/display	2.51	$p<0.05$
Sentence length	-1.12 ms/word	1.07	n. s.
Properties of previous display			
Size	7.68 ms/chaacter	3.23	$p<0.01$
Log (frequency of word 1)	0.35 ms/log freq.	0.06	n. s.
Log (frequency of word 2)	-7.43 ms/log freq.	1.14	n. s.
Log (frequency of word 3)	-2.61 ms/log freq.	0.45	n. s.

highly significant ($F(1,22)=11.4$, $p < 0.005$).[2] This suggests that, unlike the single-word version of the task the subjects showed a tendency to react as soon as the anomalous material appeared in the text.

A further test was carried out to see whether there was any evidence of spillover of syntactic processing in this task. This test was carried out as part of Experiment II in Mitchell and Green (1978) but it has not been reported previously. Earlier studies had shown that subjects tend to pause at the ends of clauses to carry out some kind of textual processing. The present test was constructed in an effort to

---

[2]The pause on the critical display was also examined separately for each subject by comparing the viewing time for this display with the average for 36 previous 3-word displays. The baseline was not ideal because the critical display only contained two words - in fact, it was the only 2-word display in the entire passage. As a result, 11 of the 12 subjects in the non-anomalous condition responded more rapidly to the test display than they did to the 3-word displays. Despite this bias, 10 of the 12 subjects in the anomalous condition took longer to respond to the 2-word test display than to the 36 control displays and for 8 of these subjects the latency was at least two standard deviations above the mean value for the 36 controls.

determine whether this kind of processing spills over into the display following the end of the clause.

At sixteen points in the passage optional relative clauses were inserted for 10 of the subjects and omitted for the remaining 10. The materials were similar to those shown in Table 2. The test phrase was identical in every case (it always consisted of the three words "was in the") and the results of the experiment showed that the mean viewing time was almost identical in the condition when it was preceded by a relative clause (846.1 ms) and when the clause was left out of the text (845.0 ms). Thus there was no evidence that any processing associated with the end of the clause is carried over into the next part of the text in the 3-word version of the subject-paced reading task.

Taken together the results of these tests suggest that in the 3-word version of the task processing spillover is much more limited than it is in the single-word task. Before leaving our evaluation of these techniques it may be worth sounding a note of caution about the status of this conclusion. The 1- and 3-word experiments considered above were based on different materials and were not specifically designed to be compared with one another. It follows that the changes in processing spillover could have been produced by experimental differences other than variations in display size. For this reason the present data do not provide decisive evidence in favour of the 3-word task. However, they do raise the possibility that 1-word tasks are particularly prone to processing spillover and this is an issue that should certainly be considered by anyone contemplating using subject-paced reading tasks.

THE RSVP TASK

In its conventional form this task presents problems that are not shared by other techniques that have been developed to measure immediate processing. The major difficulty is that the response measure (accuracy of recall) is remote from the "immediate" processes that it is designed to reflect. This means that there is ample

TABLE 2
Typical Materials Used for Testing for Spillover Effects
Following Clause Boundaries.

---

(1)... my wallet (which contained all the
money I was likely to need during my stay in
the country) *was in the* sitting room downstairs
and...

(2) Not only was I all alone but the cottage
(in which I planned to stay for a couple of
weeks) *was in the* most isolated position
imaginable.

---

opportunity for non-immediate processing to contaminate the data and the evidence suggests that this is precisely what happens.

The central methodological assumption in the RSVP task is that the accuracy with which a word is registered is a direct function of the subject's success in completing the lexical and linguistic analysis associated with this word before the next one arrives (i.e. that registration is under the *Direct Control* of stimulus analysis). However, I shall argue below the RSVP-data are influenced by factors other than the immediate difficulty of processing the words (i.e. that they are under *Buffer Control*).

Evidence that items accumulate in a buffer prior to processing comes from a consideration of order errors (and particularly transpositions) in the data. The point can be made by referring to some RSVP data which I published some years ago (Mitchell, 1976). The stimuli in this study were digits rather than words and the lists were only three items long, but neither of these details affect the argument in any material way. The stimuli were presented at various rates ranging from 1 item/sec to 10 items/sec. The stimulus duration remained constant at about 40 ms in all conditions and was always followed by a pattern mask which filled the interval until the arrival of the next stimulus. In one condition the stimuli were relatively easy to recognise (normally oriented digits) while in another they were more difficult to process (laterally inverted digits). The recall protocols in each condition were scored for item errors, for order errors and particularly for transpositions (i.e. sequences in which a string like 325 were recalled as 352). The results showed that the item errors were essentially constant over the different rates of presentation, but the frequency of order errors increased sharply with rate of presentation. The pattern of results is probably seen most clearly in the transposition data which are shown in Table 3.

Notice that the transposition errors start to make a significant contribution at a slower presentation rate when the stimuli are more difficult to recognise than they do with more familiar stimuli. These data find a straightforward interpretation in terms of a queuing model such as the one represented informally in Figure 1.

At slow rates of presentation the items are recognised as soon as they arrive in the buffer. There is no tendency for a queue to build up and so the items are processed in the order of presentation (i.e. with very few order errors). However, at

TABLE 3
Mean Percentage of Items Transposed at Different
Inter-Stimulus Intervals in an RSVP Task
(from Mitchell, 1976).

Materials	*Inter-Stimulus Intervals*					
	50 ms	100 ms	300 ms	500 ms	700 ms	1000 ms
Normal digits	12.4	7.4	1.9	1.8	0.9	1.8
Laterally inverted digits	8.3	7.4	4.7	3.5	3.5	2.8

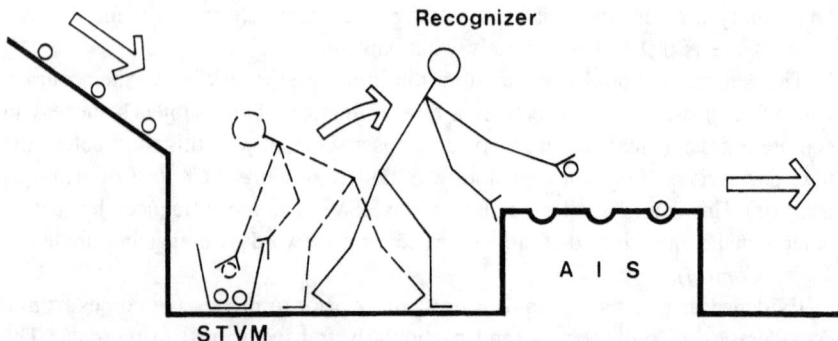

FIG. 1. An informal representation of the buffering processes in a RSVP task. The stimuli first accumulate in a visual buffer - Short-Term Visual Memory (STVM) and they are subsequently transferred to an auditory buffer - Auditory Information Storage (AIS).

faster rates the arrival of new stimuli begins to outpace the rate at which the "Recognizer" works and eventually it reaches the situation in which Items 2 and 3 drop into the buffer while "he" is still working on Item 1. The "Recognizer" is then faced with the choice of which to deal with first and sometimes makes the wrong decision producing transposition errors as a result. As expected on this account, the frequency of transposition errors begins to build up at lower rates of presentation with the stimuli that take longer to recognize (i.e. the mirror digits). Also, items towards the end of the list are more likely to be transposed in this way (see Mitchell, 1976). These data suggest that the items in the RSVP task are held in buffer storage prior to recognition. The tendency to select the wrong item from the buffer at rapid rates of presentation indicates that performance is not always under the *Direct Control* of the first item that joined the queue.

More direct evidence that performance in the RSVP task is under *Buffer* rather than *Direct Control* comes from a more recent experiment using words and sentences as materials (Mitchell, 1979). This study focussed on a different feature of *Buffer Control* namely that it is capable of producing retroactive effects so that difficulties in processing materials that occur late in the stimulus sequence may be reflected in the response measures for *earlier* stimuli. The reason that this could occur is simply that the stimuli are not necessarily dealt with in strict order of arrival and so problems associated with later material could sometimes influence the response measures for the early part of the sentence. In contrast with this, retroactive effects of this kind should not occur if the response measure is under *Direct Control*: on this hypothesis the measure should be influenced by nothing other than the difficulty of processing the current word. In the experiment to test between these two possibilities recall performance for normal 7-word sentences was compared with that in sentences in which the last three words were swapped around to make nonsensical endings. The results showed that performance in the *first four positions* was reduced significantly when this string was followed by a meaningless list of words. Since the words themselves were not altered in any way it must be concluded that the response measure was influenced by factors other than those associated with the initial processing of the material. It seems clear that this effect must either have occurred while the material was held in buffer storage prior to report or during some attempt to reconstruct a meaningful sentence from the material that had accumulated by the end of the sequence. In either case the evidence argues against the *Direct Control* model and in favor of some version of the *Buffer Control* model.

Recently, Potter, Kroll and Harris (1980) have queried the criticisms raised by this study on the grounds that "the nonsensical words could have caused the subject to forget the initial part of the sentence" (Footnote, p. 396). But this comment itself points to the locus of the weakness of RSVP tasks in the study of on-line processes in comprehension, namely that the performance measure, recall accuracy is not a pure measure of immediate processing in reading. Recall accuracy is influenced by other factors such as storage, retrieval or reconstruction of the stimulus material as well as by the initial perceptual analysis. The potential value of RSVP is in its fine-grain temporal control of presentation. To make use of this property in studying immediate processes, we must develop performance measures that are of a correspondingly fine temporal grain to use in conjunction with RSVP presentation. One possibility is to try to combine the RSVP presentation with some of the probe techniques described in our studies of priming.

EYE-MONITORING

Before going on to consider the advantages and disadvantages of RSVP and other techniques we have used, I'd like to make some comments about spillover effects in one further technique that has been used to investigate immediate processing in comprehension - the eye-monitoring technique. Investigators using this technique typically maintain that the data are more consistent with the *Direct Control* model than with the *Buffer Control* model (cf. Rayner and McConkie, 1976; Just and Carpenter, 1980). However, as I have argued in a chapter of a book on reading (Mitchell, 1982), the evidence is not entirely consistent with this view. Rayner and McConkie (1976) argued that according to the *Buffer Control* model fixations following those containing difficult materials should often be extended as additional processing spills over from one fixation to the next. The model therefore predicts that there should be a positive correlation between the durations of successive fixations. Rayner and McConkie (1976) computed these correlations and found that they "ranged from 0.10 to 0.16 with an average of 0.13" (p. 833). For some reason they took this as evidence *against* the *Buffer Control* model. However, it is easy to show that the mean of these correlations is significantly different from zero (for details see Mitchell, 1982, Section 2.8), and so the results seem to *favor* the *Buffer Control* model rather than contradicting it. Other data point to the same conclusion. Rayner (1975) found that fixations that follow troublesome materials (nonwords) tend to be longer than those following materials that are easier to process (again see Mitchell, 1982, Section 2.8 for further details) and more recently Rayner and Pollatsek (1981) have presented some evidence that saccade size is also affected by the contents of the previous fixation, while Ehrlich and Rayner (1983) have reported evidence that processing spillover sometimes occurs with "higher-level" processes such as pronoun assignment. But, Carpenter and Just (1983) report regression analyses indicating that the gaze duration on a given word is not affected by the properties of the preceding word.

At the moment, the evidence from eye fixation studies is somewhat equivocal about the presence or amount of spillover from one word to the next. One possible explanation of the discrepancy between the results of the Rayner group and the Just and Carpenter group is that the former generally reports the spillover of processing from one fixation to the next, (which may or may not be on the same word), while the latter reports little spillover of processing from one word (gaze duration) to the next. Finally, it is important to distinguish spillover due to capacity limitations and spillover that is the result of mandatory buffering that might be required because a given word sometimes cannot be interpreted until more words have been read (e.g., the pronominal assignment of a pronoun that precedes the first mention of its referent, such as "Although Jennifer liked him, Manfred was not loveable"). It is likely that future eye fixation data will provide more evidence to distinguish between *Buffer Control* and *Direct Control*.

ADVANTAGES AND DISADVANTAGES OF VARIOUS IMMEDIATE PROCESSING MEASURES

I can now turn to a broader consideration of the advantages and disadvantages of the various techniques that my colleagues and I have used.

The RSVP Task

On the basis of the detailed analysis in the previous section I would argue that there is strong reason to doubt whether the recall or comprehension data that can be obtained in this task provide a pure measure of immediate processing difficulty. In fact, I have already presented direct evidence that the measure is influenced by processes that are *not* immediate (in the sense that they must have exerted their influence at some time after the material was initially presented). Additional or different techniques are required to distinguish between performance that derives from immediate processing difficulties and those that are introduced during later memorial or reconstructive phases of the task. Recent refinements of the task by Fischler and Bloom (1980) and by Forster (1981) may well achieve this. In these new tasks the initial sequence of words is presented in the conventional way but instead of remembering these words or responding to comprehension questions the subject's task is either to pronounce the last word as quickly as he can (Forster) or to make a lexical decision about it (Fischler and Bloom). Since these changes force the subject to respond under time pressure it seems very likely that they minimize the influence of any effects other than those that act on immediate processing.

The Subject-Paced Reading Task

Although the single-word version of this task appears to be subject to the effects of processing spillover, it seems likely that these effects can be reduced substantially by presenting the material 3 words at a time, or by varying the amount of material that appears from display to display. (As mentioned before, the one spillover effect that remains can easily be dealt with by equating the lengths of any display *preceding* a critical display).

Given these precautions, this task seems to have advantages over many other methods that are currently used to investigate immediate processing in reading. It scores in three ways over versions of the task in which materials are presented sentence-by-sentence. First, it provides a means of determining the precise way in which processing load is distributed throughout the sentence and this enables us to consider hypotheses that postulate heavy processing demands at particular points in the sentence. Second, if a process can be localised to within one or two words, it becomes possible to measure its effects by recording the viewing time for a relatively small display. Since the standard deviation in the latency to a short display tends to be much smaller than that for an entire sentence, this effectively increases the sensitivity of the task and makes it possible to pick up relatively subtle experimental effects. A third advantage occurs when the experimenter tries to increase the sensitivity of the reading task by equating the materials for display size, word frequency, syntactic structure and other extraneous variables. Obviously the burden of this task is greatly reduced if there are only 2-3 words in the display rather than all of the words in the sentence.

The 3-word subject paced reading task comes out less favorably when it is compared with techniques that involve monitoring eye-movements. These techniques have all the advantages of partitioning the response to a sentence into numerous components and they are obviously much more natural than the present task. The responses (saccades) are actions that normally occur during reading and the text is continuously on display rather than being shown a few words at a time. The only real advantage of the button pressing experiments seems to be that they are simpler and cheaper to set up and to run. As an illustration of this Noel Sharkey has implemented several different versions of the button-pressing reading experiment on a PET Commodore microcomputer - a cheap and portable machine that is readily available to psychology laboratories throughout the world. By contrast, eye-movement studies are much more costly and difficult to run and analyze.

The Priming Task

This has the obvious disadvantage that making lexical decisions about isolated words is in no sense a natural part of the comprehension process. This raises the possibility that the strategies used in this kind of experiment may differ substantially from those used in normal comprehension. This means that conclusions drawn from priming experiments can never be relied upon to provide the final word on comprehension. However, they can be used to answer questions about the kinds of influence that could *potentially* play a role in comprehension. If it is possible to establish such effects it may be a relatively easy matter to determine whether comparable effects occur in more natural tasks. The main advantage of using this approach is that it is often much easier to generate materials for an artificial priming experiment than it is to prepare natural and coherent texts to test the same hypotheses in more conventional reading tasks.

SUBSTANTIVE FINDINGS OBTAINED WITH OUR TECHNIQUES

Much of our work has been concerned with attempts to clarify the way in which contextual information is used in various subprocesses of comprehension. In particular we have investigated the effect that context might have on word recognition, on parsing procedures and on the process of combining the information that appears in successive sentences. Taken together this work has led us to adopt a position in which we place much less emphasis on top-down processing than most other investigators do.

Our initial experiments examined the possibility that context speeds up the processing of individual words as they are encountered in the course of reading. Of course, we were aware that there is a widely-held assumption that this does occur, but when we looked at the literature we found that most of the empirical support for this top-down view was based on tasks which bear little resemblance to fluent reading. In many of the studies the target words were so badly degraded that they were difficult to decipher (for example, in the classic studies by Tulving and Gold (1963) and Morton (1964) the critical words were presented very briefly and although the results showed that the subjects were able to make use of contextual information to guess their identities, it is difficult to sustain the view that this reflects "ordinary" reading processes). In most previous work on top-down processing the contextual information was presented in the form of isolated sentences and in many cases the sole purpose in reading these sentences was to help subjects to make sense of the test word. There was no question of reading the material for the purposes of understanding it in any conventional way. Finally, in every study we came across there was an appreciable pause of half a second or more between the point at which the subject finished reading the context material and the point at which he was allowed to start processing the target word. It seemed to us that these experimental techniques were not at all suitable for answering questions about immediate processes in reading and so we decided to tackle the issue by using the subject-paced reading task. Using this technique we were able to examine the effects of predictability *while* the subjects were actually reading for comprehension and it was also possible to reduce (but not entirely eliminate) the unnaturally long pause between the context and the test material.

The results provided no clear evidence that context facilitates word recognition. In one experiment (Mitchell and Green, 1978, Experiment I) we looked for evidence that subjects speed up as they proceed through a sentence from the less predictable portions at the beginning to the more highly constrained material at the end. Contrary to our expectations, the results showed a slight (but nonsignificant) *increase* in reading time and this trend actually reached significance in a later experiment in the same series (Experiment IV). In another experiment (Experiment III) we varied predictability more directly by changing material in the display preceding the test phase. Again, there was no statistical support for the view that reading time was influenced by the predictability of the material.

Finally, in a variant of the subject-paced reading task in which subjects had to make lexical decisions about individually presented words of a text Mitchell and Green (1980) found that the mean decision time for 20 critical words was not significantly affected by whether they were presented as part of a passage of prose or as part of an unstructured list of words.

Taken together these results provide no evidence that context affects the speed and efficiency of word recognition in the subject-paced reading task.[3] The critical difference between these experiments and the bulk of the studies that succeed in demonstrating facilitation effects seems to be that the present technique focuses more on *immediate* processing and it cuts down the duration of the artificial pause between the context and the test material. In contrast, most other techniques introduce unnaturally large intervals either by presenting the contextual material for longer than necessary, such as by presenting it for a period that is fixed by the experimenter rather than being under the individual subject's control - as in a study by Schuberth and Eimas (1977), or by deliberately inserting a pause of a half-second or more before the target word (e.g. Perfetti, Goldman and Hogaboam, 1979; Stanovich, 1980; Kleiman, 1980). More direct evidence that a pause is crucial for demonstrating facilitation effects in word recognition comes from an experiment reported by Stanovich (1981). In this study the experimenter took positive steps to reduce the context-target pause to a minimum and the result was that the facilitation effect was reduced to a non-significant 16 ms, whereas in one of his earlier experiments using similar material (but longer pauses) the effect had been significantly larger (111 ms).

These results seem quite important for theories of reading, since there are several widely-cited models that place heavy emphasis on top-down or interactive

---

[3]Comparable results are obtained in experiments using other immediate processing techniques. For example, McConkie and Zola (1981) found a facilitation effect of only 14 ms in an eye-movement study.

processing (e.g. Goodman, 1967; Rumelhart, 1977) and these models are challenged by the evidence that top-down processing seems to disappear as the task becomes more natural. The present findings raise questions about why the context-target interval seems to be necessary for demonstrating facilitation effects. A possible answer is that the syntactic and semantic analysis that might be used to guide word recognition may take a certain amount of time before it can be brought up to date after each new word arrives. If this is true then there may be occasions when the analysis has not been completed by the time the target word has been identified, in which case it is obviously too late for it to influence the recognition process. However, this account would only apply to contextual effects that depend on the last few words for their pertinence (i.e. local contextual effects). With more stable and global effects (i.e. contextual effects that remain pertinent for several words or even sentences), it should be possible to demonstrate facilitation effects even when there are no appreciable delays. To see whether this was possible Noel Sharkey and I (Sharkey and Mitchell, 1981a) used contexts based on Schank and Abelson's (1977) Script Theory. The context consisted of two sentences designed to activate a given script (e.g. material concerning a birthday party). This was followed immediately by the presentation of a noun that was a central prop for the script in question (e.g. *candles* in the birthday party script). The subject was required to make a lexical decision about this word. The results showed that the response latency for a script-related word was significantly faster than that for a control word that was not related to the script. Further experiments showed that the priming effect was neutralized when the context caused the script to be abandoned and a new (unrelated) script to be instantiated (Sharkey and Mitchell, 1981b). These results suggest that while the word recognition processes in fluent reading may not be facilitated by forms of context that change their predictive effects rapidly from word to word, they may be affected by the constraints imposed by a more stable setting such as a script.

Given this generalization how are we to explain the anomaly effects described earlier? This obviously presents a problem since it is based on the acceptability of two or more words in sequence, and therefore corresponds more closely with the first type of effect. Our explanation of this phenomenon is that following its recognition by a procedure which is independent of local context, the new word is immediately checked against prior context to see whether it is compatible with it (Mitchell and Green, 1978, 1980; see also Forster, 1981, for a similar explanation of inhibition effects). On this hypothesis the anomaly effect occurs at some stage *after* word recognition and so using Sternberg's (1969) Additive Factors argument, it should have an additive effect with factors that influence the word recognition stage itself. In an experiment to test this Mitchell and Green (1980) varied type of context (anomalous vs normal) and stimulus quality (using stimulus degradation, which we assumed would have at least some effect on word recognition) and found, as expected, that the two effects were additive.

Up to now we have only considered the effects context may have on word recognition. However, it may also exert an influence on higher-level processes such as parsing and proposition integration. We have also used the subject-paced reading task to investigate these possibilities. In two experiments reported in Mitchell and Green (1978) we examined the effects of prior context on parsing strategies. In earlier work on this topic, Fodor, Bever and Garrett (1974) had put forward several strategies based on the notion that prior context can be used to simplify syntactic analysis of certain sentences by ruling out a substantial range of parsing options. We used the subject-paced reading task to examine two of these strategies (the *Verb Complexity* hypothesis and the *Cue Deletion* hypotheses) and we were unable to find any evidence that either effect exerted any influence on immediate processing (Mitchell and Green, 1978, Experiments II and III). Since the effects have frequently been demonstrated in memory-based tasks, we concluded that the cues highlighted by Fodor et al. are more likely to influence the storage, recovery, or reconstruction of sentences than their initial syntactic analysis.

Whether or not context plays a role in parsing there is clear evidence that it plays an important part in the problem of integrating propositions into a text base. Our initial investigations of this issue started with the relatively theoretical observation that subjects in the self-paced reading tasks tend to pause momentarily when they reach the ends of subordinate clauses and at the ends of sentences (cf. Mitchell and Green, 1978). For various reasons we suspected that these pauses were at least partly caused by processes associated with integrating the latest portion of the text with the internal representation of the earlier material. We set about testing this hypothesis in several different ways. In one study (cf. Mitchell and Green, 1977; Section 3.4.1) we compared the reading times for short fable-like stories with their sentences presented in the conventional order with those for stories in which the sentence order was scrambled. we expected that the sentences in the disorganized texts would be more difficult to integrate than those from the well-structured texts and we predicted that this increased difficulty would show itself in the form of increases in the duration of the end-of-sentence pause. This is precisely what happened. In another experiment (cf. Green, Mitchell and Hammond, 1981) we used materials taken from a study by Bransford and Johnson (1972). \These materials consisted of a short passage and two drawings which provided alternative contexts in which the material could be interpreted. One of the pictures provided a scenario (a rather unconventional serenade) which made it relatively easy to interpret and combine all the sentences in the passage while the other depicted a scene which failed to provide any reasonable basis for interpreting the text. As before, the result of the subject-paced reading experiment showed that the end-of-sentence pause was greater when the sentences were difficult to integrate (i.e. when the pictorial context was inappropriate). Further analysis showed that after controlling the individual differences in reading speed there was no evidence that reading time *prior* to the end of the sentence was affected in any way by the appropriateness of the picture. This suggested to us that textual integration might be associated *exclusively* with the ends of sentences. However, a second experiment in the same paper showed that this was not the case. At one point in the text—before the end of the clause—we introduced a test phrase that was anomalous in the context of previous sentences. We argued that if the integration processes were postponed entirely until the end of the clause, then the viewing time for this phrase would be no longer than that in a control condition in which the material was completely compatible with the earlier text. In the event, the results showed that the reading time was significantly longer when the material was anomalous. This finding, along with earlier data (e.g. Just and Carpenter, 1978) suggests that reference to earlier material can occur at certain points *within* clauses as well as at the ends of clauses and sentences.

Up to now we have concentrated on various normative or group effects in reading. However, the subject-paced reading task can also be used to investigate certain strategy effects and to investigate individual differences in the use of these strategies in reading. In one study (Green and Mitchell, 1979) we used a passage that presented an account of a frozen mammoth in Siberia, and then proceeded to evaluate a series of hypotheses concerning the way in which the creature might have got itself into this predicament. Half of the subjects were told to read the passage "normally", and the other half were told to look out for unconvincing or erroneous arguments while they were reading through the text. Since the evaluation of arguments depends on the relationship between the sentence in question and the prior text, we anticipated that the end-of-sentence pause would be increased in the Evaluation condition. In fact, although there was some support for this hypothesis, for some reason the effect was almost entirely restricted to male subjects. The female readers paused for about the same amount of time in the two conditions. This result emphasises that at least some of the higher-level processes in fluent reading must be under the subject's voluntary control, and that different types of readers may exercise this control in different ways.

The subject-paced reading task can also be adapted for use with young or inexperienced readers. For example, in one experiment (Mitchell and Green, 1977; Section 3.5) we extended one of the experiments I mentioned earlier to look for *Cue Deletion* effects in the reading profiles of 9-11 year-old children. Following Fodor, Bever and Garrett (1974) we predicted that subjects would find it easier to process sentences in which an optional surface structure cue was present (e.g., *The money which I had earned soon vanished*), than those in which the cue was deleted (*The money I had earned soon vanished*). In fact, as in the experiment with adults, we found no support for the *Cue Deletion* hypothesis. However, there *was* one surprising finding and this was that there was no evidence of an end-of-sentence effect in these subjects. An obvious interpretation of this result is that the children failed to pay proper attention to the materials. However, this seems unlikely because they paused very noticeably when they came across anomalous materials and they also performed well in a subsequent comprehension test. If this finding is replicable, and if our earlier interpretation of the end-of-sentence pause is correct, the data suggest that young readers may put much less effort into the process of organizing and linking the sentences in a text than adults do. This has direct implications for the kind of material they are likely to extract when they are presented with a passage of prose, and it would be interesting to see whether these differences are reflected in their recall data.

BRIEF CONCLUSIONS

A detailed analysis of various on-line reading tasks indicates that most of them suffer from the problem of processing spillover. However, the subject-paced reading task is less subject to this effect than most of the alternatives.

An evaluation of the subject-paced reading task and the priming task suggests that a possible advantage of both is that they may be more sensitive than reading tasks in which the material is presented sentence-by-sentence. However, they share the disadvantage that they are less natural than other techniques for investigating immediate processes in reading.

Experiments using these tasks show a more limited use of top-down processing than has been suggested by previous work. In addition textual linking tends to be concentrated at the ends of clauses and the ends of sentences, but it is not restricted to these points.

REFERENCES

Aaronson, D. & Ferres, S. The Word-by-Word Reading Paradigm: An Experimental and Theoretical Approach, this volume.

Bouma, H. & de Voogd, A. H. On the control of eye saccades in reading. *Vision Research*, 1974, *14*, 273-284.

Bransford, J. D. & Johnson, M. K. Contextual prerequisites for understanding: Some investigations of comprehension and recall. *Journal of Verbal Learning and Verbal Behavior*, 1972, *11*, 717-726.

Carpenter, P. A. & Just, M. A. What your eyes do while your mind is reading. In K. Rayner (Ed.), *Eye movements in reading perceptual and language processes*. New York: Academic Press, 1983.

Ehrlich, K. & Rayner, K. Pronoun assignment and semantic integration during reading: Eye movements and the immediacy assumption. *Journal of Verbal Learning and Verbal Behavior*, 1983, 22,75-87.

Fischler, I. & Bloom, P. A. Rapid processing of the meaning of sentences. *Memory and Cognition*, 1980, *8*, 216-225.

Forster, K. I. Visual perception of rapidly presented word sequence of varying complexity. *Perception and Psychophysics*, 1970, *8*, 215-221.

Forster, K. I. Priming and the effects of sentence and lexical contexts on naming time: Evidence for autonomous lexical processing. *Quarterly Journal of Experimental Psychology*, 1981, *33A*, 465-495.

Goodman, K. S. Reading: A psycholinguistic guessing game. *Journal of the Reading Specialist*, 1967, *6*, 126-135.

Green, D. W. & Mitchell, D. C. Connections between doing and understanding: Vigilance and fluency in reading. Paper presented to the British Psychological Society, Nottingham, 1979.

Green, D. W., Mitchell, D. C., & Hammond, E. J. The scheduling of text integration processes in reading. *Quarterly Journal of Experimental Psychology*, 1981, *33A*, 455-464.

Just, M. A. & Carpenter, P. A. Inference processes during reading: Reflections from eye fixations. In J. W. Senders, D. F. Fisher, and R. A. Monty (Eds.), *Eye movements and the higher psychological functions*. Hillsdale, N. J.: Lawrence Erlbaum Associates, 1978.

Just, M. A. & Carpenter, P. A. A theory of reading: From eye fixations to comprehension. *Psychological Review*, 1980, *87*, 329-354.

Kleiman, G. M. Sentence frame contexts and lexical decisions: Sentence acceptability and word-relatedness effects. *Memory and Cognition*, 1980, *8*, 336-344.

McConkie, G. W. & Zola, D. Language constraints and the functional stimulus in reading. In A. M. Lesgold & C. A. Perfetti, (Eds.), *Interactive processes in reading*. Hillsdale, N. J.: Lawrence Erlbaum Associates, 1981.

Mitchell, D. C. Buffer storage modality and identification time in tachistoscopic recognition. *Quarterly Journal of Experimental Psychology*, 1976, *28*, 325-337.

Mitchell, D. C. The locus of the experimental effects in the rapid serial visual presentation (RSVP) task. *Perception and Psychophysics*, 1979, 143-149.

Mitchell, D. C. *The process of reading: A cognitive analysis of fluent reading and learning to read.* Chichester: John Wiley & Sons, 1982.

Mitchell, D. C., & Green, D. W. S. S. R. C. Progress Report No. 1 on *An Experimental Investigation of the Semantic Processes During Reading*. September, 1975 (Lodged in British Lending Library).

Mitchell, D. C., & Green, D. W. Final Report on *An Experimental Investigation of the Semantic Processes During Reading*. December, 1977. (Lodged in the British Lending Library).

Mitchell, D. C., & Green, D. W. The effects of context and content on immediate processing in reading. *Quarterly Journal of Experimental Psychology*, 1978, *30*, 609-636.

Mitchell, D. C., & Green, D. W. Contextual effects in continuous reading. Paper presented to the British Psychology Society conference on Reading, Exeter University, March 22-23, 1980.

Morton, J. The effects of context on the visual duration threshold for words. *British Journal of Psychology*, 1964, *55*, 165-180.

Perfetti, C. A., Goldman, S. R., & Hogaboam, T. W. Reading skill and the identification of words in discourse context. *Memory and Cognition*, 1979, *7*, 273-282.

Potter, M. C., Kroll, J. F., & Harris, C. Comprehension and memory in rapid sequential reading. In R. S. Nickerson (Ed.), *Attention and performance VIII*. Hillsdale, N. J.: Lawrence Erlbaum Associates, 1980.

Rayner, K. The perceptual span and peripheral cues in reading. *Cognitive Psychology*, 1975, *7*, 65-81.

Rayner, K. & McConkie, G. W. What guides a reader's eye movements? *Vision Research*, 1976, *16*, 829-837.

Rayner, K. & Pollatsek, A. Eye movement control during reading: Evidence for direct control. *Quarterly Journal of Experimental Psychology*, 1981, *33A*, 351-373.

Rumelhart, D. E. Toward an interactive model of reading. In S. Dornic (Ed.), *Attention and performance VI*. Hillsdale, N. J.: Lawrence Erlbaum Associates, 1977.

Schank, R. C., & Abelson, R. P. *Scripts, plans, goals and understanding*. Hillsdale, N. J.: Lawrence Erlbaum Associates, 1977.

Sharkey, N. E., & Mitchell, D. C. Match or Fire: Contextual mechanisms in the recognition of words. Paper presented by the Experimental Psychology Society, Oxford, July 1981 (a).

Sharkey, N. E., & Mitchell, D. C. New primes for old: Passive decay versus active suppression of scripts in working memory. Paper presented to the British Psychological Society conference on Memory, Plymouth, September 1981 (b).

Schuberth, R. E., & Eimas, P. D. Effects of context on the classification of words and nonwords. *Journal of Experimental Psychology: Human Perception and Performance*, 1977, *3*, 27-36.

Stanovich, K. E. Toward an interactive-compensatory model of individual differences in reading fluency. *Reading Research Quarterly*, 1980, *16*, 32-71.

Stanovich, K. E. Attentional and automatic context effects in reading. In A. M. Lesgold & C. A. Perfetti (Eds.), *Interactive processes in reading*. Hillsdale, N. J.: Lawrence Erlbaum Associates, 1981.

Sternberg, S. The discovery of processing stages: Extensions of Donders' method. *Acta Psychologica*, 1969, *30*, 276-315.

Tulving, E., & Gold, C. Stimulus information and contextual information as determinants of tachistoscopic recognition of words. *Journal of Experimental Psychology*, 1963, *66*, 319-327.

5
Rapid Serial Visual Presentation (RSVP): A Method for Studying Language Processing

Mary C. Potter
Massachusetts Institute of Technology

INTRODUCTION

Consider the following paradox. Most readers can easily see a word presented in a tachistoscope for 50 msec, even when the word is preceded and followed by a masking pattern. Yet, when reading normally, people typically gaze at each word for over 200 msec. One potential limitation on reading rate is the eye movement system, which shifts a small area of high acuity across the text at a maximum rate of four or five fixations per second. Rapid serial visual presentation (RSVP) is a method for bypassing eye movements during reading. In RSVP, each word (or small group of words) appears in the same location, serially. By varying the rate of reading and studying the consequences, one can address various questions about reading and language processing, one of which is whether it is possible to read more rapidly than most people do, without loss of comprehension. This chapter emphasizes faster-than-normal rates of presentation in using RSVP to study reading, but RSVP is also useful at slower rates that are in the range of normal reading or listening. It gives the experimenter control over the timing of reading, in a fashion similar to the control provided by spoken stimuli.

Reading in RSVP is surprisingly natural when presentation is at a moderate rate such as 6 words per second (360 words per minute). For the typical college student, four words per second seems almost boringly slow, at least for easy RSVP text. (The generic term "RSVP" will be used even though the rate is not always rapid.) At a higher rate such as 12 words per second, one still can read all or almost all of the words, but ideas seem to pass through the mind without being adequately retained. At still higher rates such as 16-28 words per second, most viewers no longer have the subjective impression that they can see all the words or understand the sentence (although objective measures show that some processing has occurred).

In this chapter I will first provide a detailed description of RSVP methodology, and then characterize RSVP and compare it with related methods for studying reading. The main focus of the chapter deals with questions about RSVP as a method: How similar is RSVP reading to normal reading or listening? Is an RSVP sentence understood as it is read, or only afterward? What role do short-term buffers play in RSVP and normal reading? The final sections report some research findings and briefly consider some applied issues.

DETAILS OF RSVP METHODOLOGY

Choice of Parameters

The value of RSVP as a research tool is that the investigator has control over the timing of reading and over the physical display. This control also presents a major problem: one has to make a series of somewhat arbitrary choices of presentation parameters without knowing their separate effects and interactions. A systematic parametric examination, task by task, of the effects of overall rate, exposure duration per word, size of window, pauses between sentences, etc., is out of the question because of the huge parameter space.

The hypothesis to be investigated in a given experiment will usually set some of the parameters, such as the overall rate of presentation. The problem then remains of how to set parameters that are not of primary interest. If total time to read is the variable the experimenter wishes to control, how should the relative time per word be determined? An obvious choice is to present each word for an equal duration — that is the "standard" RSVP condition Forster (1970) used, when he introduced the method. Some colleagues of mine have used formulas according to which the time per word decreases in the course of a sentence. Others have used a time per word that is proportional to or montonically related to the number of letters per word.

Still another method, used by Juola, Ward, and McNamara (1982), Juola, Cocklin, Chen, and Granaas (1982), and Chen (1983), is to pick a window size — say, 10 characters — and then shrink or expand the window to encompass the word boundary nearest to the window's right-hand edge. Size 5 usually gives one word per window; size 10, two words; and size 15, three words. Each window is then shown for a constant time. The method strikes me as somewhat unsatisfactory, in that the change of a single letter in the preceding text could double a word's effective viewing time by causing it to be presented alone instead of with another word. There is thus a chance element in whether a word gets presented with its right-hand neighbor(s), its left-hand neighbor(s), or alone. It should be noted that

Juola, Ward et al. found that window size seemed to be less important than total time per word across the whole text. Juola, Cocklin et al. report that an average of 12 letters (including the space between words, and never dividing a word) is the optimal window size, using the criterion of maximal retention and understanding per unit time. For research purposes, however, it may be desirable to have exact control over the reader's time per word, so that a single word per window may be preferred.

One might imagine that the optimal condition might be to present each word for a time proportional to the gaze duration of a normal reader — for example, as determined by Just and Carpenter's (1980) regression equation. Ward and Juola (1982) tried that and found no improvement, compared to spreading the same total time evenly over the words. Just and Carpenter note that the optimal equation changes as reading rate changes, so Ward and Juola's result may not be the last word; in any case, their comprehension test may not have been sufficiently sensitive.

Each of these methods of presentation makes a theoretical commitment about reading, particularly if one assumes that processing is largely on line, driven by the visual stimulus in front of the eyes. If, however, there is any kind of buffer available that can hold more than just the current word, the issue of the precise relative timing of words might be unimportant within a rather wide range. All that would matter would be that there be time to read each word into the buffer; beyond that, only total time for higher level processing would alter performance. These issues are discussed below.

Equalizing the Visibility of Words in RSVP. Forster (1970) found that long words had an advantage in reading, when the rate of presentation was 16 words per second. He and Holmes (personal communication) tried presenting a pattern mask after each word to equalize masking, but gave it up; we also tried that, and reading was exceedingly difficult. One seemed to be obliged to attempt to "read" the mask along with the words. Another technique Holmes and Forster tried was a light ("energy") mask: the white letters of a word were followed by a window-shaped, solid white area. The claim is that this method reduces or eliminates the bias in favor of long words. In theory, the mask would simply reduce contrast, because there would be energy summation at rates faster than about 10 words per second. To my knowledge, no systematic study has been carried out to determine (a) whether the apparent advantage of longer words in RSVP is different from their advantage or disadvantage in conventional reading; and (b) whether the long-word advantage diminishes when the rate of presentation is 12 words per second or slower.

Independent Variables: The Stimulus

A list of stimulus variables in RSVP follows. There are many other possibilities, of course. Representative references are cited.

Characteristics of the Physical Stimulus. (a) Overall rate (e.g., Chen, 1983; Juola, Ward et al., 1982; Fischler & Bloom, 1980; Masson, 1983; Petrick & Potter, 1982; Potter, Kroll, & Harris, 1980). (b) The relative duration of particular words within a sentence (Ward & Juola, 1982). (c) The duration of between-sentence or within-sentence pauses (Masson, 1983; Potter et al., 1980). (d) Window parameters: The number of words or characters per "frame" (Juola, Ward, et al., 1982; Juola, Cocklin, et al., 1982) and the location of the word(s) in the window (e.g., centered or left-justified). (e) The visual clarity of the whole sequence or of individual words within it (Potter, Carpenter, & Weinberg, 1984). Clarity could be varied in a number of ways, possibly with different consequences. For example, a light mask or a pattern mask could follow the words, or contrast could be altered, or a lateral (rather than superimposed) mask could be presented. (f) Mixture of RSVP and other modalities, such as spoken words, pictures (Potter, Kroll, Yachzel, & Sherman, 1982), or conventionally displayed text.

Linguistic and Message-Level Characteristics of the Stimulus. A few such variables will be mentioned here as illustrations, but the range of possibilities is as great as in any other method of presenting language. (a) Varying the duration of individual words and of pauses, to mimic sentence prosody. (b) Contrasting two or more levels of representation required for comprehension: e.g., topic-level pragmatic knowledge versus local processing of the literal sentence (Potter et al., 1980), or gist versus details (Masson, 1983). (c) Varying the predictability and appropriateness of a target word in a sentence or paragraph (Potter et al., 1984). (d) Contrasting scrambled and ordered sentences (Forster, 1970; Juola et al., 1982a; Petrick & Potter, 1982; Pfafflin, 1974; Potter & Kroll, 1984), or scrambled versus normal order of sentences within a paragraph (Chen, 1983). (e) Deleting function words to produce telegraphic prose (Potter et al., 1982). (f) Varying the syntactic complexity of a sentence (e.g., Forster, 1970; Holmes & Forster, 1972). (g) Varying plausibility or truth (Forster & Ryder, 1971; French, 1981; Potter et al., 1982). (h) Varying explicitness of anaphoric reference (Kanwisher & Potter, unpublished experiment). (i) Varying the correlation between simultaneously displayed word groups and "idea units" (Juola, Cocklin, et al., 1982). (j) Varying language (to date, only English and French have been used in RSVP studies).

Independent Variables: The Subjects

College-age subjects have been used in virtually all RSVP experiments, to this time. In only one study (Chen, 1983) have individual differences, in this case reading ability, been examined. Age, reading proficiency, and reading style are among the variables of interest.

Dependent Variables: The Task

Again, there is no limit to the number of dependent variables, save the investigator's ingenuity. There is, however, a more acute problem in choosing an appropriate dependent variable with RSVP than there might be in ordinary reading or listening, because the stimulus material is presented so rapidly. The dependent variables that have been used will be listed under five headings: Memory; Comprehension; Search tasks; Matching or comparison tasks; and Interaction with a second task. The possible measures in each case are response latency, error rate, and pattern of errors, as appropriate.

Memory. The usual memory measures can be employed with RSVP: (a) Recall — verbatim or gist, immediate or delayed (e.g., Forster, 1970). In one study (Potter et al., 1980), measures of verbatim recall of a paragraph were highly correlated with a less stringent paraphrase or gist criterion, so it may not matter which criterion is used. Masson (1983) had subjects write a summary of the main idea of a paragraph. (b) Recognition, including verbatim or paraphrased sentences (Chen, 1983) or probe-word recognition (e.g., Petrick & Potter, 1982; Segui, Dommergues, Frauenfelder, & Mehler, 1982). In principle, a probe word could be presented in the course of the sentence, for example just above the location of the RSVP stream. A picture probe could surround the RSVP words (Kanwisher & Potter, unpublished experiment).

Comprehension. There is no single widely accepted method of measuring comprehension, apart from memory. Some possibilities follow. (a) Plausibility or acceptability judgment. Plausibility can vary from the impossible to the merely unlikely, and can hinge on syntactic, semantic, or pragmatic violations. In the sentences such as those used by Potter et al. (1982), it was possible to say exactly where the implausibility occurred, because only the final word was altered to make an acceptable sentence implausible. The ability to accept or reject the two versions of the sentence is closely identified with one's pretheoretical notion of "comprehension". (b) Sentence verification. Verification of a sentence such as *Napoleon fought a battle at Lyons* or *A canary is a bird* requires something more than a plausibility judgment. I might understand the first sentence and judge its plausibility without knowing whether it was true or false, but one could argue that plausibility and truth converge in the case of the second sentence. It may be possible to use the relative speed of a plausibility judgment versus verification to sort out the components of comprehension. (c) Self-reported time to comprehend. Despite the subjective nature of this measure, it has been used with success in conventional reading experiments. It leaves the criterion of what constitutes comprehension to the subject. (d) Integration of the text as reflected in gist recall or intrusions of certain kinds (Masson, 1983; Potter et al., 1980).

Search Tasks. A subject can be asked to detect a word specified explicitly or by some attributes such as its superordinate category (Juola, Ward et al., 1982; Lawrence, 1971), its initial letter (Forster, 1970), whether it is a word or not (a version of lexical decision), or its physical form (e.g., capital letters: Lawrence, 1971). Masson (1983, Exp. 3) had subjects search a paragraph for the answer to a question.

Matching or Comparison Tasks. The distinction here is that in a search task a target is named in advance, whereas in a matching task a post-stimulus probe is compared with the stimulus according to some specified criterion. A probe recognition task can amount to a comparison task rather than a straight memory task if probes are related to the probed material by synonymy, rhyme, or acoustic similarity. The paradigm can either be one in which the subject is instructed to respond positively to (say) semantic relatedness, or one in which relatedness interferes with rejection of the probe (Petrick & Potter, 1982).

Interaction with a Second Task. RSVP can be used to provide incidental context for the primary task. Fischler and Bloom (1980) had subjects make a lexical decision, with an RSVP sentence as the immediately preceding context. Forster (1981) contrasted lexical decision under those conditions with naming latency for the same target word. In neither case did the primary task *require* processing of the sentence. Another example is Swinney's technique (1979) in which a written word is presented for lexical decision while a sentence is being heard; unbeknownst to the subject, a priming word occurs in the sentence. This technique might be adapted to RSVP by reversing modalities or by presenting the lexical-decision word in the same visual display as the sentence. These methods have the virtue that the RSVP sentence does not have to be read to perform the task, so that any effect it has could be regarded as "automatic" rather than strategic. On the other hand, subjects may be implicitly or deliberately supplementing the primary task by making a "matching" judgment, so the question of automaticity is moot.

Pictures and RSVP

I refer below to experiments in our laboratory using a combination of RSVP and pictures. We currently use a TERAK minicomputer which has a graphics buffer that can instantaneously place a picture (a line drawing) on the screen for a variable time while an RSVP sentence is being presented. The picture can either replace a word or can surround the location where the words are appearing. (Fortunately, pictures can be recognized over a wider visual angle than can words, as recent work by Pollatsek and Rayner, 1981, shows.) The line drawings are entered into the computer memory using a Hi-Pad digitizer and hand editing. The net result is not as handsome as a good ink drawing, but a comparison between our earlier filmed sequences and the CRT format indicates that the pictures are just as "readable" on the CRT.

CHARACTERISTICS OF RSVP READING

Visual Factors in RSVP

Psychologists unfamiliar with RSVP often express surprise that visual masking does not prevent serial reading at 12 words per second and faster. As already noted, however, 83 msec per word is considerably above the typical duration threshold for masked single words, which is 50 msec or less. What masking there is tends to favor the longer words in an RSVP sentence at the expense of the shorter ones. This effect is more serious for rates above 12 words a second, when it is not clear that all the words are perceived. The range of viewing conditions to which these comments apply has not been established, but they hold for viewing a typical CRT display in an illuminated room.

Even though the words can be seen there may be apparent movement, an accordion-like effect in which successive words expand and contract. A letter that is in the same location in two successive words appears to stand still. These effects, although initially distracting, are soon ignored.

Thus, purely visual factors seem to be of relatively little importance in RSVP reading at rates of 12 words per second or slower. What limits the effective rate of RSVP reading is higher-level "masking" due to overload at levels of processing presumably shared by RSVP and normal reading. As Forster and Ryder (1971) state, in RSVP "performance depends primarily on the speed with which S can impose a meaningful organization on the input sequence" (p. 287).

Fast Processing

The claim has been made that RSVP reading is not only remarkably fast, but also that more words are processed than a reader is capable of recalling (Forster, 1970; Potter et al., 1980). It is, however, notoriously difficult to demonstrate that processing occurred, when immediate recall or recognition fails (Dagenbach & Carr, 1982; Eriksen, 1960; Merikle, 1982; and Purcell, Stewart, & Stanovich, 1982). There are at least two ways in which a dissociation between stimulus processing and reportability might come about. One is if processing sometimes or always reaches a high level (e.g., a semantic level) before entering awareness. Then, if entry into consciousness were somehow prevented, it would in principle be possible to show effects of the subliminal processing on some other response (e.g., Marcel, 1980). Another possibility is that subjects may be momentarily aware of the significance of a stimulus, but for some reason (such as distraction by other stimuli) the stimulus is forgotten before it can be reported (e.g., Potter, 1976).

Whether a word in RSVP briefly enters awareness and is then forgotten (as some viewers say) or whether it never entered consciousness but nonetheless had measurable effects, is an issue that cannot be settled here. What is of primary interest is that RSVP is capable of revealing very rapid, presumably automatic, and perhaps elementary cognitive and linguistic operations, such as those that structure a string of words into a sentence. Without those structures the words fall apart and some go unreported, even when the number of words is within the conventional span of short-term memory (Forster, 1970; Mitchell, 1979; Pfafflin, 1974; Potter, 1982; Potter & Kroll, 1984).

RSVP COMPARED WITH OTHER METHODS

The chief value of RSVP as a research tool is that the investigator controls the timing of reading, word by word. There are, of course, other methods to obtain partial control over reading time such as by instructing a subject to read at a given speed or by presenting a whole sentence or text for a fixed time. The disadvantage of the latter methods is that the reader changes the pattern of fixations in response to time pressure, skipping or skimming rather than reading every word. This performance is worth studying in its own right (cf. Just, Carpenter & Woolley, 1982; and Masson, 1982), but if the investigator wants to speed up reading without those strategic changes, RSVP may be a better method.

Comparison to Speech

RSVP reading is like listening and unlike normal reading, in that the recipient has no control over the time each word is viewed, the location of fixation, and the order in which words are fixated (there's no going back). It is of interest, therefore, to compare RSVP reading at fast and slow rates of presentation to listening to normal and compressed speech, respectively. Potter, Kroll, and Harris (1980) compared recall of RSVP and spoken paragraphs presented at the net rate of 3.3 words per second (normal brisk speech). Recall was qualitatively and quantitatively very similar with the two modes of presentation (cf. Kintsch, Kozminsky, Streby, McKoon, & Keenan, 1975; and Sticht, 1972, for a similar conclusion about the equivalence of reading and listening).

Is listening to compressed speech like reading in RSVP? It is known that speech compressed by a factor greater than 2.5, above about 8 words per second, becomes very difficult to understand (Miron & Brown, 1971; Wallace & Koury, 1982; Aaronson, 1974a, b). For single RSVP sentences, comprehension and recall is still excellent at 12 words per second (Potter et al. 1982). A direct comparison using the same materials and measures of performance would be needed to evaluate this suggestion that RSVP is easier to process than compressed speech, at high rates. The rate limiting factor with compressed speech may be that the acoustic signal becomes too degraded, since an inherent property of speech is its distribution over time. In RSVP, visual masking is not sufficiently severe at 12 words per second to prevent identification of most of the words, so the constraints on rate probably occur at high levels of processing. Nonetheless, it would be informative to compare compressed speech and RSVP over the range that both are perceptible, to see which patterns of deficits show up in both modes and which are characteristic of just one. Deficits shared by the two modes could be inferred to arise at levels of language processing common to both.

Comparison to Self-Paced Methods

RSVP may be contrasted with several methods for studying reading in which the reader has control over timing. These methods include the recording of eye movements during reading (cf. Rayner, this volume) and self-paced presentation of single words, groups of words, or sentences (cf. Aaronson; Graesser & Riha; Haberlandt; Just & Carpenter; Kieras; and Mitchell, in this volume). With these methods the main measure is the time the reader spends on each word or segment of text, whereas in RSVP the experimenter controls reading time and measures detection of a target, the accuracy and latency of a plausibility judgment, recall, or the like. The former methods thus provide a direct measure of the spontaneous response to each word or word group, whereas RSVP pushes processing to its limits and measures breakdown of performance.

The two classes of methods parallel two approaches to the study of single stimuli: reaction time versus tachistoscopic threshold. By analogy with tachistoscopic presentation, as RSVP rate is increased, the amount of processing for which there is enough time is decreased. RSVP allows one to peel away the layers of processing, by looking at what is preserved and what is lost as reading time is decreased. The two approaches — self-paced methods and RSVP — may provide converging methods to examine the temporal organization of various comprehension processes. For example, latency in self-paced reading may indicate the combined duration of all processes the reader has carried out on that word, phrase, or sentence, while RSVP may indicate which processes are omitted if there is insufficient time.

Manual Self-Presentation. One problem with self-paced presentation is that a manual response after each word of the text produces reading that is abnormally slow. Mitchell (this volume) reports an overall average of 719 msec per word, in one experiment, and Just et al. (1982) obtained 495 msec per word, compared to 289 msec per word in conventional reading of the same passage. Even with three words at a time, reading is slower than normal. It is thus difficult to know whether observations made with these techniques apply to normal reading, although Just and Carpenter (this volume) report encouraging correlations between single-word button-pressing performance and eye movement data.

Any method that slows reading is likely to reduce sensitivity to variables of interest, particularly high-level variables, because the later stages of processing can occur in the abnormally long interval between central initiation of the motor response and arrival of the next display at higher centers (abnormally long compared with eye movements). However, the response latency may be sensitive to perceptual variables such as word frequency and word length, because subjects may wait to initiate the button press until they have at least identified the word(s).

The presentation of three words at a time (see Mitchell, this volume) might increase sensitivity because the extra processing time associated with the manual response occurs only once per three words, but there are other drawbacks to this solution. One is that it becomes more difficult to allocate processing time to individual words. A potentially more serious problem is that carving up the text into arbitrary three-word segments is likely to distort processing. If the three-word segment forms a phrase, the reader is saved the problem of locating the phrase boundaries; if the segment splits a phrase or clause, extra difficulty may be encountered (in *He got out the fat chicken*, consider the difference between seeing *the fat chicken* as a single frame versus *out the fat* followed by *chicken*). Mitchell (personal communication) reports that an experiment designed to test the effect of the position of breaks found no systematic effects. Using RSVP, however, Juola, Cocklin, et al. (1982) found that it helps to break text into idea units, rather than breaking it arbitrarily.

Mixed Methods. There are some methods that fall between RSVP and self-paced procedures. Rayner (this volume) and his colleagues have combined the measurement of eye movements with masking in various ingenious ways. One method is to introduce a mask a fixed time after the beginning of each fixation. With this technique, Rayner, Inhoff, Morrison, Slowiaczek, and Bertera (1981) have shown that 50 msec at the beginning of each fixation is all a reader needs to identify the fixated word(s); eye movements are essentially normal under this condition. Like RSVP, this method tells one something about the time needed for a component process, in this case the time for initial pickup of the visual information. Their result is consistent with studies of thresholds for single words. Another method they have used is to mask only words in the periphery, or conversely only in the fovea, to study the use of peripheral information in reading.

QUESTIONS ABOUT RSVP AS A METHOD

If RSVP is to be used as a method for studying reading, or more generally, language processing, then it should be like normal reading in essential respects, apart from rate. That is, it should draw on the same processes as normal language comprehension. At rates above about 12 words per second, word perception may be seriously compromised by masking, as already discussed. Therefore, this discussion will focus on rates up to 12 words per second. Most subjects make few errors in recalling an 8-word sentence presented at that rate (Potter et al., 1982; see Table 2). Even when reading a paragraph at that rate, the word that specifies the topic is almost invariably perceived (Potter et al., 1980). Juola, Ward et al. (1982) found that subjects could pick out a word belonging to a specified superordinate category 92% of the time, in sentences or scrambled sentences presented at 10 words per second. Even at 20 words per second, the word was detected 84% of the time. That does not mean that there is no degradation of the visual input at such rates, nor can one rule out the possibility that any such degradation would interact with other levels of difficulty. Still, the evidence suggests that the major bottleneck in RSVP reading is at the high levels of processing that are common to RSVP and conventional reading.

No Peripheral Vision. An important question is whether the absence of a peripheral view of the text in RSVP distorts normal reading. The recent findings from eye movement studies by Rayner, McConkie, and their colleagues are somewhat reassuring on this point (McConkie, Blanchard, Zola, & Wolverton, 1982; cf. Rayner, 1983). They report that readers fixate the majority of words and get relatively little useful information from the periphery, except information about word size that might help in directing the next eye movement (but see Rayner, Well, Pollatsek, & Bertera, 1982, and Balota & Rayner, 1983 for recent evidence that some word-specific information is picked up from the word to the right of fixation). Nonetheless, the absence of peripheral information and information about the whole shape of the paragraph and page does make RSVP different from normal reading. If the spatial framework of a page helps to fix ideas spatially in memory (e.g., Lovelace & Southall, 1983), then clearly that also is missing in RSVP. To the extent that reading performance is similar in RSVP and normal reading, however, one can infer that the missing peripheral information is unimportant.

Eye Movements During RSVP. What about real eye movements and blinks? If an RSVP reader moves his or her eyes, the visual consequences might be major. I know of no studies of eye movements during RSVP reading. One may speculate, however, that eye movements are inhibited. In viewing a rapid sequence of pictures, eye movements virtually stop when the picture changes more often than every 500 msec (Potter & Levy, 1969). The changing words in RSVP might produce the same inhibition. Blinks could be serious, but they ordinarily last for a much shorter time than 83 msec; they might be important at higher rates of presentation. One wonders whether blinks would be inhibited when events are changing rapidly. In any case, a study is needed to discover just what the eyes do when reading with RSVP.

RSVP Reading Versus Normal Reading and Listening

Comprehension of RSVP Sentences. Potter et al. (1982) compared single RSVP sentences presented at 12 words per second with the same sentences displayed conventionally for the same total time. This rate is equivalent to 720 words per minute, which is more than twice as fast as a typical college student normally reads. The subjects first judged whether or not the sentence was plausible and then wrote it down. Plausibility hinged on the last word of the sentence, as in *The fox chased the chicken around the yard/kitchen*. The sentences were 8 to 14 words long. The chief measures of performance were the latency and accuracy of the plausibility judgment (which was assumed to require comprehension) and recall accuracy (which measured perception and memory, in addition). On all these measures, the RSVP sentences were better than the normally displayed sentences viewed for an equal time (Table 1). A third group that viewed the normal sentences for an additional 300 msec (about a 33% increase in duration) performed as well as the RSVP readers except that the plausibility decisions remained slower.

RSVP Paragraphs. The results were somewhat different when paragraphs were presented (Potter et al., 1980). For the recall of the first half of the paragraph, conventional presentation for the same total time produced better performance than RSVP presentation, at each of the three rates we used: 3.3, 6.7, or 10 words per second. (The rate within a RSVP sentence was 4, 8, or 12 words per second, but a pause between sentences equivalent to two words reduced the overall rate.) For recall of the second half of the paragraph, the conventional and RSVP presentations produced similar performance only at the slowest rate of 3.3 words per second (a comfortable 200 words per minute). At higher rates RSVP readers recalled more than the conventional presentation group. In other words, RSVP enabled readers to get through a paragraph faster, but at a cost in the completeness of processing.

More important, however, were the results of a second manipulation, the presence or absence of a key to the otherwise obscure topic of the paragraph. The paragraphs were modeled on Bransford and Johnson's (1972) paragraph about washing clothes. Instead of using a title to convey the topic (e.g., doing one's

TABLE 1
RSVP versus Conventional Reading of Single Sentences:
Proportion of Words Omitted in Recall and Response Time
(in msec) to Judge the Plausibility of the Sentence
(Potter, Kroll, Yachzel, & Sherman, 1982)

Condition	Recall Errors	Plausibility Judgment (a)	
RSVP (12 wps) (b)	.13	1371	(.14)
Reading (12 wps)	.25	2028(c)	(.24)
Reading (9 wps) (d)	.12	1781(c)	(.13)

Notes:
(a) Error rate is shown in parentheses.
(b) Words per second.
(c) Measured from the equivalent of the last word, in RSVP.
(d) The time available for reading each sentence was 12 wps plus 300 msec, so the range was 8.3 wps for the shortest sentences to 9.6 wps for the longest sentences.

laundry), the topic was provided in a sentence presented at the beginning, middle, or end of the paragraph — or it was omitted. The task was to recall the paragraph immediately after presentation. In RSVP, the key information increased recall of whatever part of the paragraph followed it, showing that the key concept was understood and that the scenario it activated could be used to interpret the following text. This positive effect was of similar magnitude at all three RSVP rates, including 12 words per second (Fig. 1).

To our surprise, in normal reading the key topic had *no* effect on recall of the first half of the paragraph, although there was a marked positive effect on the second half (Fig. 2). Evidently readers set their reading rate by a joint criterion of comprehension and speed, so that even when they were trying to read very fast, they read obscure text more slowly than clear text. The part they did get through was thus remembered equally well, with or without the topic. The effect of knowing the topic was to permit them to read faster and so get through more of the second half of the paragraph in the time available. Incidentally, in no condition was there any evidence that the key topic aided reconstruction of earlier parts of the paragraph. Having the topic after a given part of the paragraph was no better than never having a topic (see Fig. 1 and 2). (Reconstructive recall occurs when recall is delayed and there has been further forgetting.)

Apart from RSVP's control over the rate of reading, there was little apparent difference in comprehension of RSVP and conventional paragraphs. The same

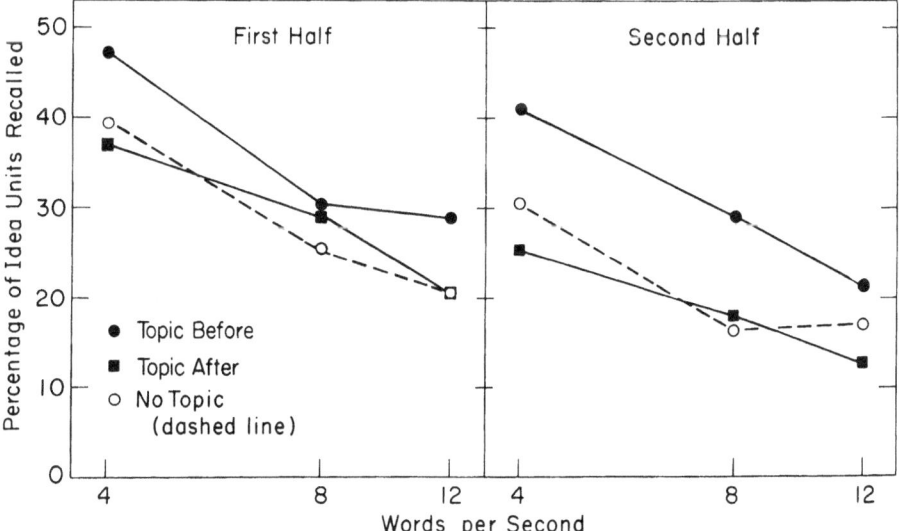

FIG. 1. Immediate recall of each half of an RSVP paragraph as a function of the rate of presentation and whether information about the otherwise obscure topic was included before that half, after that half, or never (adapted from Potter, Kroll, & Harris, 1980).

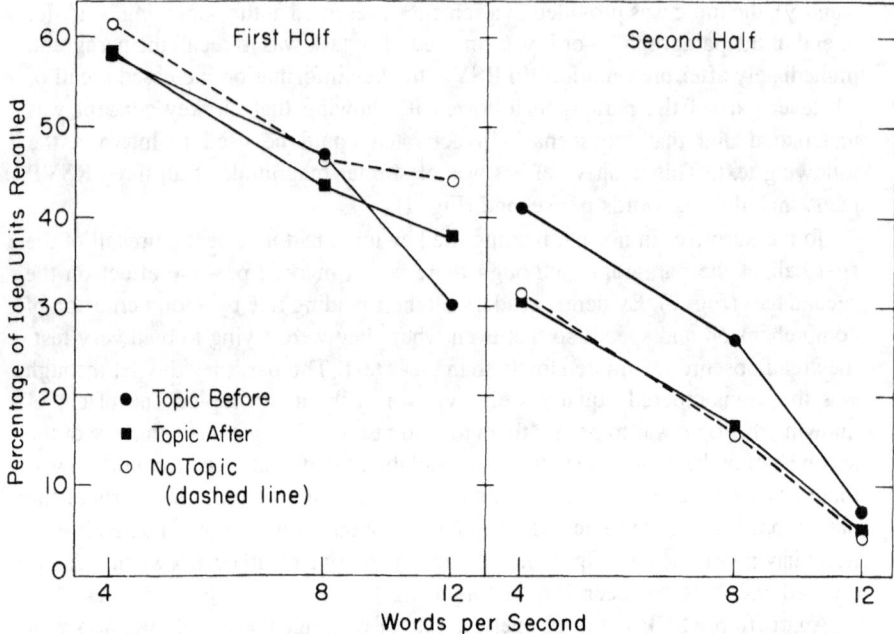

FIG. 2. Immediate recall of each half of conventionally presented paragraphs displayed for total times equivalent to the three RSVP rates; see the caption of Fig. 1 for details (adapted from Potter, Kroll, & Harris, 1980)

qualitative patterns of errors were observed. A further comparison with listening to the paragraphs at the slowest rate (3.3 words per second) gave similar results, as already noted.

Masson (1983) has recently reported a series of experiments comparing RSVP and conventional reading or skimming, using a large number of standardized paragraphs. The subjects answered questions or wrote a summary of the paragraph. RSVP produced poorer performance than normal reading when there was no pause between sentences, but equal performance when a pause was introduced (the significance of pauses is considered later). Juola, Ward et al. (1982), who used brief pauses between sentences, observed an overall effect of total time to read but minimal differences between conventional paragraph reading and RSVP in which one, two, or three words (on the average) appeared in each RSVP window. Chen (1983) has recently reported similar results: RSVP and conventional paragraphs were no different, overall. However, he found an interaction such that poorer readers actually benefitted from RSVP, whereas good readers showed a (nonsignificant) decrement.

Conclusion: RSVP and Convention Reading (or Listening) are Similar. In short, apart from shifting control over rate from reader to the experimenter, RSVP does not appear to distort normal language processing. As the recall and summarization results indicate, what a reader comprehends is fairly similar in RSVP and conventional reading. Thus, it is an appropriate tool for controlling the distribution of processing time in the study of reading comprehension.

Immediate Versus Post-Presentation Processing

The most important methodological question about RSVP is the extent of processing during presentation. In normal reading, a substantial amount of processing is completed as the eyes fixate a given word; there is now strong evidence that a reader carries the analysis of a word and its relation to the prior context as far as possible, before looking at the next word (see Just & Carpenter, this volume). If, in contrast, an RSVP sentence is simply stored in a buffer and processed at leisure after presentation (as Mitchell, 1979, suggested), that would represent a significant distortion of normal reading. There are a number of reasons for thinking that readers do carry out a good deal of processing during RSVP at 12 words per second or even faster — much more than simply identifying the words, for example. My working hypothesis is that much or all of the processing that normally occurs as one reads a sentence also occurs during RSVP, although it is abbreviated as rate increases. The processing that remains to be completed at the end of a normal sentence also remains at the end of an RSVP sentence. Some of the evidence bearing on that hypothesis follows.

Effects of Sentence Length. In the experiments of Potter et al. (1982), described earlier, suppose readers were merely storing up the words of an RSVP sentence and processing them afterward. One would then expect a monotonic increase in latency to judge plausibility, with increasing length of the sentence, because running through the buffer would take longer for longer sentences. That was not what we found. Although 8-word sentences were indeed evaluated slightly faster than longer sentences (by about 62 msec), sentences of 10, 12, and 14 words did not differ significantly (Table 2). Nor did judgment errors increase systematically with length.

TABLE 2
Response Time and Errors in Judging the Plausibility
of RSVP Sentences of Different Lengths
Presented at 12 Words per Second
(Potter, Kroll, Yachzel, & Sherman, 1982)

	Length (Words)			
	8	10	12	14
RT (msec)	1299	1382	1372	1328
Proportion of Errors	.09	.13	.12	.14

Recall Errors. In the same experiments, the pattern of errors in immediate recall was also consistent with on-line processing, in that words least relevant to the main topic of the sentence were the ones likely to be omitted. For example, as Forster (1970) noted, adjectives and adverbs are less likely to be recalled than other words. Potter et al. (1982) found that adjectives were likely to be retained, however, when the sense of the sentence would have been markedly changed by their omission. To explain this, one has to assume that the sentence was understood during presentation; otherwise, there would have been no basis for selective retention. An alternative is that all the words were momentarily available at the end of the sentence in the form of an as yet unrelated list, and that selection occurred during reconstruction from this list buffer. This alternative can be rejected because of the small capacity for retaining unrelated words (e.g., Potter, 1982).

A convincing demonstration of the effect of meaning on retention of a critical adjective is provided by Dommergues, Frauenfelder, Mehler, and Segui (1979). They presented RSVP sentences with adjective-noun compounds such as *chaise lounge* (literally *chair long*, whose compound meaning includes the sort of air mattress used on water). In one version of the sentence, both the compound sense and the noun sense (*chair*) were plausible; in the other version, only the compound sense was plausible. In the latter case, the adjective was rarely omitted; in the former case, it frequently was. Controls in which the adjective was omitted, or replaced by a nonword anagram, showed very few intrusions of the adjective, demonstrating that the effect was not due to guessing.

RSVP Paragraphs and Immediacy. Of course, if there *were* substantial processing still to be done after presentation of a sentence, it would be very difficult to understand several RSVP sentences in sequence. As described earlier, when subjects viewed RSVP paragraphs (Potter et al., 1980) reading comprehension did not fall apart as that hypothesis would predict, but kept up with presentation (note, however, that there was a pause equivalent to two words at the end of each sentence). Not only did subjects process individual sentences, they also managed to make some sense of the overall topic, when it was provided (Fig. 1). Although the overall amount recalled dropped substantially as rate increased, the bottleneck apparently came after comprehension. Rapid presentation, like rapid conventional reading, seems to induce forgetting (cf. Chen, 1983, for a similar conclusion).

Extra Processing at the End of a Sentence. As noted, in the paragraphs experiment there was a pause after each sentence equivalent to two words. We included the pause because we had the impression that some extra processing time was needed at the end of a sentence. Just and Carpenter (1980) have shown that a short pause occurs at the end of a sentence in normal reading, as Mitchell and Green (1978) also observed in self-paced sequential reading. Masson recently reported (1983) that RSVP reading was inferior to conventional reading when no such pause was provided, but (as we also found) was equally good with the pause. (Masson's experiments were, however, somewhat ambiguous about whether the pause itself or the increase in total time was responsible for the improvement.) It is not the case that no processing remains to be done at the end of an RSVP sentence. The present working hypothesis is that the type of processing that remains to be completed at the end of an RSVP sentence also remains at the end of a normal sentence.

Pictures in RSVP Sentences and the Buffer Hypothesis. Potter et al. (1982) looked at the effects of substituting a pictured object for an equivalent word in RSVP sentences. Processing the picture sentences turned out to be very nearly as easy as processing all-word sentences. Since the pictures could not have been phonologically recoded during presentation (at least, not in the proper sequence), it is unlikely that they were stored in a phonological buffer. A visual buffer for a sequential string of up to 14 items is also unlikely. Pictures and words are, however, compatible at a conceptual level. Thus the ease of understanding these sentences strongly implies immediate processing to a conceptual level.

Reading or Guessing? Even at 12 words per second, many readers of RSVP have the sensation that they are guessing some of the words without seeing them, in particular the function words. (There is no reason, of course, to accept this conscious impression as valid without further evidence. In tachistoscopic experiments, it is a common enough experience to think one is guessing but still be correct.) As we know from recent word on eye movements (for example, Ehrlich & Rayner, 1981), normal reading is not a psychological guessing game — and the same seems to be true of RSVP. Certainly if one leaves blanks in place of the predictable function words in an RSVP sentence, readers do not fill in the missing words with perfect accuracy (Potter & Kroll, 1984; cf. Table 3). That is not to say that expectations play no role, only that RSVP reading does not amount to telegraphic reading.

Scrambled Sentences. Forster (1970), Pfafflin (1974), and Potter and Kroll (1984) all found that recall of a scrambled RSVP sentence was much poorer than the same sentence presented in normal order, even when there were as few as seven or eight words in the sentence. That result strongly suggests that the structure provided by a sentence was used during presentation. If phrase and sentence-level processing had been postponed until the end of the sentence, all the words would have had to be held in a buffer until that point; why so many should then be lost from a near-span list is difficult to explain. French (1981) also found that scrambling reduced recall of seven-word sentences, using a rate of 14 words per second. At 24 words per second, however, scrambling mattered less than the plausibility of the sentence (the more plausible sentences tended to have thematically associated words). That suggests that the ability to make use of sentence structure breaks down at very high RSVP rates, leaving only associative structure.

Two other studies compared normal and scrambled RSVP sentences using more immediate tasks than recall. Juola, Ward et al. (1982) had subjects search for a word target in RSVP sentences, and found a small but significant advantage when the sentence was normally ordered. Petrick and Potter (1982) presented 12-word sentences at 12 words per second, followed after 83 or 250 msec by a probe word (the timing of the probe did not interact with the other variables). The task was to decide whether the probe had appeared in the sentence. Responses to probes of scrambled sentences were in general less accurate and slower than responses to probes of normally ordered sentences. There was also an interaction with the type of distractor that suggested less reliance on a semantic representation and more on an acoustic or speech-like representation, in the case of scrambled sentences (see Table 4). These results offer further support for on-line processing of sentence structure and meaning (cf. also Segui et al., 1982).

Retroactive Interference in RSVP: Mitchell's Experiment. Mitchell (1979; see also Mitchell, this volume) reported an experiment in which 7-word RSVP sentences were presented at 20 words per second and immediately recalled. When the last three words of the sentence were altered to make nonsense of the sentence, recall of the first four words was reduced by 8-18%, compared to the same four words in the intact sentence. Thus, recall reflected not only immediate processing, but also (to some extent) events that occurred subsequent to presentation. Mitchell did not use a conventional-reading control; I would expect that such a control would also show a deficit in retention, if subjects only had time to read the sentence once. Clearly, recall is a measure that can be disrupted by post-stimulus distraction.

This finding does not represent a fatal criticism of RSVP as a method for studying immediate processing, however. It certainly does not prove that the bulk of RSVP processing occurs after the sentence or paragraph has been presented, any more than would be the case for normal reading. Although any measure taken after all the words of the RSVP sentence have been presented cannot directly indicate the processing of each individual word, there are still strong reasons (reviewed in this section) for believing that the measures reflect processing that occurred during presentation.

Other Evidence for On-Line Processing. Fischler and Bloom (1980) found that an acceptable RSVP sentence context preceding the target word in a lexical decision task produced faster responses than an anomalous context, for sentences presented as rapidly as 28 words per second (the effect was larger at 4 and 12 words per second than at higher rates, however). The overall response times were similar to those in experiments using isolated words, so there was no indication that subjects engaged in post-presentation processing of the sentences, prior to making the lexical decision. Thus, at least some of the subjects some of the time must have succeeded in processing the sentences on-line. Potter, Carpenter, and Weinberg (1984) obtained similar effects in a word-naming task, when the sentence context was presented at 5 words per second.

Conclusion: Processing is Largely On-Line. In RSVP, not all the processing that would be done at slow rates of reading gets done, which is why RSVP is of interest as an experimental method. What processing there is, however, appears to occur primarily during, not after, RSVP. At higher rates than 12 words per second, it is possible that there is more post-sentential processing, but it is more likely that there is simply less processing altogether. Even at rates of 12 words per second and slower, there is undoubtedly some part of processing that can only take place at the end of a sentence, because only then is all the relevant syntactic and semantic information available. We have no reason at this point for supposing that this end-of-sentence processing is different for RSVP than for normal reading (or listening).

Immediate recall, which has been the chief task used with RSVP, is not strictly immediate, even if it does reflect on-line processing. More use could be made in the future of tasks that probe the representation of the sentence at a given point during its presentation.

Short-Term Buffers in RSVP and in Conventional Reading

The evidence from short-term memory research indicates that no more than five unrelated words can be held verbatim, on the average, even when they are presented slowly. As rate increases to 12 words per second, capacity drops to about 2.6 words (Potter, 1982). In rapid visual presentation of unrelated items such as digits, the order of presentation is particularly vulnerable to forgetting; even when the items are retained almost perfectly, almost all order information is lost at rates above 6 items per second (Mitchell, 1976; Scarborough & Sternberg, 1967; for a similar result with auditory sequences, cf. Aaronson, Markowitz & Shapiro, 1971). Thus, there is no buffer capable of retaining the words of a sentence of normal length in raw form. If it is to be understood and retained, the sentence must undergo some processing (beyond the mere identification of the words) during presentation.

Nonetheless, buffers of smaller capacity then a full sentence may play a role in reading. I have speculated elsewhere (Potter, 1983) that one or more visuospatial buffers (organized retinotopically, spatiotopically, or on the basis of individual objects) retain the information in a single fixation or RSVP frame for a short period even after the next visual event has reached the retina. This buffering may mean that the relative duration of single words in RSVP is less important than the total presentation time for small segments of text such as a phrase or clause.

Ward and Juola (1982) offer some support for that conclusion. They report an experiment in which word durations in RSVP were (a) constant; or (b) adjusted to be proportional to the mean times conventional readers spend looking at each word; or (c) adjusted to conform to a regression analysis by Just and Carpenter (1980) of the data in (b). In a fourth condition, the paragraphs were presented conventionally. In a test of recognition memory no differences were obtained among the four conditions of presentation, although as usual there was a substantial effect of total reading time. It is of course possible that there were differences in comprehension between these various presentation conditions that were not large enough to be detected by the test of recognition memory they used; more sensitive tests should be devised, before the null hypothesis is accepted.

Phonological buffering is familiar from the traditional studies of acoustic coding in short-term memory. Such a buffer has been assumed in many contemporary models of reading, although its exact nature is still in doubt (Baddeley & Lewis, 1981). Petrick and Potter (1982) show that a phonological and semantic representation are each available in RSVP reading at 12 words per second, just as in reading conventionally at slower rates (Table 4). There is no reason as yet to suppose that buffers in RSVP are any different from buffers used in conventional reading; they may be present as a backup for recovery when "left to right" processing fails.

It should be noted that buffers containing syntactic and semantic information about several words or constituents (not always the most recent ones) are assumed in almost any computer model of language processing. In one parsing model, for example (Marcus, 1980), there is a three-cell constituent buffer and a push-down stack (note that this buffer plays an active role in processing; it is not simply a memory device). Thus the question is not whether there are buffers in RSVP, but whether RSVP buffers are different from those in normal reading. The tentative answer is "no", but there has been little research directed to just this question.

RESEARCH USING RSVP

Few studies of language processing used RSVP before Forster named the technique (1970). A comprehensive review of research since that time is beyond the scope of this chapter. Instead, I will describe some findings that are particularly relevant to the use of RSVP as a research tool in the study of reading.

Is Language Comprehension Rapid but Memory Consolidation Slow?

The most important finding to emerge from RSVP research is that language processing can be extraordinarily rapid, capable of occurring at 12 words per second or even faster. The evidence for rapid comprehension comes from the work just reviewed. The level of comprehension reached during RSVP reading does not necessarily produce a lasting trace, however. In the paragraph reading experiments of Potter et al. (1980), increasing the rate of reading from 3 to 10 words per second did not prevent comprehension, but did cause a substantial drop in recall (Fig. 1). The bottleneck came at a point in processing after individual word recognition and apparently after comprehension of individual sentences and the general topic. The processing that was impaired by rapid presentation may have been memory consolidation per se, or may have been deeper or more detailed processing of meaning.

The method used to assess comprehension was recall of a critical topic-giving word and the influence of that word on recall of other parts of the ambiguous paragraph, including the intrusion of plausible inferences. These measures of comprehension may not have been sufficiently sensitive to distinguish between failure of consolidation and failure to draw bridging inferences and the like, when rate was increased. It was clear, however, that much more than simple word retrieval was accomplished even at the highest RSVP rate used in those experiments (10 words per second, overall). A similar conclusion was reached by Forster (1970, 1975) and by Chen (1983).

We may read and speak at a relatively slow rate because an adequate level of retention requires processing time beyond that required for comprehension, where "comprehension" includes not only word identification but also the retrieval of word meaning and pragmatic or script-based knowledge. The rate at which RSVP sentences are understood may be closer to the rate of thought than is normal reading, and the memory trace correspondingly ephemeral. If the main effect of RSVP is on consolidation, not on cognitive processing itself, then recall of RSVP text may not be a suitable method for revealing levels of text processing (although it might tell us something about memory). Researchers interested in studying the momentary extent of processing might use single RSVP sentences (whose recall presumably directly reflects the extent of processing) or might present probes during RSVP reading.

What the Language Processor Finds Difficult

Forster, Holmes, and their colleagues have used RSVP to examine the effects of various syntactic and pragmatic variables on language comprehension. Forster (1970) presented six-word sentences at 16 words per second, and found that syntactically simple one-clause sentences were more accurately recalled than two-clause sentences (cf. also Holmes, 1973). Forster and Ryder (1971) replicated Forster's results and showed that bizarre and anomalous sentences are harder to recall than plausible sentences. Since the two effects did not interact, they concluded that syntactic analysis is autonomous, separate from pragmatic factors (cf. French, 1981). Likewise, Forster and Olbrei (1974) found that active sentences were more readily judged as grammatical than were passive sentences, and there was no effect of the pragmatic factor of reversibility. In seeming contrast, however, Holmes and Forster (1972) found that the added difficulty of complement verbs showed up only in sentences rated very natural.

Holmes, Arwas, and Garrett (1977) found that recall of an ambiguous word in an RSVP sentence was less probable than recall of an unambiguous control word. I also found that ambiguous words lowered comprehension and overall recall accuracy when the nondominant meaning was the appropriate one (Potter, 1981).

TABLE 3
RSVP Sentences with Redundant Words Replaced by Blank Frames
("telegraphic") versus Full RSVP Sentences:
Proportion of Words Omitted in Recall and Response Time
(in msec) to Judge the Plausibility of the Sentence

Condition	Recall Errors		Plausibility Judgment (b)
	Presented Words	Deleted (a) Words	
Telegraphic	.14	.39	2158 (.13)
Full sentence	.09	.09	1257 (.07)

Notes:
(a) Deleted only in the telegraphic condition.
(b) Error rate is shown in parentheses.

Potter and Kroll (1984) presented RSVP sentences that had "inessential" words (chiefly function words) removed so that they read like telegrams, as in *(The) hunters hoped (to) find (a) deer (and) shoot (it)*. Not surprisingly, comprehension and recall were impaired, although less so when the missing words were replaced by blanks than when the remaining words were run together. Perhaps more surprising was how small the impairment was (Table 3): much smaller than the impairment due to scrambling, for example. (Subjects in the telegraphic group were asked to write out a full sentence that the "telegram" might have been taken from.) Readers managed to make sense of most of the sentences, suggesting that there are default assignments of roles to words that operate when explicit syntactic markers are absent. Telegraphic RSVP could be used in future research to sort out what these default assignments are, and whether they persist as biases even when syntactic markers are present.

Added to this list of processing difficulties revealed by RSVP is the observation that noun-noun constructions like *store door* or *chicken fat* are difficult to process in RSVP, at least when the first noun is a possible head noun for the phrase (Potter & Kroll, 1984). The experiment in question was designed to test the perceptibility of word order in RSVP at 12 words per second, using reversible pairs in sentences such as *The fat chicken* (or, *chicken fat*) *was removed from the refrigerator*. On 45% of the trials, one or both words were omitted in recall, demonstrating the difficulty of parsing this sort of construction. When both words were recalled, their order was correct 74% of the time.

In summary, syntactic complexity (no clauses rather than one, complement verbs, noun-noun phrases) and pragmatic implausibility each increase recall errors in RSVP. Whether the two classes of effects are additive or interactive is less clear. Telegraphic RSVP sentences are harder to read than full sentences—but the surprise is how well readers do. Ambiguous words also increase errors. These results validate the use of RSVP as a way to measure processing difficulty.

Input to the Language Processor is Not Exclusively Lexical

Potter et al. (1982) tested the effect of substituting a picture for a word in an RSVP sentence. The readers made a plausibility judgment and then recalled the sentence, as described earlier. The hypothesis to be tested was that words are interpreted conceptually, not just lexically, as they are read. If the hypothesis is correct, pictured concepts would successfully substitute for words, even when there was too short a time (at 12 words per second) to name the pictures. Processing the sentences with pictures was very nearly as easy as processing all-word sentences. That suggests that sentences are encoded content word by content word (or phrase by phrase) into a conceptual (nonlexical) format, a format in which the remaining processes of comprehension are carried out.

The sequential nature of speech and other factors in speech production and perception put constraints on the organization of natural languages that are probably different from the constraints on conceptual thought. It is not *a priori* apparent how much of the machinery of language comprehension is specific to the language code and how much is part of the general machinery of thought. The tentative conclusion from the ease of understanding pictures in sentences presented very rapidly is that extra-linguistic conceptual processes play a major role early in processing.

Speech Recoding is Fast and Ubiquitous

Recent research has put increasing emphasis on the value of speech recoding in reading (Baddeley & Lewis, 1981). Widely cited estimates of recoding time have suggested that recoding occurs no faster than three or four (to a maximum of six) words a second (Landauer, 1962; Lovelace, Powell & Brooks, 1973). It is widely believed that those readers who "hear what they are reading" are held to that maximum rate, which is about 250 words per minute.

If recoding is important and if it were as slow as claimed, then RSVP at rates over 6 words per second would make recoding impossible and change the nature of

TABLE 4
The Effect of Presenting a Negative Probe Similar to a Word in the Preceding RSVP Sentence: Increase in Response Time to Reject the Probe (in msec) and Increase in Error Rate, Relative to Unrelated Probes (Petrick & Potter, 1982)

Sentence Condition	Probe Similarity	
	Acoustic	Semantic
6 wps (a)	95 (.05)	77 (.04)
12 wps	84 (.03)	121 (.10)
12 wps, scrambled	152 (.07)	54 (.07)

Notes:
(a) Words per second.

reading. Petrick and I (Petrick & Potter, 1982) carried out a series of experiments in which subjects responded to a probe word following after an RSVP sentence — all they had to do was decide whether or not the word was in the sentence. Just as others have shown for slow rates of presentation, probes acoustically similar to a word in the sentence proved difficult to reject (Table 4). This indicates that even when reading at 12 words per second subjects were retrieving a phonological representation of the words. Acoustic interference was as great at 12 as at 6 words per second, suggesting that the acoustic code was equally well-formed at the two rates. There was also substantial interference from semantically related probe words, which indicates that subjects understood the words as well as retrieving their sounds. As mentioned earlier, scrambling the sentence reduced semantic interference and increased acoustic interference (Table 4); response time and errors were increased overall. All this suggests that speech recoding is not only prevalent among readers, but is also capable of occurring much more rapidly than previously thought. Thus, hearing the words during reading may not deserve the bad press it has received.

APPLIED QUESTIONS ABOUT RSVP

The focus of this chapter has been on RSVP as a method for studying reading and language processing. Those research issues should be separated from questions about the value of RSVP as a method for reading rapidly, for evaluating reading ability, for treating reading disabilities, and the like. (Although investigators need to know that reading is relatively "normal" if they plan to use it as research tool, it is unnecessary to show that RSVP is a *better* way to read than conventional reading.)

Is RSVP an efficient way to read fast? Masson's work (1983) suggests that RSVP is not better than conventional skimming, and may be worse for some purposes. Potter et al. (1980) found RSVP to be an effective way to ensure that every word is read, but less effective than normal rapid reading when overall retention was measured (Fig. 1 and 2). Juola, Ward et al. (1982) found RSVP to be equivalent to conventional reading. In none of those experiments did subjects have much practice in RSVP reading, however, so it remains possible that RSVP would permit faster than normal rates after extensive practice. What is doubtful is whether practice would speed up the higher processes (including consolidation) that seem to be required for adequate retention. Nonetheless, RSVP might prove to be an efficient way to search through lists or texts for specific words, names, or ideas that might be missed by a skimmer.

Apart from speed, one can speculate that serial presentation (not necessarily rapid) would be preferred by some people because it paces the reader and prevents regressions. For the same reason, it might prove to be a way of teaching better reading habits, of overcoming difficulties with the control of eye fixations in reading, or of inducing more successful reading in some dyslexics. Chen (1983) found that the half of his college subjects who were less good readers remembered *more* from RSVP paragraphs than from conventional paragraphs viewed for the same total time; the better readers showed a slight but not significant drop, with RSVP. Finally, the ability to magnify single words without producing scanning difficulties could aid people with impaired eyesight. Were any of these applications to prove useful, it would be necessary to develop ways that a reader could control the rate of RSVP and also replay portions of text.

A practical reason for interest in RSVP is that cheap, small devices might be developed that are capable of presenting one word clearly, but not a full sentence or page of text. A wrist "teletype" might be more legible in RSVP than in the form of a moving window, for example.

A further question that falls between theoretical and applied interests is the extent of individual differences in the ability to read in RSVP, including age differences. We suspect that RSVP provides a very sensitive test of reading ability; some bilinguals we have observed informally have had marked difficulty with RSVP at 12 words per second even though their English appears to be excellent. Further, the ability to read at such rates seems to decline with age, although once more this is a casual impression rather than an established observation. If this loss is real, it will be of interest to discover whether it has to do with peripheral visual sensitivity, more central processes, or both. We know of no research using RSVP among children below high school age; serial presentation might help to separate scanning ability from specific reading ability, in young readers.

CONCLUSIONS

RSVP allows the investigator to control the timing of words in a sentence or text while presenting the material at rates equivalent to or faster than normal reading or listening. The evidence reviewed here indicates that visual adequacy may be maintained at rates sufficient to produce deficits at higher levels of processing. Thus, RSVP may be used to test hypotheses about sentence and text processing. The control the experimenter has over stimulus presentation and the consequent ability to push reading to its temporal limits makes the RSVP method a useful complement to eye movement methodology and other self-paced methods of presentation used in the study of reading.

ACKNOWLEDGEMENTS

Preparation of this chapter was supported by Grant BNS80-15597 from the National Science Foundation. I thank Marcel Just, Ken Forster, Judith Kroll, and Don Mitchell for comments.

REFERENCES

Aaronson, D. A. Stimulus factors and listening strategies in auditory memory: A theoretical analysis. *Cognitive Psychology*, 1974, *6*, 108-132. (a)

Aaronson, D. A. Stimulus factors and listening strategies in auditory memory: An experimental demonstration. *Cognitive Psychology*, 1974, *6*, 133-158. (b)

Aaronson, D. A., Markowitz, N., & Shapiro, H. Perception and immediate recall of normal and "compressed" auditory sequences. *Perception & Psychophysics*, 1971, *9*, 338-344.

Baddeley, A. D., & Lewis, V. J. Inner active processes in reading: The inner voice, the inner ear, and the inner eye. In A. M. Lesgold & C. A. Perfetti (Eds.), *Interactive processes in reading*. Hillsdale, N. J.: Lawrence Erlbaum Associates, 1981.

Balota, D.A., & Rayner, K. Parafoveal visual information and semantic contextual constraints. *Journal of Experimental Psychology: Human Perception and Performance*, 1983, *9*, 726-738.

Bransford, J. D., & Johnson, M. K. Contextual prerequisites for understanding: Some investigations of comprehension and recall. *Journal of Verbal Learning and Verbal Behavior*, 1972, *11*, 717-726.

Chen, H. C. *Reading normal versus rapid, sequential text formats: Effects of text structure and reading ability*. Technical Report No. 122, Institute of Cognitive Science, University of Colorado, 1983.

Dagenbach, D., & Carr, T. H. *On semantic activation from unidentified and undetected words*. Paper presented at the Psychonomic Society Meeting, Minneapolis, 1982.

Dommergues, J. Y., Frauenfelder, U., Mehler, J., & Segui, J. L'integration perceptive des phrases. *Bulletin de Psychologie*, 1979, *32*, 893-902.

Ehrlich, S. F., & Rayner, K. Contextual effects on word perception and eye movements during reading. *Journal of Verbal Learning and Verbal Behavior*, 1981, *20*, 641-655.

Eriksen, C. W. Discrimination and learning without awareness: A methodological survey and evaluation. *Psychological Review*, 1960, *67*, 279-300.

Fischler, I., & Bloom, P. A. Rapid processing of the meaning of sentences. *Memory & Cognition*, 1980, *8*, 216-225.

Forster, K. I. Visual perception of rapidly presented word sequences of varying complexity. *Perception & Psychophysics*, 1970, *8*, 215-221.

Forster, K. I. The role of semantic hypotheses in sentence processing. In F. Bresson & J. Mehler (Eds.), *Problemes actuels en psycholinguistique*. Paris: Centre National de la Recherche Scientifique, 1975.

Forster, K. I. Priming and the effects of sentence and lexical contexts on naming time: Evidence for autonomous lexical processing. *Quarterly Journal of Experimental Psychology*, 1981, *33A*, 465-495.

Forster, K. I., & Olbrei, I. Semantic heuristics and syntactic analysis. *Cognition*, 1974, *2*, 319-347.

Forster, K. I., & Ryder, L. A. Perceiving the structure and meaning of sentences. *Journal of Verbal Learning and Verbal Behavior*, 1971, *10*, 285-296.

French, P. Semantic and syntactic factors in the perception of rapidly presented sentences. *Journal of Psycholinguistic Research*, 1981, *10*, 581-591.

Holmes, V. M. Order of main and subordinate clauses in sentence perception. *Journal of Verbal Learning and Verbal Behavior*, 1973, *12*, 285-293.

Holmes, V. M., Arwas, R., & Garrett, M. F. Prior context and the perception of lexically ambiguous sentences. *Memory & Cognition*, 1977, *5*, 103-110.

Holmes, V. M., & Forster, K. I. Perceptual complexity and underlying sentence structure. *Journal of Verbal Learning and Verbal Behavior*, 1972, *11*, 148-156.

Juola, J. F., Ward, N. J., & McNamara, T. Visual search and reading of rapid serial presentations of letter strings, words, and text. *Journal of Experimental Psychology: General*, 1982, *111*, 208-227.

Juola, J. F., Cocklin, T., Chen, H. C., & Granaas, M. *Effects of segmentation size and structure on reading RSVP text*. Paper presented at the Psychonomics Society Meeting, Minneapolis, 1982.

Just, M. A., & Carpenter, P. A. A theory of reading: From eye fixations to comprehension. *Psychological Review*, 1980, *87*, 329-354.

Just, M. A., Carpenter, P. A., & Woolley, J. D. Paradigms and process in reading comprehension. *Journal of Experimental Psychology: General*, 1982, *111*, 228-238.

Kintsch, W., Kozminsky, E., Streby, W., McKoon, G., & Keenan, J. Comprehension and recall of text as a function of content variables. *Journal of Verbal Learning and Verbal Behavior*, 1975, *14*, 196-214.

Landauer, T. K. Rate of implicit speech. *Perceptual & Motor Skills*, 1962, *15*, 646.

Lawrence, D. H. Two studies of visual search for word targets with controlled rates of presentation. *Perception & Psychophysics*, 1971, *10*, 85-59.

Lovelace, E. A., Powell, C. M., & Brooks, R. J., Alphabetic position effects in covert and overt alphabetic recitation times. *Journal of Experimental Psychology*, 1973, *99*, 405-408.

Lovelace, E. A., & Southall, S. D. Memory for words in prose and their locations on the page. *Memory & Cognition*, 1983, *11*, 429-434.

Marcel, T. Conscious and preconscious recognition of polysemous words: Locating the selective effects of prior verbal context. In R. S. Nickerson (Ed.), *Attention and performance VIII*. Hillsdale, N. J.: Lawrence Erlbaum Associates, 1980.

Marcus, M. P. *A theory of syntactic recognition for natural language*. Cambridge: M. I. T. Press, 1980.

Masson, M. E. J. Cognitive processes in skimming stories. *Journal of Experimental Psychology: Learning, Memory, and Cognition*, 1982, *8*, 400-417.

Masson, M. E. J. Conceptual processing of text during skimming and rapid sequential reading. *Memory & Cognition*, 1983, *11*, 262-274.

McConkie, G. W., Blanchard, H., Zola, D., & Wolverton, G. S. *Letter perception during reading*. Paper presented at the Psychonomic Society Meeting, Minneapolis, 1982.

Merikle, P. M. Unconscious perception revisited. *Perception & Psychophysics*, 1982, *31*, 298-301.

Miron, M., & Brown, E. The comprehension of rate incremented aural coding. *Journal of Psycholinguistic Research*, 1971, *1*, 65-76.

Mitchell, D. C. Buffer storage modality and identification time in tachistoscopic recognition. *Quarterly Journal of Experimental Psychology*, 1976, *28*, 325-337.

Mitchell, D. C. The locus of the experimental effects in the rapid serial visual presentation (RSVP) task. *Perception & Psychophysics*, 1979, *25*, 143-149.

Mitchell, D. C., & Green, D. W. The effects of context and content on immediate processing in reading. *Quarterly Journal of Experimental Psychology*, 1978, *30*, 609-636.

Petrick, M. S., & Potter, M. C. *Acoustic and semantic encoding during rapid reading*. Manuscript in preparation, 1982.

Pfafflin, S. M. The total time hypothesis, recall strategies, and memory for rapidly presented word strings. *Memory & Cognition*, 1974, *2*, 236-240.

Potter, M. C. Short-term conceptual memory for pictures. *Journal of Experimental Psychology: Human Learning and Memory*, 1976, *5*, 509-522.

Potter, M. C. *Reading picture puns*. Paper presented at the Psychonomic Society Meeting, Philadelphia, 1981.

Potter, M. C. *Very short-term memory: In one eye and out the other*. Paper presented at the Psychonomic Society Meeting, Minneapolis, 1982.

Potter, M. C. Representational buffers: The eye-mind hypothesis in picture perception, reading, and visual search. In K. Rayner (Ed.), *Eye movements in reading: Perceptual and language processes*. New York: Academic Press, 1983.

Potter, M. C., Carpenter, E., & Weinberg, E. The effects of sentence context on pronunciation latency. Manuscript in preparation, 1984.

Potter, M. C., & Kroll, J. F. How different is RSVP from conventional reading? Manuscript in preparation, 1984.

Potter, M. C., Kroll, J. F., & Harris, C. Comprehension and memory in rapid sequential reading. In R. Nickerson (Ed.), *Attention and performance VIII*. Hillsdale, N. J.: Lawrence Erlbaum Associates, 1980.

Potter, M. C., Kroll, J. F., Yachzel, B., & Sherman, J. Pictures in sentences: Understanding without words. Manuscript in preparation, 1982.

Potter, M. C., & Levy, E. I. Recognition memory for a rapid sequence of pictures. *Journal of Experimental Psychology*, 1969, *81*, 10-15.

Purcell, D. G., Stewart, A. L., & Stanovich, K. E. *Another look at semantic priming without awareness*. Paper presented at the Psychonomic Society Meeting, Minneapolis, 1982.

Rayner, K. (Ed.) *Eye movements in reading: Perceptual and language processes*. New York: Academic Press, 1983.

Rayner, K., Inhoff, A. W., Morrison, R. E., Slowiaczek, M. L., & Bertera, J. H. Masking of foveal and parafoveal vision during eye fixations in reading. *Journal of Experimental Psychology: Human Perception and Performance*, 1981, *7*, 167-179.

Rayner, K., Well, A. D., Pollatsek, A., & Bertera, J. H. The availability of useful information to the right of fixation in reading. *Perception & Psychophysics*, 1982, *31*, 537-550.

Scarborough, D. L., & Sternberg, S. *Processing items and their order in sequential visual displays*. Paper presented at the meeting of the Eastern Psychological Association, Boston, 1967.

Segui, J., Dommergues, J. Y., Frauenfelder, U., & Mehler, J. L'integration perceptive des phrases: Aspects syntaxiques et semantiques. *Bulletin de Psychologie*, 1982, *35*, 579-585.

Sticht, T. G. Learning by listening. In J. B. Carroll & R. O. Freedle (Eds.), *Language comprehension and the acquisition of knowledge*. Washington, D. C.: Winston, 1972.

Swinney, D. A. Lexical access during sentence comprehension: (Re) consideration of context effects. *Journal of Verbal Learning and Verbal Behavior*, 1979, *18*, 645-659.

Wallace, W. P., & Koury, G. *Comprehension following speed listening at 500 words per minute*. Paper presented at the Psychonomic Society Meeting, Minneapolis, 1982.

Ward, N. J., & Juola, J. F. Reading with and without eye movements: Reply to Just, Carpenter, and Woolley. *Journal of Experimental Psychology: General*, 1982, *111*, 239-241.

6 Priming and On-Line Text Comprehension[1]

Gail McKoon and Roger Ratcliff
Northwestern University

There are a number of procedures that can be described as involving priming. What they have in common is an attempt to influence a subject's response to a test item by presenting some priming information immediately prior to the test item. Where the procedures differ is in the kind of priming information presented and the kind of response required to the target test item. The priming information is sometimes a single word, sometimes a whole sentence or paragraph; sometimes in the same modality as the target, sometimes not. The target can be a single word or a sentence. For a single word, the subject's task may be item recognition, perceptual identification, lexical decision, or naming the word aloud. For a sentence, the task is verification ('is the sentence true or false?'). In all of these tasks, the measurement of interest is the amount of facilitation or inhibition in response time to the target as a function of priming information.

The priming task we have found most useful for examining the processes of comprehension is item recognition. Subjects are required to respond 'yes' or 'no' according to whether a target word was or was not present in previously read textual information. We like this task for two reasons. First, it requires reference to information about the text, whereas in lexical decision or naming, a response can be made without reference to the text. Second, response times in item recognition are relatively long (around 600-700 msec) so that the effects of priming can be relatively large (as large as 100 msec). Such large effects ensure enough sensitivity

---

[1]Preparation of this chapter was supported by NIH grant HD16381 and by NSF grant BNS-8203061. We wish to thank David Kieras and Marcel Just for their useful comments on an earlier version of the chapter.

to examine differences in amount of priming as a function of various experimental conditions.

We have used priming in item recognition to investigate two different aspects of comprehension: these are the state of activation of concepts during comprehension and the organization of information in memory that results from comprehension. To measure activation, the priming information is the text being read and the target is a single word presented immediately after the text, with no delay between text and target. The idea behind this procedure is that, if the reader uses a concept in processing the text, then response time to that concept as a target will be affected.

To examine the representation of a text in memory, testing is delayed and a list of single words is presented for recognition. Measuring the relative distance between two concepts in the representation is accomplished by presenting the concepts in the test list; one, designated the target, immediately follows the other, designated the prime. The idea here is that, if the prime is close to the target in memory, then response time for the target will be affected.

These two different procedures will be described in more detail by presenting examples of experiments that use them. The first experiment examines the activation of the referent of an anaphor, and the second examines the representation in memory that results from anaphoric reference.

EXPERIMENT 1: ACTIVATION OF CONCEPTS

Consider the text shown in Table 1 (from McKoon & Ratcliff, 1980b). In version 1, the final sentence begins with an anaphor, *the criminal*, so reading this sentence should produce activation of the referent, *burglar*. But reading the other version of the final sentence, where there is no anaphor, should not produce activation of *burglar*.

To measure this difference in the state of activation of *burglar*, and to examine the time course of this difference, subjects read texts like that shown in Table 1 (a more complete description of this research is given by Dell, McKoon, & Ratcliff, 1983). The texts were presented word-by-word across a CRT screen, with each word in a sentence turning on 250 msec after the previous one (about normal reading rate). By the end of the sentence, all of the words were displayed. Then the sentence disappeared and the next sentence was presented in the same way. By presenting texts this way, a test word could be presented at any point, after any word of the text. A test word was identified to the subject by presenting it all in capital letters; just before it was presented, any part of a sentence that was on the CRT screen disappeared. As soon as the subject responded to the test word ('yes' or 'no' according to whether it had appeared in the text being read), the test word disappeared from the screen and, after a subject-paced pause, presentation of the next text began.

As can be seen in Table 1, subjects read either the first or second version of the text. The test word was the referent of the anaphor in version 1 (*burglar*), another

TABLE 1
An Example of the Paragraphs
Used in the Experiments (1)

Referent of the anaphor: "burglar"
Word in the same proposition as the referent: "garage"
Control word: "bottles"

Sentence 1:
　A burglar surveyed the garage set back from the street.

Sentence 2:
　Several milk bottles were piled at the curb.

Sentence 3:
　The banker and her husband were on vacation.

Sentence 4: (Version 1, anaphor):
　The criminal slipped away from the streetlamp.
　　　1　　　　2　　　3　　　4　　　5　　　6
Sentence 4: (Version 2, no anaphor):
　A cat slipped away from the streetlamp.
　1　2　　　3　　　4　　　5　　　6

---

(1) The number subscripts represent test positions.

word in the same proposition as the referent (*garage*), or a word unrelated to the anaphor or referent from one of the two middle sentences (*bottles*). Across several experiments, the test word was presented in six different positions in the final sentence. The combined results of these experiments are presented in Table 2, which shows the amount of facilitation given to the test word by the final sentence that mentions the anaphor, relative to the amount given by the other final sentence. It can be seen that the anaphor gives rise to very rapid activation of its referent, that it gives rise to equally rapid activation of other concepts in the same proposition as the referent, and that activation of the referent but not the other concepts remains to the end of the sentence. Our interpretation of these results is that an anaphor causes very fast activation of propositions containing a referent and then continued activation of the concept selected as the referent. This continued activation of the referent may be necessary for the establishment in memory of connections between information mentioned in the text about the referent and information mentioned about the anaphor.

EXPERIMENT 2: ORGANIZATION OF INFORMATION IN MEMORY

In version 1 of the text shown in Table 1, the final sentence mentions an anaphor for a concept from the first sentence. Thus, when this version of the text is read, information about the anaphor should be connected in memory to information about the referent. For example, the concept *streetlamp* should be connected to the concept *burglar*, because it was the burglar who slipped away from the streetlamp.

TABLE 2
Amount of Facilitation (in msec)
in Each Condition of Experiment 1

	\multicolumn{6}{c}{Test Position}					
	1	2	3	4	5	6
Test Word Referent	-3	28	30	34	24	36
Same prop. word	1	30	35	—	3	-6
Control	—	—	1	—	11	4

In the other version of the text, there is no anaphor in the final sentence, so *burglar* and *streetlamp* should not be connected.

To examine this difference in the way information is organized for the different versions, subjects read texts like the one in Table 1. There was a series of trials, and each trial consisted of a study phase and a test phase. In the study phase, two texts were presented, one at a time, for 8 sec each. Then the test phase began immediately. Single words were presented, one at a time, for recognition ('was the word in either of the texts presented in the study phase, yes or no?'). After 10 test words and a subject-paced pause, the next trial began.

One noun from the final sentence of each text, usually the object of the sentence, was designated a target. This word was placed in some randomly chosen position in the test list, except not in positions 1 or 2. The immediately preceding word in the test list, the prime, was the subject noun from the first sentence of the text (the referent of the anaphor in the final sentence of version 2). For the example shown in Table 1, the prime was *burglar* and the target was *streetlamp*. The amount of facilitation given by the prime to the target should differ, depending on which version of a text was read. If the final sentence mentioned an anaphor of the prime, then prime and target should be closely connected in memory and the amount of facilitation should be relatively large. If the final sentence did not mention the anaphor, facilitation should be less. In fact, these are the results that were obtained: response time for the target was 644 msec when version 1 was read and 686 msec when version 2 was read.

AUTOMATIC AND STRATEGIC PROCESSES IN PRIMING

In order to fully understand results from experiments like those above about the activation of concepts and the organization of memory, it is necessary to understand the distinction between automatic and strategic processes and how this distinction applies to priming. Thus, this section of the chapter will be devoted to a discussion of these processes and experiments designed to investigate them.

There are currently two different notions of automaticity. One is that of Schneider and Shiffrin (1977) and it concerns the relationship between a stimulus and the response to that stimulus, and how that relationship can become automatic with practice. The other notion of automaticity, the one which will be used here for discussing priming, concerns the relationship between one concept and another, that is, whether one concept automatically activates another.

This notion of automaticity has been defined by Posner (1978) with respect to three criteria, which can be observed in priming experiments. The first concerns the probability that the subject will encounter a priming pair in which the two items of the pair are related in a way apparent to the subject (e.g. *A - a* or *bread-butter*). If this probability is varied (say, from almost all items in a test list being primed by a related item to almost none), then for an automatic process, the size of the priming effect will be unaffected. A strategic process, on the other hand, is sensitive to probability manipulations. Second, automatic processes have a very fast onset whereas strategic processes have a slower onset. Finally, the third criterion involves a cost-benefit analysis. Automatic processes give benefits but have no associated costs. In other words, a related prime would give facilitation to a target but an unrelated prime would not lead to inhibition. However, strategic processes do involve costs; a related prime gives facilitation as with an automatic process, but an unrelated prime results in inhibition.

Posner and Snyder (1975) developed this view with respect to letter matching and Stroop tasks, and a comprehensive discussion was presented by Posner (1978). We applied this view to the processes involved in item recognition, and in particular, the processes involved in recognition of concepts from texts, with three experiments (Ratcliff & McKoon, 1981).

All three experiments used a study-test procedure. In the study phase, a list of unrelated sentences was presented for study and in the test phase, which followed the study phase immediately, a list of single words was presented for recognition. For each word in the test list, a subject was required to respond 'yes' or 'no' according to whether that word had appeared in any of the sentences presented in the study phase. In the first experiment, the probability of a related priming pair was varied, where a related priming pair was two words from the same sentence presented sequentially in the test list. Results showed that varying probability in this way had no effect on the amount of facilitation given by the priming word to response time for the target word. Thus, the first criterion for automaticity is satisfied. In the second experiment, the time course of processing was examined. In this experiment, subjects responded to the target but did not make a response to the prime, in order that the time between presentation of the prime and presentation of the target could be varied. The prime was presented for a variable amount of time (the SOA), then it disappeared and the target was presented immediately. There were three kinds of priming pairs: related (prime and target words from the same sentence), unrelated (prime and target words from different sentences), and neutral (a string of random letters priming a word). Facilitation and inhibition were measured with respect to the neutral condition. It was found that for related pairs, facilitation occurred by 150 msec SOA, but that for unrelated pairs, inhibition did not occur until 450 msec SOA. These findings reflect the second and third criteria, that the automatic process producing facilitation is fast relative to a slower strategic process producing inhibition. The third experiment was designed to examine the time course of strategic processing in a task with specific instructions about strategic processing. In the study phase, subjects were presented with two unrelated sentences. Then in the test phase, there was only one priming pair, a prime (to which they did not respond) and a target. Subjects were told, truthfully, that on 75% of trials, the prime and target would not be from the same sentence so that when they saw a prime from one sentence, they should try to switch to recall the other sentence in preparation for the target. At 100 msec SOA, there was facilitation for related (same sentence) pairs, at 700 msec SOA there was inhibition for related pairs, but only at 1800 msec SOA was there facilitation for the unrelated (different sentence) pairs. These results show that, while strategic inhibition can occur by 700 msec, strategic facilitation probably requires at least 1000 msec. Other, less artificial strategic processes might take somewhat less time to produce facilitation, but, nevertheless, it is clear that strategic processes arise quite late in processing.

Taken together, these experiments demonstrate that, under properly controlled conditions, the priming effects observed in recognition of words from texts are automatic effects. Thus, when priming is used to examine the activation of concepts, under conditions where the SOA from the priming information in the text to the target is short, then any facilitation observed for the target can be assumed to be due to automatic processes. For example, in the data shown in Table 2, facilitation is observed for the target *burglar* when the SOA from presentation of the anaphor (*criminal*) to presentation of the target is only 250 msec; so activation of *burglar* by *criminal* is taken to be an automatic process.

Under appropriately controlled conditions, automatic processes are also responsible for effects observed when priming in word recognition is used to examine the organization of concepts in memory. Appropriate conditions are those in which the SOA from prime word to target word (in the test list) is relatively short. This can be accomplished in two ways. If the subject gives a recognition response to both the prime and the target words, then the SOA between them is the response time for the prime plus the time from that response until presentation of the target (150 msec in our experiments); assuming mean response time for primes at 700 msec, this gives a total SOA of about 850 msec. This SOA is almost certainly too short for both processing and responding to the prime AND strategically processing the relationship between the prime and target. Such strategic processing, by itself, would take on the order of 1000 msec according to the results of the experiment mentioned above. Thus, we argue that a procedure in which subjects give recognition responses to both primes and targets shows automatic facilitation effects. However, the SOA between prime and target can be more tightly controlled with the alternative procedure in which the subject does not make a response to the prime; the prime is simply presented for some experimenter - determined time, then it disappears from the CRT screen, and the target is presented. With this procedure, the SOA can be made as short as necessary so that any observed facilitation can be ascribed to automatic processing.

In summary, experimental evidence shows that priming in item recognition can be used to observe the effects of automatic processes, both the automatic processes of activation of concepts during comprehension and the automatic processes of activation of one concept by another concept in the memory representation of a text. The fact that priming can show automatic effects will be used in the next section of this chapter, where priming is compared to other procedures for investigating comprehension.

PRIMING COMPARED WITH OTHER ON-LINE MEASURES

Priming in item recognition as a procedure for investigating comprehension can be compared both to other procedures for investigating comprehension and to other kinds of priming procedures. These will be discussed in order in this section.

The first dimension on which priming differs from other, more wholistic, measures such as reading time (for words, phrases, or sentences) or eye-movement time is level of analysis. With reading time and eye-movement time, all of the components of processing that increase processing time are measured simultaneously. But with priming, the emphasis is on measurement of components of processing that are not directly observable in reading times or eye movements, components such as the activation of concepts other than those explicitly mentioned in the text and the effect of activation on the memory representation of the text. While reading and eye-movement times can indicate when increased processing is required, they cannot indicate what the effect of that processing is. With respect to inference, for example, reading time may be longer because the subject searches for a to-be-inferred concept but does not find it. Or the concept may be found and activated but not connected to the new propositions as it should be. Even if the proper connections are made, they may not be stored in the long-term memory representation of the text. In general, these kinds of component processes may not be directly reflected in reading and eye-movement times.

Priming, on the other hand, is designed explicitly to measure component processes. For example, the inference that *the criminal* refers to a previously-mentioned burglar involves activating the to-be-inferred concept (*burglar*), connecting information mentioned about the criminal to information mentioned about the burglar, and storing these connections in memory. On the one hand, the activation process can be examined by presenting a test word for recognition, as was done in Experiment 1, and on the other hand, the connections among concepts in memory can be examined by measuring the amount of priming between words in a recognition test, as was done in Experiment 2. Thus, the two procedures allow the separation of two components of comprehension.

The second respect in which priming differs from other on-line procedures is that priming is not, strictly speaking, an on-line measure. What priming measures is the state of activation of concepts (or state of working memory, in some theoretical frameworks) at the point of interruption during reading or after a delay from the end of reading. Thus, rather than measuring the total time taken for reading, priming can measure the effects of on-line processes, effects that might be hidden in other measures. Specifically, presentation of a test word immediately after a text (or part of a text) is designed to measure the effect of comprehension of the text on the state of activation of the concept expressed by the test word. Similarly, presentation of a prime and target pair in a list of test words is designed to measure the connections between the two words that were established during comprehension. Because in both procedures it can be shown that obtained effects reflect automatic processes, it can be argued that the effects reflect comprehension, not strategies in which subjects engage at the time of test. Thus, priming is a way of investigating what happens in memory as a result of comprehension processes.

Priming in item recognition can be compared not only to other kinds of on-line procedures but also to other kinds of priming procedures. These include priming in lexical decision and word naming. For example, in experiments conducted by Swinney (1979), subjects listen to spoken text and at unexpected times are given a letter string for a lexical decision. In other experiments (cf. West & Stanovich, 1982), subjects read text and then are given a word to name aloud. If response time for a certain word is speeded, either in lexical decision or naming aloud, then it may be that a concept related to that word was activated by comprehension of the text. Thus these procedures may provide converging evidence on the activation of concepts during comprehension. However, recognition requires reference back to the text just processed, whereas lexical decision and word naming do not. Whether this difference leads to processing differences is a question which requires further research.

The final topic to be considered in a comparison of priming to other techniques is the limitations of priming. The use of priming techniques is not new, but the application to text processing is relatively undeveloped. The recognition priming technique that we have used has been presented in only about 10 published papers. To date, we have found that any problem that has arisen in the use of priming can be overcome, at the cost of some time and effort. We will list these problems and the solutions we have found.

One problem is to understand exactly what is being measured by the amount of priming between two concepts. Is it the distance between the concepts in the surface form of the text, in the meaning structure of the text, or in semantic memory (i. e. nothing to do with the text at all)? It is possible to address this problem by careful design of materials. For example, paragraphs whose surface and meaning representations are different (Ratcliff & McKoon, 1978; McKoon & Ratcliff, 1980a) show that priming reflects the meaning representation. That priming is not due entirely to semantic association can be shown in several ways: by varying the distance between the same two words in different versions of a text (McKoon & Ratcliff, 1980a) or by presenting the words in different sentences of a list of random sentences in order to measure any effects of semantic association (McKoon & Ratcliff, 1980a; 1980b; 1981).

A second problem is to be sure that priming is measuring the effects of comprehension and not strategies in which subjects engage at the time of test in order to improve their performance (or to speed the experiment to an early end). This problem was discussed earlier, and we argued that it is possible to examine the automatic and strategic components of priming and determine under what conditions priming is automatic, and thus determine when it reflects the effects of comprehension.

The last two problems are practical ones. First, a priming experiment is costly in subjects and materials. Optimally, there should be 8 to 10 observations per subject per condition. With the various control conditions and filler items to provide a balance of positive and negative test items and to keep the subject from perfectly predicting what the test items will be, the amount of work is not trivial. Although it is possible to use materials more than once in an experiment with the same subject, there are severe limitations on such repetitions (Dell, Ratcliff, & McKoon, 1981). Second, priming can only be used to investigate those components of processing which can be reflected in a single test item, either a single word or a single sentence (see McKoon & Ratcliff, 1980b, for the use of priming with sentences). So far, we have not found either of these practical problems as daunting as we would have expected, and we find that the gains in experimental results outweigh the costs in design.

REFERENCES

Dell, G., McKoon, G., & Ratcliff, R. The activation of antecedent information during the processing of anaphoric reference in reading. *Journal of Verbal Learning and Verbal Behavior*, 1983, 22, 121-132.

Dell, G., Ratcliff, R., & McKoon, G. Study and test repetition effects in item recognition priming. *American Journal of Psychology*, 1981, 94, 497-511.

McKoon, G., & Ratcliff, R. Priming in item recognition: The organization of propositions in memory for text. *Journal of Verbal Learning and Verbal Behavior*, 1980, 19, 369-386. (a)

McKoon, G., & Ratcliff, R. The comprehension processes and memory structures involved in anaphoric reference. *Journal of Verbal Learning and Verbal Behavior*, 1980, 19, 668-682. (b)

McKoon, G., & Ratcliff, R. The comprehension processes and memory structures involved in instrumental inference. *Journal of Verbal Learning and Verbal Behavior*, 1981, 20, 671-682.

Posner, M. *Chronometric explorations of mind*. Hillsdale, N. J.: Lawrence Erlbaum Associates, 1978.

Posner, M., & Snyder, S. Attention and cognitive control. In R. L. Solso (Ed.), *Information Processing and Cognition*. Hillsdale, N. J.: Lawrence Erlbaum Associates, 1975.

Ratcliff, R., & McKoon, G. Priming in item recognition: Evidence for the propositional structure of sentences. *Journal of Verbal Learning and Verbal Behavior*, 1978, 17, 403-417.

Ratcliff, R., & McKoon, G. Automatic and strategic priming in recognition. *Journal of Verbal Learning and Verbal Behavior*, 1981, *20*, 204-215.

Schneider, W., & Shriffin, R. Controlled and automatic human information processing: I. Detection, search, and attention. *Psychological Review*, 1977, *84*, 1-66.

Swinney, D. A. Lexical access during sentence comprehension: (Re)consideration of context effects. *Journal of Verbal Learning and Verbal Behavior*, 1979, *18*, 645-659.

West, R. F., & Stanovich, K. E. Source of inhibition in experiments on the effect of sentence context on word recognition. *Journal of Experimental Psychology: Learning, Memory, and Cognition*, 1982, *8*, 385-399.

7 Eye Movements and Reading Comprehension

Keith Rayner and Patrick J. Carroll
University of Massachusetts, Amherst

The study of the processes involved in skilled reading has fascinated experimental psychologists for over a hundred years. As Huey (1908) indicated, if we could understand the nature of the reading process, we would have understood the workings of the mind itself, thereby unravelling one of the most complex mysteries of mankind. It is not surprising that researchers from a number of disciplines have been interested in reading and that, within experimental psychology, researchers have approached the study of reading from a variety of perspectives.

The study of reading within cognitive psychology has concentrated primarily on understanding the perceptual and linguistic aspects of skilled reading. As is obvious from the contributions to this book, a major break-through in the study of reading has been in technological and methodological areas. With the development of extremely sensitive eye movement recording devices and with the ability to interface these with rapidly changeable visual displays under computer control, reading has achieved an exceptional status within cognitive psychology. At the present time, reading is perhaps the only complex, dynamic activity able to be observed under reasonably naturalistic and nonintrusive conditions while still under precise experimental control.

In this chapter, we will review a number of studies and theoretical developments dealing with the comprehension of text. We will focus on studies conducted in our laboratory, but we will try to make connections with related work from other laboratories. Prior to reviewing work dealing with language comprehension, we will try to provide a general framework for understanding the problems and issues associated with the use of eye movement data.

ISSUES AND PROBLEMS IN THE USE OF EYE MOVEMENT DATA IN STUDYING READING COMPREHENSION

Much has been made in recent years of the claim that eye movements provide an on-line measure of important processes taking place during reading. In fact, evidence has slowly been accumulating that lends some credence to this claim. Nevertheless, the burden of relating eye movement data to the processes they are meant to reveal, as well as the task of establishing the limits of this relationship, still rest with those building a theory on this foundation.

The use of eye movement data to study reading comprehension raises many questions. There are three major issues which we have judged to be central to justifying our claim that the behavior of the eyes can be used as a window to the language comprehension process. The first two issues are conceptual or empirical, while the third is practical in nature. The first empirical question concerns the characteristics of the perceptual span or the useful field of vision during an eye fixation. The second empirical question is about the duration of the fixation and the degree to which the behavior of the eye reflects ongoing mental activity. The third, practical problem revolves around the nature of the eye tracking equipment and difficulties associated with evaluating the data such systems provide. These issues have been addressed elsewhere (see Rayner, 1979; McConkie, Hogaboam, Wolverton, Zola, and Lucas, 1979; McConkie, 1981), but we will discuss them here specifically with regard to reading comprehension.

Perceptual Span Problem. As a person reads a passage of text, a series of eye movements are made. The reader *fixates* for about 200-250 msec and then makes a jump forward or a *saccade* of 7-8 character spaces. It is during the fixation periods that new information is brought into the processing system, yet the fixations are so brief that we are generally not aware of them as distinct events. About 10-20 of the time, the reader makes an eye movement back to a region that has already been read. These *regressions* are typically quite short, 2-5 character spaces, but can at times be to previous sentences and lines of text. While the values we have cited represent averages, they are often considered as stable indices of the eye movement pattern during reading. In reality, there is considerable variability not only between readers, but also within any given reader (Rayner, 1978; Rayner & McConkie, 1976). Similarly, the difficulty of the text and the level of comprehension expected of the reader can affect some or all of these factors. A primary goal for experimenters interested in using eye movements to monitor the reading process has been to account for this variability.

The perceptual span problem is essentially the question of how much information a reader can see and use during a single fixation. There are actually two different perceptual span problems. One of these concerns the area in which detailed information can be picked up, leading to letter and word identification.

The second problem is that of defining the area which contributes to the control of eye movements.

A great deal of recent research makes it very clear that the perceptual span is generally larger than a single word. However, it is the case that the perceptual span is relatively small and that information leading to semantic identification of a word cannot be obtained far beyond the word being fixated. We shall not review all the research documenting the characteristics of the perceptual span (see Rayner, 1978; 1981; 1983 for reviews), but a number of studies are quite consistent in indicating that the perceptual span extends from the beginning of the currently fixated word (but not more than 4 characters to the left of fixation) to 15 characters to the right of fixation. Much of the information available beyond about 6 characters to the right of fixation is rather gross and may be used primarily in determining where to fixate next.

The dramatically limited range of the perceptual span is certainly reason to believe that we can identify with some assurance what is being processed, at least at the lowest levels, at any given moment in time. Frequently, the area of useful vision corresponds neatly with the characteristics of the word being fixated, particularly in the case of content words. Unfortunately, many or most fixations cannot be so neatly categorized. Even a reader who can give a verbatim report of a sentence does not fixate on some of the words. Short words are often skipped and long words are sometimes fixated in the last few character spaces. Clearly, the perceptual span for detailed information is not limited to the word in the center of fixation, but can include part of the following word or even one or two whole words if they are short.

Much of the work currently being done on language processing assumes that the location of a fixation on a word permits the inference that the duration of that fixation (or those fixations if there are more than one) is determined by processing difficulty for that word. We feel that this is a useful first approximation. Nevertheless, it is likely that information about a word not in the center of fixation but still within the perceptual span is not discarded. An adequate theory of language processing will need to account for the fate of this other information.

The Eye-Mind Problem. To what extent are the fixation periods of the eye synchronous with higher level cognitive processes? During oral reading, if the lights in the room are suddenly turned off, the reader will be able to report a few more words because the voice lags behind the eye by a couple of words. The use of eye movement data to study reading raises the analogous question of whether or not there is a lag between the eye and the cognitive processes acting on the words being fixated.

It has not always been popular to believe that the answer to this question is obvious. Some (Bouma & deVoogd, 1974; Kolers, 1976) have argued that there is not a close link between the eye fixations and cognitive processes. If eye movements are rhythmic or random or if the fixation duration is determined entirely by visual characteristics of the text, their use as tools for studying language comprehension is severely limited.

A great deal of recent research argues that eye control is responsive to language variables. A number of studies have shown that fixation duration varies as a function of such lexical and semantic factors as frequency of the word (Just & Carpenter, 1980; Rayner, 1977), its informativeness (Rayner, 1977; Wanat, 1971), and its predictability (Ehrlich & Rayner, 1981). Fixation duration has also been shown to vary as a function of the extent to which the word is constrained by context (Ehrlich & Rayner, 1981; Zola, 1982) and the semantic relatedness of preceding words in the sentence (Carroll, 1983). Psycholinguistic studies have demonstrated that eye movements and fixation durations are influenced by syntactic organization of individual sentences (Frazier & Rayner, 1982; Holmes & O'Regan, 1981; Ehrlich & Rayner, 1983; Rayner, Carlson, & Frazier, 1983).

This evidence shows that there is a lawful relationship between certain aspects of the text and the pattern of eye movements. The interpretation of these effects is determined by the kind of process model we use to describe them. Rayner (1977; 1978) has distinguished two general classes of processing models which lead to very different expectations of the nature of reading. The *Cognitive Lag Hypothesis* refers to the position that higher level processing cannot keep up with the visual intake of information. Processing for meaning would, consequently, lag behind the eye. The eye movement data would need to be understood in relation to the characteristics of the buffer or buffers containing information taken in but not fully processed. The alternative view, called the *Process Monitoring Hypothesis*, suggests that fixation durations directly reflect at least some higher level processing on the word being fixated. An extreme version of this view can be seen in Just and Carpenter's (1980) *Eye-Mind Assumption* and *Immediacy Assumption*, which claim that all possible processing is done during the fixation and the eye does not move until that work is completed.

Recent research in our laboratory has led us to favor a position somewhere between the Cognitive Lag and Process Monitoring views. Rayner and Pollatsek (1981) demonstrated that events unambiguously occurring on a fixation influenced the duration of that fixation. By delaying the onset of the text (for a variable amount of time) at the beginning of each fixation, they found that, as text delay increased, fixation duration showed a corresponding increase. However, they also found that information from prior fixations can influence the timing of a fixation and the length of a saccade, leading them to suggest a mixed control model of eye movements in reading. In a separate research program, Ehrlich and Rayner (1983) have shown that all higher level comprehension processes are not completed in the duration of a single fixation. In general, the results of the experiments described above indicate that fixation duration accurately reflects lexical access of a particular word, but that certain higher order processes lag behind the fixation.

The results of these and other studies lead us to believe that a satisfactory model of the relationsip between eye behavior and language comprehension processes is only beginning to be developed. At the same time, we feel there is considerable reason for optimism that this relationship will not be so intricate that it cannot be fairly precisely defined by careful experimental investigation.

Technical and Methodological Issues. The study of reading during this last decade has been closely linked to technological advances in systems designed to track and time the eye. What may be less obvious to those unfamiliar with this technology is the fact that the kinds of theories espoused by different researchers frequently reflect the characteristics of the apparatus used to develop the theories. While at some point in time, precision becomes an absolute necessity for proper theory building, a case can surely be made that, during early development of theories of eye movements in reading, it is something of a mixed blessing.

Many eye movement recording systems are accurate to only 1 or 2 degrees of visual angle. In most reading studies, about three character spaces correspond to one degree of visual angle. With such systems, the experimenter cannot determine the position of the eye, even in terms of which word is being fixated, with a great deal of confidence. Another concern is that the rate of some systems for sampling the position of the eye is limited to every 17 or 33 msec. The magnitude of some higher level comprehension effects is in this same range, so the introduction of that much variability into the data can often disguise the evidence for real differences. This sampling rate also precludes the use of on-line changes in the text. To avoid flicker or even the perception of the unchanged stimulus, the system must be able to calculate the position of the eye and then change the display based on that position within a few milliseconds of the end of a saccade. Consequently, such systems cannot take advantage of some of the most productive techniques developed for studying reading.

The most reasonable response to the limits of a system is to do as Just and Carpenter have done and adjust the level of analysis to the capabilities of the recording apparatus. Rather than concentrating on the individual fixation as a measure of processing, they have relied on a measure called *gaze duration*, the total amount of time spent looking at a word prior to any movement away from it. In addition, the instructions they give the reader seem to lead to very close study of the text, virtually guaranteeing that each word will be fixated at least once.

The type of eye tracking system we have used in our research has a great deal of visual and temporal resolution. It is accurate to 10 minutes of arc (about half a character space) and provides a continuous signal of the eye's location. This position is sampled every millisecond to determine if the eye is fixated or in a saccade. Our algorithm for distinguishing these two states of the eye is based on a comparison of the vertical and horizontal output of the recording system for each four consecutive milliseconds with the prior four milliseconds. In short, this sort of system is able to provide an extremely precise record, both temporal and positional, of the behavior of the eyes.

The capabilities of our apparatus have led us to a somewhat different approach to the eye movement data than that of Just and Carpenter. We have been able to put considerable confidence in the actual values of the fixation duration and saccade length. Because of this, we have increasingly moved to studies experimentally manipulating individual words, grammatical cues, and structural boundaries. We are able to have fairly relaxed reading instructions, making measures such as likelihood of fixating a particular item a potent variable (cf. Ehrlich & Rayner, 1981).

We started this section by mentioning that precision is a mixed blessing. We mean this in the sense that vast amounts of very accurate data stand as a roadblock to early, global theorizing. We are still very much in the stage of testing the claims of specific, rather local processing mechanisms. Yet, the value of a general theoretical commitment can be seen in the scientific controversy initiated by the general theory of reading of Just and Carpenter (1980). To the extent that such work creates interest in the problems of reading and focuses researchers on the important theoretical issues, it is certainly healthy and stimulating. We now turn to a review of studies dealing with language processing and reading comprehension that have relied on the use of eye movement data.

EYE MOVEMENTS AND LANGUAGE PROCESSING

In this section, we will review in more detail some experiments that have demonstrated that fixation duration and fixation location can be used to study on-going language processing during reading. We will divide this work into two areas. The first area comprises a number of studies of the semantic integration of text and the impact of semantic context in the process of comprehending sentences. The second area focuses on some psycholinguistic questions, describing some work which has attempted to understand the influence of the reader's structural knowledge of language and the relationship of this knowledge to processes affected by semantic and pragmatic information.

Semantic Integration. It has been known for a long time that there are global effects of context on eye movement behavior. For example, as text becomes increasingly difficult, the average saccade length decreases, the average fixation duration increases, and the frequency of regressions increases. Vanacek (1972) used statistical approximations to normal text and found decreases in fixation duration as text became more like normal. Vanacek's method, while demonstrating certain global context effects, fails to distinguish among different sorts of comprehension processes which may be confused or slowed by the altered text.

A recent study by Inhoff (1983) has supported some of Vanacek's findings, but shown that the text need not be altered in some general and radical way. He

TABLE 1
An Example of One Passage Used by Inhoff (1983).
The Passage is from *Alice in Wonderland*.

"WE LEARNED FRENCH AND MUSIC."
"AND WASHING?" ASKED THE BIBER.
"CERTAINLY NOT," ANSWERED ALICE.
"THEN YOURS WASN'T A REALLY GOOD SCHOOL,"
SAID THE BIBER,
IN A TONE OF GREAT RELIEF.
"NOW AT OURS, THEY HAD,
AT THE END OF THE BILL,
FRENCH, MUSIC, AND WASHING EXTRA."
AND WHAT WERE THE REGULAR COURSES?"
ASKED ALICE CURIOUSLY.
"REELING AND WRITHING, OF COURSE,
AND THEN THE DIFFERENT BRANCHES
OF ARITHMETIC; FOR EXAMPLE,
AMBITION, DISTRACTION, UGLIFICATION."
"NEVER HEARD OF UGLIFICATION"
SAID ALICE QUICKLY.
"NEVER HEARD OF UGLIFICATION"
EXCLAIMED THE BIBER.
"BUT I SUPPOSE YOU KNOW
WHAT TO BEAUTIFY IS?"

---

monitored subjects' eye movements as they read passages from *Alice in Wonderland* such as the one shown in Table 1. As can be seen, some words in the passage are easily understood, as is true when Alice says she took "French and music" in school. By contrast, the concepts of "reeling" and "writhing" would make more sense in the context of a battlefield or a snake pit than of a school (though the connection may not be entirely coincidental). Inhoff reasoned that words that were consistent with the reader's prestored knowledge base and with the thematic context should be read relatively easily. On the other hand, words that were unexpected and did not conform to the reader's experience with the normal workings of the world should require more effort for processing. In order to better identify the source of possible processing difficulties, Inhoff used an experimental condition in which a very small mask (covering only the letter in the center of fixation) moved in synchrony with the eye. Presumably, this mask interfered with initial word identification, but had little effect on integration of the words into the sentence or passage.

Table 2 shows some of the results of Inhoff's study. In essence, he found that unusual items took longer to read than words more likely within the context. The difference was even greater when there was a mask covering part of the target word. While a lexical access explanation of the results may be possible, the thrust of these and other findings in this study seems to point to an interpretation saying that the interaction is based on the reader's attempts to make the unexpected concepts fit

TABLE 2
Fixation Duration of Individual Words from Inhoff (1983).
First Pass Refers to the Initial Reading Time; Total Viewing Time
Includes Regressive Fixation Durations.

		Word Frequency	Predictability in Context	
			low	high
First pass	no mask	low	464	281
		high	351	254
	mask	low	513	322
		high	430	253
Total viewing time	no mask	low	576	320
		high	402	274
	mask	low	787	402
		high	553	301

into the representation of the text, itself a reflection of the reader's knowledge of the world.

Inhoff's experiment is, from a methodological standpoint, an example of a study where the materials are chosen to have certain characteristics and no alterations are made by the experimenter. The model for a different sort of experiment using materials which allow replacement of critical items within a factorial design was provided by Zola (1982; see also McConkie & Zola, 1981). Zola's experiment was designed to examine the effects of semantic context on word perception. Subjects were asked to read short passages, several sentences long, while their eye movements were recorded. Each passage had two versions which differed only by a single adjective, which either highly constrained or predicted the immediately following noun or was relatively neutral with respect to it. For example, subjects read a passage about the movie industry. One of the sentences in this passage read as follows: "Since movie theaters must have buttered popcorn to serve their patrons. . ." When subjects were given the passages up through the word *buttered* in a modified cloze task, they responded with the word *popcorn* 83% of the time. On the other hand, when the word *buttered* was replaced by the word *adequate*, subjects chose *popcorn* as their completion only 8% of the time. Each passage was read by different groups of subjects in the constraining and neutral forms. In some conditions, Zola systematically introduced spelling errors in the critical noun (e.g., the *c in popcorn* was replaced with an *e* or *t*). He found that the probability of fixating the target noun was not influenced by the type of adjective or by whether or not there were misspellings. The probability of fixating on the target noun in the four conditions (formed by crossing the adjective constraint and error variables) averaged about .97. The mean fixation duration and total time spent fixating the critical noun (determined by adding together all fixations on the word) were significantly longer in the cases in which there was a misspelling. In cases in which there was no misspelling, the average fixation duration on the critical noun in the high-redundancy condition was 221 msec and in the low redundancy condition it was 237 msec. The mean total fixation time (the sum of forward fixations and regressions to the target) was 290 and 313 msec in the high and low redundancy conditions, respectively.

On the basis of the results of this experiment, Zola (1982) concluded that the reader encounters all the visual detail that is afforded by the text. The fact that the misspellings influenced fixation duration even when they were in the middle letter of a seven letter word is consistent with the view that the reader responds to all of the visual detail that is available. With regard to context, Zola concluded that contextual and redundancy patterns do not influence eye movement patterns and that, while context did decrease the fixation duration on the highly redundant noun, the "savings" was slight.

Zola's experiment is important both because it showed that this type of stimulus, involving experimental manipulation of a single target item, is viable with on-line measurement techniques and because the study represents the first attempt to use eye movement data to measure local context effects on word perception during silent reading. However, there appear to be two problems with the study. First, Zola's target words were all seven to eight letters long. This is problematic because Rayner and McConkie (1976) have demonstrated that with normal reading speeds of 250-400 words per minute, words that are seven or eight letters long will be fixated 95% of the time. If this tendency to fixate fairly long words is sufficiently strong, it could compete with the contextual effects, thereby disguising the potential facilitation by the context. In fact, given that the critical noun was fixated 97% of the time, it is clear that word length is a very strong factor influencing eye movement control. Second, the target word in Zola's experiment only became highly redundant as a result of the immediately preceding word. The effect of context is, with thematically consistent passages, probably more likely to be built up and maintained over time than open to constant and immediate changes (cf., Foss, 1982).

Cognizant of the potential limitations of Zola's experiment, Ehrlich and Rayner (1981) conducted two experiments that differed from his in two ways. First, the target words were all five letters long. The probability of fixating five-letter words has been found to be about .64 (Rayner & McConkie, 1976). Second, the context for the critical target word was built up throughout the passage rather than keeping the passage neutral until the word immediately prior to the target. In Ehrlich and

Rayner's experiments, subjects read passages of text and then answered questions about the text. As they read, their eye movements were recorded. In their first experiment, Ehrlich and Rayner prepared alternative passages, such that a particular word (for example, *shark* in Table 3) was highly constrained by the context in one passage but not in the other. Half of the time, the spelling of the target item was altered by replacing one of its letters with another letter, thus creating a different word (so that, in this case, *shark* became *sharp*). The respelling produced a word which was anomalous in the context of the passage. Table 4 presents the fixation duration data and the probability of fixating on the target word as a function of contextual constraint and of the appropriateness of the target word to the passage. As is clear in Table 4, there were highly reliable effects of both context and of the presence of a spelling change in the target word.

TABLE 3
Passages from the First Experiment of Ehrlich and Rayner (1981).
Constraint Refers to the Predictability of the Target
(italicized) Word in the Context.

High Constraint

He saw the black fin slice through the water and the image of sharks' teeth came quickly to his mind. He turned quickly toward the shore and swam for his life. The coast guard had warned that someone had seen a *shark* off the north shore of the island. As usual, not everyone listened to the warning.

Low Constraint

The young couple were delighted by the special attention they were getting. The zoo keeper explained that the life span of a *shark* is much longer than those of the other animals they had talked about. The scientists decided that this man would make a great ally.

Note: The target word is italicized in the examples, but was not in the experiment.

TABLE 4
Average Fixation Duration (msec) on a Target Word as a
Function of Contextual Constraint and Whether or
Not There was a Respelling. Values in Parentheses Indicate
the Probability of Fixating the Target Word.
Data are from Ehrlich and Rayner (1981).

First Pass	High Constraint	Low Constraint
Normal	221 (.51)	254 (.62)
Respelling	313 (.56)	324 (.79)
Total		
Normal	248 (.54)	305 (.71)
Respelling	476 (.73)	541 (.87)

In the second experiment, Ehrlich and Rayner prepared passages that were also highly constraining for a particular word. However, in this experiment, either the predicted word (for example, the word *horse* in a passage that was clearly about horses) or a word that differed from the target word by a minimally confusable letter in the middle letter position (e. g., the word *house* used as a replacement for *horse*) and which did not result in an anomalous reading of the sentence was used as the target. This latter word, therefore, while not being semantically inappropriate, was not consistent with nor predicted by the context. Table 5 presents the probability of fixating on the target word and the fixation duration data as a function of predictability of the target word. In this experiment, the probability of fixating the target word on forward (left-to-right) saccades did not differ between the two conditions. However, when regressive eye movements were considered, there was a higher probability of fixating on the target word when it was not strongly constrained by the context. As in the first experiment, fixation duration was shorter (55 msec) when the predictable word was present in the passage than when the neutral word was used.

Ehrlich and Rayner interpreted their results as indicating that contextual information allows a reduction in the readers' reliance on visual information. If it is assumed that there is a threshold associated with word identification during reading, more powerful context might reduce the threshold in comparison to less powerful context. Hence, there would be somewhat reduced fixation durations when the word in question was directly fixated. The lower threshold notion could also explain why the target word was fixated less frequently in the high constraint condition than in the low constraint condition in the first experiment. If the reader were fixated to the left of the beginning of the target word, the visual information picked up from the target word would be the same regardless of experimental condition. However, since the threshold for word identification is lower in the high constraint condition, the visual information acquired nonfoveally may be sufficient to convince the processing system that the word has been identified. The combination of the contextual information and the visual information would lead

TABLE 5
Probability of Fixating on the Target Word
and Average Fixation Duration (msec) as a Function
of Whether the Target Word was Predictable or Unpredictable.
Values in Parentheses for the Probability of Fixating
Include Regressions. Values in Parentheses for Fixation
Duration Indicate Total Reading Time for Target Word. Data
are from Ehrlich and Rayner (1981).

	Probability of Fixating	*Fixation Duration*
Predictable	.68 (.72)	228 (269)
Unpredictable	.68 (.82)	283 (429)

the reader to skip over the target word more frequently in the high constraint condition. In the second experiment, the quality of the information picked up from parafoveal vision is again constant whether the predicted or the non-predicted word is present in the paragraph. For a given context, there should be no difference in forward fixations to the target. However, when the target is fixated, the contextual constraints should have an effect, as was shown by longer fixation durations for the non-predictable word. In addition, the larger number of regressions to that word when it was not predictable might indicate that some of the effects found here are a reflection of work the processing system is doing on integrating the accessed word into a meaning representation of the text.

A third experiment, conducted by Carroll (1983), also used the target word method to look at context effects. The level of context important in Carroll's materials lay somewhere between that in the two previously described experiments. Unlike Ehrlich and Rayner, he concentrated on effects from within a single sentence, but the distance of the contextually constraining information from the target was varied and constraints never came from the word immediately preceding the target, unlike Zola's experiment. Carroll's experiment attempted to extend two robust effects from the reaction time literature to a sentence context. Both semantic priming and exemplar typicality have been shown to have strong reaction time effects in categorization and sentence verification tasks (see, for example, Rosch, 1975). These effects have been attributed to the structure of semantic memory, that is, to processes which occur when we access the meaning of some word. If reading for meaning involves the same memory structures tapped in the reaction time experiments, and if this processing has some control over the eye movement control mechanism, then the same sorts of effects should be visible in the fixation duration.

Table 6 presents an example of the materials used in Carroll's study. The stimuli consisted of sentence frames which remained constant and two locations which could be changed. The category name (in this case, *bird*) could be replaced by a neutral item (*thing*) and the exemplar could be either an exemplar rated as very typical (*sparrow*) or one rated as less typical (*vulture*). As much as possible, the sentences were otherwise neutral with regard to the critical semantic relation up to that point in the sentence where the exemplar was first encountered. Only first pass fixations (that is, no regressions from later words) were of interest.

The most obvious prediction from the literature on typicality and priming for these materials would be that the fixation time on the exemplar should be shorter for the highly typical word than for the less typical word in the category context. In the neutral context, however, there should be no effect of typicality, particularly since the exemplars were controlled for frequency and word length. In other words, *vultures* and *sparrows* are equally good *things*, but not equally good *birds*. The results, shown in Table 7, were somewhat surprising. Both priming and typicality showed significant effects, but the predicted interaction failed to materialize. The typicality effect was, in fact, slightly greater in the unprimed condition. Carroll

TABLE 6
Sample Materials from Carroll (1983) Showing Changes in One
Sentence According to the Three Experimental Variables.

SHORT DELAY

PRIMED
High Typicality: The salesman said that the *cloth* was actually *cotton* which had been dyed.

Low Typicality: The salesman said that the *cloth* was actually *canvas* which had been dyed.

UNPRIMED
High Typicality: The salesman said that the *stuff* was actually *cotton* which had been dyed.

Low Typicality: The salesman said that the *stuff* was actually *canvas* which had been dyed.

LONG DELAY

PRIMED
High Typicality: The salesman said that the *cloth* which they thought was so pretty was actually *cotton* which had been dyed.

Low Typicality: The salesman said that the *cloth* which they thought was so pretty was actually *canvas* which had been dyed.

UNPRIMED
High Typicality: The salesman said that the *stuff* which they thought was so pretty was actually *cotton* which had been dyed.

Low Typicality: The salesman said that the *stuff* which they thought was so pretty was actually *canvas* which had been dyed.

TABLE 7
Average Fixation Duration on the Target Noun as a Function
of Rated Typicality and Whether or not a Category Prime
was Presented. The delay variable (cf. Table 6) showed no effect.
Data are from Carroll (1983).

	TYPICALITY	
	HIGH	LOW
Primed	226	244
Unprimed	252	276

interpreted these findings as reflecting two different sorts of processing. According to his account, the priming effect probably did result from facilitation arising from the appearance of the category name. The typicality effect, he suggested, may reflect the work in integrating the different exemplars into the sentence context. (For a further discussion of semantic memory literature consistent with this interpretation, see Carroll, 1983).

One point which we have mentioned several times now is that the eye movement pattern may reflect some higher level semantic integration of the sentence. As it stands, this is a fairly general statement, but some work has been done to attempt to focus on these processes a little more precisely. Just and Carpenter (1978) found that fixation was longer on an agent in a sentence in which there was an indirect inference linking two concepts than when there was a direct inference; regressive fixation patterns showed the same pattern as forward fixations. In another study, Carpenter and Just (1978) found that readers tend to make regressive fixations to the referent of a pronoun. In this study, the referent of the pronoun was ambiguous, such that either of two nouns in a preceding sentence could qualify as an appropriate referent. On over 50% of the trials, readers looked back to at least one of the two nouns in the sentence preceding the pronoun. The occurrence of the regressive fixation probably indicates the point in time at which the assignment of the referent was made. This assignment could occur as soon as the pronoun was encountered, or it could occur after the entire clause or sentence was read. The results of the study show both effects. In a more general sense, the fact that the regression occurred as soon as the pronoun was encountered on many trials is support for the position that eye movement data can directly reflect on-going comprehension processes.

The study of anaphora is interesting because it reflects the construction of a semantically coherent sentence or passage. Ehrlich (1983) and Ehrlich and Rayner (1983) have recently reported further experiments examining pronoun assignment using eye movement data. In their experiments, the distance between a pronoun and its antecedent was varied. Ehrlich and Rayner found that subjects regressed to the antecedent only about 5% of the time, unless there was an inconsistency between the referent and the pronoun (for example, a passage about a person called Tom Norman which then referred to *she*). Ehrlich and Rayner concluded that readers regress to a pronoun when instructions or task demands lead them to do so. This explains the far greater likelihood of regressions in the Carpenter and Just study, because the instructions in that experiment asked subjects to determine if a target sentence was consistent with the prior sentences. Another cause for regressions with regard to pronoun assignment may be when there is serious difficulty in determining pronoun-antecedent relations.

A finding of equal interest in the Ehrlich and Rayner study is that, when the distance between the pronoun and antecedent was not great, pronoun assignment occurred during the fixation which the pronoun was encoded. When the distance between the pronoun and the referent was greater (when the referent occurred some distance back in the text), pronoun assignment was delayed as the reader searched through memory trying to determine the appropriate referent. In such cases, readers continued to move their eyes, but the saccades were shorter and the fixation durations were considerably longer than when pronoun assignment was completed on the fixation on the pronoun. Table 8 shows the results of one of the Ehrlich and Rayner experiments, demonstrating the lengthening of fixations under greater distances between pronoun and referent.

We believe that the experiments reported in this section are important because they are a first step in making sense of the relationship between a very sensitive on-line measure, eye behavior, and complex levels of language processing. The types of effects available to be studied are rich and varied, but not completely undecipherable. We feel, also, that rather precise predictions can be made about the location of certain effects and that it is possible to collect sufficient data even in the difficult eye tracking environment to test hypotheses using well accepted empirical methods.

Studies of Sentence Structure. Psycholinguists have been struggling for decades under cumbersome methods for studying the processing of syntactic aspects of language comprehension. Syntax cannot be separated from sentence processing, as can single word effects, nor can it be simply related to end of sentence measures, as is possible with general comprehension or interpretation. The interesting questions about structure concern how it is realized moment by moment and how and when recovery is made from misinterpretation. As Graesser, Hoffman, and Clark (1980) recently discovered, for instance, syntactic effects may prove among the most elusive events for general comprehension time measures or other similar methods to identify.

Eye movement data, on the other hand, have proven to be reasonably sensitive to syntactic considerations. Wanat (1971), Rayner (1977), and Holmes and O'Regan (1981) have all reported that the main verb in simple sentences received longer fixations than did nouns. Rayner (1977) suggested that these longer fixation times on the verb may be explained by the central role it plays in understanding the sentence. The verb specifies the action which the main nouns in the sentence enter into; thus, the longer fixation durations might reflect the work the reader is doing in interpreting the relationship between the subject noun and the verb.

TABLE 8
Mean Fixation Duration (msec) as a Function of
the Distance Between the Pronoun and its Antecedent.
Data are from Ehrlich and Rayner (1983), Experiment 2.

Distance	Prior	Identity	*Fixation* 1 After	2 After	mean
Near	224	248	224	207	226
Intermediate	230	253	234	206	231
Far	220	242	269	296	257
mean	225	248	243	236	238

It has also been demonstrated that certain types of syntactic structures result in more and longer fixation durations (Klein & Kurkowski, 1974; Wanat, 1971; Holmes & O'Regan, 1981). For example, Wanat (1971) found more and longer fixations on left embedded sentences than in corresponding right embedded sentences. Since there was no difference in the number of regressions and the duration of regressive fixations, Wanat was able to isolate the difficulty with the left embedded sentences to particular regions. Recently, Holmes and O'Regan (1981) found differences in fixation durations and eye movement patterns when native French readers read subject and object relative clause sentences in French. The crucial syntactic form which French makes possible is the transposed object relative clause which has a surface form almost identical to the subject relative clause, but in meaning is merely a variation on the object relative clause. When the first pass through the relative clause was examined, Holmes and O'Regan found that the pattern of fixations for the transposed object relative was more similar to that of the subject relative than that of the object relative. On the other hand, the overall probability of regressing to a constituent was primarily determined by deep structure. Subject relatives were read with fewer regressions than either type of object relative. Holmes and O'Regan also point out that differences in the starting point for the regressive sequences between the two types of object relatives suggest a particular combination of deep and surface structure properties in determining when the eye regresses.

The study of structurally ambiguous sentences has traditionally proven to be one of the most useful sorts of stimuli for researchers interested in syntactic processing. The use of eye movement data with such sentences actually began fairly early. Mehler, Bever, and Carey (1967) recorded eye movements as subjects read structurally ambiguous sentences. Their general finding was that readers tend to fixate the beginnings of surface structure constituents. Table 9 presents two samples from this experiment along with the number of fixations in different regions of the sentence. For example, subjects tended to fixate more often on the word *dog* when it was interpreted as in the beginning of the noun phrase *dog candies* (as in the second sentence in Table 9) than when it was interpreted as the head of the noun phrase *her dog* (as in the first sentence).

While this study represents a first attempt to relate patterns of eye movements to syntactic structure, there are a number of problems with it as has been pointed out by Wanat (1971), Rayner (1978), and Frazier (1983). First, first pass fixations were not measured separately from regressive fixations, raising the possibility that the observed correlation between the position of fixations and the surface structure assigned to the sentence was due entirely to second pass fixations. Frazier (1983) pointed out that readers may initially compute a contextually inappropriate reading of a noun phrase and realize the need to revise it when they reach information which specifies the correct reading. These readers may then regress to the beginning of the ambiguous phrase, leading to the observed correlation of fixations and structure. Second, data on fixation durations were not reported. Third,

TABLE 9
Average Number of Fixations on Each Region of a Sentence as a Function of Structure Provided by Prior Context. The Parentheses Indicate That *dog* is the Second Word in an NP in the Top Sentence and First Word in the NP in the Lower Sentence.
From Mehler, Bever, and Carey (1967).

They	gave		(her		dog)		can	dies.
14.3	3.5	3.7		2.6	8.7	2.1	10.3	9.8
They	gave		her		(dog		can	dies.)
13.5	3.6	7.9		3.6	14.3	2.8	10.4	10.7

the finding has been found not to be very robust insofar as O'Regan (1975) was unable to replicate it. Finally, as Rayner (1978) and Frazier (1983) have pointed out, the hypothesized correlation is conceptually problematic since it is not clear how readers could determine either the position or the number of left brackets (beginnings of constituents) before they had performed an analysis of the structural consequences of the words they had not yet fixated. The general rule of fixating the first half of the immediate constituent implies that the reader can make this determination on the basis of nonfoveal information. If this level of identification can be made from parafoveal vision (and the perceptual span studies reviewed earlier indicate that it cannot), it is difficult to see why a reader would then fixate on a region that has already been interpreted.

A number of studies recently conducted in our laboratory have examined eye movement patterns as subjects read structurally ambiguous sentences. Frazier and Rayner (1982), following some suggestions of Frazier (1978), have suggested that the reader initially parses a sentence according to a few simple strategic preferences, themselves based on the limitations of short term memory. This strategic approach avoids the problem encountered by Mehler et al. (1967) of needing to postulate that the reader knows what is coming up before the visual system could have taken in that information. In addition, they allow rather clear predictions of where the reader will detect an error during the first analysis of a sentence and what would be necessary to correct the original analysis. Two very general parsing strategies, *Late Closure* and *Minimal Attachment* (described in some detail in Frazier, 1978), were investigated in this study. According to the late closure strategy, whenever possible, readers should attach incoming lexical items to the clause or phrase currently being constructed (i.e., to the lowest possible nonterminal node dominating the last item analyzed). According to minimal attachment, the reader should prefer an analysis reading leading to the simplest structural description of the sentence consistent with the well-formedness of the language (technically, incoming materials should be attached to the phrase structure being constructed using the fewest possible nodes).

For this study subjects read sentences such as those found in (1). Sentence (1a)

1a. While Mary was mending the sock fell off her lap.
1b. While Mary was mending the sock it fell off her lap.

can lead to a misreading if "*the sock*" is interpreted as the direct object of "*was mending.*" Sentence (1b) leads to no such misreading. Frazier and Rayner compared general reading performance for garden path sentences, such as (1a), with sentences such as (1b) in order to study subjects' recovery from erroneous parsing. The eye movement data allowed them to examine reading performance in different regions of the sentence while keeping separate different passes of the eye through a given region. They found that the fixation in the disambiguating region of the garden-path sentence was longer than normal. In studying the reanalysis processes involved in recovering from parsing errors, the pattern of regressions and fixation times seemed to indicate that the subject neither moves step by step backwards until the course of error has been discovered nor does the reader return to the beginning of the sentence to start again. Rather, the confused reader apparently uses whatever information is available at the time the error is detected to restructure the sentence appropriately. The kinds of decisions made by the reader can be predicted by the parsing strategies mentioned earlier; thus, it is possible to explain differences among ambiguous sentences in difficulty of reanalysis.

A recent study by Rayner, Carlson, and Frazier (1983) used eye movement data to explore the various contributions of syntactic, pragmatic, and semantic information in sentence comprehension. In the first experiment, they used temporarily ambiguous sentences (from the perspective of a left-to-right processor) which varied in pragmatic plausibility and structural preferences. Examples of their stimuli can be seen in Table 10. Given the choice of reading the string in (2a) as a simple active sentence or as a type of relative clause (the reduced relative, meaning "the florist who was sent the flowers..."), people tend to prefer the simple active alternative. The preference for the reduced relative reading of sentence (2b) is

2a. The florist sent the flowers...
2b. The performer sent the flowers...

only slightly better than chance, indicating that the pragmatic information about whether performers get or send flowers influences the reading of such strings. Reading time was separated by different passes through the sentence as well as different segments of the sentence. The results indicated that the initial analysis of the sentence followed structural preferences, not pragmatic preferences.

In their second experiment, they used sentences such as those in (3).

3a. The spy saw the cop with binoculars, but the cop didn't see him.
3b. The spy saw the cop with a revolver, but the cop didn't see him.

Sentence (3a) is ambiguous with respect to the person holding the binoculars, while sentence (3b) leaves little doubt that *the cop* had a revolver. The minimal

TABLE 10
Examples of the Four Types of Sentences Varying
in Pragmatic Plausibility and Grammatical Structure
from Rayner, Carlson, and Frazier (1983).

Reduced Implausible:

Susan said that the florist sent the flowers was very pleased with herself.

Reduced Plausible:

Susan said that the performer sent the flowers was very pleased with herself.

Unreduced Plausible:

Susan said that the performer who was sent the flowers was very pleased with herself.

Active Implausible:

Susan said that the performer sent the flowers and was very pleased with herself.

---

attachment strategy mentioned earlier suggests that the instrumental reading of *with binoculars*, putting them in the hands of *the spy*, should be preferred. Of course, if this is true, the parser should also prefer the instrumental reading of sentence (3b), making the revolver a viewing instrument even though this reading is somewhat bizarre. While the ultimate reading of the sentence was consistent with pragmatic considerations of real world plausibility, the eye movement data indicated that a conflict between pragmatic and structural preferences leads to longer reading times and some need for reanalysis.

SUMMARY

On the whole, early attempts to study reading comprehension and language processes through eye movements were unsuccessful (see Blumenthal, 1970). The endeavors that were undertaken around 1900-1920 failed to reveal any interesting facts about the reading process in general or about language processes specifically. Recent work in psychology and linguistics has led to a description of language more compatible with mentalistic processing models than was the case in that earlier period. Similarly, the description of the memory system underlying our knowledge of words and concepts gives us hope of separating the effects of word identification, sentence structure, and higher level inference processes. The view of language comprehension as the outcome of a system composed of processing components allows us to look at the independent contribution of various processing modules as well as their interrelationships and processes coordinating their activity.

The studies we have reviewed in this chapter lead us to believe that eye movement data can be used to study moment-by-moment processing of language. The primary characteristic of much of the work we have reviewed is that we have been able to identify in advance specific locations in the text where processing should be more difficult or easier depending on contextual constraints, syntactic structures, or semantic relations. In effect, this research has indicated that the processing load is reflected in the pattern of the eye's behavior. The advantage of our method is that the data can be collected on-line as the subject reads the text; it is not necessary to rely on measures either that infer processes presumed to have taken place at a specific point using end of sentence tasks or that are based on global measures such as total reading time where one is not sure which part of the sentence actually led to changes in reading time. Subjects can read at their own pace, secondary tasks need not be employed, and the situation is relatively normal.

This is not to say that even the basic groundwork has yet been fully laid. We have referred above to the pattern of the eye's behavior, which is composed of fixations defined by their duration and movements defined by length and direction. But this pattern must be mapped onto a textual stimulus which must be described at several levels corresponding to levels of a processing system of great complexity. Only the first steps have been made to unravel the interconnection among combinations of eye movements (cf. Kliegl, Olson, & Davidson, 1983; Hogaboam, 1983). At present, we are still forced to sum multiple fixations on a particular word without any idea yet of the validity of such a measure (are two 250 msec fixations equal to one 500 msec fixation?). Similarly, sets of fixations within a minor constituent, such as a simple noun phrase, have not been separated from fixations crossing constituent boundaries.

Our purpose here has not been to assert that the problems left are simple or even that the basic parameters controlling the reading system are well defined. Rather, our optimism springs from the recent success researchers have had using the eye movement technique to study language and, perhaps even more, from an intuition born of hours of studying eye movement patterns on text that there is a great deal more to be learned beneath the surface we have scratched.

ACKNOWLEDGMENT

Preparation of this chapter and much of the research described was supported by grant BNS79-17600 from the National Science Foundation. The second author was also supported by a predoctoral fellowship from the National Institute of Mental Health. We would like to thank Lyn Frazier for her helpful comments.

REFERENCES

Blumenthal, A. L. *Language and psychology.* New York: Wiley, 1970.

Bouma, H. & de Voogd, A. H. On the control of eye saccades in reading. *Vision Research,* 1974, *14,* 273-284.

Carroll, P. J. A study of semantic and syntactic control of fixation in reading. Unpublished doctoral dissertation, University of Massachusetts, 1983.

Ehrlich, K. Eye movements in pronoun assignment: A study of sentence integration. In K. Rayner (Ed.), *Eye movements in reading: Perceptual and language processes.* New York: Academic Press, 1983.

Ehrlich, K., & Rayner, K. Pronoun assignment and semantic integration during reading: Eye movements and immediacy of processing. *Journal of Verbal Learning and Verbal Behavior,* 1983, *22,* 75-87.

Ehrlich, S. F. & Rayner, K. Contextual effects on word perception and eye movements during reading. *Journal of Verbal Learning and Verbal Behavior,* 1981, *20,* 641-655.

Foss, D. J. A discourse on semantic priming. *Cognitive Psychology,* 1982, *14,* 590-607.

Frazier, L. On comprehending sentences: Syntactic parsing strategies. Unpublished doctoral dissertation, University of Connecticut, 1978. (Available from IU Linguistics Club, 310 Lindley Hall, University of Indiana, Bloomington, Indiana).

Frazier, L. Processing sentence structure. In K. Rayner (Ed.), *Eye movements in reading: Perceptual and language processes.* New York: Academic Press, 1983.

Frazier, L. & Rayner, K. Making and correcting errors during sentence comprehension: Eye movements in the analysis of structurally ambiguous sentences. *Cognitive Psychology,* 1982, *14,* 178-210.

Graesser, A. C., Hoffman, N. L., & Clark, L. F. Structural components of reading time. *Journal of Verbal Learning and Verbal Behavior,* 1980, *19,* 135-151.

Hogaboam, T. Reading patterns in eye movement data. In K. Rayner (Ed.), *Eye movements in reading: Perceptual and language processes.* New York: Academic Press, 1983.

Holmes, V. M. & O'Regan, J. K. Eye fixation patterns during the reading of relative-clause sentences. *Journal of Verbal Learning and Verbal Behavior,* 1981, *20,* 417-430.

Huey, E. B. *The psychology and pedagogy of reading.* New York: Macmillan, 1908.

Inhoff, A. W. Attentional strategies during the reading of short stories. In K. Rayner (Ed.), *Eye movements in reading: Perceptual and language processes.* New York: Academic Press, 1983.

Just, M. A. & Carpenter, P. A. A theory of reading: From eye fixations to comprehension. *Psychological Review,* 1980, *87,* 329-354.

Klein, G. A. & Kurkowski, F. Effect of task demands on relationships between eye movements and sentence complexity. *Perceptual and Motor Skills,* 1974, *39,* 463-466.

Kliegl, R., Olson, R. K., & Davidson, B. J. On problems of unconfounding perceptual and language processes. In K. Rayner (Ed.), *Eye movements in reading: Perceptual and language processes.* New York: Academic Press, 1983.

Kolers, P. A. Buswell's discoveries. In R. A. Monty & J. W. Senders (Eds.), *Eye movements and psychological processes.* Hillsdale, N. J.: Lawrence Erlbaum Associates, 1976.

McConkie, G. W. Evaluating and reporting data quality in eye movement research. *Behavior Research Methods and Instrumentation,* 1981, *13,* 97-106.

McConkie, G. W., Hogaboam, T. W., Wolverton, G. S., Zola, D., & Lucas, P. A. Toward the use of eye movements in the study of language processing. *Discourse Processes,* 1979, *2,* 157-177.

McConkie, G. W. & Zola, D. Language constraints and the functional stimulus in reading. In A. M. Lesgold and C. A. Perfetti (Eds.), *Interactive processes in reading.* Hillsdale, N. J.: Lawrence Erlbaum Associates, 1981.

Mehler, J., Bever, T. G. & Carey, P. What we look at when we read. *Perception & Psychophysics,* 1967, *2,* 213-218.

Rayner, K. Visual attention in reading: Eye movements reflect cognitive processes. *Memory & Cognition*, 1977, *4*, 443-448.

Rayner, K. Eye movements in reading and information processing. *Psychological Bulletin*, 1978, *85*, 618-660.

Rayner, K. Eye movements and cognitive psychology. On-line computer approaches to studying visual information processing. *Behavior Research Methods and Instrumentation*, 1979, *11*, 164-171.

Rayner, K. Eye movements and the perceptual span in reading. In F. J. Pirozzolo and M. C. Wittrock (Eds.), *Neuropsychological and cognitive processes in reading*. New York: Academic Press, 1981.

Rayner, K. The perceptual span and eye movement control during reading. In K. Rayner (Ed.), *Eye movements in reading: Perceptual and language processes*. New York: Academic Press, 1983.

Rayner, K., Carlson, M., & Frazier, L. The interaction of syntax and semantics during sentence processing: Eye movements in the analysis of semantically biased sentences. *Journal of Verbal Learning and Verbal Behavior*, 1983, *22*, 358-374.

Rayner, K. & McConkie, G. W. What guides a reader's eye movements? *Vision Research*, 1976, *16*, 829-837.

Rayner, K. & Pollatsek, A. Eye movement control during reading: Evidence for direct control. *Quarterly Journal of Experimental Psychology*, 1981, *33A*, 351-373.

Rosch, E. Cognitive representation of semantic categories. *Journal of Experimental Psychology: General*, 1975, *104*, 192-233.

Vanacek, E. Fixations dauer und fixations frequenz bein stillen lesen von sprachapproximationen. *Zeitschrift fur Experimentelle und Angewandle Psychologie*, 1972, *19*, 671-689.

Wanat, S. *Linguistic structure and visual attention in reading*. Newark, Del.: International Reading Association, 1971.

Zola, D. The perception of words in reading: An exploratory treatise. Unpublished doctoral dissertation, Cornell University, 1982.

8 Using Eye Fixations to Study Reading Comprehension

Marcel Adam Just and Patricia A. Carpenter
Carnegie-Mellon University

This chapter describes some of the methodological innovations and refinements that we have introduced in the study of on-line comprehension processes over the past few years. Our goal was to characterize the psychological processes that occur as the reader processes the successive words of a text. During such reading, there is generally not much observable behavior that can be quantified, analyzed and related to mental processes. One naturally-occurring behavior that is observable is the reader's pattern of eye fixations: which words are fixated, how long they are fixated, and on occasion, which words are refixated. These measures can be used to trace and characterize the underlying comprehension processes. This presentation method, data collection, and data analysis of eye fixations during normal reading can be called the reading eye-fixation paradigm. Using this paradigm, we have been able to examine the comprehension processes by which a person perceives a word, understands its meaning, and relates that word to the preceding context. In this chapter, we will first discuss the methodological issues that have developed in the course of our research on reading, describing the reading eye-fixation paradigm, including the measurement and analysis aspects of the paradigm. In addition, we will describe an alternative paradigm, the Moving Window paradigm, and compare it to the reading eye-fixation paradigm. The second half of the chapter summarizes five major substantive results that have been discovered with this paradigm. These include the immediacy principle, the processes in error detection and recovery, several lexical-level processes, wrap-up processes at the ends of sentences, and the analysis of individual differences in reading ability.

In describing a particular methodology, we will try not to be just advocates but also evaluators of its use. A methodology can be thought of as a tool, and the use of eye fixation experiments to study reading comprehension can be thought of as one more tool in a larger kit that cognitive psychologists have at their disposal. Eye fixation methods are not necessarily better than other methods for examining all issues. As in the choice of mechanical tools, the choice ought to be based on appropriateness to the issue. Hammers are neither better nor worse than pliers, but there are certainly jobs for which hammers are more appropriate. Eye fixation methodologies as well as many others have a role in an experimental science. We will try to describe the place of eye fixation experiments in the study of reading comprehension.

METHODOLOGICAL ISSUES

In the sections below, we describe four facets of the methodologies we have been using. The first is a more detailed description of the procedure used in the reading eye-fixation paradigm, a relatively natural situation in which people read a text while their point of regard is recorded. The second is a discussion of the size of the unit of stimulus and unit of behavior that have been most fruitful in analyzing the task and the data. The third is a discussion of the treatment of the data at various stages of analysis. The fourth is a discussion of some useful variants of the methodology.

The Prose Reading Experiments

In a number of experiments, we have measured the amount of time that readers spend looking at each word of a text. The goal of the experiments is to account for the time course of the ongoing comprehension processes that occur as the subject reads. This chronometric approach reveals where and how long readers pause, where they speed up, what causes them difficulty, and when they first detect the difficulty. Eye fixations occur naturally during reading, and current technology allows them to be recorded without intruding on the reader. Moreover, the reading task itself is undisturbed, and unaccompanied by unusual secondary tasks, such as monitoring for a second stimulus or making lexical-decision judgments. Finally, reading processes are studied as they occur on-line, rather than inferring their nature retroactively from recall data or judgments made at the completion of reading. So the paradigm involves the non-intrusive measurement of a naturally occurring behavior during an ecologically sensible task.

The Procedure. In the procedure that we use most often, the reader sits in an armchair and reads a text displayed on a video monitor while his or her eye fixations are monitored and recorded from a distance. This procedure is relatively similar to normal reading in several respects. The reader sits unencumbered and reads text displayed in screensful that roughly correspond to short pages. The texts can be natural in content and length, such as excerpts from magazines or books, or they can be generated for experimental purposes with more controlled characteristics. The readers are usually told that they will be asked questions about the text or will be asked to summarize it, but they are asked to read normally, without intentionally memorizing anything. The text is arranged in conventional paragraph layout with each character of print subtending roughly the same visual angle as in common reading conditions. Each doubled-spaced screen contains 11 lines of 80 character spaces, or about 150 words. Longer texts are presented on successive screens.

Before the data recording begins, a calibration procedure establishes the correspondence between the reader's point of regard and the light reflections from his eye. This brief procedure requires that the subject look at nine specific locations on the screen while the tracker records the nature of the reflections during each of the nine gazes. To ensure that the calibration remains intact throughout the entire experiment, it is automatically checked just before displaying each new screenful of text. To initiate the display of a screenful, the reader must look at an asterisk located at the upper left-hand corner of the screen (where the first word will eventually appear) and at the same time press a "ready" button. If the reader's measured point of regard is not within one degree of the fixation point, then the text is not displayed, and the experimenter must recalibrate. If the accuracy is adequate, then the text appears on the screen and remains there until the reader indicates that he or she has finished reading by pressing a "done" button. Then the fixation point reappears and the subject initiates presentation of the next screen as just described. Some aspects of the situation are not a part of typical reading, such as reading on a monitor, pressing a button to see the next page of print, and having to fixate an asterisk at the beginning of every page. Nevertheless, this situation provides for experimental control without loss of ecological validity.

Usefulness of the Approach. We have found eye fixation studies to be most useful when trying to trace psychological processes, both in reading and problem solving. Tracing psychological processes in the context of eye fixation studies refers to determining the sequence and duration of mental processes that operate on separate external stimuli. This can be contrasted with approaches that focus on mental structure rather than process, such as scaling studies in general and multidimensional scaling in particular, clustering analyses, and factor-analytic analyses of abilities and traits. In general, eye fixation studies tell us more about cognitive processes than cognitive structures, although assumptions must be made about both in order to test specific aspects of either. Eye fixation studies are best suited to study processes that range from 20 msec to about 1000 msec, with particular suitability between 200 and 600 msec because the grain of the eye fixation durations is roughly in the 200 to 600 msec range.

Limitations of the Approach. The most obvious limitation is that the methodology can be costly in terms of instrumentation, training of personnel, and intensity of data analysis. A conceptual limitation, shared with all chronometric approaches, is that eye fixation behavior does not directly indicate the end product of the comprehension process, what the reader has learned from the text. It is usually worthwhile to supplement eye fixation monitoring with another measure like recall, question-answering, or retrospective protocols that indicate more about what has been comprehended. Another initial limitation is that we have used the methodology as an exploratory tool, searching for correlations between characteristics of the text and of the eye fixation behavior. These initial correlational studies (Just & Carpenter, 1980) are generally followed by experimental studies in which the stimulus properties corresponding to the independent variables of interest are systematically manipulated (e.g., Carpenter & Daneman, 1981; McDonald & Carpenter, 1981).

The Units of Analysis: Word Gaze Durations

The Dependent Measure. The main dependent measure we have used is the gaze duration, rather than the duration of individual eye fixations. The gaze duration is the total looking time on a word, uninterrupted by intervening fixations on other words. For example, if a reader made three successive fixations on a given word, then the gaze duration would simply be the sum of the durations of the individual fixations. If a word is difficult to process for one reason or another, subjects respond by making more fixations on that word and by making individual fixations longer in duration. Previous research has shown that in most reading tasks, the number of fixations varies much more than does the duration of individual fixations (Tinker, 1951). The gaze duration measure captures both of these responses.

Our work has shown that the total time a reader spends looking at a word (i.e. the gaze duration) is systematically related to the characteristics of that word and to the context that precedes it. For example, we can specify how much the gaze duration increases as a function of the word's frequency. It is the gaze durations, rather than durations of individual fixations, that are so systematically related to the word's characteristics. This sensitivity of the gaze duration holds not only for low-level properties of the word, such as its length and frequency, but also to its semantic role in the sentence, such as whether it introduces a new topic, is an anomalous word, or indicates that the reader had been led down a garden path.

From the turn of the century, when the first eye fixation studies were done, until well into the 1970's, most eye fixation studies of reading attempted to describe the distributional properties of individual fixations, such as their durations, frequency, or the physical distance between them (i.e. the size of the saccades). There was often an attempt made to relate the general characteristics of the text, task, or reader to these distributional properties. A typical conclusion from a study of this type was that difficult texts result in an increase in the number or duration of fixations.

Our work introduced two related innovations. First, we tried to relate the looking at a given word to the characteristics of that word. This relation was mediated by specific, hypothesized comprehension processes, such as lexical access or inference making. This stands in contrast to the then prevailing practice of relating the distributional properties of fixations to the general properties of the text. The second innovation was the use of the gaze duration measure, which we found to have a precise quantitative relation to the hypothesized process. We have been able to go beyond the statement that some dependent measure increases or decreases and give precise quantitative relations. For example, the analysis of gaze durations has indicated that lexical access takes 50 msec longer as the normative frequency of a word decreases by 1 log unit, and that particular inferences during the comprehension of agents and instruments take an additional 75 msec. These two innovations are precisely what allows eye fixations to be treated as external indices of internal cognitive processes. Subsequent research has analyzed a number of specific comprehension processes, such as inference making, lexical access, encoding, parsing, and error detection and recovery (cf. Carpenter & Just, 1977, 1978; Just & Carpenter, 1978, 1980).

In a developing science, the problem often lies in finding the appropriate level of aggregation. Reductionistic approaches relentlessly push towards finer units of analysis, but sometimes grosser units are more appropriate. For example, if one wanted to study how metereological conditions govern the amount of precipitation, it would be preferable to measure rainfall in inches rather than counting raindrops. In quantifying precipitation, the size of individual raindrops is not important; only the aggregate of their volume matters. One can of course measure and count individual raindrops and then sum them up but this is not just a waste of resources, but a misdirection of focus. There are certainly interesting questions to be asked about the size of individual raindrops and the durations of individual eye fixations, but we have found that gaze durations rather than fixation durations provide the closest correspondence to cognitive processes in comprehension.

The Word as the Stimulus Unit. One important facet of our approach is that we have treated each word of a text as the functional stimulus unit (rather than letters or phrases or clauses). The advantage of this approach is that it has led us to the discovery that the reading of each word evokes the full range of comprehension processes that attempt to interpret that word and integrate it with its context. Focusing on stimulus units larger than a word (such as phrases) would miss the immediacy of the comprehension processes that do not wait until the ends of phrases to go into operation. The choice of the unit of analysis must primarily depend on the level of the theory being developed, which in our case, has focused on comprehension processes. In most cases, stimulus units smaller than a word would be unsatisfactory for an analysis focused on linguistic processes, since most linguistic processes cannot be evoked by a single letter. Moreover, units smaller than a word would be difficult to relate to eye fixations because several letters are clearly visible during each fixation.

The unit of analysis in characterizing the stimuli (i.e. the word) is particularly compatible with the unit of analysis in characterizing the behavior (i.e. the gaze duration). Although gaze durations can be measured on units of any size, the word is the smallest unit on which it can sensibly be used. In any science, there is a need to match the measuring tools to the process under investigation. One aspect of the match is that the time course of the measure should roughly correspond to the time course of the process being studied. For example, to study the movement of a flower that is blossoming one uses time-lapse photography, while to study the movement of a muscle one uses a much higher sampling density. Gaze durations on words of a text provide an appropriate measure of the ongoing comprehension processes because they have similar temporal grains.

Limitations of the Word as a Stimulus Unit. A cost that is involved in using gaze durations rather than fixation durations, is that gaze durations are partially defined by the stimulus, and are not simply an inherent property of the behavior. In English, a reasonable solution is to measure the gaze duration on each word. The solution is not perfect because words, when defined by spacing in the orthography, only roughly correspond to psychological entities of meaning. English words can be composed of prefixes, compounds, and affixes (e.g., un-touch-able) and it is plausible that subunits (perhaps corresponding to the linguistic unit called the morph) sometimes are processed separately. The assignment of morphs to words is somewhat arbitrary, as in the case of *bedroom* being treated as a single word but *living room* as two separate words. Polymorphemic words present a greater problem in agglutinating languages like Turkish, which contain many morphs per word ("agglutinating" means "sticking together", and refers to individual morphs being stuck together to form words). For example, the phrase made up of three separate English words, "word recognition priming", is translated into a single Dutch word, "woordherkenningsvoorbereiding". Should the gaze be measured on this entire word, or more likely, on some subset of the component morphs (word - recognition - pre - ready - ness)? The answer may best be provided empirically, by determining whether the gaze durations are best accounted for by the properties of the sub-word components or by the properties of the entire word. This is less of a problem in languages like English that minimize the number of morphs per word. Thus, the functional unit will depend on the nature of the meaning elements in a given language and on the writing system that expresses those elements.

Most Content Words are Fixated. Our analysis treats each word as a unit and it appears that at least for content words, readers do also. An analysis of the locations of eye fixations shows that skilled adult readers sample an age-appropriate text fairly densely, usually fixating adjacent words or skipping no more than one word. In the reading of technical prose from *Newsweek*, 83% of the content words were fixated, and for simple prose (a long narrative from *Reader's Digest* read by college students), 74% of the content words were fixated. Approximately 40% of the function words were fixated in both cases.

To determine how many words readers did not directly fixate, we counted the lengths of the runs of successive unfixated words. If the reader fixates two adjacent words, then the length of the run of unfixated words is zero. If the reader skips exactly one word, then the length of the run is one, and so on. Figure 1 shows the average number of runs of each length for each 1000 words of text from the data base described by Just & Carpenter (1980). When readers move their eyes forward in the text from one word to some other word, most of the time (93%) they fixate the very next word or skip over only one word. For every 1000 words of text, the

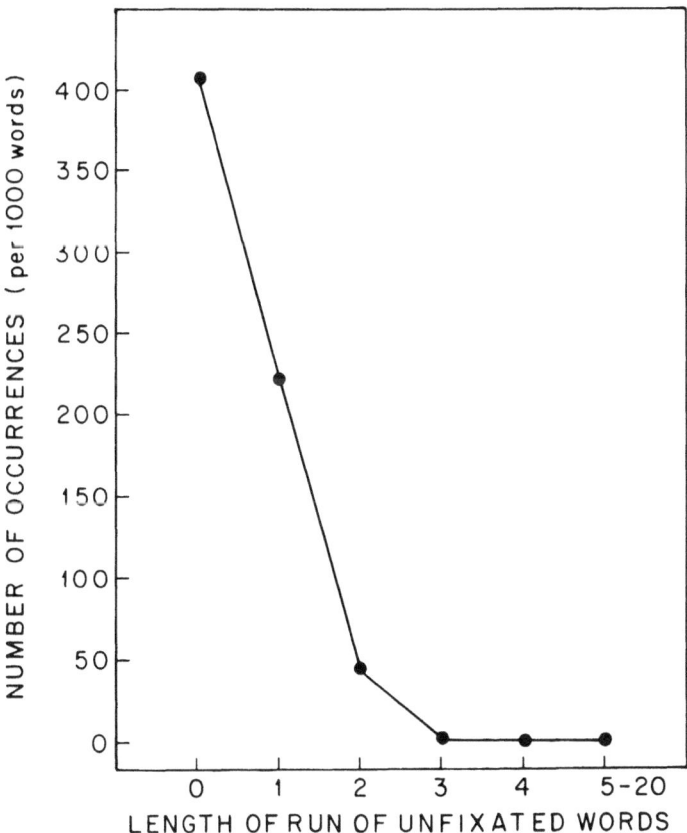

FIG. 1. The length of the run of unfixated words between successive fixations, conditionalized on a passage of 140 words.

mean number of words fixated at least once was 678. On average, these 678 fixated words were distributed as follows: the gazes were on adjacent words in 410 cases, involved one skipped word between consecutive gazes in 221 cases, two skipped words in 43 cases, three skipped words in 3.6 cases, and almost never involved more than three skipped words. The words that were likely to be skipped were short, function words, like *a, of, the, to,* and so on. Overall, readers fixated only 38% of the function words (conjunctions; articles; prepositions; modal, auxiliary, and copula verbs). By contrast, they fixated 83% of the content words (adjectives, adverbs, nouns, verbs, pronouns). Thus the gaze duration on individual words provides a good measure of the processing time for content words.

The Semantic Span of Apprehension is Small. It would be useless to measure the point of regard if people had a very large span of apprehension, and processed many of the words in a text without fixating them. Fortunately for this methodology, the span of apprehension, the width of stimulus that is semantically processed during a given fixation, is small. Before defining "span of apprehension" more precisely, several distinctions must be made. First, the span of apprehension must be defined functionally, not physiologically. We must ask not how far into the periphery *can* readers see, but how far out do they actually process? Second, there are different levels of processing for which there are different spans. For example, information about the presence of spaces and the length of a word is available much farther from the point of regard than is information about the identity of the word (Rayner, 1975).

The functional span of apprehension for semantic processing during normal reading is small, between 2 and 4 degrees of visual angle, which usually contain 3 letters per degree. This conclusion is supported by a number of empirical findings. First, Rayner (1975) reports a semantic span that extends 6 letters to the right of the current point of regard. However, even this modest span may be an overestimate, because a technical flaw in the instrumentation which changed the display after the saccade rather than during it, may have artifactually caused the span to be overestimated (McConkie, Zola, Blanchard & Wolverton, 1982). When more reliable instrumentation is used, there is a strong indication that the semantic span is limited to not much more than the currently fixated word (McConkie et al., 1982). Finally, our analyses have also indicated that the semantic span is small; as we will describe in a later section, the gaze duration on a given word is affected very little by the properties of the preceding or following word.

One possible explanation for the small size of the semantic span is that the cognitive load incurred by processing the currently fixated word leaves inadequate resources to process peripheral information, and it is more economical to directly fixate the next word. In other words, cognitive load may cause tunnel vision. A second reason that the semantic span is small is that the print surrounding the words in the periphery lessens visual acuity. Thus, visual noise also causes tunnel vision (Bouma, 1978; Mackworth, 1965).

While the semantic span is small, not all words are directly fixated and there clearly is some processing of these non-fixated words. People sometimes process the word "the" without fixating it, as we know because they skip over it (i.e. don't fixate it) more often than other three-letter words. Three-letter function words have a significantly lower probability of fixation (.40) than do three-letter content words (.57), $F(1,265) = 45.37$, p.01. (This analysis was restricted to 267 three-letter words in the text that neither began nor ended a line or a sentence). The probability of fixation was .29 for 37 *and's*, .40 for 122 *the's*, .47 for 47 other three-letter function words (such as *was, may, can, but, for, off, has*), and .57 for 61 three-letter content words (such as *act, red, use, ant, run, two, not*). Since the choice of which words to fixate is probably made largely on information from the unfixated words themselves, some processing of unfixated words must be occurring. However, such processing is likely to be infrequent. It may occur primarily when the rightmost part of one word is fixated and the shape of a very short familiar word is visible on the right, suggesting some peripheral processing of short, frequent function words like *the, and, of, and to*.

Data Analysis

Averaging Over Readers. Whether the dependent measure is individual eye fixations or gaze durations, the experimenter must decide whether to average unconditionally, over all readers, or to average conditionally, over only those readers who fixated at a particular location or word. If individual fixations are used as the dependent measure, the experimenter must still choose an area over which fixations by any reader are considered equivalent. If gaze durations are used as the dependent measure, the area is usually a word, although it could be larger or smaller. The unconditional mean averaged over all subjects reflects both the probability of fixation in that location and the processing time. In the case of content words, most of which are fixated, the unconditional mean gaze duration provides a reasonable estimate of the processing time spent on the word. The advantage of the unconditional average is its algebraic property, namely that unconditionalized averages can be summed to determine the average time spent on a larger unit of text. For example, the average time spent on a sentence will be the sum of the unconditionalized average times on each word. If the goal is to account for the total time processing a text, it is desirable to use the unconditionalized gaze durations. However, the unconditionalized averages do not reflect the processing time of individual readers if there are a substantial number of readers who do not fixate the word, as in the case of short function words. To estimate the processing time on function words, the gaze durations must be conditionalized on there having been a fixation at that location. Conditionalized mean gaze durations must also be used to obtain estimates of processing time even on content words if the content words are not reliably fixated, as in speed reading or skimming.

While in theory, the averaging issue may be one of the most fundamental aspects of data analysis, in practice it is preceded by several steps of data reduction to identify fixations, saccades, and noise, and to aggregate the fixations into gazes. The following section describes our procedures. It is followed by a discussion of some of the issues in the use of regression techniques to analyze the gaze durations.

Data Reduction. The ability to determine exactly where a reader is looking has existed since the beginning of this century. But one aspect of current research that differentiates it from the early work is that the new computer technology provides the automatic scoring of the vast amounts of data that are generated during reading. Although it was possible 50 years ago to tell how long a reader spent on one particular word, it was not feasible to compute how long each of 15 readers spent on each word in a 2000 word passage. This is feasible with current instrumentation.

The first step is to transform sequential observations of the reader's point of regard into individual fixations. Much of the initial data reduction is determined by the nature of the tracker being used. Our tracker determines the point of regard at a high sampling rate (60 times per second), and outputs an X and Y coordinate to the PDP 11 every 16.7 msec. A program on the PDP 11 immediately maps these coordinates into the 80 x 22 character grid used on the display monitor, and aggregates the 16.7 msec observations into units that resemble fixations. A new "fixation" is defined whenever the change in horizontal position between two successive time slices exceeds the width of two characters (about .67 degrees of visual angle) or the change in vertical position exceeds the height of one character (about 1 degree). All the time slices aggregated into a single "fixation" are attributed to the location specified by the modal X and Y coordinates of the contributing observations. The duration of the "fixation" is simply the sum of the 16.7 msec time slices.

The next phase of the data reduction aggregates fixations that differ in Y-coordinate (i.e. line number) due to measurement inaccuracy or noise. This program is performed by an off-line Fortran program on a PDP 11 after the experimental task has ended. The program assumes that after reading to the end of one line, readers are most likely to look at the beginning of the next line, although this assumption can be overridden by strong evidence to the contrary. The program also makes use of the information that the text is double spaced, and only every second line on the screen contains print. Also, the duration of any blinks that are preceded and followed by fixations on the same location are attributed to that location. A word must receive some minimum fixation (usually set at 33 or 50 msec) to count as having been fixated. This cutoff eliminates observations of 16 or 33 msec that are due to measurement noise or sampling the eye position during a saccade. The output of the program is a series of fixations whose durations have conventional values, usually greater than 200 msec. This output is compared to the videotape record by a human scorer who makes certain that the program did not make any unwarranted or unwise decisions.

The next step is to compute the total gaze duration on each word for each reader. This is done by a program that accesses the coordinates of each word of the text and aggregates over successive fixations on the same word. Fixations on inter-word spaces are attributed to the word on the right. This is because the perceptual span for readers of English is asymmetric about the point of regard, with a clear bias towards the right (McConkie & Rayner, 1976; Schiepers, 1980). The program distinguishes between the first gaze on a word and subsequent gazes, i. e. subsequent to intervening gazes on other words. The subsequent gazes are the result of regressive fixations. The amount of regressive fixations depends on the nature of the text, the reader and the task. Instructions to monitor for possible inconsistencies will elicit many regressions, whereas instructions not to reread result in very few regressions to earlier words in the text.

After this, the gaze duration data can be averaged, either conditionally or unconditionally. Averages can be computed for forward gazes, regressions, or the total time on a word. In addition, it is possible to compute the probability of fixating each word, as well as the probability of regressions. After the averages of interest have been computed, they can be analyzed using conventional statistical techniques.

Regression Analysis. The mean gaze durations or conditionalized mean gaze durations can be related to the properties of the words by a multiple regression analysis in which the gaze durations are the dependent variable and the properties of the words are the independent variables. As our research indicates, there is not much sequential dependency between adjacent words, so the observations on each of the words are treated as independent observations. The emphasis in the early experiments and analysis is not on hypothesis testing, but rather on determining the characteristics of the performance in order to build better versions of the theory. Thus, the analysis of temporal parameters focuses on their magnitude and their degree of variability. Later experiments test some specific hypotheses derived from the theory.

The regression analysis has some clear benefits. It allows large amounts of data from naturally occurring texts to be analyzed, and allows us to code many independent variables that can be varying unsystematically within the text. With such large data bases, with many observations from many subjects, over many words, one can obtain relatively stable estimates of various parameters. In experimental studies, regression analysis allows the effects of extraneous variables to be partialled out before the effects of the independent variables of interest are assessed. For example, to determine the effect of any syntactic variable on the gaze on a word, the effects of word encoding and lexical access can be partialled out with the independent variables of word length and frequency.

Our regression analyses also have some limitations. As in any correlational study, one can't be certain that a relation between the variation in an independent and the dependent variable is causal. Also, there is always a possibility, and in this case likelihood, of correlation among the independent variables, occasionally making some of the parameter estimates difficult to interpret. For example, word length and word frequency are correlated, and a regression analysis with both those independent variables in the equation will not separate the contributions of those two independent variables. Of course, other techniques allow one to assess the independence of the contributions, such as graphical techniques that simply plot out the effect of one variable at each level of the other. This latter kind of analysis, reported later in this chapter, shows clear evidence of the independence of word length and word frequency effects on the gaze duration of a word.

The use of regression analysis does not have as many problems as one might expect. For example, one might expect very large sequential dependencies among successive words, so that if one word takes a long time to process, one might expect a very long processing time on the next word, because of a spill-over in processing. But in fact, such spill-overs rarely occur. If a particular word in a text takes a long time to process by most subjects, the word that immediately follows generally does not take any extra time to process, as we will describe in more detail below.

The Interpretation of Regression Weights. The way a regression weight is interpreted depends on whether the theory specifies that the process operates concurrently with other processes or sequentially. If it is believed that two processes are executed sequentially, the interpretation of the regression weights is straightforward; the regression weight indicates the amount of extra processing time per stimulus unit. For example, a regression weight of 32 msec associated with word length is interpreted as an extra 32 msec of encoding time per letter. However, a regression weight is given a different interpretation if the underlying process is assumed to be executed concurrently with other processes. In that case, the regression weight indicates the increase (or decrease) in the total processing time when that process is executed; the weight does not indicate the total duration of the process. For example, if the regression weight for sentence-final words is 100 msec, we can infer that these words are associated with extra processing whose absolute duration is unknown but which extends 100 msec longer than the other concurrent processes.

The Moving Window Paradigm

Although eye fixation studies provide excellent measures of how long readers spend looking at each word, they require expensive instrumentation and experienced experimenters. To make this type of data more accessible to our laboratory and others, we have developed a new experimental paradigm that more economically provides information about processing time on each word (Just, Carpenter & Woolley, 1982). In the new paradigm, called the Moving Window, a reader presses a button to see each successive word in a text, and the previous word is removed when a new word appears. The reading time is simply the time interval during which a word is exposed. The words appear in the same position that they would in normal text. Before the word is presented, each letter is represented by a series of dashes, so that word-length information is available in peripheral vision. Thus, as the reader moves through the text, it is as though there were a moving window that allowed the reader to see the actual characters, rather than the dashes. The window, however, is not continuous, nor need it be a fixed size. It is defined in terms of some unit of the text, such as a word, phrase, or a mixture of words and phrases.

The Moving Window paradigm resembles normal reading in that it preserves the left-to-right motion of normal reading. Moreover, word length, punctuation, and location information are available in the parafovea and periphery. It differs from normal reading in two major respects. First, the reading rate is typically slower than in normal reading. With a single-word window, the rates we have obtained for college students reading scientific texts is 140 wpm compared to a normal rate of 240 wpm. This means that readers spent much longer on each word, 450 msec compared to an average of 330 msec on a fixated word in normal reading. The slower rate reflects the necessity of individually exposing and fixating each word, whereas in normal reading, a large proportion of short function words are not individually fixated (60%) and some content words (20%) are skipped as well. It may also reflect the fact that the timing and programming of the eye movements themselves is more automatic than is the timing and programming of the finger movements that are required in the Moving Window paradigm. A second difference is that in the Moving Window paradigm, readers cannot regress to previously read text, whereas they can and occasionally do regress in normal reading.

In one series of experiments, we compared the parameters obtained with the Moving Window paradigm - with a window size of one word - to those obtained with eye fixations (Just et al., 1982). The reading times on individual words in the moving window condition are highly correlated with gaze durations, although they are about 200 msec longer. Many of the properties of the text that affect gaze durations similarly affect these reading times. The regression weights are generally similarly reliable in both cases; however, there are some important differences. First, the word length and word frequency effects are decreased by a factor of two. In normal reading, the gaze duration increased 32 msec/letter and 33 msec/log frequency. In the Moving Window condition, the corresponding parameters were both 15 msec. However, almost all of the other effects are much larger in the Moving Window condition than in normal reading. In the Moving Window condition, readers spend much longer on novel words, on the first word of a line, on the last word of a sentence or paragraph, on the first mention of the topic, and on the first topic word. In addition, the intercept is much larger, presumably reflecting the non-automaticity of the button pressing and the necessity of exposing individual words. The same considerations probably account for the fact that word-level factors account for less of the variance in the Moving Window condition; the

R-squared is .79 for the gaze duration data and .56 for the Moving Window condition. Thus, the Moving Window implicates similar variables as are found in normal reading, but their quantitative characteristics are considerably changed. The usefulness of the paradigm is that it preserves the immediacy of processing using a methodology that is much more accessible than recording eye fixations.

In the same series of experiments, we explored two additional button-pressing paradigms. In one, called the Stationary Window, the words were individually exposed at the same location, a task that Aaronson and Scarborough (1976) used. This paradigm gave fairly similar results to that obtained in the Moving Window condition, although the individual parameters deviated even more from those obtained from gaze duration estimates. In another condition, called the Cumulative paradigm, the text was exposed a word-at-a-time, but earlier words continued to be available so that the text cumulated on the screen. The cumulative condition did not resemble the gaze duration data and was generally much less well-fit by the regression model. The most likely reason was that some readers repeatedly pressed the response button in a burst of button presses to obtain a group of words, which they then read. Thus the time between successive presses did not correspond closely to the processing time on individual words.

Several possible modifications may make the Moving Window paradigm more closely resemble normal reading. Earlier, we mentioned two major differences between normal reading and the Moving Window paradigm. The first is that in normal reading, only 40% of the function words and 80% of the content words tend to be fixated, whereas in the Moving Window paradigm we explored, each word was individually exposed and fixated. Of course, it is not necessary to present each word individually. In other experiments, we have exposed short function words, such as *a*, *the*, and *to*, with content words. This has the advantage of decreasing the number of individual button presses that the reader has to make to advance through the text, and making the distribution of fixations more closely resemble those in normal reading. It is an empirical question whether a function word should be presented with the preceding word or following word, or whether there is any consistent pattern in their perceptual processing. The function word is usually syntactically related to the following word (such as the article and the following noun phrase, the preposition and subsequent phrase, and the infinitive and subsequent verb), so that presenting it with the subsequent word maintains the phrase structure boundaries. However, there also is evidence that readers of left-to-right languages read to the right. That is, they process farther to the right of their point of fixation than to the left. Thus, readers may pick up short function words while fixating earlier words. There are currently no data to choose between the two positions.

A second modification of the paradigm would allow for regressions, perhaps by allowing the reader to display preceding words by pressing a different button. Such a modification, of course, would not allow regressions that skip several preceding words. Although we have not explored this particular modification, its usefulness most likely depends upon how much the text, instructions and reader's ability normally encourage regressions.

Linguistic Influences on Picture Scanning

While our major methodologies have focused on the temporal course of processing, we have explored one novel method for determining the content of a mental representation. This paradigm explores how a linguistic construction is represented by determining how it influences the way a subsequent picture is inspected. In this paradigm, the subject first reads a text, generally just one sentence, and then scans a picture to retrieve some information from it, perhaps to determine whether the sentence is true or false of the picture, or to answer a question posed by the sentence. The subject must have some a priori knowledge about the location of two or more elements in the picture. The preceding sentence treats the two elements differentially, and the experiment determines how the linguistic structure affects the inspection of the picture. An example of how we have used this paradigm will illustrate its usefulness. In our first use, we investigated how inherently negative quantifiers (such as *few* and *hardly any*) were represented, contrasting them with positive quantifiers (such as *a minority* or *most*) (Carpenter & Just, 1972). Subjects read a sentence (such as *Most of the dots are red.*) and verified it as true or false of an accompanying picture of two subsets of dots, a large subset and a small subset, each of the subsets being a different color. The subject knew *a priori* that the small subset was always at the top of the picture and the large subset at the bottom. When the quantifier referred to the large subset (e.g. *most*), subjects simply looked at the large subset, and when it referred to the small subset (e.g. *a minority*), they looked at the small subset. The interesting result occurred for quantifiers that are linguistically negative, such as *few*. The linguistic analysis of these negative quantifiers suggested that they might be mentally represented as a negation of some property of the large subset, such that *Few are red* might be represented, roughly, as (NEG (MANY RED)). The results confirmed this analysis. After reading such quantifiers, subjects tended to first inspect the large subset of dots. By contrast, superficially similar quantifiers that are linguistically affirmative (such as *a minority*) led to an initial inspection of the small subset. Thus the inspection of the picture indicated how a preceding sentence had been represented.

The paradigm has also been used to determine the focus of sentences like *It is John who is following Mary* to determine whether the subject initially scans the picture for the information that is marked as new or old by the sentence (Carpenter & Just, 1977). It has also been used to examine the time and stages in processing explicit negatives, such as *The plus is not North* (Carpenter & Just, 1976).

The general approach is to design a task that leaves the subject some interesting choice of sequence or duration of inspection, for example, the choice of where to fixate or how much time to spend. The task must not completely determine the duration or sequence. For example, it is not interesting to find that viewers look at the face of a person when asked to judge the person's age (Yarbus, 1967). On the other hand, the task must not be too unstructured, or subjects will not be systematic, and the processes will be determined by random and idiosyncratic characteristics of the subject and the display. The interesting property of this paradigm is its potential to reflect aspects of the content of the internal representation. One of its limitations is that in addition to the influence of the sentence, the picture and task also influence the viewer's inspection pattern. The success of the paradigm may depend upon minimizing the latter influences, and yet balancing these constraints to allow for interesting choices by the subject.

SUBSTANTIVE RESULTS

This section describes five main substantive results. The first is the immediacy of processing. The second concerns the detection of errors in the comprehension process and error recovery heuristics. The third result is the large word-level effects on gaze duration. The fourth is the wrap-up processing at the ends of sentences. The fifth is the finding that individuals' working memory capacity is strongly related to their reading ability.

Immediacy of Processing

Immediacy of processing refers to the fact that a reader (or listener) tries to interpret each word of a text as he encounters it, rather than waiting to make an interpretation until a number of words have been encountered (Just & Carpenter, 1980). "Interpret" refers to several levels of cognitive processing, such as encoding the word, accessing its meaning, assigning it to its referent, and determining its semantic and syntactic status in the sentence and the discourse. "Encounter" refers to the time when the cognitive system (not the visual system) first has access to the word. Although interpreting each word without knowing what will follow occasionally produces an incorrect interpretation, effective error recovery heuristics minimize the cost of a misinterpretation, as we will describe later. It is important to note that although the attempt at interpretation is immediate, the text can force postponement by withholding essential information. In such cases, the postponement is out of necessity rather than out of strategic choice. Immediacy stands in contrast to a strategy of collecting several words (in units we will refer to as *bins*) before processing any one of them. Even though the evidence we will present indicates that readers interpret immediately rather than using a binning strategy, we will describe two kinds of binning strategies that have been proposed, and that were quite plausible before the relevant data became available.

Suppose that three successive words of a text, A, B, and C, constitute one bin. Then a binning strategy (i.e. non-immediate interpretation) would have the interpretation of A wait until all three of the words were available to the cognitive system. One variant of a binning strategy is to interpret all of the bin's constituents when the bin is complete. For example, it has been suggested that clauses are the functional units (bins) in syntactic analysis and that syntactic and semantic analyses are postponed until the end of a clause is reached (Fodor, Bever, & Garrett, 1974). Binning the words of a clause before analyzing them is an instance of using a bin whose size varies with the length of the clause. This kind of bin is stationary, because the position of a given word in a bin never changes (e.g. the second word in the clause is always the second element of the bin). Another example of a variable size stationary bin is Kimball's (1973) scheme in which the syntactic interpretations of the successive words of a phrase are held in a buffer (bin) until the end of the phrase is reached, and at that time all the constituents of the phrase are shunted off for semantic processing.

A second kind of binning is exemplified by a "look ahead" strategy (Kimball, 1973; Marcus, 1980), in which readers look one or two words ahead before deciding the syntactic status of a given word. Looking N words ahead of the current word means using a moving bin of size $N + 1$. In a moving bin strategy, only some of the earliest constituents of the bin are interpreted, and then some new words are entered into the bin.

In contrast to binning strategies, immediate interpretation knows no bins, and starts the interpretation of A and continues it to completion (as far as possible) before B is considered. Several of the phenomena accounted for by binning strategies are accounted for slightly differently according to the immediacy principle. For example, the processing time is often longer on the last word of a sentence, and possibly on the last word of a clause. According to the immediacy principle, the extra processing time on the last word of a sentence is a phenomenon that emerges because important information is often unavailable before the end of a sentence, so in general, more processing occurs there. A binning strategy would attribute the effect to a strategic postponement of the processing until the end of the sentence is reached.

Another relevant phenomenon is that some words have a retroactive influence on the interpretation of preceding words. According to the immediacy principle, readers try to interpret each word as they encounter it, before knowing exactly what will follow. The fact that readers are sometimes surprised by what follows, as in *The old train the young*, indicates that an initial interpretation had already been made after encountering *train*. By contrast, a look-ahead strategy would never be led down the garden path by this sentence, because looking ahead just one word beyond *train* would indicate the correct interpretation. The immediacy principle does not deny the use of context that follows, but it proposes that interpretation is not invariably postponed until the succeeding context is known. For example, the extensive meaning of the adjective *large* cannot be computed without knowing what concept it modifies (e.g. *large insect* versus *large house*). A reader might have no choice but to wait until he reads the head of the noun phrase to know what *large* modifies, in which case the extensive interpretation would have to be postponed. But very often a reader can guess the referent on the basis of the previous context. If a passage repeatedly referred to a *large house*, even the extensive meaning might be computed immediately on fixating the word *large*. The immediacy principle requires that the interpretation of the current word be computed as soon as possible, rather than routinely waiting until all possibly relevant information from succeeding words has been collected.

Bouma and deVoogd (1974) have argued for both perceptual and cognitive bins on the grounds of empirical evidence they have collected. They found that readers' self-reported ability to comprehend a text was unaffected by a wide range of variation in the spatial and temporal arrangement of the words. They presented a few words of a text at a time, varying both the number of words per display and the duration of the display. Readers reported being able to read the text under a variety of conditions, so Bouma and deVoogd concluded that the processing was impervious to the temporal distribution of the input because the words were being buffered before being cognitively processed. One binning mechanism might be an iconic store that allows the cognitive system to lag behind the perceptual system by about two words. Another binning mechanism might be a store in which activated word meanings are held until a lagging syntactic or semantic analysis operates on them. However, before one can conclude that processing is impervious to the pacing of the input, it is necessary to determine that the text has been understood similarly across conditions. Although the readers in this experiment reported being able to comprehend the text, there was no careful assessment of exactly what they understood. In fact, readers said they were unable to read under these conditions if they expected a comprehension test at the conclusion of the reading. This suggests that the comprehension was unusual, at best, and grossly below normal, at worst. Thus, the critical criterion of demonstrating analogous levels of comprehension across different conditions was not satisfied in this experiment.

The immediacy of the effects in our data (i.e. the gaze duration response occurs on the very word that provides the stimulus) suggests that mandatory binning does not occur. Interpretive processes of many levels occur as soon as they are enabled. Lower level processes are usually enabled as soon as the word is encoded. However, the point at which higher level integrative processes are enabled is unpredictable. But if the higher level processes are possible to execute immediately (i.e. without the benefit of information to follow), then they *are* executed immediately. This finding clearly shows that binning is not mandatory or fixed.

What the various bin theories have failed to recognize is that in naturalistic language use the interpretation of a word can extremely often be computed immediately. By focusing on sentences out of context, these theories have failed to appreciate that the semantic and pragmatic context, plus biases constructed over years of a person's language use make the reader's interpretations correct much more often than incorrect. By focusing on infrequent sentence types, they have failed to discover the strategy of immediate interpretation that succeeds on an overwhelming proportion of the sentences that people actually process outside of the laboratory.

The Eye-Mind Assumption

This assumption posits that the interpretation of a word occurs while that word is being fixated, and that the eye remains fixated on that word until the processing has been completed to some criterion. So the time it takes to process a newly-fixated word is directly indicated by the gaze duration. Of course, interpreting a word often involves the use of information from preceding parts of the text, without any backward fixations. So during any given fixation, a reader may be considering previous words as well as the current word. Although the immediacy of interpretation and the eye-mind assumption are somewhat related, they can be distinguished. The eye-mind assumption is specific to the visual modality, posits a lack of delay between the perceptual and cognitive systems, and presupposes immediacy of interpretation. After all, if the processing of a word occurs while the word is being fixated, and before the next word is considered, then interpretation must be immediate. If the eye-mind assumption is true, then the immediacy must be in effect. But it is possible for the eye-mind assumption to not hold (or to be inapplicable, as in listening comprehension), and the immediacy strategy could still be used. For example, if there were a constant eye-mind lag of two words caused by a fixed transmission delay between the visual and the cognitive systems, the representation of each word could still be interpreted immediately as it is encountered by the cognitive system. But in fact there is no such lag, and both immediacy and the eye-mind assumption apply in reading.

Evidence for Immediacy and Eye-Mind. The clearest support for immediacy and the eye-mind assumption is the copious evidence that the time spent looking at a word is strongly influenced by the characteristics of that word (e.g., Just & Carpenter, 1980). Evidence for immediacy has been obtained for several levels of processing, such as the lexical (Just & Carpenter, 1980), syntactic (McDonald & Carpenter, 1981), and text levels (Dee-Lucas et al, 1982). That is, an increase in the processing demands at each of these levels introduced by a given word produces an increased gaze duration on that word.

Additional tests of immediacy and eye-mind can be made by determining whether the gaze duration on a given word is influenced by the characteristics of the preceding word. If the eye were exactly one word ahead of the mind, then the semantic processing of word $N-1$ would occur during the gaze on word N, and the duration should be a function of the properties of word $N-1$. Not in all cases are both word N and $N-1$ fixated, so two separate cases were considered. In one regression analysis, the dependent variable was the mean gaze duration on word N, given that the reader fixated both word $N-1$ and word N. In another analysis, the dependent variable was the mean gaze duration on word N given that the reader fixated word N but skipped word $N-1$. In each case, three regression analyses were run, differing in the independent variables: (1) the length and frequency of only word N, (2) both the length and frequency of word N and of word $N-1$, and (3) the length and frequency of only word $N-1$. Length and frequency were used as independent variables because their large effects should be detected easily. The data-base was from Just & Carpenter (1980) and was restricted to words that did not begin or end a line or a sentence, since such words tend to be processed differently (Just & Carpenter, 1980; Rayner, 1977, 1979).

The major result, shown in Table 1, is that the gaze duration on word N is not affected by the length or frequency of the preceding word. The account of the variance in gaze durations on word N is not significantly improved by considering the characteristics of word $N-1$. This result holds regardless of whether the reader did or did not fixate word $N-1$. These results suggest that the reader generally has finished encoding and accessing the preceding word before fixating the next. This finding provides strong support for the eye-mind assumption and for immediacy of interpretation.

A similar analysis shows that the mind is not processing the word to the right of the fixated word, as a look-ahead strategy based on peripheral encoding might suggest. If the reader usually semantically processed word $N+1$ while fixating word N, the length and frequency of word $N+1$ should influence the time on word N. Again, two cases were analyzed separately, those cases in which the readers fixated both word N and $N+1$, and those in which they fixated word N and skipped word $N+1$. As Table 1 shows, the length and frequency of word $N+1$ have no appreciable effect on the gaze duration on word N, even when word $N+1$ is skipped. This result indicates that readers usually do not encode and lexically access words to the right of the word that they are fixating, suggesting that the span of semantic processing is fairly small.

Error Recovery Heuristics

One consequence of immediate interpretation is that it will occasionally turn out to be incorrect and will have to be revised. We have found that readers detect

TABLE 1
Variance in the Conditionalized Mean Gaze
Duration on Word N Accounted for by Regression

Independent Variables: Length and Frequency of	Reader Fixated Word $N-1$	Reader Didn't Fixate Word $N-1$
1) Word N	23.8%	25.1%
2) Word N and $N-1$	24.0%	25.6%
3) Word $N-1$	0.4%	0.2%
	Reader Fixated Word $N+1$	Reader Didn't Fixate Word $N+1$
1) Word N	24.2%	18.1%
2) Word N and $N+1$	24.7%	19.9%
3) Word $N+1$	0.4%	0.5%

syntactic and semantic anomalies on the first inconsistent word, as the immediacy principle predicts. After detecting an anomaly, the reader needs effective error recovery procedures to "fix" an interpretation. This section describes the paradigm we have used to explore both how errors in interpretation are detected, and how they are repaired.

Semantic Anomalies. The experimental paradigm involves the use of "garden path" passages, in which the initial context strongly primes one interpretation of an ambiguous word or phrase, but the subsequent text is inconsistent with that interpretation. The following passage gives such an example (Carpenter & Daneman, 1981):

> The young man turned his back on the rock concert stage and looked across the resort lake. Tomorrow was the annual, one-day fishing contest and fishermen would invade the place. Some of the best bass guitarists in the country would come to this spot. The usual routine of the fishing resort would be disrupted by the festivities.

If asked to read this passage aloud, most people initially give *bass* in line 3 the pronunciation corresponding to the "fish" meaning, the meaning primed by the earlier references to fishing. But the "fish" interpretation is inconsistent with the subsequent disambiguating word, *guitarists*, and a resolution requires the reinterpretation of *bass* to mean "low music register". These processes, the initial interpretation, the detection of the inconsistency, and its resolution, can be seen in a reader's pattern of eye fixations. To assess the effects, we compared readers in the garden path condition to a condition in which readers initially interpreted *bass* as "low music register", an interpretation that is consistent with *guitarist* and consequently requires no error detection or recovery. Detecting the inconsistency and attempting to recover took extra processing time and was reflected in longer gazes on the inconsistent word or phrase, and more regressions to the previous ambiguous word and to the inconsistent phrase itself.

The Mind-Voice Lag. Oral reading protocols, coordinated to the eye fixations, demonstrate that there is a delay between the voice and the comprehension processes, but very little delay between the eye and the comprehension processes. The voice lags behind the eye, giving rise to an eye-voice span. However, the error detection does not have to wait until the inconsistency is verbalized; the reader typically detects the inconsistency when he fixates the first word that is inconsistent. Thus the eye and mind are close together in time, while the voice lags behind both of them.

Relative Frequency and Priming. The relative frequencies of the two interpretations of an ambiguous word influenced both the initial interpretation of the ambiguous word and the subsequent error recovery process. One set of ambiguous words, like *bass, bow, wind*, have interpretations that are both relatively frequent.

The reader's pronunciation of these words indicated that they usually were interpreted in a way that was consistent with the prior context. Another set of ambiguous words, like *sewer, minute, buffet*, and *row*, have one interpretation that is very infrequent. The infrequent meaning was seldom produced, even when it was strongly primed. The fact that the very infrequent meanings are seldom chosen reflects the strong bias that readers have towards common interpretations; even context effects cannot entirely compensate for this bias. This result suggests that context may play a different role in helping to select one interpretation of a polysemous word, depending on whether or not the various interpretations are approximately equally likely. If the two meanings have similar frequencies, both meanings may be retrieved, with context selecting the more appropriate one (Swinney, 1979). But if the two meanings have very different frequencies, the less common meaning may not be retrieved and a strong context is necessary to bring it to threshold (see also Simpson, 1981).

Error Recovery Patterns. The patterns of eye fixations suggested that in recovering from an inconsistency, readers focused on words or phrases that have caused difficulty initially. They did not reread the sentence from the beginning, nor did they go backward from the inconsistency. The error recovery process was more guided and economical.

This guidance was most apparent in cases in which the incorrectly rejected interpretation was very infrequent, such as in the case of *sewer, minute, buffet, tears and row*. For half of the readers, the context that preceded the ambiguous word primed the more common interpretation. For example, the *sewer* passage described the good and bad qualities of a neighborhood. For one group, a context sentence primed the "drain" meaning of *sewer* by mentioning that there was a very bad smell. For the other group, the context primed the infrequent interpretation of *sewer* by mentioning that there were lots of tailors in local shops. Either context sentence was followed by the target sentence: *There is also one sewer near our home who makes terrific suits.*

Readers in both groups tended to initially interpret *sewer* as "drain". However, the effect of the prime was apparent in the time spent on the ambiguous word. Readers who had the "tailor" prime spent more time on the ambiguous word, presumably because the more available "drain" interpretation acts like a new topic. By contrast, readers who had the "drain" context sentence had less difficulty interpreting and integrating the "drain" interpretation of *sewer*.

Interestingly, it was readers who had the "tailor" prime who were more likely to recover the correct, but infrequent "tailor" meaning of *sewer* after encountering an inconsistency, ... *who makes terrific suits.* (Recovery was assessed from their oral reading and by questions asked after the passage was read, such as "Who made terrific suits?"). The eye fixation protocol shows that these readers spent more time on *sewer* after the disambiguation. The readers who had less trouble initially accessing and integrating *sewer*, because they had been primed to interpret it as "drain", spent less time on *sewer* after encountering the inconsistency, spent more time on the disambiguating phrase, and were less likely to recover. This suggests that error recovery processes focus on places that contain a trace of earlier difficulties.

Parsing Ambiguous Phrases

Immediacy not only characterizes the detection of anomalies, it also characterizes the process of parsing words at their constituent boundaries. The detection of boundaries depends in part on the ability to find a referent for the candidate constituent. This decision, in turn, seems to be made on-line, rather than waiting for the ends of sentences. This point is illustrated very clearly in a study that examined parsing processes in a translation task (McDonald & Carpenter, 1981). Bilingual translators read passages in English and translated them into spoken German as quickly as possible as they read. Embedded in the passages were idioms such as *kick the bucket* and *hit the nail right on the head*. Such phrases are of interest because they have different parsings and different interpretations depending on whether they are used idiomatically or literally. When interpreted idiomatically, each such phrase is a single constituent; when interpreted literally, each phrase has more than one constituent, such as *(((hit) (the nail)) (right (on (the (head)))))*. We constructed passages that primed either one interpretation or the other, and found that translators produced very different patterns of eye fixations in the two cases, reflecting the different constituent boundaries of the two types of interpretations. Translators visually scanned each major constituent of a sentence twice. During the first pass, which presumably reflected English comprehension, the translators read at normal speed and paused at the constituent boundary. Then, the gaze returned to the beginning of the constituent for a second, much slower pass during which the translator output the German equivalent. The place at which the translator stopped between the first and second passes indicated how he or she parsed a segment of text.

A typical passage, one that primed a literal translation of *hit the nail right on the head*, described a man, David, who was having problems building a bookshelf and asked his friend, Mike, to help him: *Mike picked up the hammer to show David some basic woodworking techniques. Mike hit the nail right on the head . . .* During the first pass, the translators scanned to the end of *Mike hit the nail*, stopped, and returned to the beginning of the sentence to translate it. They parsed this as a clause. However, when the context primed an idiomatic meaning, the individual words did not have plausible literal referents. In those cases, the translators did not stop and translate idioms at an internal phrase boundary; they continued until they reached the end of the idiom. The differential parsing pattern reflected in the eye fixations predicted whether the oral translation would be literal or idiomatic. The study suggests that the interpretation of such ambiguous phrases is determined as the phrase is read, as part of the reader's attempt to integrate the currently processed information with the preceding representation.

Large Effects of Lexical Processing on Gaze Duration

The analysis of gaze durations has uncovered a number of lexical-level effects that reflect encoding and lexical access mechanisms, as well as lexical-level inferences. In fact, most of the variance in the gaze durations across the words of a passage seems to be accounted for by processes that operate at the lexical level such as the processes that recognize word forms (word recognition) and look up their meanings in an internal lexicon (lexical access). This is not to say that higher levels of processing, such as the syntactic or text level cannot have a large effect on a given word or group of words. But overall, these other levels produce either a smaller or less variable effect on the gaze duration. After describing the various word-level effects, we will consider their relative "importance".

Word Length. One very striking result from the analysis of the reading times is that gaze duration increased linearly with word length, whether length was measured in number of letters or number of syllables. Figure 2 shows both the mean gaze duration and the conditionalized mean gaze duration on a word as a function of its length (measured in number of characters) and the logarithm of its normative frequency. The data base is from Just & Carpenter (1980). The number of letters accounted for more of the variance than did number of syllables. The word length effects are extremely robust. Not only have they been found with these scientific texts, but similar effects were found in another study involving long narratives (2,000 words) taken from *Reader's Digest* and long expository passages from *Scientific American* (Just, Carpenter & Masson, 1981). Some very short and frequent words, like *the* and *and* might be coded as a single chunk; but overall, frequency has effects that are independent of length.

Word Frequency. As Figure 2 illustrates, over the entire range of lengths, less frequent words were fixated for a longer duration. This was true for both the unconditionalized and conditionalized gaze duration. The effect followed a log function; that is, small differences among infrequent words had comparable effects to large differences among frequent words. The effect of frequency, like that of word length, is robust. A very similar function was found in the Moving Window paradigm described earlier and in an eye fixation experiment with long narrative and expository texts.

Novel Words. Some words in the scientific passages, such as *staphylococci* and *thermoluminescence*, were probably entirely new to the readers. These words were fixated for an especially long time, 802 msec beyond what would be predicted by their infrequency and their length. We hypothesized that when such a word is

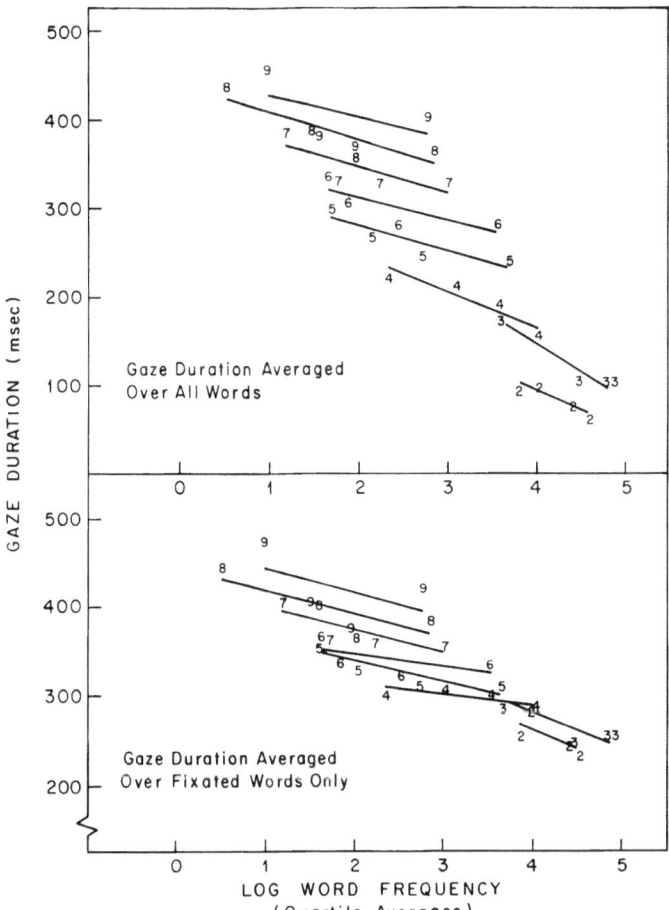

FIG. 2. (a.) The mean gaze duration on a word as a function of the logarithm of its frequency and its length in number of characters (the parameter on the curves). Each point represents the mean of a quartile of the words of that length. (b.) The same function except that the dependent measure is the conditionalized mean gaze duration. (From Thibadeau, R., Just, M. A., & Carpenter, P. A. A model of the time course and content of human reading. Pittsburgh, PA.: Carnegie-Mellon University, 1981.)

encountered, the reader tries to infer its meaning and construct a dictionary entry with information that includes its orthographic, phonological, syntactic, and semantic properties (as far as they can be determined). This entry will help the reader identify the word if it is encountered again later in the text, and the entry will aid the reader in later recalling the word.

Size of the Lexical Effects. Word length and frequency account for a relatively high proportion of the variation in the mean gaze duration on words. In the experiment involving scientific texts, the two variables alone account for 69% of the variance, the other variables alone account for 37%, and all 11 variables together account for 79%. The other variables coded whether the word introduced a topic, began a line, was at the end of a sentence or paragraph, was totally new, was a digit, a modified noun, an inferrable function word, or the first content word in the passage. For the conditionalized mean gaze duration, length and frequency alone account for 40%, the other nine variables alone account for 39%, and all 11 variables account for 60%. (The variances accounted for are not additive because some variables are intercorrelated).

This does not mean that one or the other process is more important or central, but merely that the word-level processes control more of the systematic variability in word gaze durations. This statement would have to be modified if some alternative account (other than the ones we have tried) of the higher levels accounted for more of the variance. But as a first approximation, our analyses suggest that word recognition and lexical access are the main determinants of word gaze durations.

There is a temptation to equate proportion of variance accounted for by a variable with the theoretical importance of the underlying process, but such an inference is unwarranted for at least three reasons (see Sechrest and Yeaton, 1979, for a discussion of "effect size" issues). First, the variance accounted for by a factor is not an inherent property of the factor; it depends on the variation of that factor relative to other factors in the task. The current texts involved words of widely varying lengths and frequencies. If a text were constructed of words of a small range of lengths and frequencies, then word length and frequency would account for a much lower proportion of the variance. Second, these variables may account for a relatively high proportion of the variance because we know how to measure them; as the metrics improve for describing higher level factors, they may account for more of the variance. Finally, it is clear that encoding and accessing words are not sufficient processes for reading; it is also necessary to interrelate concepts to form the meanings of phrases, clauses, sentences, the text, and the referential domain. So these higher level processes must be occurring, even if they are not making large contributions to the variance in word gaze durations.

In spite of these caveats, there is a theoretically interesting implication of the finding that length and frequency effects are generally more robust than the effects of the other variables. The processes influenced by length and frequency appear to be more uniform across readers and texts; a given word is encoded and accessed relatively similarly by all readers. In contrast, the higher level processes may be more variable across readers in several aspects, such as their time of enablement, their duration, and their content. One way to make the variance due to higher level processes more systematic is to experimentally manipulate when the higher level process is executed or to make it especially difficult, so that almost every reader will take extra time at the same place. The studies of error detection and recovery are examples of this approach.

End of Sentence Processing

While it is clear that readers attempt to interpret words as they are encountered, there also is evidence that some processes are executed at ends of sentences. We have labeled this the sentence wrap-up effect. One source of evidence came from a study in which the texts involved verb-based inferences (Just & Carpenter, 1978). For example, one set of readers received a text that described the discovery of the body of a millionaire who had *died*. Another group read that he had been *killed*. Both groups read a later sentence that described the search for *the murderer*. The first group of readers took longer to read the sentence involving *murderer*, because they had to make a more difficult inference to relate *died* and *murderer*. Part of the longer reading time for the later sentence was localized to the word *murderer* itself, agreeing with the immediacy principle. However, part of the extra reading time was spent at the end of the sentence. End of sentence effects were also evident in the processing of garden path sentences with ambiguous words like *sewer* and *bass* (Carpenter & Daneman, 1981). Readers sometimes initiated regressions after the first inconsistent word, but at other times, not until the end of the sentence. In some instances, they may have expected that the rest of the sentence would resolve the difficulty. We also found end of sentence effects in the scientific passages (Just & Carpenter, 1980). Finally, end of sentence effects were found in a study involving narrative texts, but only in those sentences that involved a switch in surface topic from the preceding sentence (Dee-Lucas et al., in press).

All evidence cited above for wrap-up processes at ends of sentences has come from correlational studies, in which the effects of other variables such as normative word frequency and word length were statistically controlled using multiple linear regression. Recently, we have also assessed end of sentence effects in an experimental study (Daneman & Carpenter, in press). The experiment used texts that were identical up to the sentence boundary. For example, one text was *He found a bat. It was very large and...* and the comparison text was *He found a bat that was very large and...* In one set of conditions, the target word was ambiguous (such as *bat*); in another set of texts, the target was an unambiguous control word, but one that constituted a topic switch (like *bird*). The sentences were presented word by word in the Moving Window paradigm described earlier. There was a significant increase in the time on a word that occurred at the end of a sentence, compared to the time on the same word when it was not sentence terminal. The size of the effect was between 150 to 200 msec in the silent and oral reading conditions, respectively. Thus, sentence wrap-up effects can be relatively large.

End of sentence effects appear to occur if a sentence contains an extra processing burden. In the scientific passages, the additional processing was caused by the large proportion of novel and important concepts. In the narrative passages, additional processing was required when a sentence introduced a new topic. In the garden path experiments, the extra processing was caused by the ambiguity and the error recovery. By contrast, we have examined other texts and tasks in which readers do not spend extra time at the end of sentences. The texts had a relatively low proportion of novel concepts and described very predictable events (Just, et al., 1981). This contrast suggests that ends of sentences themselves do not necessarily require additional processes and that they may only be places to finish up integrative processes that could not be completed in mid-sentence. Furthermore, task requirements and individual differences in functional working memory capacity may also affect the probability of some wrap-up processes being held over until the end of the sentence.

Individual Differences

Recently, we have explored how individual differences in reading skill interact with the text to determine whether a reader recovers from a misinterpretation (Daneman & Carpenter, 1980, in press). Our proposal is that the functional capacity of working memory plays an important role in reading comprehension performance. Traditional tests of short-term memory, such as digit span and word span tests, do not correlate with reading comprehension performance. The reason for the low correlation may be that such tests are primarily tests of passive storage capacity. For example, in a digit span test, the subject must recognize and encode very familiar digits and try to maintain some record of their order of occurrence. This traditional test reflects a view of short-term memory as primarily a storage place with a fixed number of slots, with the number varying among individuals. In contrast, current conceptions of working memory view it as having both processes and storage components (Baddeley & Hitch, 1974; Hunt, 1978). What is needed to test the proposal regarding functional capacity was a task that requires more taxing processes, especially processes that are related to reading itself. We developed a reading span test that includes both processing and storage components (Daneman & Carpenter, 1980). In the test, the subject reads a set of sentences and, at the end of the set, recalls the final word of each sentence. The subject's reading span is the number of sentences for which he or she can successfully recall the final words. We have found that among college students, the range of reading spans is usually 2 - 5.5 sentences. Unlike the traditional digit span and word span tests, reading span does correlate with global reading comprehension test scores; a correlation typically lies between .45 and .6. The correlation between reading span and comprehension is even higher (.7 to .9) when the comprehension test taps specific comprehension abilities, such as the ability to answer a question about a fact mentioned in the passage or the ability to relate a pronoun to a distant prior referent.

Reading span also correlates with the ability to recover from inconsistencies in garden path passages. Readers with low spans recover less often than do readers with intermediate or high spans. Poorer readers have particular difficulty if a sentence boundary intervenes between the ambiguous word and the subsequent inconsistency. For example, these poorer readers have more difficulty with *There is also one sewer near our home. He makes terrific suits.* than with *There is also one sewer near our home who makes terrific suits.* The explanation is that ends of sentences are often places where readers do additional wrap-up processes that may tax working memory and purge it of at least part of the verbatim representation (Jarvella, 1971; Just & Carpenter, 1980). The processing of a sentence boundary taxes the readers with a small working-memory capacity, making it less likely that they recover from an inconsistency whose resolution requires information from a preceding sentence.

CONCLUSION

We conclude by mentioning some new directions in which we have been applying the eye fixation methodology. We have begun exploring how readers with specific reading characteristics, such as dyslexics or trained speed readers, differ from normal readers. Using the reading eye fixation paradigm, we have been able to specify which particular processes differentiate these readers from normal readers. We have also examined reading of Chinese, a language whose structure and orthography is very different from English. And we have explored several nonlinguistic tasks, in which people solve visually presented problems, and we use their eye fixation behavior as a trace of the problem-solving process. It is plausible that computer-based eye-trackers will soon become no more expensive than the tachistocopes of yesterday, and there will be an eye-tracker in every cognitive laboratory. At that point, the only possible bottleneck will be a lack of scientific ingenuity.

ACKNOWLEDGMENT

This research was partially supported by grant MH-29617 from the National Institute of Mental Health. The chapter was written while the authors were Fellows at the Netherlands Institute for Advanced Study.

Meredyth Daneman, Diana Dee-Lucas, Janet McDonald and Robert Thibadeau collaborated in many aspects of the research reported here and their contributions are gratefully acknowledged.

REFERENCES

Aaronson, D., & Scarborough, H. S. Performance theories for sentence coding: Some quantitative evidence. *Journal of Experimental Psychology: Human Perception and Performance*, 1976, 2, 56-70.
Baddeley, A. D., & Hitch, G. Working memory. In G. H. Bower (Ed.) *The psychology of learning and motivation* (Vol. 8). New York: Academic Press, 1974.

Bouma, H. Visual search and reading: Eye movements and functional visual field: A tutorial review. In J. Requin (Ed.), *Attention and performance VII*. Hillsdale, N. J.: Lawrence Erlbaum Associates, 1978.

Bouma, H., & deVoogd, A. H. On the control of eye saccades in reading. *Vision Research*, 1974, *14*, 273-284.

Carpenter, P. A. & Daneman, M. Lexical retrieval and error recovery in reading: A model based on eye fixations. *Journal of Verbal Learning and Verbal Behavior*, 1981, *20*, 137-160.

Carpenter, P. A., & Just, M. A. Reading comprehension as eyes see it. In M. A. Just & P. A. Carpenter (Eds.), *Cognitive processes in comprehension*. Hillsdale, N. J.: Lawrence Erlbaum Associates, 1977.

Carpenter, P. A., & Just, M. A. Eye fixations during mental rotation. In J. W. Senders, D. F. Fisher & R. A. Monty (Eds.), *Eye movements and the higher psychological functions*. Hillsdale, N. J.: Lawrence Erlbaum Associates, 1978.

Carpenter, P. A., & Just, M. A. Integrative processes in comprehension. In D. LaBerge & S. J. Samuels (Eds.), *Basic processes in reading: Perception and comprehension*. Hillsdale, N. J.: Lawrence Erlbaum Associates, 1977.

Carpenter, P. A., & Just, M. A. Linguistic influences on picture scanning. In J. Senders & R. Monty (Eds.), *Eye movements and psychological processes*. Hillsdale, N. J.: Lawrence Erlbaum Associates, 1976.

Carpenter, P. A., & Just, M. A. Semantic control of eye movements during picture scanning in a sentence-picture verification task. *Perception & Psychophysics*, 1972, *12*, 61-64.

Daneman, M., & Carpenter, P. A. Individual differences in integrating information between and within sentences. *Journal of Experimental Psychology: Learning, Memory and Cognition*, in press.

Daneman, M., & Carpenter, P. A. Individual differences in working memory and reading. *Journal of Verbal Learning and Verbal Behavior*, 1980, *19*, 450-466.

Dee-Lucas, D., Just, M. A., Carpenter, P. A., & Daneman, M. What eye fixations tell us about the time course of text integration. In R. Groner, & P. Fraisse (Eds.), *Cognition and eye movements*. Amsterdam: North Holland and Berlin: Deutscher Verlag der Wissenschaften, in press.

Fodor, J. A., Bever, T. G., & Garrett, M. F. *The psychology of language: An introduction to psycholinguistics and generative grammar*. New York: McGraw-Hill Co., 1974.

Hunt, E. Mechanics of verbal ability. *Psychological Review*, 1978, *85*, 109-130.

Jarvella, R. J. Syntactic processing of connected speech. *Journal of Verbal Learning and Verbal Behavior*, 1971, *10*, 409-416.

Just, M. A., & Carpenter, P. A. Inference processes during reading: Reflections from eye fixations. In J. W. Senders, D. F. Fisher, & R. A. Monty (Eds.), *Eye movements and the higher psychological functions*. Hillsdale, N. J.: Lawrence Erlbaum Associates, 1978.

Just, M. A. & Carpenter, P. A. A theory of reading: From eye fixations to comprehension. *Psychological Review*, 1980, *87*, 329-354.

Just, M. A., Carpenter, P. A., & Masson, M. Eye fixations and cognitive processing during rapid reading. Pittsburgh, PA: Carnegie-Mellon University, 1981.

Just, M. A., Carpenter, P. A., & Woolley, J. D. Paradigms and processes in reading comprehension. *Journal of Experimental Psychology: General*, 1982, *111*, 228-238.

Kimball, J. P. Seven principles of surface structure parsing in natural language. *Cognition*, 1973, *2*, 15-47.

Macworth, N. H. Visual noise causes tunnel vision. *Psychonomic Science*, 1965, *3*, 67-68.

Marcus, M. P. *A theory of syntactic recognition for natural language*. Cambridge, MA: The MIT Press, 1980.

McDonald, J. L., & Carpenter, P. A. Simultaneous translation: Idiom interpretation and parsing heuristics. *Journal of Verbal Learning and Verbal Behavior*, 1981, *20*, 231-247.

McConkie, G. W., & Rayner, K. Asymmetry of the perceptual span in reading. *Bulletin of the Psychonomic Society*, 1976, *8*, 365-368.

McConkie, G. W., Zola, D., Blanchard, H. E., & Wolverton, G. S. Perceiving words during reading: Lack of facilitation from prior peripheral exposure. Champaign, ILL.: University of Illinois, 1982.

Rayner, K. The perceptual span and peripheral cues in reading. *Cognitive Psychology*, 1975, *7*, 65-81.
Rayner, K. Visual attention in reading: Eye movements reflect cognitive processes. *Memory and Cognition*, 1977, *5*, 443-448.
Rayner, K. Eye movements in reading: Eye guidance and integration. In P. A. Kolers, M. E. Wrolstad. & H. Bouma (Eds.), *Processing of visible language* (Vol. 1), New York: Plenum Press, 1979.
Sechrest, L., & Yeaton, W. E. Estimating magnitudes of experimental effects. Unpublished manuscript, Florida State University, 1979.
Simpson, G. B. Meaning dominance and semantic context in the processing of lexical ambiguity. *Journal of Verbal Learning and Verbal Behavior*, 1981, *20*, 120-136.
Swinney, D. A. Lexical access during sentence comprehension: (Re) consideration of context effects. *Journal of Verbal Learning and Verbal Behavior*, 1979, *18*, 645-659.
Tinker, M. Fixation pause duration in reading. *Journal of Educational Research*, 1951, *44*, 471-479.
Yarbus, A. L. *Eye movements and vision*. New York: Plenum Press, 1967.

APPENDIX

Description of the Eye Tracker

The eye tracker we use (Applied Science Laboratories Model 1998, processor-based system with a head-tracking mirror) was purchased in 1977 and integrated into a fully operational laboratory by 1978. The system has three main components. The first component is a sensor, a video camera fitted with a sensitive vidicon tube that is focused on one of the subject's eyes. The eye is illuminated by a low intensity infra-red light source that is co-axial with the camera lens, and the light that is reflected from the cornea and pupil is registered by the video camera. The second main component is an electronic device that pre-processes the signal produced by the camera, converts it into a digital format, and recognizes the outline of the pupil and the corneal reflex. The third component is a fast minicomputer (Computer Automation LSI 2/20) that uses the digital representation of the video image to compute the subject's point of regard. In addition to these three components of the eye tracker, a laboratory computer (a PDP 11/04) collects the eye fixation data from the tracker and stores it. In addition, the PDP 11 controls the stimulus display, using a video character generator (and graphics controller) that can display 22 rows of 80 characters. The entire system operates at 60 Hz, with one master video synchronization pulse, such that the sensor camera produces 60 fields per second, the tracker computes the point of regard on each of the fields, and communicates the data (in the form of an X and Y coordinate) to the PDP 11.

The eye tracker relates the position of the pupil and the corneal reflex to a particular point of regard. If a person's head is fixed in one position, and he moves his eyes around to look at various places, then the corneal reflection of a fixed light source will move around in monotonic relation to the fixated points in space. The minicomputer's program contains a function that maps from corneal reflex positions to points of regard. This function was developed by the manufacturer in a generalized form, with specific parameters computed for each subject. These parameters are obtained during a brief calibration procedure, by having the program note the position of the corneal reflex as the subject is asked to fixate nine pre-defined locations distributed across the viewing field.

Head movements as well as eye movements can cause a change in position of the corneal reflex. Consequently, the tracker must use a second reference point to distinguish between the two types of movement. The second reference point is provided by the position of the pupil (actually, the center of the pupil) which indicates head movements. The program uses these two reference points to determine the point of regard even if the subject moves his head. The tracker allows head movement within about 1 square inch, beyond which the pupil falls outside of the viewing field of the camera. The allowable head movement is increased considerably (to about 36 square inches) by a servo-controlled mirror through which the camera views the eye. Whenever the program detects the pupil moving across a boundary of the camera's viewing field, it re-positions the mirror to re-center the pupil in the field.

The system is accurate to about 1 degree of visual angle in the horizontal axis (approximately the width of three characters) and about 1.5 degrees in the vertical (approximately 1.5 times the height of each character). Because the vertical accuracy is not quite sufficient to distinguish fixations on adjacent lines of the display, the text is displayed on every second line. The visual angle of the print is roughly similar to common reading situations. A videotape recording is usually made of the text with superimposed cross-hairs indicating the point of regard. The reader sits in an armchair with a headrest, sometimes using an elasticized head band to reduce head movements during reading.

9 An Application of Multiple Regression Techniques to Sentence Reading Times

Arthur C. Graesser
California State University, Fullerton
and
James R. Riha
Claremont Graduate School

In this chapter we will demonstrate how multiple regression techniques can be used to analyze reading times for sentences in passages. We will examine the extent to which sentence reading times can be predicted by a large number of predictor variables, which are properties of words, sentences, and passages. We will also examine the extent to which readers' comprehension scores be predicted by the readers' allocation of processing resources to various units, components, and dimensions of text during reading. It is beyond the scope of this chapter to discuss all the assumptions, virtues, and limitations of multiple regression techniques. Some of this information is provided in Knight (this volume). Our primary goal is to discuss some of our discoveries, problems, and solutions when we applied multiple regression techniques to reading times.

OVERVIEW OF METHODOLOGY

This section will present an example study in some detail. We will discuss issues and problems in applying multiple regression, in addition to reporting some substantive results that can be obtained.

Our method of collecting sentence reading times is very straightforward. Individuals read sentences in passages, one sentence at a time. As each sentence is presented on a display scope, the reader pushes a button when finished reading the sentence. The sentence reading times are critical data that we want to explain. Why do some sentences take longer to read than others? Multiple regression analyses permitted us to examine the extent to which several variables predict sentence reading times.

The regression equation is one of the informative products of a multiple regression analysis. In our application, the regression equation generates a set of predicted sentence reading times that optimally match the obtained reading times. There is a slope coefficient for each predictor variable in the regression equation. We were particularly interested in these slope coefficients because they estimate the processing time that is uniquely associated with specific predictor variables. Multiple regression analyses were also performed on the reading times of individual readers, resulting in a profile of slope coefficients for each reader. We could ultimately compare the profiles of different readers.

Most researchers believe that comprehension is somehow related to the way readers allocate their cognitive resources to different text components during reading. At this point in the science, however, researchers understand very little about the relationship between resource allocation and comprehension (see Reynolds & Anderson, 1981). In order to investigate this relationship, we administered a comprehension test on the passages after the subjects read them. The readers' comprehension scores were ultimately correlated with the slope coefficients of the reading time regression equations. These analyses provided some informative clues as to why some readers have poor comprehension of what they read. Thus, the profile of slope coefficients for individual readers are useful in the sense that they can predict and diagnose comprehension problems.

MATERIALS AND PROCEDURE

The analyses reported in this chapter will focus on one study. In this study, 48 college students completed two tasks. The subjects read sentences in 12 passages and then completed a comprehension test approximately 15 minutes after the last passage was read.

Collection of Sentence Reading Times

At the beginning of the experimental session we told subjects that they would be reading passages and that they would later be asked questions about each of the passages. Subjects read the sentences from each passage one sentence at a time. A single sentence was presented on a display scope and the subject pressed a button on the computer terminal when the subject was finished reading each sentence. Approximately .5 second after the button was pressed and the screen was cleared, the next sentence in the passage appeared on the display scope. In this way we collected sentence by sentence reading times for each sentence in the passage. A computer recorded the reading times at millisecond accuracy.

Each passage was introduced by its title and ended with an *End of Passage* signal. Subjects were told that they could pause and rest between passages, but they should never pause while reading sentences within a passage. The subjects pressed a response button when they were ready to read a new passage. The order in which the 12 passages were presented and read was counterbalanced across subjects using a 12x12 Latin square. All subjects read one practice passage before reading the 12 experimental passages.

Passages

One virtue of our methodology is that we can apply it to any passage. This freedom allows us to retain a respect for ecologically valid prose, that is, passages that readers normally encounter in the real world. The 12 passages in our study were selected from story books and encyclopedias. Thus, the passages were ostensively representative of the passages that individuals normally read. The passages were of medium length (200 to 400 words) and covered a variety of topics. We segregated the passages into sentences with 9 to 16 words. The number of sentences per passage varied from 17 to 32, yielding a total of 275 sentences among the 12 passages.

The passages varied in text genre and topic familiarity. Three passages were in the narrative genre and were familiar to most college students (*Snow White*, *Noah*, and *Jonah*). Three passages were unfamiliar narratives (*Bodisat*, *The Serpent and the Judge*, and *The Princess and the Pea*). Three passages were expository passages discussing a topic that was familiar to most college students (*Earthquakes*, *Emotions*, and *Earth's Motions*). Three passages were unfamiliar expository passages (*Armadillos*, *Harvestor Ants*, and *Coal Energy*). Additional details about these passages are reported in previous studies (Graesser, 1981; Graesser, Hauft-Smith, Cohen, Pyles, 1981; Graesser, Hoffman, & Clark, 1980). Table 1 shows the sentences in the passage entitled *Earth's Motions*.

TABLE 1
Earthquake

1. Only a score of severe earthquakes wrench the earth in an average year.
2. There are approximately a million minor tremors during the same period.
3. They provide a continuous source of data for analysis of the earth's interior.
4. Nearly all major earthquakes originate in two long, relatively narrow zones.
5. One zone borders the Pacific, on the coast of the Americas and Asia.
6. The second major belt runs east to west across Europe and Asia.
7. The first is the site of 80 percent of all the world's earthquakes.
8. It's path is lined with most of the world's volcanoes.
9. For this reason it is known as the "Pacific Ring of Fire".
10. The second zone is responsible for 15 percent of the earthquakes.
11. Nearly all earthquakes originate in fractures of solid rock of the earth's crust.
12. These fractures, called faults, occur when stresses develop within the earth.
13. A spectacular example is the San Andreas Fault in California.

14. The land mass east of the San Andreas Fault is steadily inching south.
15. Every so often the motion goes beyond the underlying rocks stretching ability.
16. When this happens, the rock ruptures as it did on April 18, 1906.
17. The ground shifted as much as 15.5 feet along 200 miles.
18. The resulting earthquake along the San Andreas Fault demolished most of San Francisco.
19. It was the most extensive earth shift ever recorded for a single quake.
20. The movement along Pacific coast faults shook California in 1857, 1922, and 1940.
21. We know others can be expected because of the inevitability of the future movements.
22. They suggest our foothold on this old globe is tenuous.

Comprehension Test

The comprehension test contained 120 3-alternative, forced choice (3AFC) questions. There were 10 equations for each of the 12 passages. The questions were sufficiently challenging to test for comprehension, as opposed to simple word recognition. The computer presented the questions and recorded the subjects' answers. An overall comprehension score was computed, which was simply the number of correct responses out of 120.

PREDICTOR VARIABLES

There obviously is a large number of variables that contribute to reading time. The 15 predictors that we selected certainly do not exhaust the total set. Some of our predictors correspond to *units* in the text. For example, letters, syllables, words, and propositions are units in text that we can easily identify. Sentence reading times are expected to increase with the number of units that readers must encode. Other predictors are scaled products of theoretical *components*. For example, the syntactic complexity of a sentence was scaled according to some properties of a model of syntax. This syntax scale is a product of the text plus a theoretical mechanism. Other predictors of reading time correspond to *dimensions* of knowledge and cognition. These dimensions do not map onto text in a simple way. For example, reading times will undoubtedly be influenced by the extent to which sentences evoke mental images and the extent to which readers are familiar with the passage topic. Dimensions such as imagery and familiarity are products of the text plus the readers' knowledge and certain cognitive mechanisms that are not well understood.

In the best of all scientific worlds, all of our predictors would be scaled products of text and theory. Unfortunately, there are far too many gaps in our scientific understanding of reading. Our theories and models of comprehension are not developed to the point where we can specify in detail what implicit structures and cognitive mechanisms are invoked at "deep" levels of comprehension. Consequently, some of our predictor variables were scaled by asking college students to give normative ratings on sentences in passages. For example, imagery, interestingness, and topic familiarity were measured by normative ratings. Perhaps the science will eventually mature to the point where these dimensions are rooted in an explanatory, theoretical scale. Until that time, we will resort to normative rating scales.

Our 15 predictors of reading time can be segregated into word-level, sentence-level, and passage-level categories. Table 2 lists the 15 predictor variables along with the means and standard deviations for the 275 sentences. In this section we will describe how each variable was measured.

Word-level Predictors

The five word-level predictors include units and dimensions at or within the level of the word. Four of these predictors were very easy to measure; we simply counted the number of units within the sentence. We scaled each sentence on the number of letters, syllables, words, and new argument nouns. New argument nouns are those nouns in a sentence that introduce a person, object, location, or concept in the passage for the first time. Previous studies have reported that introducing a new argument in a passage requires additional processing time (Graesser, et al., 1980; Kintsch, Kozminski, Streby, McKoon, & Keenen, 1975). Sentence reading times are obviously expected to increase as a function of the number of letters, syllables,

TABLE 2
Predictors of Reading Time

Predictor Variables	Descriptive Statistics	
	Mean	Standard Deviation
Word-level		
Letters	54.1	10.4
Syllables	17.6	4.3
Words	11.9	1.1
Word Frequency	4.5	1.0
New Argument Nouns	.7	.9
Sentence-Level		
Syntax	.59	.10
Propositions	5.1	1.3
Sentence Staticness	.74	.23
Sentence Interestingness	4.3	.6
Sentence Imagery	4.6	.9
Passage-Level		
Passage Familiarity	3.7	.9
Passage Narrativity	4.3	2.0
Passage Staticness	.75	.14
Passage Interestingness	4.5	.7
Passage Imagery	4.5	.5

words, and new argument nouns. We would expect positive slope coefficients for these predictor variables.

The fifth word-level predictor is word frequency. The word frequency predictor captures the well-known finding that words of high frequency in a language require less processing time than rare words and words of medium frequency (Foss, 1969; Just & Carpenter, 1980; Mitchell & Green, 1978; Morton, 1969). Because sentences are the basic unit of analysis in this research, we needed a measure of word frequency that would span entire sentences. Our measure of word frequency for a sentence involved four steps. First, we identified each content word in the sentence. The content words include nouns, verbs, adjectives, and adverbs, but not articles, pronouns, prepositions, and conjunctions. Second, we obtained word frequency estimates for each content word, using the Kucera and Francis (1967) norms. If a word was not listed in the table of norms, we assigned it the frequency of .01 per million words. Third, we computed the natural logarithm of the frequency for each content word, following the practice of other researchers (Just & Carpenter, 1980; Mitchell & Green, 1978). It is therefore assumed that the processing time for a word decreases linearly as a function of the log of word frequency. Fourth, we computed a mean logarithm score from all of the content words in a sentence. We expected a negative slope coefficient for word frequency in our multiple regression analyses.

Sentence-level Predictors

These predictors capture processes and products of mechanisms which embellish, integrate, and interrelate words in sentences. The scaling of some sentence-level predictors requires a commitment to a specific theory or model. The measurement and meaning of some of these predictors are not as straightforward as the word-level predictors.

The essence of our syntax measure lies in prediction. Specifically, the reader formulates a prediction about the syntactic class of word $n + 1$ in a sentence after the reader knows about words 1 through n. For example, if a sentence starts out *the old*, we normally expect that the next word will be a noun. Researchers have developed augmented recursive transition network grammars which attempt to capture these syntactic predictions for the English language (Stevens & Rumelhart, 1975; Woods, 1970). According to our measure of syntax, the syntactic complexity of a sentence increases to the extent that the syntactic classes of words in the sentence fail to match the readers' expectations.

We adopted Stevens & Rumelhart's network when we scaled our 275 sentences on syntactic complexity. Stevens and Rumelhart's network specifies a set of alternative syntactic classes for each word in a sentence given that the previous words have been parsed. Although the network accepts a set of alternative syntactic classes at various points in the sentence, only one of the alternatives is expected by subjects with a high likelihood (see Stevens & Rumelhart, 1975, Table 6.1).

Readers apparently predict only one syntactic class at any given point in the sentence, although they can accommodate several alternative classes. We defined the theoretically predicted syntactic class of word $n + 1$ in a sentence as the first choice syntactic class, given that words 1 to n are accurately parsed. The network and data reported by Stevens and Rumelhart (1975, Table 6.1) were adopted for formulating these theoretically predicted syntactic classes. The syntactic complexity of a sentence was measured by computing the proportion of words in a sentence which did not turn out to be in the predicted syntactic class.

Propositions are units that contain one predicate and one or more arguments. For example, the sentence *the economic depression increased suicide* has two propositions. One proposition is INCREASE (DEPRESSION, SUICIDE); *increase* is the predicate that relates two arguments, *depression* and *suicide*. The other proposition is ECONOMIC (DEPRESSION); *economic* is a predicate that qualifies the single argument, *depression*. Propositions usually express a complete thought. In recent years, several psychologists have defined what propositions are and how sentences can be segregated into propositional units (Bovair & Kieras, 1981; Carpenter & Just, 1975; Clark & Clark, 1977; Graesser, 1981; Kintsch, 1974; Norman & Rumelhart, 1975), so we do not need to describe propositions in detail here. There are differences among researchers, however, as to what constitutes a proposition. The propositional system that we adopted is virtually identical to the one described by Bovair and Kieras (1981).

Sentence Staticness was measured by computing the proportion of propositions in a sentence which refer to states, as opposed to actions and events. Actions and events involve state changes, e.g., *the president cut the budget* and *inflation increased unemployment*. States involve ongoing properties that remain unchanged throughout a passage, e.g., *the president was rich* and *the pentagon is large*. Reading times are expected to increase with sentence staticness (Graesser, 1981).

We had to resort to normative ratings when we measured sentence interestingness. Twenty subjects rated each sentence in the 12 passages on a 7-point interestingness scale. The scale varied from 1, "the information conveyed in this sentence is very uninteresting," to 7, "the information conveyed in this sentence is very interesting." Subjects rated these sentences in the context of the passages. A mean interestingness rating was then computed for each sentence. We are uncertain about the impact of sentence interestingness on reading times. Richard Anderson (personal communication) has found that children spend more time reading interesting sentences than uninteresting sentences. However, these were isolated sentences rather than sentences embedded in text. Moreover, college students might show different trends than children. College students may expend more processing resources on uninteresting input when they are expected to master all the material. Alternatively, interesting sentences might demand more processing resources than uninteresting sentences with predictable content (Black, Schwartz, & Lehnert, 1981). The problem is complicated further by the fact that readers vary considerably as to what they think is interesting (Asher, 1980).

Normative ratings were also collected to scale sentences on sentence imagery. Twenty subjects rated each sentence on a 7-point imagery scale. The scale varied from 1, "information does not at all evoke a mental image," to 7,"information evokes a very vivid mental image." Mean ratings were computed for each sentence, averaging over subjects. Previous research does not present a consistent picture on the influence of imagery on reading times. Some researchers have reported that high imagery sentences take longer to read, presumably because additional time is needed to construct a vivid mental image (Eddy & Glass, 1981). Other researchers have reported that concrete sentences with high imagery are read faster than more abstract, imageless sentences (Holmes & Langford. 1976). However, subjects read unrelated sentences in these studies. The comprehension of isolated sentences may be substantially different than the comprehension of sentences embedded in a passage context.

Passage-level Predictors

These predictors correspond to properties of a passage as a whole. Each sentence within a specific passage received the same score for any given predictor.

Normative ratings were collected when we measured most of the passage-level predictors. Passage interestingness measured how interesting a passage is to an average reader. Twenty subjects rated each passage on a 7-point interestingness scale, varying from 1, "passage is very uninteresting," to 7, "passage is very interesting." Regarding passage imagery, 20 subjects rated each passage on a 7-point imagery scale, varying from 1, "passage evokes no mental image at all." to 7, "passage evokes a very vivid mental image." Passage familiarity measured the extent to which readers are familiar with the topic discussed in the passage. Twelve subjects rated each passage on a 7-point familiarity scale, varying from 1. "very unfamiliar with the topic discussed in the passage," to 7, "very familiar with the topic discussed in the passage."

From one perspective, we would expect reading times to be shorter for passages on very familiar topics (Johnson & Kieras, 1982; Kintsch et al., 1975: Sanford & Garrod, 1980). When readers are familiar with a topic, they have a richer knowledge base and this should facilitate the speed of interpreting and interrelating sentences. This knowledge would also narrow the readers' expectations of what will be mentioned in the text (Bisanz & Voss, 1981). From another perspective, however, passages on familiar topics may take longer to read. Such passages invoke more inferences, placing more demands on processing resources (Britton. Holdredge, Curry, & Westbrook, 1979). Passages on familiar topics may also be more absorbing.

Passage narrativity measures the extent to which a passage is in the narrative genre, as opposed to the expository genre. Twelve subjects rated the passages on a 7-point narrativity scale, varying from 1, "passage conveys static information" to 7, "passage conveys active information with actions and events unfolding in time." We expected that high narrative passages (such as a story) are read faster than static expository passages (such as an encyclopedia article). Indeed, Graesser (1981; Graesser, Hoffman, & Clark, 1980) reported that narrativity was the most robust predictor of reading times among seven predictors that were examined. Given the importance of this narrativity variable, we desired an independent method of measuring the narrativity construct. Colleagues have wondered whether narrativity ratings are a valid measure; subjects may have used some other dimension when generating narrativity ratings, such as interestingness or readability. Our alternative measure of narrativity was passage staticness. Passage staticness was measured by computing the proportion of propositions in a passage that refer to states as opposed to actions and events. Passage staticness should be inversely related to passage narrativity.

Other Predictors

There obviously are other predictors of reading time. We should briefly point out some of these other predictors and explain why we ended up neglecting them.

One obvious predictor is the number of inferences that are activated by each sentence. We would expect reading times to increase as a function of the number of generated inferences (Just & Carpenter, 1980; Olson, Mack & Duffy, 1980). Reading times for sentences may increase as a function of the number of inferences which are needed to bridge a particular sentence with the previous passage context (Clark, 1977). We originally wanted to include an inference component as a predictor of reading time. Unfortunately, our attempts were blocked because of theoretical and practical limitations. Our present theories of comprehension are not yet developed to the point of specifying in detail what inferences are generated and how many inferences are generated when any given passage is comprehended. We would need an exhaustive inventory of world knowledge before we could even begin to approach the problem of inference on a theoretical level. An adequate understanding of inference generation will not emerge from a linguistic analysis of the text. Most inferences are generated by world knowledge schemas that are suggested by the text (Schank & Abelson, 1977).

There are empirical methods for estimating the number of inferences generated by sentences in text. Researchers have asked subjects to think aloud while they read or listen to passages (Bisanz & Voss, 1981; Olson et al., 1980). Think-aloud protocols uncover many inferences and expectations that readers potentially generate during comprehension. In our laboratory, we have developed a question-answering method of exposing passage inferences and expectations (Graesser, 1978, 1981; Graesser & Goodman, in press; Graesser, Robertson, & Anderson, 1981). Unfortunately, there are practical limitations to collecting think-aloud and question-answering protocols. These analyses are very time consuming. We would need 2 years or more to collect and analyze the protocols for our 12 passages.

Other potential predictors are motivated by models of reading and comprehension. These models involve detailed symbolic analyses of comprehension. Some of these models specify mechanisms in short-term memory or working memory which (a) parse sentences, (b) segment sentences into propositions, (c) relate propositions structurally, (d) integrate new propositions with old propositions, and (e) related propositional structures with passage themes (van Dijk, 1980; Kieras, 1981; Kintsch & van Dijk, 1978; Miller & Kintsch, 1980; Spilich, Vesonder, Chiesi, & Voss, 1979; Vipond, 1980). One fruitful direction in our reading time research would involve scaling our sentences on dimensions that capture different aspects of these mechanisms. For example, some sentences impose more demands on short-term memory and working memory than other sentences. Sentences could be scaled according to memory load. Sentences also vary in the number of processing operations that are executed when sentences are interpreted.

Unfortunately, we confronted some problems when we attempted to scale sentences on dimensions suggested by available comprehension models. One major problem was that the models could not handle many of our sentences. When researchers have reported and tested these models, they have focused on specific families of sentences that the models can process successfully. The scope of these models is limited, but this limitation is tolerated in order to pursue some impressive research directions. Unfortunately, the scope limitation was a barrier when we attempted to scale our sentences according to dimensions suggested by the models. Sometimes we tried to expand the models in order to accommodate our sentences. However, we confronted too many barriers of uncertainty when we had to decide on how to deal with specific cases. There was one other problem that we faced with some of the models. Some models address characteristics of a passage as a whole. For example, in Kintsch's model, microstructure is first constructed from all of the sentences in a passage. After the microstructure is built, macrostructure operators are applied to segments within the microstructure in order to construct a macrostructure representation. We were unable to trace what impact various processes had on individual sentences during comprehension. We were unable to translate processes operating on passages to processes operating on individual sentences.

Our syntax predictor was the only predictor which capitalized on a detailed symbolic model. The syntactic complexity of sentences was scaled according to products of an augmented transition network (ATN) grammar. However, even our measure of syntactic complexity failed to capture some potentially powerful aspects of the ATN grammar. For example, we might have used the ATN grammar to scale sentences according to (a) the number of decision and processing operations that are invoked when a sentence is parsed, (b) the number of times that the ATN parser must back up during parsing, and (c) the mean number of symbolic units that must be held in working memory when a sentence is parsed word by word. The ATN grammar was not general enough to handle all our sentences when we tried to scale the sentences on these dimensions. However, the ATN grammar was sufficiently general when scaling sentences according to our proposed metric, i.e., the proportion of words in a sentence that do not match theoretically predicted syntactic classes. The syntax scale that we derived from the ATN grammar was sufficient to handle all of our sentences, but at the cost of losing valuable information about the mechanism of the ATN parser.

9. MULTIPLE REGRESSION AND SENTENCE READING TIMES   193

We also tried to categorize and scale sentences on dimensions suggested by recent text grammars (Mandler & Johnson, 1977; Stein & Glenn, 1979; Thorndyke, 1977; Rumelhart, 1977) and other theories of global passage structure (van Dijk, 1980). For example, Haberlandt, Berian, and Sandson (1980) have examined the extent to which Mandler and Johnson's story grammar can explain sentence reading times for 12-sentence narrative passages. Unfortunately, we encountered two barriers when pursuing this direction. First, any given text grammar could be successfully applied to only a subset of passages. For example, story grammars were not designed to analyze expository prose. Second, many of our sentences did not easily map onto statement categories proposed by text grammars and other theories of text structure.

It should be obvious by now that our 15 predictors of reading time hardly exhaust the set of theoretically interesting predictors. However, we have incorporated a large number of predictors, and can illustrate how multiple regression analyses can be used to study sentence reading times.

PROBLEMS AND ISSUES IN APPLYING MULTIPLE REGRESSION

Collinearity Between Predictors of Reading Time

The predictors of reading time are expected to be intercorrelated to some extent. The correlation matrix in Table 3 shows all possible bivariate correlations for the 15 predictor variables. A few of the correlations are extremely high, but most are quite modest. Of the 105 correlations, 45 were not significant at the .05 level ($r = .12$). There were 73 correlations with absolute values of .30 or less, 30 in the .31 to .63 interval, and 2 with extremely high values of .86 and .87.

The two extremely high correlation coefficients present problems of collinearity between pairs of predictor variables. As a rule of thumb, a bivariate correlation of .8 or higher is a sign of collinearity problems (Nie, et al., 1975). When a predictor variable has a high correlation with another predictor, it is difficult or impossible to estimate its unique contribution to the dependent variable. There was an extremely high positive correlation between letters and syllables ($r = .86$). This correlation is of course quite expected. The other extremely high correlation was a negative correlation between passage narrativity and passage staticness ($r = .87$). This correlation is informative in at least one respect. The subjects' narrativity ratings were guided primarily by an active/static dimensional judgement (the dimension that we asked the subjects to rate the passages on) rather than some extraneous dimensions.

What does an investigator do when there is a severe collinearity problem? There are two possible solutions. One solution is to pursue some advanced multivariate analyses, such as correlational analyses with latent variables, causal modeling, factor analysis, or path analysis (Bentler, 1980; Joreskog, 1978; Joreskog & Sorbom, 1978; Kenny, 1979). A multivariate analysis with latent (unmeasured)

TABLE 3
Correlation Matrix

	Reading Time	L	Syl	W	WF	NA	Syn	P	SS	Sin	Sim	Fam	N	PS	Pin
Word-Level															
Letters (L)	.61														
Syllables (Syl)	.67	.86													
Words (W)	.34	.40	.36												
Word Frequency (WF)	-.28	-.34	-.26	.00											
New Argument Nouns (NA)	.28	.22	.17	.05	.23										
Sentence-Level															
Syntax (Syn)	.00	-.04	-.08	.01	.06	-.09									
Propositions (P)	.45	.44	.39	.42	-.09	.22	.23								
Staticness (SS)	.39	.37	.43	.16	-.04	.16	-.05	.37							
Interestingness (Sin)	-.16	.01	-.01	.04	-.04	-.02	-.04	.00	-.03						
Imagery (Sim)	-.55	-.45	-.51	-.06	-.03	-.03	.06	-.16	-.33	.34					
Passage-Level															
Familiarity (Fam)	-.13	-.14	-.11	-.03	.06	-.03	-.16	-.11	.13	.23	.08				
Narrativity (N)	-.59	-.53	-.63	-.13	.23	-.14	.09	-.26	-.54	.02	.52	-.09			
Staticness (PS)	.54	.52	.56	.15	-.20	.14	-.04	.28	.62	.03	-.47	.21	-.87		
Interestingness (Pin)	-.54	-.53	-.60	-.16	.07	-.10	.02	-.25	-.29	.20	.51	.42	.49	-.47	
Imagery (Pim)	-.07	-.07	-.06	.00	-.02	.03	-.10	.07	.08	.50	.11	.43	-.17	.13	-.53
	Reading Time	L	Syl	W	WF	NA	Syn	P	SS	Sin	Sim	Fam	N	PS	Pin
		WORD-LEVEL					SENTENCE-LEVEL					PASSAGE-LEVEL			

variables would isolate latent variables that capture the commonality between collinear measured variables. We did not analyze the reading time data with these multivariate methods because we encountered some difficulties. Regarding multivariate analyses with latent variables, we could not identify sensible latent variables on theoretical grounds which explained the collinearity problems. Regarding multivariate analyses with structural properties, there were too many alternative structures to test which interrelate measured variables and/or latent variables. Available theories do not sufficiently constrain the set of alternative structures to test. Although we did not pursue multivariate solutions to our reading time data, this is one direction for future research.

The second solution to a collinearity problem is to eliminate one of the two variables from subsequent analyses. This is the solution that we chose. Of course, another problem emerges when this solution is adopted. Which of the two variables should be eliminated? There are several criteria to consider when deciding which variable to drop. Our primary criterion was to eliminate the predictor which does the poorest job of predicting reading times. Before we elaborate on this criterion, we should report some preliminary analyses on the reading times.

In the left column of Table 3 we have listed the bivariate correlations between reading times and the 15 predictor variables. For each sentence we computed a mean reading time, averaging over subjects. The mean sentence reading times were correlated with each of the 15 predictor variables. Of the 15 correlations, 13 were significant at the .05 level. As we expected, there were positive correlations between reading times and letters, syllables, words, new argument nouns, propositions, sentence staticness and passage staticness. As expected, there were negative correlations between reading times and word frequency, familiarity, and narrativity. We mentioned in the previous section that we were uncertain about the impact of interestingness and imagery on reading times. According to the bivariate correlations, reading times decreased with higher sentence interestingness, with higher sentence imagery, and with higher passage interestingness. The syntax variable and the passage imagery variable did not correlate significantly with reading times.

The above bivariate correlations between reading times and the predictor variables provided some basis for eliminating predictor variables when a pair of predictors are collinear. Consider first the collinearity between letters and syllables. The correlation between number of syllables and reading time is slightly higher than the correlation between number of letters and reading times. Therefore, we eliminated letters and preserved syllables. Other considerations also led us to eliminate letters. We performed a standard multiple regression that predicted the mean sentence reading times as a function of all 15 predictor variables (with all predictors in the regression equation). The outcome of this regression analysis revealed that syllables significantly predicted reading times (i.e. the semipartial correlation was significant) whereas letters was a nonsignificant predictor. Our final reason for eliminating letters and preserving syllables is based on nonstatistical considerations. The time to process letters should be much shorter than the time to process syllables (see Graesser, 1981). Indeed, letter processing time is so fast that a few milliseconds might not be detectable in our reading time task in which an average sentence has a reading time of 3884 milliseconds.

The other collinearity problem existed between passage narrativity and passage staticness. Since reading times showed a slightly higher correlation with narrativity than with passage staticness, we decided to eliminate the passage staticness variable. A multiple regression analysis was performed examining reading times as a function of the 15 predictor variables. Narrativity was a significant predictor while passage staticness was nonsignificant. Narrativity predicted reading times better than passage staticness so we ended up eliminating passage staticness in subsequent analyses.

We have discussed collinearity problems that emerge when observing bivariate correlations between pairs of predictor variables. A potential collinearity problem for any given predictor could be assessed in another way. To what extent is a given predictor collinear with the remaining *set* of predictors? We will examine this question in a later section.

Eliminating Nonsignificant Predictor Variables

We have already described one criterion for eliminating predictor variables. When examining the correlation matrix in Table 3, we spotted two extremely high correlations that reflected collinearity problems between pairs of predictors. We ultimately eliminated letters and passage staticness as predictor variables in order to resolve these collinearity problems. We were then left with 13 predictor variables.

Another criterion for eliminating predictor variables is to eliminate variables that do not significantly predict reading times in the multiple regression analysis. We elected to be cautious when eliminating variables by this second criterion. Why should we be cautious? One reason for the caution is statistical. When we assess whether a given predictor has a significant effect on reading time, we are assessing the statistical significance of its squared semipartial correlation. This squared semipartial correlation estimates the amount of reading time variance uniquely explained by one predictor variable, after partialling out the contributions from all other predictors. A squared semipartial is a very conservative estimate of the impact of a predictor on reading times because the cards are stacked against the predictor variable. The predictor does not receive any credit for whatever commonality it has with other predictor variables. When there are a large number of predictor variables, a potentially significant predictor might end up showing nonsignificant effects in multiple regression analyses because (a) the predictor has a small, modest, or statistically unreliable collinearity with several other predictors and (b) the contributions of the other predictors on reading times are completely partialled out before assessing the unique impact of the predictor variable on reading time.

There is a second reason for being cautious about eliminating nonsignificant predictors. There may be interesting individual differences among readers; these differences would be concealed in analyses on mean sentence reading times which average over subjects. If half of the subjects have significantly negative slope coefficients and half significantly positive slope coefficients for a predictor, then an analysis of mean sentence reading times might show a zero slope coefficient for the predictor. It is obviously important to examine multiple regression analyses on individual reader's times in addition to mean sentence reading times which average over subjects.

Our cautious method of eliminating predictor variables involved multiple regression analyses with a reduced subset of predictor variables. Specifically, we performed three separate multiple regression analyses: (a) reading times with word-level predictors, (b) reading times with sentence-level predictors, and (c) reading times with passage-level predictors. Consequently, the squared semipartial correlation for a predictor variable was computed after partialling out only 3 or 4 other predictor variables instead of all 12 other predictor variables. This method minimized the previously discussed artifacts that arise when there is a large number of predictor variables and when there is some unsystematic collinearity among the predictor variables. In addition to segregating the multiple regression analyses into these three groups (word, sentence, and passage predictors), we used a very high alpha-level (.50) as a criterion for eliminating a predictor. A predictor was eliminated only if the F-score was less than 1.0.

When we used the above method we ended up eliminating two more predictor variables. We eliminated sentence interestingness because it had an F-score of less than 1.0 in the multiple regression with sentence-level predictors. Also, this variable was rarely significant when we performed analyses on individual subjects. We eliminated passage imagery because it had a very low F-score in the multiple regression analysis with passage-level predictors. This variable was also rarely significant in individual subject analyses. At this point, we were left with 11 predictor variables. There were four word-level predictors (syllables, words, word frequency, and new argument nouns), four sentence-level predictors (syntax, propositions, sentence staticness, and sentence imagery), and three passage-level predictors (familiarity, narrativity, and interestingness). The subsequent analyses in this chapter will examine these 11 predictors in more detail.

Multicollinearity

To what extent is each predictor variable collinear with the set of remaining predictor variables? An assessment of multicollinearity is an important preliminary analysis before we examine the reading times in detail. If values on one predictor variable can be completely predicted by the remaining set of predictor

TABLE 4
Multicollinearity Analyses
for 11 Predictor Variables

Variable	R	R^2
Word-Level		
Syllables	.79	.62
Words	.52	.27
Word Frequency	.44	.20
New Argument Nouns	.35	.12
Sentence-Level		
Syntax	.37	.13
Propositions	.62	.38
Sentence Staticness	.62	.39
Sentence Imagery	.64	.41
Passage-Level		
Familiarity	.59	.35
Narrativity	.76	.58
Interestingness	.76	.58

variables, then it would be impossible to assess how reading times are uniquely influenced by the predictor variable in question.

In order to assess the multicollinearity of a given predictor variable V, we performed a multiple regression with V as the dependent variable. In other words, we examined the extent to which other predictor variables can predict values on variable V. We performed multicollinearity analyses on each of our 11 predictor variables. The outcome of these analyses is shown in Table 4. The right column lists the amount of variance (R^2) of predictor variable V that is explained by the other predictor variables in the regression equation. If R^2 approached 1.00, then the predictor V would be completely collinear with the set of other predictor variables and it would be impossible to isolate a unique contribution from variable V. The R^2 values in Table 4 indicate that each variable has a moderate degree of multicollinearity with the other variables. However, each variable does have some unique variance that cannot be explained by other variables. The highest multicollinearity index involved syllables ($R^2 = .62$). Although 62% of the syllable variance could be predicted by the other 10 variables, there was some proportion of the syllable variance (38%) that could not.

Choice of Analysis

There are a number of ways to perform multiple regression analyses on a set of data. However, only a subset of these multiple regression analyses are appropriate for the questions we want to address. We will report analyses that seem appropriate and point out some of the advantages and disadvantages of each.

9. MULTIPLE REGRESSION AND SENTENCE READING TIMES   199

One question that arises is what criterion to adopt for eliminating predictor variables which have small effects or no effect on the reading times. We adopted a very cautious approach to eliminating variables. Specifically, we preserved all 11 variables in all of our analyses. The rationale for our position on this matter is related to the goals of our analysis of reading times. Our goal is *not* to arrive at a small set of predictor variables which capture the lion's share of the predictable reading time variance. Instead, our goal is to estimate processing times associated with several predictor variables. We want each predictor to have its chance at contributing whatever reading time variance it can explain. The fact that we will preserve all 11 variables in the regression equation eliminates some decisions about which multiple regression method to use. Specifically we do not have to decide whether to adopt a forward stepwise method, a backward method, a hierarchical method, or some other method of choosing variables.

A second question is which dependent measure to predict. We can analyze the mean sentence reading time per sentence, averaging over subjects. We can also perform a separate multiple regression on each subject, which allows us to examine individual differences among readers. Finally, we can compute Z-score transformations of the reading times. We first obtain Z-scores of the sentence reading times for each subject separately. Then we compute a mean Z-score for each sentence, averaging across subjects. We have performed multiple regression analyses on all of these measures. We will refer to these three measures as (a) mean sentence reading times, (b) individual subjects' reading times, and (c) sentence Z-scores.

Each reading time measure has both advantages and disadvantages. The individual subjects' reading times clearly provide the most detailed data base for studying reading. However, these reading times suffer from uninteresting sources of variance. For example, an individual subject sometimes has lapses of attention and occasionally pauses for thought and reflection in the middle of reading a passage. When these events occur, a sentence receives a very long reading time for very uninteresting reasons. Because of these sources of error, the individual subjects' reading times may not be very sensitive. Mean sentence reading times are minimally influenced by these sources of error, because these lapses and pauses would be distributed unsystematically among all of the sentences. One shortcoming of mean sentence reading times, however, is that such analyses do not reveal differences among readers. Another shortcoming is that those subjects with more robust and systematic patterns of scores end up influencing multiple regression analyses more than subjects with more subtle patterns of scores. This last problem can be minimized somewhat by analyzing sentence Z-scores because all subjects are weighted equally. However, sentence Z-scores do not permit an analysis of individual differences and do not provide slope coefficients that correspond to processing time.

We will report analyses on mean sentence reading times and individual subjects' reading times. We conducted an analysis on sentence Z-scores, but we will not report it, because the outcome of this analysis was redundant with the mean sentence reading time analysis. When considering tests of significance, the Z-score analysis and mean sentence reading time analysis were virtually identical. The slope coefficients are more informative in the mean sentence reading time analysis than the Z-score analysis, so we will report the analysis on mean sentence reading times.

RESULTS

Analysis of Mean Sentence Reading Times

Basic Analysis. The mean sentence reading times varied from 2.261 to 7.221 seconds, with a mean of 3.884 and a standard deviation of .897. The 11 predictor variables accounted for a significant 63.0% of the reading time variance, $F(1,63) = 40.77$.

Table 5 shows some statistics and parameter values for each of the 11 predictor variables. There are four values for each predictor variable. The first value is the slope coefficient. The slope coefficient estimates the amount of change in reading time associated with one unit of change in the predictor variable. For example, there was a .038 slope for syllables; each additional syllable in a sentence is associated with an increase of 38 milliseconds in reading time. The second column in Table 5 lists the beta weights for each predictor. A beta weight is a standardized slope coefficient. The beta weights estimate how robustly the reading times are predicted by specific predictor variables. The third column in Table 5 lists the r^2 value for the squared semipartial correlations of each variable. The squared semipartial correlation assesses the amount of reading time variance predicted by one predictor variable, after partialling out contributions from all other predictor variables. The F-scores listed in the fourth column assess the significance of the squared semipartial correlations.

The F-scores in Table 5 reveal that 8 of the 11 predictors significantly predicted mean sentence reading times. The three nonsignificant predictors ($F<1$) were syntax, sentence staticness, and passage familiarity. The squared semipartials were small or modest for the significant predictors, ranging from .005 for passage interestingness to .046 for sentence imagery. The fact that these semipartial values are small is quite expected because they are extremely conservative estimates of the unique impact of each predictor on reading times.

The direction of the slope coefficients and beta weights indicate whether reading times increase or decrease with increasing values on the predictor variables. The signs of the slopes were consistent with the bivariate correlations reported earlier. Reading times increased with the number of syllables, number of words, number of new argument nouns, and number of propositions. The reading times decreased with word frequency, sentence imagery, passage narrativity, and passage interestingness.

9. MULTIPLE REGRESSION AND SENTENCE READING TIMES

TABLE 5
Multiple Regression Analysis on
Mean Sentence Reading Times

Predictor	Slope Coefficient	Beta Weight	Semipartial r^2	F-score of semi-partial
Word-Level Syllables	.038	.184	.013	9.16
Words	.116	.142	.015	10.40
Word Frequency	-.136	-.152	.019	13.20
New Argument Nouns	.124	.128	.015	10.33
Sentence-Level				
Syntax	-.221	-.025	.001	.38
Propositions	.103	.151	.014	10.02
Staticness	-.025	-.006	.000	.02
Imagery	-.295	-.278	.046	32.67
Passage-Level				
Familiarity	-.022	-.022	.001	.23
Narrativity	-.077	-.174	.013	8.98
Interestingness	-.138	-.107	.005	3.40

The beta weights permit us to rank order the predictor variables according to their robustness in predicting the reading times. According to the beta weights, the significant predictors would be ordered as follows, starting with the most robust predictor: sentence imagery, syllables, passage narrativity, word frequency, propositions, words, new argument nouns, and passage interestingness.

Check of Linearity Assumption. In the above multiple regression analysis, we assumed that there is a linear relationship between each predictor variable and reading time. This assumption proved to be quite satisfactory. When mean sentence reading times are plotted as a function of different values of a predictor variable, the shape of the plot was linear. We performed a series of multiple regression analyses to confirm this observation. In the first set of analyses we examined a logarithmic transformation for each variable. We performed 11 different multiple regression analyses; in each analysis one of the 11 predictors was recomputed with a logarithmic transformation whereas the other 10 predictors remained linear. In all 11 analyses, the beta weights were lower for the transformed variable than the beta weight in Table 5. In all 11 analyses the total R value was lower than the corresponding R value for multiple regression analyses which adopted strictly linear assumptions. We also examined exponential transformations and parabolic (curvilinear) transformations and found them to be less satisfactory than the linear functions.

Interactions. The question arises as to whether predictor variables interact in their effects on reading times. Multiple regression analyses can be used to examine potential interactions. We examined first-order interactions on the 8 significant predictor variables. A first-order interaction involves two predictor variables, e.g., words and imagery. In order to test for a first-order interaction between words (W) and imagery (I), we would add another component to the multiple regression analysis; the additional component is a product of the two variables, W x I. We performed a series of multiple regression analyses that examined one first-order interaction at a time. Since there were 8 predictor variables, there were 28 first-order interactions to examine and 28 multiple regression analyses to perform.

The multiple regression analyses revealed that 2 out of the 28 first order interactions were significant at the .05 level. One significant interaction was between words and new argument nouns, $F(1,265) = 5.62$. We traced the source of this interaction by examining the slope values of the word (W), new argument noun (NAN), and W x NAN components. New argument nouns had smaller processing times when there were more words in a sentence. This interaction was modest, but enough to achieve statistical significance. The second significant interaction was between propositions and passage narrativity, $F(1,265) = 4.11$. When we examined the source of the interaction, we found that the time to process propositions was slightly faster in narrative passages than in expository passages. These two first-order interactions did not substantially improve prediction of reading times. The two interactions together increased the total R^2 from 63% to 64% of the variance. We will not examine these interactions in subsequent analyses because these interactions were subtle and they were not antagonistic interactions (e. g., with cross-over patterns).

It is possible to examine second-order interactions and higher n-order interactions using multiple regression. We did not perform such analyses, however, because there are a horrendous number of interactions to inspect and there was no theoretical rationale for examining specific interactions.

Analysis of Individual Subjects' Reading Times

Predictors of Individual Data. A multiple regression analysis with all 11 predictor variables was performed on the sentence reading times of each subject, producing 48 multiple regression analyses altogether. A total R^2 was computed for each subject, specifying the amount of variance predicted by the best fit predictive equation with the 11 predictor variables. The mean R^2 per subject was 24.4%. The predictive equations explained a significant amount of the reading time variance for 47 out of 48 subjects (at $p<.05$).

Table 6 summarizes the outcome of these 48 multiple regression analyses. The first two columns in Table 6 list mean slope coefficients for each predictor variable and standard deviations for these slope coefficients. Columns 3 and 4 are the beta weight means and standard deviations. Column 5 lists the proportion of subjects who had significant squared semipartial correlation coefficients (at $p<.10$) for the predictor variable. We pointed out earlier that analyses of individual subjects' reading times would suffer from uninteresting sources of error, such as attention lapses and pauses for thought. With this consideration in mind, we adopted a liberal ($p<.10$) level for testing of significance. The last column lists the proportion of subjects who had positive slope coefficients for a predictor variable.

We adopted two criteria for deciding whether a predictor variable has a nonsignificant effect on reading times (in the context of analyses on individual subjects). One criterion is the proportion of subjects who had significant F-scores. If this proportion is low, then the predictor is not likely to be significant. There is a problem in using this single criterion alone, however. A predictor might have a small but consistent effect on reading times among subjects; the small effect might be masked by large error components that yield nonsignificant F-scores. We therefore adopted a second criterion which reflected intersubject consistency. A predictor variable would have an inconsistent effect on reading times if half of the subjects had positive slope coefficients and half had negative slope coefficients. In summary, a nonsignificant predictor variable would have a low proportion of significant squared semipartial correlations (i.e., column 5 in Table 6) and a .50 proportion of positive slope coefficients (i.e., column 6 in Table 6).

Using the above criteria for assessing significance, 2 out of the 11 predictor variables failed to predict the reading times of individual subjects. One of the nonsignificant predictors was sentence staticness. Only .08 of the subjects had significant semipartial correlations; .50 of the subjects had positive slopes and .50 had negative slopes. The other nonsignificant predictor was syntax. Only .16 of the

TABLE 6
Multiple Regression Analyses on
Reading Times of Individual Subjects

Predictor	Slope Coefficient		Beta Weight		proportion significant at $p<.10$	proportion with + slope
	Mean	SD	Mean	SD		
Word-Level						
Syllable	.038	.030	.100	.099	.29	.92
Word	.116	.119	.084	.093	.31	.94
Word Frequency	-.136	.182	-.069	.108	.48	.15
New Argument Nouns	.124	.165	.060	.089	.42	.83
Sentence-Level						
Syntax	-.221	1.237	-.004	.089	.16	.44
Propositions	.103	.124	.073	.087	.29	.83
Staticness	-.025	.519	-.013	.091	.08	.50
Imagery	-.295	.256	-.134	.117	.63	.04
Passage-Level						
Familiarity	-.022	.387	.000	.171	.50	.52
Narrativity	-.077	.143	-.090	.163	.54	.25
Interestingness	-.138	.619	-.076	.166	.38	.38

subjects had significant semipartial correlations; .44 of the subjects had positive slopes and .56 had negative slopes. The fact that these two variables were nonsignificant agrees with our analysis of mean sentence reading times (see Table 5).

The analysis of mean sentence reading times (see Table 5) indicates that passage familiarity did not significantly influence reading times. However, our analyses of individual subjects' reading times do not agree with this conclusion. For passage familiarity, .52 of the subjects had positive slopes and .48 had negative slopes. However, these slope coefficients were significant for a large proportion of the subjects (.50), including those subjects with negative slopes and those subjects with positive slopes. Half of the subjects spent more time reading passages on familiar topics, whereas the other half spent more time reading passages on unfamiliar topics. These individual differences explain the null result when mean sentence reading times were analyzed. This discrepancy indicates that interesting trends are sometimes concealed in the analyses of mean sentence reading times that average over subjects.

There were 8 significant predictor variables in the analysis of mean sentence reading times. These predictors were also significant when we analyzed individual subjects' reading times. Among these 8 predictors, the proportion of subjects with significant squared semipartials ranged from .29 to .63. For those predictors with positive mean slope coefficients, the proportion of subjects with positive slopes ranged from .63 to .94. For those predictors with negative mean slope coefficients, the proportion of subjects with negative slopes ranged from .75 to .96. There were some individual differences in slope values for the passage interestingness variable. Roughly two-thirds of the subjects spent more time reading uninteresting passages whereas one-third spent more time reading interesting passages.

The Reliability and Validity of Reading Time Slope Coefficients

Are the slope coefficients reliable estimates of the processing time associated with the predictors? Would the same slope coefficients occur if the study were replicated on a different group of college students? We can answer this question in two ways. First, the direction of the slope values for individual subjects (see Table 6) showed a high degree of intersubject reliability for 7 out of the 9 significant predictor variables. These 7 predictors were syllables, words, word frequency, new argument nouns, propositions, sentence imagery, and passage narrativity. On the average, 87% of the subjects' slope coefficients agreed in direction (+ versus -) with the mean slope coefficient. We would conclude, therefore, that the directions of the slope coefficients are quite reliable for these 7 variables. However, there are substantial individual differences among subjects when considering passage familiarity and passage interestingness. The slopes for these predictors may be unstable from experiment to experiment.

The issue of reliability can also be examined with respect to the magnitude of the slope coefficients. We can address this issue informally by comparing the outcomes reported in this chapter with the outcomes of a previous study (Graesser, 1981). In this previous study, sentence reading times were collected on the same passages, but with a different group of 36 college students. Multiple regression analyses were performed on mean sentence reading times. The predictor variables included the same predictors that were significant in the study reported in this chapter, except for word frequency, sentence imagery, and passage interestingness variables. Of the 6 predictor variables that overlapped between these two studies, most of the slope coefficients were quantitatively similar (see Graesser, 1981, the multiple choice condition in Table 2.4). The slope for syllables was .043 in the previous study, which is quantitatively compatible with the .038 slopes in Tables 5 and 6. When comparing the two studies, the slope coefficients for words were .117 and .116, the slope coefficients for propositions were .118 and .103, and the slope coefficients for new argument nouns were .090 and .124. The passage narrativity variable had slopes of -.103 and -.077 in the two studies. Even the relatively unstable variable of passage familiarity had similar slope coefficients in the two studies, -.018 and -.022. The fact that the slope values were quite compatible between these two studies supports the conclusion that the slope coefficients reported in this chapter are very reliable.

Are the slope coefficients reported in this chapter valid estimates of processing time? One way to answer this question is to compare our slopes with the slopes from other studies which used different passages and different measures of reading time. There are a few studies in which researchers have used multiple regression analyses to assess different predictors of reading time. In these studies, researchers have collected sentence by sentence reading times (Haberlandt et al., 1980; Kieras, 1981), phrase by phrase reading times (Mitchell & Green, 1978), and eye movements (Carpenter & Just, 1981; Just & Carpenter, 1980). These studies have not included the exact same sets of predictors that we have. Therefore, we would not expect the slope coefficients to be exactly the same across studies for those predictors that overlap. At best, the slope coefficients would be roughly similar in magnitude.

Five of our predictor variables have been examined by other researchers who have analyzed reading times using multiple regression techniques. These variables include syllables, words, word frequency, new argument nouns, and propositions. Just and Carpenter (1980) have reported a .052 slope for syllables which compares favorably with our .038 slope. Our .116 slope for words is roughly comparable to Haberlandt et al.'s .161 slope for words (see Table 5 in Haberlandt et al., 1980). Haberlandt et al. reported a .113 slope for propositions, which is quite close to our .103 slope. Haberlandt et al.'s slope for new argument nouns was .168, which is in the ballpark of our .124 second slope. The logarithm of word frequency has been examined in a number of studies (Just & Carpenter, 1980; Mitchell & Green, 1978). In these studies the analyses spanned word units. There was a slope of -.030 seconds per unit of log frequency in the Mitchell and Green study (see Tables III and IV) and a slope of -.053 in Just and Carpenter (1980). The analyses in our study spanned sentences rather than individual words. There were 4.7 content words per sentence, on the average, and our log frequency slope was -.138. When dividing -.138 by 4.7, we obtain a slope value of -.029 per word, which is roughly comparable to values reported by other researchers.

To summarize, we have performed an informal comparison of our slopes and slopes reported by other researchers who have used different passages and different methods of measuring reading time. The slope coefficients were surprisingly similar in these comparative analyses. It appears that our slope coefficients are valid estimates of processing time. Of course, more systematic comparisons among materials and tasks are needed before we can defend this claim more strongly.

Predicting Comprehension Scores from Slope Coefficients in Reading Time Analyses

In this section we will examine the extent to which comprehension scores can be predicted by individual subjects' reading times. After subjects read each passage they completed a comprehension test consisting of 120 3-alternative, forced choice questions. The comprehension scores ranged from 50 to 100, with a mean of 84.5 and a standard deviation of 9.5.

There are several ways to examine the relationship between reading times and comprehension. Perhaps the simplest method is to compute correlation coefficients between comprehension scores and the reading time measures and parameters we reported in the previous section. We have examined such correlations for the mean sentence reading times for subjects and the subjects' slope coefficients for the 9 significant reading time predictors. These correlations are presented in Table 7. There was a significant negative correlation between comprehension scores and sentence reading times. The faster readers tended to perform better on the comprehension test. In contrast, the slope values did not significantly predict comprehension scores. If the final word rested on these data, we would conclude that comprehension scores cannot be predicted by the way readers distribute their processing resources among different text components.

A substantially different conclusion emerged when we performed more fine-grained analyses which segregated fast readers from slow readers and good comprehenders from poor comprehenders. Fast readers may be fast because they have high verbal aptitude; these subjects would have relatively high comprehension scores. Other fast readers may have low comprehension scores because they gloss over too many details that are needed to comprehend the material. Similarly, some slow readers may have high comprehension scores because they read carefully, whereas other slow readers may have low comprehension scores because their verbal aptitude is low.

We segregated subjects into different groups on the basis of their mean sentence reading times and their comprehension scores. We used a median split criterion to segregate fast from slow readers. The fast readers' mean sentence reading times varied from 2.939 to 3.573 seconds, with a mean of 3.280. The slow subjects' reading times varied from 3.710 to 6.630 seconds, with a mean of 4.487. Within

TABLE 7
Correlation between Comprehension Scores
and Reading Time Measures

Reading Time Measure	Correlation
Mean Sentence Reading Time	-.33*
Slope Coefficients	
Word-Level	
Syllables	-.11
Words	.05
Word Frequency	-.05
New Argument Nouns	.13
Sentence-Level	
Propositions	.04
Imagery	.00
Passage-Level	
Familiarity	-.11
Narrativity	-.02
Interestingness	-.05

*significant at $p<.05$

each of these two groups of subjects, the 24 subjects were segregated into subgroups with low, medium, versus high comprehension scores. Poor comprehenders had comprehension scores of at least .5 standard deviation units below the mean for the group. Good comprehenders had scores of .5 standard deviations units above the mean for the group. This criterion produced four groups of subjects. There were 7 fast readers with poor comprehension (mean reading time = 3.299 and mean comprehension score = 80.4), 8 fast readers with good comprehension (mean reading time = 3.351 and mean comprehension score = 95.3), 9 slow readers with poor comprehension (mean reading time = 4.322 and mean comprehension score = 69.8), and 7 slow readers with good comprehension (mean reading time = 4.413 and mean comprehension score = 89.7).

Table 8 presents mean slope coefficients for slow readers, segregating good versus poor comprehenders. We performed t-tests in order to assess whether slopes differed for subjects with poor versus good comprehension. The slopes of three predictor variables showed significant differences: new argument nouns, propositions, and sentence imagery. Compared to slow readers with good comprehension, the slow readers with poor comprehension did not devote as much time to processing new argument nouns, propositions, and abstract sentences with low imagery. There were no differences in slope coefficients for highly automatized text units (involving syllables, word, and word frequency predictors), nor were there any differences at the passage level (involving passage familiarity, narrativity, and interestingness predictors). Perhaps slow readers with poor comprehension might improve their comprehension with special training and instruction. These readers would be instructed to pay more attention to (a) nouns that introduce new people, objects, locations, and concepts in the passage, (b) the

TABLE 8
Slope Coefficients for Slow Readers
with Low versus High Comprehension Scores

	Comprehension	
	Low	High
Word-Level		
Syllables	.038	.051
Words	.149	.169
Word Frequency	-.118	-.102
New Argument Nouns	.077	.246*
Sentence-Level		
Propositions	.071	.158*
Imagery	-.243	-.473*
Passage-Level		
Narrativity	-.092	-.103
Interestingness	-.208	-.095
Familiarity	-.055	-.101

*significant difference between low and high comprehenders, according to a t-test at $p<.05$.

segregation of sentences into phrases and clauses, i.e., propositions, and (c) abstract sentences.

Table 9 presents mean slope coefficients for fast readers with good versus poor comprehension. A series of t-tests revealed that only one predictor variable, passage interestingness, had significantly different slope coefficients for fast readers with good versus poor comprehension. Readers with good comprehension spent more time reading uninteresting passages. Perhaps the fast readers with poor comprehension could improve their comprehension with special instruction.

TABLE 9
Slope Coefficients for Fast Readers
with Low versus High Comprehension Scores

	Comprehension	
	Low	High
Word-Level		
Syllables	.042	.028
Words	.091	.144
Word Frequency	-.032	-.152
New Argument Nouns	.051	.048
Sentence-Level		
Propositions	.077	.063
Imagery	-.156	-.178
Passage-Level		
Narrativity	-.057	-.608
Interestingness	-.011	-.286*
Familiarity	-.126	-.095

*significant difference between low and high comprehenders, according to a t-test at $p<.05$

Specifically, they would be instructed to spend more time reading the uninteresting material.

Our investigation of the relationship between comprehension and reading time is hardly conclusive. We need to examine a larger sample of readers before we can defend our conclusions more strongly. Perhaps the major contribution of this section is methodological. We have demonstrated how reading problems can be diagnosed by inspecting slope coefficients in a subject's reading time profile, the subject's overall reading speed, and the subject's comprehension score. It is an open question as to whether a reader's comprehension can be improved by special instructions and training based on his or her reading time profile.

SUMMARY

Our multiple regression analyses of sentence reading times have provided useful information about reading and comprehension. We have estimated the impact of several different text components on reading time. We now have some idea about which components are time consuming and which components have little or no impact on reading time. The slope coefficients and beta weights from our analyses provide estimates of the unique contributions of specific predictor variables. Most of the previous studies on reading time have examined only a few variables at a time, whereas our approach offers a more complete perspective by examining many variables.

The slope coefficients in this study provide ballpark estimates of how long it takes to "process" specific units and components of text. For an average reader, it takes 38 milliseconds to process each syllable, 116 milliseconds to process each word, 124 milliseconds to foreground a noun concept when it is first introduced in a passage, and 103 milliseconds to process each proposition. A relatively rare word like *ellipse* takes 168 milliseconds more time to process than a relatively frequent word like *earth*. A 12-word sentence takes 1770 milliseconds longer to process if it is very abstract than if it evokes a very vivid mental image, 462 milliseconds longer to process if it is in a very expository passage than if it is in a very narrative passage, 828 more milliseconds to process if it is in a very uninteresting passage than if it is in a very interesting passage, and 132 more milliseconds to process if it is in a passage about a very unfamiliar topic than in a passage on a very familiar topic.

Our multiple regression analyses of sentence reading times permitted us to examine individual differences among readers. We identified differences between fast and slow readers regarding the allocation of processing resources to different text components. We identified specific ways that comprehension scores can be predicted by resource allocation characteristics, i.e., the profile of slope coefficients from reading time analyses. The relationship between comprehension and resource allocation during reading definitely requires further investigation. Nevertheless, we have demonstrated how our multiple regression techniques can be used to examine this relationship.

THEORETICAL CONCLUSIONS AND ISSUES

Research in reading and comprehension has blossomed during the past decade. Along with this collective enthusiasm, researchers have introduced many new codes and processing components that seem fundamental to reading and comprehension mechanisms. Models have also come to be quite complex. It is well beyond the scope of this section to review and evaluate all these developments. Instead, we will selectively focus on some issues that are particularly relevant to our investigation of sentence reading times.

Resource Allocation and Automatic Processes

Most models of reading assume that readers have a limited supply of cognitive resources which somehow are allocated to the processing of different components of text. The notion that there is not an infinite supply of processing resources reflects a general constraint on the human information processing system (Kahneman, 1973; Norman & Bobrow, 1975). Processing resources must be distributed among components in a way that falls within the capacity limitations. If resources are not distributed effectively, or if the text is too demanding on processing resources, then comprehension will suffer. For the present purposes, we will avoid the complex questions of what cognitive processing resources are, what capacity limitation means exactly, and where the bottlenecks exist in the human information processing system. It suffices to say that most models of reading assume that there is a limited capacity short-term memory or working memory where sentences are interpreted (Just & Carpenter, 1980; Kieras, 1981; Kintsch & van Dijk, 1978; Lesgold, Roth & Curtis, 1979; Perfetti, 1979; Rumelhart, 1977).

Most models of reading also distinguish between processing mechanisms that are activated and executed automatically versus those that are not automatized. The distinction between automatized and nonautomatized processing components applies to reading as well as other activities in the human information processing system (LaBerge & Samuels, 1974; Perfetti, 1979; Posner & Synder, 1975; Shaffer & LaBerge, 1979; Shiffrin & Dumais, 1981; Shiffrin & Schneider, 1977). In the context of reading, automatized processors involve the interpretation of overlearned familiar text units, such as letters, syllables, high frequency words, and syntax. Processors that conceptually interrelated words in sentences and sentences in passages would not be executed automatically.

One finding that has emerged in this study and other studies (Graesser, 1981; Graesser, et al., 1980; Kieras, this volume; Just & Thibadeau, this volume) is that syntactic processing is either executed very quickly or does not significantly predict reading time. The fact that syntax seems to be a flimsy predictor of reading time does not imply that syntax is unimportant in reading. Syntactic processing may be a highly automatized mechanism which is not very demanding on processing resources. Alternatively, some other components, such as words and propositions, might incorporate syntax as part of their processing mechanisms.

Posner and Warren (1972) identified four characteristics of components that are executed automatically. If we applied these characteristics to reading, we would make the following claims: (a) the processing of automatized components does not require consciousness, focal attention, and effort; (b) readers cannot consciously introspect on the processing of automatized components; (c) the processing of automatized components is relatively unaffected by the reader's goals; (d) the processing of automatized components does not usually suffer interference from other processing components. The definition of automaticity has become more complicated in recent years with the abundance of research on the topic (see Shiffrin & Dumais, 1981). However, there are two implications about reading that can be drawn from virtually all definitions of automaticity. The processing of familiar linguistic units and components (e.g., letters, syllables, words, syntax) should be accomplished relatively quickly and be relatively impervious to the readers goals. In contrast, processing components associated with "deeper" levels of analysis (e.g., semantics, conceptual interpretation of unfamiliar text, etc.) should be more time consuming and sensitive to the goals of the reader. There is one other implication which addresses the issue of whether components are processed serially or in parallel. Automatized components are often activated and executed in parallel whereas nonautomatized components tend to have serial processing characteristics (Carpenter & Just, 1981; Just & Carpenter, 1980).

The distinction between automatized and nonautomatic (controlled) processes was supported in an earlier study that we conducted on sentence reading times (Graesser, 1981; Graesser, Hoffman, & Clark, 1980). We assigned readers to two different instructional set conditions in order to vary the readers' goals. Some readers were told that they would recall the passages after reading them, whereas other readers were told that a multiple choice test would be administered after the passages were read. We performed multiple regression analyses on sentence reading times in order to examine how the readers in the two groups differed. We found differences between instructional conditions when we examined the slope coefficients of those components associated with deeper levels of processing, such as new argument nouns, passage familiarity, and passage narrativity. The slopes were steeper in the recall condition than in the multiple choice condition. Readers in the recall condition allocated more resources to the deeper levels, presumably in order to integrate and organize information in the passage as a whole. In contrast, there were no differences between groups when we examined the slopes for the shallow, automatized components, such as letters, syllables, words, and syntax. This outcome supports the claim that the processing of automatized units at shallow perceptual levels is not substantially influenced by the encoder's goals (Posner, 1978; Posner & Warren, 1972; Schneider & Shiffrin, 1977). Graesser et al. (1980) also reported that slow readers have steeper slopes than fast readers when observing text components at shallow levels; however the slopes are the same for components at deeper levels of processing. This outcome supports some claims that slow readers have deficits in interpreting automatized language codes rather than deficits in integrating information at deeper levels of conceptual analysis

(Aaronson & Scarborough, 1977; Hunt, Lunneborg, & Lewis, 1975; Lesgold & Curtis, 1981; Perfetti & Roth, 1981).

Interpretation of Processing Times

What does it mean to "process" a unit, component, or dimension of text? "Process" is a general term that glosses over intricate mechanisms and many types of code. Even the processing of a syllable involves several mechanisms and several different codes. A syllable processing mechanism might involve (a) pattern match operations which identify syllable codes in long-term memory on the basis of orthographic features, letter codes, and phonemic codes, (b) search processes for syllable codes in long-term memory, and (c) execution of a motor "program" involving the phonetic and/or articulatory realization of a syllable. Syllable processing also includes the formulation of several different codes: (a) primitive orthographic features, (b) abstract letter codes, (c) phonemic and phonetic codes, (d) syllable unit codes, and (e) articulatory codes. In a similar fashion, the other predictor variables could be decomposed into subprocesses and subcodes.

We acknowledge that the idea of a unit, component, or dimension of text being "processed" is vague. However, we have at least provided ballpark estimates of the processing time associated with each of our predictor variables.

Models of reading vary substantially with respect to assumptions about how processing components interact and communicate with one another. The earliest models had the simplest assumptions. These models assumed that units are interpreted and components are executed in a bottom-up, sequentially ordered fashion. Assuming there is a hierarchy of levels, letters are interpreted first, then syllables, then words, then syntax and propositions, and so on. The most extreme bottom-up models proposed that the interpretation of units at level n in the hierarchy did not begin processing until all units at level $n-1$ were completely interpreted (Gough, 1972; Selfridge, 1959; Smith & Spoehr, 1974). More recent bottom-up models assume that units at level $n-1$ need to be partially interpreted before units at level n begin to be processed (LaBerge & Samuels, 1974; McClelland, 1979).

Multiple regression analyses are relatively easy to interpret from the perspective of models assuming bottom-up, sequentially ordered processing stages. The processing of units and components at any particular level requires some execution time and these times combine additively in determining reading times for sentences. The slope parameters from a multiple regression analysis provide estimates of the processing times for units and components at each level.

Interactive models of reading assume that components communicate with one another in a highly interactive fashion. The components interact with one another in a limited capacity working memory, which is sometimes called a message center or blackboard (Carpenter & Just, 1981; Just & Carpenter, 1980; Reddy, 1980; Newell, 1980; Rumelhart, 1977). Processing components are activated by patterns of information that accumulate in the message center. Information in the message center is globally accessible to processing components and knowledge sources at all levels. When a component (or knowledge source) is activated by information in the message center, the component executes its specialized operations and sends its output to the message center. This new information in the message center creates the conditions which enable other processing components to be activated. One consequence of an interactive mechanism is that a higher level component (e.g., a word) may be activated before lower level components are finished being interpreted (e.g., the letters in the word). Another consequence is that the execution of a higher level component may modify, facilitate, interfere, or preclude the activation and interpretation of a lower level component. In most interactive models of reading, the interactive characteristics of the message center are not entirely unconstrained. Generally speaking, the message center must have at least some products from components at lower levels before higher level components are activated. Lower level components are usually activated and executed more quickly than higher level components.

There presently are several interactive models in the theoretical arena and research to support them (Carpenter & Just, 1981; Drewnowski & Healy, 1977; Just & Carpenter, 1980; Just & Thibadeau, this volume; Lesgold & Perfetti, 1978, 1981; Levy, 1981; Marslen-Wilson & Welsh, 1978; Perfetti & Roth, 1981; Potter, Kroll, & Harris, 1980; Reddy, 1980; Rumelhart, 1977; Rumelhart & McClelland, 1981, 1982). The interactive models differ in subtle ways which we do not need to elaborate in the present context.

From the perspective of interactive models of reading, our multiple regression analyses are rather difficult to interpret. When units and components from many different levels are executed in parallel, the slopes and beta weights cannot be interpreted in a systematic way; it is entirely vague as to what codes and mechanisms are associated with a measured predictor variable. The slope coefficients would be crude estimates of the processing time associated with a component. However, there are a few general implications that can be safely drawn from an interactive model. Consider a component that has the following characteristics: (a) it requires a relatively long time to execute, (b) its execution can not be entirely circumvented by components being executed at other levels, and (c) its execution provides output which components at other levels frequently need to enable their activation and execution. Such a component would have relatively high beta weights and/or slope values. Consider processing components that (a) are highly automatized, (b) are activated and executed in parallel, and (c) do not require products from components at other levels. These components should have small slope coefficients. There are other implications of an interactive model. When activities of component n frequently facilitate the activation and execution of components at level m, the slopes and beta weights for level m will be low compared to conditions in which n has little impact on m.

LIMITATIONS OF THE APPROACH

Like all methods, our multiple regression methodology does have its fair share of shortcomings. Our application of multiple regression techniques to reading time does not reveal how the various components are organized and interrelated. For example, the overall architecture of the reading mechanism would probably place the syllable processing component closer to the word processing component than to the component which explains the role of passage familiarity. There are some esoteric multivariate methods available to test plausible structural configurations that interrelate the processing components (Bentler, 1980; Kenny, 1979; Joreskog & Sorbom, 1978). One direction for future research is to examine causal modeling with both measured variables and latent variables (i.e., hypothetical variables that are not measured). We did not apply these sophisticated multivariate methods in this chapter because available theories of reading do not converge on one or even a small set of system configurations.

Both multiple regression analyses and esoteric multivariate methods do not provide the foundation for investigating interactions among knowledge sources and text units at a symbolic level. The methods are too crude to discover or test (a) how knowledge sources communicate with one another in an interactive capacity, (b) how information and control is passed from one processing component to other processing components, and (c) the codes and operations that are characteristic of specific processors. Available theories of reading and comprehension have detailed assumptions about processing mechanisms, codes, and interactions among components. Examining statistical interactions among variables may reveal little or nothing about the details of a symbolically interactive model of reading. Instead, computer simulation methods are needed to investigate the specific properties of an interactive mechanism (Carpenter & Just, 1981; Just & Carpenter, 1980; Kieras, 1981; McClelland, 1979; Reddy, 1980; Rumelhart & McClelland, 1981, 1982; see chapters by Kieras and Just & Thibadeau in this volume). Of course, it is no small task to develop a computer simulation of reading.

Nevertheless, our multiple regression analyses do provide ballpark estimates of the processing time associated with text components. In a previous section we concluded that the slope coefficients of most of our predictor variables are quite reliable and perhaps even valid. These slope coefficients may be informative to researchers in a number of ways. First, the slopes generally improve a researcher's perspective on what components impose demands on the limited supply of processing resources during reading. Second, the slopes can be used to search for best-fit parameters in computer models with highly interactive characteristics. Third, when investigators are confronted with third variable artifacts in data, the slopes provide some information as to whether a pattern of reading times is substantially contaminated by a potential confounding variable.

So far we have examined the impact of 15 variables on sentence reading times. There obviously are other variables that contribute to reading times and these can be readily incorporated into multiple regression analyses. Whenever we want to examine the extent to which a new variable predicts reading times, we scale our sentences on that variable and add the variable to our predictive equation. We do not need to design, conduct, and analyze another experiment to test this new variable. We can simply reanalyze the data that we have already collected.

Our multiple regression analysis of reading times is simply another method of studying reading time and comprehension. It is not a perfect method, but it does provide some information that other methods cannot easily provide. Multiple regression will never replace computer simulation methods and experimental methods that have traditionally embraced analysis of variance. We believe that multiple regression and other multivariate analyses merely offer another perspective for studying reading and comprehension.

ACKNOWLEDGMENT

The research reported in this chapter was supported in part by a grant from the National Institute of Mental Health (MH-33491) awarded to the first author. Requests for reprints should be sent to Arthur C. Graesser, Department of Psychology, California State University, Fullerton, California 92634.

REFERENCES

Aaronson, D., & Scarborough, H. S. Performance theories for sentence coding: Some quantitative models. *Journal of Verbal Learning and Verbal Behavior*, 1977, *16*, 277-304.

Asher, S. R. Topic interest and children's reading comprehension. In R. J. Spiro, B. C. Bruce, and W. F. Brewer, (Eds), *Theoretical issues in reading comprehension*. Hillsdale, N. J.: Lawrence Erlbaum Associates, 1980.

Bentler, P. M. Multivariate analyses with latent variables: Causal modeling. In M. R. Rosenweig and L. W. Porter (Eds.), *Annual review of psychology*. Palo Alto, California: Annual Reviews, 1980.

Bisanz, G. L., & Voss, J. F. Sources of knowledge in reading comprehension: Cognitive development and expertise in a content domain. In A. M. Lesgold & C. A. Perfetti (Eds.), *Interactive processes in reading*. Hillsdale, N. J.: Lawrence Erlbaum Associates, 1981.

Black, J. B., Schwartz, S. P., & Lehnert, W. G. Interestingness and memory for stories. Proceedings of the Third Annual Conference of the Cognitive Science Society, Berkely, CA., August, 113-114.

Bovair, S., & Kieras, D. E. A guide to propositional analysis for research on technical prose. Technical Report No. 8, University of Arizona, 1981.

Britton, B. K., Holdredge, T. S., Curry, C., & Westbrook, R. D. Cognitive capacity usage in reading identical texts with different amounts of discourse level meaning. *Journal of Experimental Psychology: Human Learning and Memory*, 1979, *5*, 262-270.

Carpenter, P. A., & Just, M. A. Sentence comprehension: A psycholinguistic processing model of verification. *Psychological Review*, 1975, *82*, 45-73.

Carpenter, P. A., & Just, M. A. Cognitive processes in reading: Models based on readers' eye fixations. In A. M. Lesgold & C. A. Perfetti (Eds.), *Interactive processes in reading*. Hillsdale, N. J.: Lawrence Erlbaum Associates, 1981.

Clark, H. H. Inferences in comprehension. In D. LaBerge & S. L. Samuels (Eds.), *Basic processes in reading: Perception and comprehension*. Hillsdale, N. J.: Lawrence Erlbaum Associates, 1977.

Drewnowski, A., & Healy, A. F. Detection errors on *the* and *and*: Evidence for reading units larger than the word. *Memory and Cognition*, 1977, *5*, 636-647.

Eddy, J. K., & Glass, A. L. Reading and listening to high and low imagery sentences. *Journal of Verbal Learning and Verbal Behavior*, 1981, *20*, 333-345.

Foss, D. J. Decision processes during sentence comprehension: Effects of lexical item and position upon decision times. *Journal of Verbal Learning and Verbal Behavior*, 1969, *8*, 457-462.

Gough, P. B. One second of reading. In J. F. Kavanagh & J. G. Mattingly (Eds.), *Language by ear and by eye*. Cambridge, Mass.: M. I. T. Press, 1972.

Graesser, A. C. How to catch a fish: The representation and memory of common procedures. *Discourse Processes*, 1978, *1*, 72-89.

Graesser, A. C. *Prose comprehension beyond the word*. New York: Springer-Verlag, 1981.

Graesser, A. C., & Goodman, S. M. Inferences, question answering, and the representation of expository text. In B. Britton and J. B. Black (Eds.), *Understanding expository text*. Hillsdale, N. J.: Lawrence Erlbaum Associates, in press.

Graesser, A. C., Hauft-Smith, K., Cohen, A. D., & Pyles, L. D. Advanced outlines, familiarity, text genre, and retention of prose. *Journal of Experimental Education*, 1980, *48*, 209-220.

Graesser, A. C., Hoffman, N. L., & Clark, L. F. Structural components of reading time. *Journal of Verbal Learning and Verbal Behavior*, 1980, *19*, 131-151.

Graesser, A. C., Robertson, S. P., & Anderson, P. A. Incorporating inferences in narrative representations: A study of how and why. *Cognitive Psychology*, 1981, *13*, 1-26.

Haberlandt, K., Berian, C., & Sandson, J. The episode schema in story processing. *Journal of Verbal Learning and Verbal Behavior*, 1980, *19*, 635-650.

Holmes, V. M., & Langford, J. Comprehension and recall of abstract and concrete sentences. *Journal of Verbal Learning and Verbal Behavior*, 1976, *15*, 559-566.

Hunt, E., Lunneborg, C., & Lewis, J. What does it mean to be high verbal? *Cognitive Psychology*, 1975, *7*, 194-227.

Johnson, W., & Kieras, D. E. The role of prior knowledge in the comprehension of simple technical prose. Technical Report No. 11, University of Arizona, 1982.

Joreskog, K. G. Structural analysis of covariance and correlation matrices. *Psychometrica*, 1978, *43*, 443-477.

Joreskog, K. G., & Sorbom, D. *LISREL IV Users Guide*. Chicago: National Educational Research, 1978.

Just, M. A., & Carpenter, P. A. A theory of reading: From eye fixations to comprehension. *Psychological Review*, 1980, *87*, 329-354.

Kahneman, D. *Attention and effort*. Englewood Cliffs, N. J.: Prentice-Hall, 1973.

Kenny, D. A. *Correlation and causation*. New York: Wiley, 1979.

Kieras, D. E. Component processes in the comprehension of simple prose. *Journal of Verbal Learning and Verbal Behavior*, 1981, *20*, 1-22.

Kintsch, W. *The representation of meaning in memory*. Hillsdale, N. J.: Lawrence Erlbaum Associates, 1974.

Kintsch, W., & van Dijk, T. A. Toward a model of text comprehension and production. *Psychological Review*, 1978, *85*, 363-394.

Kintsch, W., & Keenan, J. Reading rate and retention as a function of the number of propositions in the base structure of sentences. *Cognitive Psychology*, 1973, *5*, 257-274.

Kintsch, W., Kozminsky, E., Streby, W. J., McKoon, G., & Keenan, J. M. Comprehension and recall of text as a function of content variables. *Journal of Verbal Learning and Verbal Behavior*, 1975, *14*, 196-214.

Kucera, H., & Francis, W. *Computational analysis of present-day American English*. Providence, R. I.: Brown University Press, 1967.

LaBerge, D., & Samuels, S. L. Toward a theory of automatic information processing in reading. *Cognitive Psychology*, 1974, *6*, 293-323.

Lesgold, A. M., & Curtis, M. E. Learning to read words efficiently. In A. M. Lesgold & C. A. Perfetti (Eds.), *Interactive processes in reading*. Hillsdale, N. J.: Lawrence Erlbaum Associates, 1981.

Lesgold, A. M., & Perfetti, C. A. Interactive processes in reading comprehension. *Discourse Processes*, 1978, *1*, 323-336.

Lesgold, A. M., & Perfetti, C. A. (Eds.) *Interactive processes in reading*. Hillsdale, N. J.: Lawrence Erlbaum Associates, 1981.

Lesgold, A. M., Roth, S. F., & Curtis, M. E. Foregrounding effects in discourse comprehension. *Journal of Verbal Learning and Verbal Behavior*, 1979, *18*, 291-308.

Levy, B. A. Interactive processing during reading. In A. M. Lesgold and C. A. Perfetti (Eds.), *Interactive processes in reading*. Hillsdale, N. J.: Lawrence Erlbaum Associates, 1981.

Mandler, J. M., & Johnson, N. S. Remembrance of things parsed: Story structure and recall. *Cognitive Psychology*, 1977, *9*, 111-151.

Marslen-Wilson, W. D., & Welsh, A. Processing interactions and lexical access during word recognition. *Cognitive Psychology*, 1978, *10*, 29-63.

McClelland, J. L. On the time relations of mental processes. *Psychological Review*, 1979, *86*, 287-330.

Miller, J. R., & Kintsch, W. Readability and recall of short prose passages: A theoretical analysis. *Journal of Experimental Psychology: Human Learning and Memory*, 1980, *6*, 335-354.

Mitchell, D. C., & Green, D. W. The effects of content on immediate processing in reading. *Quarterly Journal of Experimental Psychology*, 1978, *30*, 609-636.

Morton, J. The interaction of information in word recognition. *Psychological Review*, 1969, *76*, 165-178.

Newell, A. Harpy, production systems and human cognition. In R. Cole (Ed.), *Perception and production of fluent speech*. Hillsdale, N. J.: Lawrence Erlbaum Associates, 1980.

Nie, N. H., Hull, C. H., Jenkins, J. G., Steinbrenner, K., & Bent, D. H. *Statistical packages for the social sciences* (2nd edition). New York: McGraw-Hill, 1975.

Norman, D., & Bobrow, D. On data-limited and resource-limited processes. *Cognitive Psychology*, 1975, *7*, 44-64.

Norman, D. A., & Rumelhart, D. E. *Explorations in cognition*. San Francisco: Freeman, 1975.

Olson, G. M., Mack, R., & Duffy, S. *Strategies for story understanding*. Paper presented at the meeting of the Cognitive Science Society, Yale University, New Haven, 1980.

Perfetti, C. A. Leels of language and levels of process. In F. I. M. Craik & L. Cermak (Eds.), *Levels of processing in human memory*. Hillsdale, N. J.: Lawrence Erlbaum Associates, 1979.

Perfetti, C. A., & Roth, S. Some of the interactive processes in reading and their role in reading skill. In A. M. Lesgold & C. A. Perfetti (Eds.), *Interactive processes in reading*. Hillsdale, N. J.: Lawrence Erlbaum Associates, 1981.

Posner, M. I. *Chronometric explorations of the mind*. Hillsdale, N. J.: Lawrence Erlbaum Associates, 1978.

Posner, M. I., & Synder, C. R. Attention and cognitive control. In R. L. Solso (Ed.), *Information processing and cognition: The Loyola symposium*. Hillsdale, N. J.: Lawrence Erlbaum Associates, 1975.

Posner, M. I., & Warren, R. E. Traces, concepts, and conscious constructions. In A. W. Melton & E. Martin (Eds.), *Coding processes in human memory*. Washington, D. C.: Winston, 1972.

Potter, M. C., Kroll, J. F., & Harris, C. Comprehension and memory in rapid sequential reading of words in text. In R. S. Nickerson (Ed.), *Attention and performance VIII*. Hillsdale, N. J.: Lawrence Erlbaum Associates, 1980.

Reddy, R. Machine models of speech perception. In R. A. Cole (Ed.), *Perception and production of fluent speech*. Hillsdale, N. J.: Lawrence Erlbaum Associates, 1980.

Reynolds, R. E., & Anderson, R. C. The influence of questions on the allocation of attention during reading. Technical Report No. 183, Center for the Study of Reading, University of Illinois, Champaign-Urbana, ILL., 1981.

Rumelhart, D. E. Toward an interactive model of reading. In S. Dornic (Ed.), *Attention and performance VI*. Hillsdale, N. J.: Lawrence Erlbaum Associates, 1977.

Rumelhart, D. E. Understanding and summarizing brief stories. In D. LaBerge & S. L. Samuels (Eds.), *Basic processes in reading: Perception and comprehension*. Hillsdale, N. J.: Lawrence Erlbaum Associates, 1977.

Rumelhart, D. E., & McClelland, J. An interactive model of context effects in letter perception: Part 2. The contextual enhancement effect and some tests and extensions of the model. *Psychological Review*, 1982, *89*, 60-94.

Rumelhart, D. E., & McClelland, J. Interactive processes through spreading activation. In A. M. Lesgold and C. A. Perfetti (Eds.), *Interactive processes in reading*. Hillsdale, N. J.: Lawrence Erlbaum Associates, 1981.

Sanford, A. J., & Garrod, S. Memory and attention in text comprehension. In R. S. Nickerson (Ed.), *Attention and performance VIII*. Hillsdale, N. J.: Lawrence Erlbaum Associates, 1980.

Schank, R. C., & Abelson, R. *Scripts, plans, goals, and understanding*. Hillsdale, N. J.: Lawrence Erlbaum Associates, 1977.

Schneider, W., & Shiffrin, R. M. Controlled and automatic human information processing: Detection, search, and attention. *Psychological Review*, 1977, *84*, 1-66.

Selfridge, O. G. Pandemonium: A paradigm for learning. In D. V. Blake & A. M. Vittey (Eds.), *The mechnisation of thought processes*. London: H. M. Stationery Office, 1959.

Shaffer, W. O., & LaBerge, D. Automatic semantic processing of unattended words. *Journal of Verbal Learning and Verbal Behavior*, 1979, *18*, 413-426.

Shiffrin, R. M., & Dumais, S. T. The development of automatization. In J. R. Anderson (Ed.), *Cognitive skills and their acquisition*. Hillsdale, N. J.: Lawrence Erlbaum Associates, 1981.

Shiffrin, R. M., & Schneider, W. Controlled and automatic human information processing: II. Perceptual learning, automatic attending, and a general theory. *Psychological Review*, 1977, *84*, 127-190.

Smith, E. E., & Spoehr, K. T. The perception of printed English: A theoretical perspective. In B. H. Kantowitz (Ed.), *Human information-processing: Tutorials in performance and cognition*. Hillsdale, N. J.: Lawrence Erlbaum Associates, 1974.

Spilich, G. J., Vesonder, G. T., Chiesi, H. L., & Voss, J. F. Text processing of domain related information for individuals with high and low domain knowledge. *Journal of Verbal Learning and Verbal Behavior*, 1979, *18*, 275-290.

Stein, N. L., & Glenn, G. G. An analysis of story comprehension in elementary school children. In R. O. Freedle (Ed.), *New directions in discourse processing* (Vol. 2). Norwood, N. J.: Ablex, 1979.

Stevens, A., & Rumelhart, D. E. Errors in reading: Analyses using an augmented transition network grammar. In D. A. Norman & D. E. Rumelhart (Eds.), *Explorations in cognition*. San Francisco: Freeman, 1975.

Thorndyke, P. W. Cognitive structures in comprehension and memory of narrative discourse. *Cognitive Psychology*, 1977, *9*, 77-110.

van Dijk, T. A. *Macrostructures*. Hillsdale, N. J.: Lawrence Erlbaum Associates, 1980.

Vipond, D. Micro- and macroprocesses in text comprehension. *Journal of Verbal Learning and Verbal Behavior*, 1980, *19*, 276-296.

Woods, W. Transition network grammars for natural language analysis. *Communications of the Association for Computing Machinery*, 1970, *13*, 591-606.

10 Components of Sentence and Word Reading Times

Karl Haberlandt
Trinity College

In reading a person translates strings of graphic symbols into meaning by using a variety of processes. The reader decodes letters, forms word percepts, accesses word meanings, parses sentences, integrates sentences, and forms an overall interpretation of the text. Investigators of reading assume that the cognitive load associated with these processes fluctuates with time and that different factors contribute to the fluctuations. It is the goal of reading research to capture the momentary changes in processing load and to isolate the factors contributing to it. Various "on-line" methods have been devised to measure the pattern of processing over time and statistical techniques have been developed to analyze those measurements. The present chapter first discusses general assumptions underlying the use of some recent on-line methods. Then it turns to techniques of data analysis, specifically to linear multiple regression. It does so by way of giving a brief theoretical background on my research which deals with the influence of several components on reader processing load as it is reflected by the pattern of word and sentence reading times. Linear multiple regression was used in order to partition the contribution of these components to the variance in reading times. The reading times were collected in two subject-paced conditions, a "single-sentence" and a "single-word" condition. Within conditions, there were two orienting tasks, recall and question-answering. The analysis of reading times from these experiments revealed that readers' processing load increased with the normative word frequency, with stimulus length of both words and sentences, with the introduction of new concepts, with the shift to a new narrative episode, and, importantly, with content differences between stories. In addition, some task-specific factors increasing processing load were identified. After controlling for these and other factors, processing load decreased as the reader progressed with reading a story. In the third part of this chapter these data will be used to illustrate methodological aspects of stimulus presentation as well as of data analysis.

GENERAL ASSUMPTIONS OF ON-LINE METHODS

The major on-line methods used in current reading research include the eye fixation method (e.g., Just & Carpenter, 1980; Rayner, 1977), different single-word procedures (Aaronson & Scarborough, 1977; Just, Carpenter, & Woolley, 1982), and the single-sentence procedure. These methods are based on certain assumptions several of which I shall consider in the first section of this chapter along with some of their problems and limitations. In outlining these assumptions I shall use the single-sentence procedure as point of departure and introduce the others as needed. In the single-sentence procedure passages are presented one sentence at a time on a video-terminal with the reader advancing through the passage by pressing a button in order to expose the next sentence and with "Sentence Reading Time" defined as the interval between button presses. The first assumption, made since sentence reading time was first introduced as a dependent variable by Miller & McKean (1964; see also Danks, 1968; Kintsch & Keenan, 1973; Haviland & Clark, 1974; Kieras, 1974; Manelis & Yekovich, 1976) is that it provides a measure of the comprehension process in the reader. This means the reader is assumed to press the button when he or she has "understood" the sentence where the criterion for "understanding" is left up to the reader. Furthermore, it is argued that if the reading times show reliable differences in accordance with an experimental manipulation, it is unlikely that the readers moved through the passages indiscriminately. According to this view it is not necessary to assess the reader's level of comprehension independently. On the other hand, some researchers find it useful to record additional indices of comprehension as measured in an orienting task such as question-answering, summarization, or recall (e.g., Kieras, 1981). Since "comprehension" may depend critically on the task given to the reader and since it may interact with the task, it is necessary to evaluate reading time levels and the reading time pattern relative to the type of task as Aaronson and Scarborough (e.g., 1976), Just et al. (1982) and Kieras (1981) have done.

Regardless of whether additional indices of comprehension are used or not, reading time is still a controversial measure according to some critics including McKoon and Ratcliff (1980, p. 671). These authors have pointed out that "reading time can indicate when increased processing is required, but it cannot indicate what that processing is" (see also Graesser, 1981, p. 216; Hogaboam & McConkie, 1981). While these critics have a valid point here, it is also the case that nobody actually claimed that reading times taken by themselves reveal comprehension processes directly just as nobody claims that percentage of recall, d', latencies, or any other dependent variable reveals processing directly. Reading times have the same status as other dependent variables. They are either used in order to evaluate a hypothesis of processing or to aid in the formulation of new hypotheses as I shall describe later. They are also used in conjunction with measures obtained using other methods such as question-answering, recall, think-aloud protocols, norming studies (Graesser, 1981) and more recently computer simulation (Thibadeau, Just, & Carpenter, 1982; Kieras, 1981).

Second, it would be convenient if a researcher could assume that sentence reading time was a measure of the processing of the current sentence n. There are, however, two reservations calling this assumption into question. The first reservation was raised by McConkie, Hogaboam, Wolverton, Zola, and Lucas (1979) who argued that the interval between button presses also includes a "post-comprehensional" process or "thinking time". However, the task context used by McConkie et al. was a sentence verification experiment and the degree to which latencies contain a "post-comprehensional" process may vary as a function of the task context. The second reservation is more difficult to deal with. We know that there are sequential effects from previous sentences on current sentences. Indeed, many of our theoretically motivated research manipulations exploit these sequential effects, for example where an investigator varies the "inference distance" between adjacent sentences (e.g., Bower, Black, & Turner, 1979). Unfortunately, there are also unexpected "spillover effects" from a prior text n-1 to text n (Haberlandt & Bingham, 1978) such that the reading time of text n was longer the more difficult the preceding text was. The best way to deal with such artifactual spillover effects is through careful counterbalancing of the sequence of stimulus items.

The third assumption is that sentence reading times are a composite of several time intervals including the time to press the button and the durations of more molecular responses such as fixations of the eye on individual words. Since sentence reading time does not reveal such durations, it is not sensitive to intra-sentence modulations of processing including potential "tradeoffs" which involve an increase in processing difficulty in one part of the sentence while decreasing it in another. The only solution to this problem is the use of molecular measures such as reading times of single words (Aaronson & Scarborough, 1976; Just, Carpenter, & Woolley, 1982), eye fixation durations, or reading times of phrases (Mitchell & Green, 1978). In the long run, the verdict on these methods will be whether or not the results they yield are compatible. Comparison of results using different methods is an important empirical task which has only been addressed recently (Just et al., 1982). It will require the attention of reading researchers in the future and is, at least in part, a purpose of the present chapter.

The methods and the data analyses described in the remainder of the chapter were developed in the framework of research of certain local factors in reading comprehension and of the narrative problem solving schema first introduced by Rumelhart (1975) and later developed by Mandler & Johnson (1977; see also Stein

& Glenn, 1979; Thorndyke, 1977). In order to provide the background for the analyses, first the story schema and a processing assumption, the boundary hypothesis, will be discussed.

BACKGROUND FOR RESEARCH ON STORY COMPREHENSION

The Story Schema

The stories used in the present studies consisted of a Setting and two "episodes" with each episode conforming to the narrative problem solving schema described by Mandler & Johnson (1977). The episode is defined from the point of view of a protagonist who faces a problem and attempts to solve it. The solution path of the problem is described in terms of "nodes". Adopting Mandler & Johnson's (1977), notation, the episodes of our stories had the following six nodes, Beginning (B), Reaction (R), Goal (G), Attempt (A), Outcome (O), and Ending (E). In the Beginning the problem confronting the protagonist is introduced. Next the protagonist makes a Reaction in response to the events related in the Beginning, formulates a Goal to cope with the problem, and makes an Attempt to achieve the Goal. The Attempt is followed by the Outcome, which recounts a specific local result of the Attempt, and by the Ending, which provides a more general summary. We used 12 stories each consisting of two well-formed episodes. One of these stories is reproduced in Table 1.

While the processing assumptions presented next were first formulated with respect to such simple stories, they are, in principle, applicable to more complex stories.

TABLE 1
Sample Story Consisting of a Setting and Two Episodes

S Mike and Dave Thompson lived in Florida.
  They lived across from an orange grove.
  There was a river between their house and the grove.
B One Saturday they had nothing to do.
R They were quite bored.
G They decided to get some oranges from the grove.
A They took their canoe and paddled across the river.
O They picked a crate full of oranges and put it in the canoe.
B While they were paddling home the canoe began to sink.
R Mike and Dave realized that they were in great trouble.
Q They had to prevent the canoe from sinking further.
A They threw the oranges out of the canoe.
O Finally the canoe stopped sinking.
  Now all of the oranges were gone.
E Their adventure had failed after all.

The Boundary Hypothesis

The hypothesis guiding the present research was that readers have knowledge of the narrative problem solving schema and that they use it when reading such simple two-episode stories for the purpose of recall or answering questions. The specific prediction, called the boundary hypothesis, was that readers would use the boundary sentences of an episode, namely the Beginning and Ending, to do extra processing above and beyond word recognition and sentence parsing. Consequently, reading times *controlled for other factors*, should be longer at boundary sentences than at other sentences of the stories. The extra processing at the boundaries is presumably a result of certain encoding operations. Thus, at the Beginning the reader is assumed to identify the protagonist, to encode the problem facing the protagonist, and to initialize new memory locations for the current episode. It should be relatively easy for a reader to identify the Beginning of a new episode because it is typically signalled by such surface cues as *One day...*, *One afternoon...*, *While playing one day* and so on. There are also thematic cues including changes from a description of states or habitually occurring events to a description of unique events, changes of activities or scripts, introduction of a new perspective and/or of a new protagonist. The advent of a new episode may also coincide with a shift in the local topic between adjacent sentences such that the surface subject of the Beginning sentence was not mentioned in the preceding sentence (Dee-Lucas, Just, Carpenter, & Daneman, 1982). At the Ending the reader is assumed to condense the information of the current episode, transfer it to long-term memory and clear working memory.

In order to provide generality across orienting tasks the boundary effect was evaluated using two tasks, a recall and a question-answering task. Furthermore, in order to determine the locus or loci of the slow-down within the boundary sentences a single-word procedure was used in addition to the single-sentence procedure described above.

READING TIME ANALYSIS BY MULTIPLE REGRESSION

Background for Multiple Regression Analysis

Because comprehension and, hence, reading time is affected concurrently by many factors, the key issue in evaluating the boundary hypothesis was the issue of "control for other factors". Originally I controlled for just one of these factors, namely sentence length. I did so by dividing sentence reading times by the number of words in the sentence. Figure 1 and the following considerations will show that this was a poor estimate of sentence processing. In the left panel of Figure 1 sentence reading times, observed in a recall situation, are graphed as a function of the number of words. The function has a slope of about 200 milliseconds and an intercept of about 1100 milliseconds.

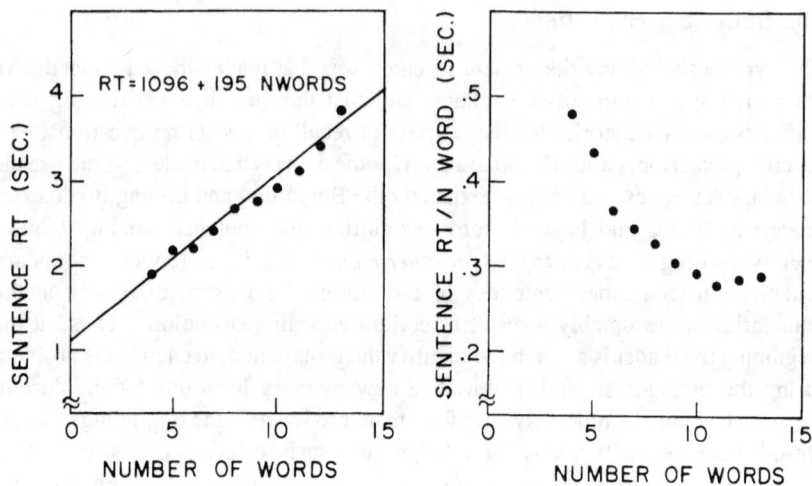

FIG. 1. Sentence reading times (left panel) and sentence reading times divided by the number of words (right panel) as a function of the number of words in the sentence.

In dividing the sentence reading times by the number of words, one is also dividing the intercept of the function. Consequently, with shorter sentences the intercept makes a larger contribution to the new reading time measure thus producing longer estimates than when the number of words is relatively large (see right panel of Figure 1). Hence sentence reading times divided by the number of words are not a suitable measure when the sentences differ widely in their number of words. Similarly, sentence reading time divided by the number of syllables is not a suitable measure (Black, Turner, & Bower, 1979.) Indeed, in at least one case sentence reading times and reading times divided by the number of syllables gave contradictory interpretations of the same data (see Bower et al., 1979, Exp. 6). Of course, there are many other factors influencing sentence reading times. Inspection of our reading times indicated, for example, that later sentences of a story were read faster than earlier sentences (Haberlandt, 1980), and a review of the literature yielded many more factors including those listed in Table 2.

Due to the joint influence of these factors on reading times, an analytical tool was required that could handle their concurrent contribution to reading times. The tool I chose was multiple linear regression. Simply put, a multiple regression predicts the dependent variable from a set of independent variables such that the squared deviations between observed and predicted values are at a minimum. Opting for multiple regression as a tool, the investigator faces a number of choices, to be discussed in turn. First, which predictor or independent variables does one choose and which regression model does one adopt? Second, how should one measure the contribution of each component to the variance in reading time, if at all? Third, how does one draw inferences from the data and how does one measure the significance of an effect? In addressing these questions it should be remembered, that there is no single answer to any of them with each answer involving

TABLE 2
Selected Factors Influencing Sentence Reading Times

Sentence Level Factors

Word frequency (Danks, 1968; Kieras, 1974; Rayner, 1977; Mitchell & Green, 1978).
Number of propositions (Danks, 1968; Kintsch & Keenan, 1973).
Imagery value of words (Paivio, 1971; Kieras, 1974; Thorndyke, 1975).
Meaningfulness of words (Kieras, 1974).
Interword associations (Danks, 1968; Kleiman, 1980).
Syntactic factors: voice, negation (Just & Carpenter, 1971), amount of embedding, marking of adjectives.
Reader's knowledge of syntactic structure (Wisher, 1976).
Specificity of information (Sanford & Garrod, 1980).

Text Level Factors

Number of reinstatement searches (Lesgold, Roth, & Curtis, 1979).
Difficulty of finding referent (Haviland & Clark, 1974; Caramazza et al., 1977; Yekovich et al., 1979).
Degree of coherence (Kieras, 1978; Haberlandt & Bingham, 1978).
Entailment of information (Carpenter & Just, 1977).
Importance of a sentence to the text (Cirillo & Foss, 1980).
New arguments (Kintsch et al., 1975; Graesser, 1980).
Topic change (Dee-Lucas, Just, Carpenter, & Daneman, 1982).
Perspective shift (Black, Turner, & Bower, 1979).
Content, familiarity, narrativity, action vs. intent (Kintsch et al., 1975; Graesser et al., 1980).

some problems. For this reason statisticians recommend that researchers compare multiple regression results observed in repeated experiments, an approach adopted here.

Choice of Independent Variables and Regression Model. There are at least four sources for independent variables to be used in a multiple regression on sentence reading times. First, some variables are provided by an analysis of the features of the sentences and of the text itself. The variables chosen here were those we could quantify relatively easily such as the number of words, the serial position, the normative word frequency, the number of propositions, and the number of new arguments in a sentence where new arguments were concepts mentioned for the first time in the sentence.[1] Save for one exception to be discussed later on, we did not use in any one regression analysis such variables as the number of characters, the number of syllables and the number of words jointly, because these measures were highly correlated giving rise to the problem of multicollinearity. Second, independent variables may be provided by a simulation model, e.g., Kieras (1981) used ATN transitions and number of memory links provided by his model as independent variables, and Thibadeau et al. (1982) used processing cycles generated by their READER model as independent variables. Third, independent

---

[1]In a separate analysis the complexity of each sentence expressed by its Yngve depth was also entered as an independent variable. This variable had no significant effect and its presence did not change the contribution of other effects.

variables may be provided from other experiments. For example, we used importance ratings of each sentence, obtained in a separate norming experiment, as a predictor variable. In the norming experiment, raters were asked to judge the importance of each sentence on a scale from 1 to 12 where 1 represented "very important". In further analyses we also used the percentage of recall of a sentence and the sentence reading times obtained in one experiment as independent variables on the reading time of the same sentence in another experiment (for further details see Haberlandt et al., 1980).

The fourth source of an independent variable is the hypothesis guiding the experiment, which was in this case the boundary hypothesis. I generated different sets of indicator weights to reflect the hypothesized additional processing of the six sentences in an episode. One variant of the boundary hypothesis was that the extra processing due to the use of the episode schema, would be greater at the Beginning and Ending and least in the two innermost nodes with intermediate levels at the Reaction and the Outcome. The set of weights corresponding to this symmetrical hypothesis was 1, 0, -1, -1, 0, 1 for the six successive nodes, respectively. (Alternative hypotheses with corresponding sets of indicator weights will be considered later.) Of the variables produced by these sources, one typically selects those which one expects to contribute significantly to the variance in reading times. Based on these considerations I selected for the single-sentence experiment the following independent variables for analyses of sentence reading times, the number of words, the serial position, the normative frequency of content words, the number of propositions, the number of new arguments, the mean importance rating, and the indicator weights for the boundary effect. (For a discussion of independent variables in analyses of word reading times see page 234.) The next two tables give the means (and standard deviations) of five of these variables for the 12 nodes of the stories and the zero-order correlations among all of the seven independent variables.

Inspection of Table 4 indicates that the correlations between the independent variables were small, except for the correlation between the number of words and the number of propositions. Thus, the problem of multicollinearity was judged to be of minor impact. For the present analysis we included the number of words and of propositions jointly because research by Kintsch (1974), Graesser et al. (1980) and Kieras (1981) indicated that the number of propositions influences sentence reading times independently of the number of words. However, additional analyses revealed that excluding the number of propositions as a factor did not change the qualitative multiple regression results. Excluding the word factor increased the contribution of the proposition and boundary effects but did not change the others substantially. The seven components contained in Table 4 were entered as independent variables in a simultaneous multiple regression. The simultaneous model was chosen because there were no predictions of the relative priority of the independent variables (Cohen & Cohen, 1975).

TABLE 3
Means and Standard Deviations (in Parentheses)
of Independent Variables
in Single-Sentence Experiments

Node	Words	Propositions	Frequency	New Arguments	Importance
B	10.8 (2.9)	4.4 (1.4)	271 (162)	.92 (1.0)	5.4 (3.0)
R	7.9 (2.5)	2.1 (.7)	127 (182)	.58 (1.0)	9.7 (2.4)
G	7.7 (2.4)	2.8 (1.0)	257 (284)	.25 (.6)	8.3 (2.2)
A	8.2 (1.6)	2.8 (.7)	178 (108)	.67 (.7)	7.8 (1.9)
O	7.0 (2.5)	3.0 (1.0)	119 (112)	.75 (.8)	6.3 (1.7)
E	7.3 (1.8)	2.9 (.8)	178 (142)	.50 (.7)	9.6 (2.4)
B	9.2 (2.6)	3.7 (1.4)	172 (101)	.75 (.5)	6.3 (1.1)
R	8.0 (2.4)	2.2 (.8)	150 (130)	.33 (.5)	10.3 (1.7)
G	7.2 (1.3)	2.7 (.7)	174 (138)	.25 (.5)	9.6 (1.6)
A	7.8 (1.2)	3.5 (1.3)	167 (150)	.67 (1.0)	8.6 (1.9)
O	9.0 (5.2)	3.8 (1.6)	245 (216)	.75 (1.0)	7.8 (1.2)
E	9.5 (2.1)	3.9 (1.2)	296 (168)	.58 (.9)	9.6 (1.7)

The Relative Contribution of an Effect. A regression yields a number of related coefficients, which are either provided by most extant computer programs or which can be readily computed from the output of those programs (see Cohen & Cohen, 1975, Appendix 3). The regression provides, among other coefficients, "Multiple R" which expresses the association between the dependent variable and an optimal combination of two or more independent variables. Multiple R^2 is the proportion of the variance in the dependent variable predicted by the set of independent variables entered into the equation. The other coefficients provided by the regression for each predictor variable are the raw score partial regression coefficient, B, and three squared correlation coefficients r^2_i, pr^2_i, $sr_2{}^i$. These four coefficients are typically used to estimate the contribution of the individual predictor variable. The meaning of these coefficients is nicely described by Cohen

TABLE 4
Correlations Between Independent Variables Used in
Single-Sentence Experiments

	Position	Frequency	Propositions	Importance	New Arguments	Boundary
Words	-0.018	0.199	0.661	-0.070	0.439	0.227
Position		0.056	0.119	0.158	-0.037	0.000
Frequency			0.228	-0.115	-0.034	0.085
Propositions				-0.007	0.275	0.251
Importance					0.048	-0.123
New Arguments						0.122

and Cohen (1975, pp. 78-84). However, one of these coefficients, the squared *semipartial* correlation coefficient, sr^2_i, deserves special attention. It corresponds to the increase in the variance of the dependent variable accounted for if the independent variable, X_i, had been added as *last* variable in a stepwise regression. The squared partial correlation is the proportion of the variance in Y associated with X_i but not with the other variables. The squared, semipartial and partial, correlation coefficients are measures of the relative contribution of an effect to the reading times. They are a useful "diagnostic" rather than an indicator of absolute "effect size". Specifically, the squared semipartial correlation coefficient associated with a factor indicates what the overall fit, expressed by R^2, would be if that factor were excluded from the equation. In some cases a single factor may contribute a relatively large amount to R^2 as we shall see in a recall experiment described later on. The R^2 measure by itself does not reveal such unequal contributions of effects and thus it is less informative than when the squared semipartial coefficients are also reported.

Assumptions Underlying Regression Analysis and Tests of Significance. If we used a multiple regression merely to describe a sample of data from a given experiment, the semipartial and partial correlation coefficients would provide an adequate account of the sample. However, we would like to draw inferences about the presence or absence of an effect in the population by computing F or t ratios. The schema of an F test in multiple regression is simple enough with F being defined as regression variance relative to residual variance.

(1) $F = MS$ regression/MS residual.

While it is simple to define and to compute F, certain assumptions about the independent variables and about the residuals must be understood, if not be met, in order to interpret F properly. One assumption about the independent variables is that they be orthogonal. However, frequently the independent variables are not orthogonal. For example in our research the number of propositions and the number of words in a sentence were correlated. In such cases, it is recommended by statisticians to repeat the analysis deleting one of the variables and to observe the extent to which the coefficients of interest change (cf. Weisberg, 1980, Ch. 6).

Another assumption is that the values of the dependent variables are normally distributed and have an equal variance at each level of an independent variable. This assumption underlies F-tests in general. While this "normality assumption" may not actually be met by a given set of reading time or latency data to be analyzed by multiple regression, it has been shown that F- and t-tests are "robust" when the assumption is violated (e.g., Keppel, 1973; Winer, 1971). As a result, statisticians consider the use of these tests in multiple regression analysis as justified (e.g., Kerlinger & Pedhazur, 1973; Cohen & Cohen, 1975).

The assumptions concerning residuals are that residuals be normally distributed, that they have a mean of zero and a common variance. These assumptions are relatively easy to check by plotting residuals against predicted Y values (see Weisberg, 1980). In Figure 2 residuals obtained from sentence reading times

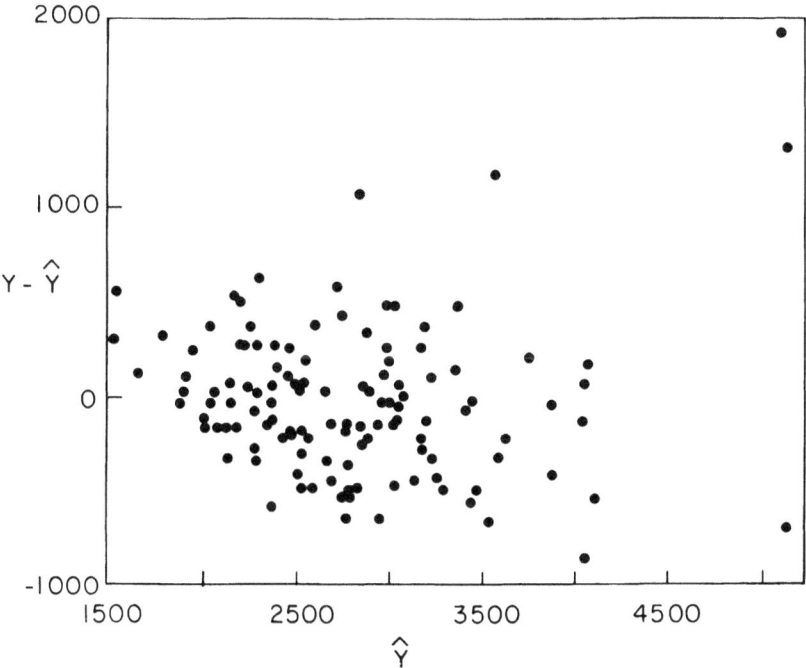

FIG. 2. Residuals, Y-$\hat{Y}$, plotted as a function of estimated reading times, $\hat{Y}$, from the recall experiment single-sentence condition.

observed in one of our recall experiments are plotted against predicted sentence reading times. The residuals were computed in a simultaneous linear regression with the 7 independent variables described above.

This plot illustrates that the residuals and the Y values were not correlated, that the residuals had a zero mean, that their variance did not differ with different values of Y, and that there were no systematic effects in the distribution of residuals. Based on the robustness of the F-test regarding violations of normality and the fact that the residuals did not correlate with predicted reading time values, the use of multiple regression and of F-tests was judged as legitimate.

Results of Reading Time Analysis

With the background on multiple regression and regression coefficients their application in an analysis of reading times collected in four experiments will be described in the subsequent three sections. Section 1 presents data from two experiments using the single-sentence condition. Section 2 presents data from two experiments using the single-word condition, and Section 3 is concerned with differences across stories as revealed by an "item" analysis.

Single-Sentence Condition. There were a recall and a question-answering experiment using the single-sentence condition. In the recall experiment subjects read the stories one sentence at a time with the instruction to recall a story as close to verbatim as possible. Subjects wrote down their recall protocols on receiving a recall prompt which was given immediately following the last sentence of a story. Two groups of 32 subjects each participated in the recall experiment. Each subject read six stories contributing a total of 72 reading times, one for each of the 12 episode nodes of the stories. Note that here as elsewhere in my research processing times of Setting sentences, (marked S in Table 1), were not analyzed because these times were assumed to include extraneous processes such as getting readjusted to reading from a video-terminal. Across the two groups then there were reading times of 144 sentences. In the question-answering experiment, after reading a story, subjects were handed a set of ten relatively easy questions and asked to answer them. In this experiment 32 subjects read 12 stories contributing a total of 144 reading times. Thus there were 144 reading times in both experiments using the single-sentence procedure. These 144 reading times were the dependent variable for the regressions I performed. Two types of analysis were performed on the data from the single-sentence experiments, an "item" analysis focussing on individual stories and an "aggregate" analysis applied to data from all stories. In the item analysis for each story the 12 raw reading times of each subject were used as dependent variables. So the total number of data points for this analysis was 12 x 32 where 32 is the number of subjects in the experiment (Results from this analysis will be given in Table 11). For the aggregate analysis a vector of 144 mean reading times was constructed by averaging reading times across subjects for each node of each of the 12 stories. Differences between stories were also examined using the vector of the data for the aggregate analysis. This was done by coding each of the 12 stories with a unique pattern of weights (see pp. 239-240). In order to get an impression of the overall reading speed in each of the experiments the aggregate data were reduced further by averaging sentence reading times across the 12 stories. These data are shown in Table 5.

A multiple regression with the independent variables listed in Table 6 was performed on each matrix of 144 data points. Partial regression coefficients, correlation coefficients, and t-values derived from these regressions are displayed in Table 6. In the recall experiment the predictor variables accounted for .73 of the variance as indicated by R^2 with a standard error of estimate of 415. In the question-answering experiment the corresponding values were .69 and 342, respectively.

Inspection of the other results indicates, that in both experiments the same components, save for one, contributed significantly to the variance in the reading times. First, in both experiments sentence length and word frequency made a significant contribution to reading times, findings first reported over a decade ago (see Danks, 1968). Second, as observed by Kintsch et al. (1975), Manelis & Yekovich (1976), and Graesser et al. (1980) reading times increased proportionally with the number of propositions in the sentence. Third, in both experiments reading times decreased with the serial position of a sentence. Fourth, there was a

TABLE 5
Means of Sentence Reading Times

Node	Single Sentence		Single Word	
	Recall	Questions	Recall	Questions
B	4062	3088	5899	3946
R	2964	2327	4548	3495
G	2657	2131	4452	3185
A	2657	2224	4522	3353
O	2706	2149	4230	3053
E	2521	2173	4147	2980
B	3124	2613	4971	3602
R	2557	2136	4287	3336
G	2320	1842	3838	2948
A	2557	2112	4130	3059
O	2691	2505	4823	2947
E	2868	2414	4560	3384
Mean	2807	2310	4534	3274

significant boundary effect in both studies. The boundary effect tested here assumed an equal extra processing load at the Beginning and at the Ending, with the former being a new-episode or "initialization" process and the latter a rehearsal process, which was assumed to be specific to a recall situation. In order to evaluate the "initialization" and the rehearsal processes separately, two alternative versions of the boundary hypothesis were formulated, a new-episode effect and a rehearsal effect. The weights were 1,0,0,0,0,0 for the six nodes, respectively, expressing the former effect and 0,0,0,0,0,1 expressing the latter effect. In a multiple regression with the same set of independent variables included in Table 6 and the reformulated boundary effect, it was observed that in both experiments the Beginning process was statistically significant while there was no significant extra load at the Ending. The coefficients for these effects are exhibited in Table 7.

TABLE 6
Regression Coefficients for Single-Sentence Experiments

	Recall					Questions				
Variable	B	r^2	pr^2	sr^2	t	B	r^2	pr^2	sr^2	t
Words	145	.581	.309	.122	7.80	132	.598	.353	.171	8.61
Position	- 62	.077	.204	.070	5.90	- 23	.023	.051	.017	2.72
Frequency	- 1	.001	.025	.007	1.88	- 1	.001	.067	.023	3.13
Propositions	151	.373	.104	.031	3.97	86	.363	.053	.017	2.75
New Arguments	153	.223	.064	.018	3.04	47	.166	.010	.003	1.14N
Importance	9	.098	.002	.001	.58N	- 8	.081	.003	.001	.63N
Boundary	113	.099	.047	.013	2.50	117	.116	.068	.023	3.14

Note: N indicates t is not significant ($p<.05$)

TABLE 7
Load at Beginning and Ending of an Episode

Factor	Recall					Questions			
	B	r^2	pr^2	sr^2	t	B	r^2	pr^2	sr^2
Beginning	304	.207	.058	.016	2.89	241	.166	.051	.017	2.70
Ending	59	.004	.003	.000	<1	72	.000	.005	.002	<1

The contributions of the other components were of similar magnitude as in the previous analyses.

Based on this analysis the boundary effect reported previously (Haberlandt, 1980; Haberlandt et al., 1980) is more properly described as a new-episode effect occurring at the Beginning of the episode, both in question-answering and in recall. Thus, processing a shift of perspective, of activity frame, of protagonist and of topic (see page 223) appear to be more pronounced than the putative rehearsal process. Of course, this is not to say that there is no rehearsal in the recall experiment, only that rehearsal is no more prominent at the Ending of an episode than in other sentences.

In a separate analysis the effects of syntactic complexity expressed by Yngve depth was evaluated. There was no evidence of syntactic structure on sentence reading times in either experiment. The failure to observe an effect of syntactic structure may have been due to a number of different reasons including that the present sentences were too simple, that Yngve depth was not an appropriate metric of syntactic complexity, and that sentence reading time was not the appropriate measure for revealing syntactic effects.

There were also some discrepancies between the two experiments and between the present data and results from other labs. The discrepancy in the present experiments involves the new argument effect which was significant in the recall, but not in the question-answering experiment. As we shall see later on, however, this effect was quite inconsistent across different stories even within the recall experiment. Next, the reading time data from both experiments reveal a serial position effect. Because Graesser et al. (1980) argued that the serial position effect was a result of repeated arguments, that factor was partialed out here. But the effect was still significant in the present 12-node passages suggesting that perhaps a related, if not repeated, argument effect was responsible. The related argument effect implies that concepts in a prior sentence facilitate processing of *related* concepts in a later sentence (see also conclusion, page 244). Finally, while Cirilo & Foss (1980) found that reading time was a function of the importance of a statement, we failed to observe such an effect. This difference could be a result of difference in stimulus materials with Cirilo & Foss' stories being longer and more complex than the present stories, or it could result from different ways of defining and scaling importance, an issue considered again in the conclusion.

The Single-Word Condition. One of the assumptions of the present work was that sentence reading times contain a time component equal to the sum of more molecular responses such as word reading times. Consequently, any effect uncovered by the analysis of sentence reading times should also be detectable in the single-word condition, provided that the number of additional key presses, one for each word, does not change the reader's reading strategy. With the greater resolution of word reading times it should be possible to localize within sentences some of the effects observed in the single-sentence conditions.

Of particular interest were the serial position effect and the new-episode effect. As noted above, unlike Graesser et al. (1980), we observed that sentence reading times decreased with the serial position of a sentence. Using the single-word procedure we sought to determine whether or not the speed-up across serial positions was evenly distributed over entire sentences such that all words were read faster in later than in earlier sentences. Alternatively, only certain sections of a sentence might be read faster as the story progresses while the rest of the sentence continues to be read at the same rate independent of serial position. Concerning the new-episode effect, the single-word condition enables us to inquire into the slowdown in reading time as the reader begins to process a new episode. The two possibilities are again that all words or just some words of the first sentence of an episode are read more slowly.

Two single-word experiments were performed, a recall and a question-answering experiment. In the recall experiment subjects ($N = 28$) were asked to recall the story as close to verbatim as possible. Recall was oral with the protocols being recorded on a cassette recorder. In the question-answering experiment subjects ($N = 26$) were given a set of relatively easy questions after they finished reading a story. Both experiments used the Moving Window condition developed by Just, Carpenter, & Woolley (1982). In the Moving Window condition the video-terminal was initially filled with dashes where a word would appear. A reader proceeded through a story by pressing a button. This caused word n to be replaced by the dashes corresponding to it and word $n+1$ to appear replacing its dashes. In this manner the reader exposed words left to right on one line and then on succeeding lines until the end of the story. Just et al. (1982) called this the Moving Window condition in order to contrast it from the Stationary Window condition where all words are presented successively in the same place on the screen (Aaronson & Scarborough, 1977). Just et al. (1982) found that the Moving Window condition approximated the natural reading situation better than the Stationary Window condition, because the former at least provided perceptual cues about the length and location of the next word and about the length of the story as a whole. Furthermore, as in natural reading the eye moves from left to right and makes return sweeps when advancing to the next line.

The unit of analysis in the single-word experiments were word rather than sentence reading times and the independent variables I used here reflect this shift. Rather than coding sentences I coded individual words with word-level features expected to affect word reading times. These included the number of characters, the log occurrence frequency, and whether or not the word was a content word. Specifically, for each word the following values were used as independent variables, the number of characters, the occurrence frequency of the word, and the codes 1 and 0 for content words and other words, respectively. In addition, words were coded according to the position they occupied in a sentence, specifically the first and last words of each sentence were coded with 1 with all other words coded with 0. Furthermore all words of a node were coded in terms of the serial position of the node in the story. Thus serial position weights ranging from -11 to 11 in steps of 2 were assigned to all words of the 12 nodes, respectively (see "serial pos. allw," in Table 8). Because of the apparent prominence of the serial position effect of last-word reading times, the last words of a node were coded with an additional set of weights ranging from -11 to 11 (see "serial pos, lw," in Table 8) with all other words coded with 0. Next, each content word was coded according to the number of times it was repeated in the story. The new-episode hypothesis was expressed in terms of codes as described below. As in the single-sentence experiments different stories were also coded (see p. 240). For the purpose of illustrating the overall reading speed in the single-word experiments word reading times were accumulated for each sentence of the stories and averaged across stories and subjects. These reading times are displayed in columns 4 and 5 of Table 5.

The regression results on word reading times from the recall and question-answering experiments are presented in Table 8. In the recall experiment the independent variables accounted for a proportion of $R^2 = .79$ of the variance with a standard error of estimate of 103. The R^2 value was relatively large due to one effect, the last-word effect. This effect was reflected by a regression coefficient of 282 milliseconds and by a squared semipartial coefficient of $sr_i^2 = .594$. Thus, excluding the last-word factor, the other factors accounted for a proportion of about .20 of the variance. In the question-answering experiment the fit of the regression equation was expressed by $R^2 = .33$ with a standard error of estimate of 43. After excluding the last-word effect, the remaining variables accounted for a proportion of about .21 in the reading time variance, this proportion being comparable to that observed in the recall experiment. The last word effect and its size in the recall experiment are attributable to the task that subjects recall the passages "as close to verbatim" as possible. The extent of this effect is illustrated in Figure 3 in which mean reading times are graphed for the words of the 12 episode nodes of the passage reproduced in Table 1. Mean reading times of last, first, and other words averaged across all passages are exhibited in Figure 4.

Last-word effects, which could not be observed using the single-sentence procedure, were reported by Aaronson & Scarborough (1976) using a single-word method and by Just & Carpenter (1978) who used the eye fixation method (for further reports on end-of-sentence effects see Mitchell & Green, 1978; Dee-Lucas et al., 1982; Just & Carpenter, 1980; Just et al., 1982). According to Just &

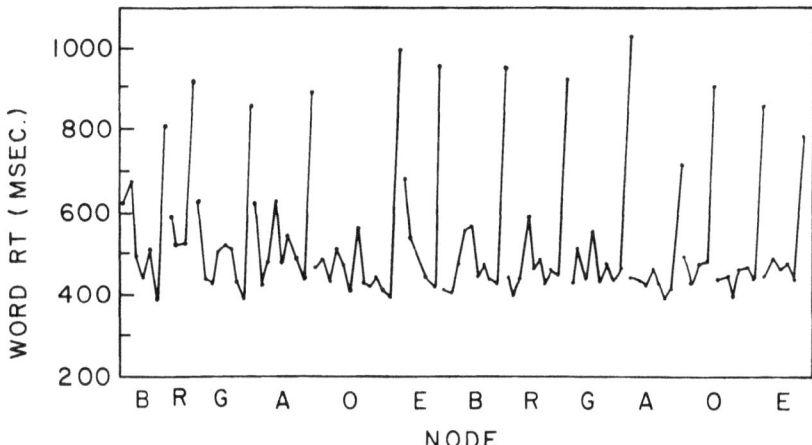

FIG. 3. Profile of mean word reading times for one passage from the single-word condition recall experiment. The word reading times correspond to individual words subsumed under 12 episode nodes of the Mike and Dave story reproduced in Table 1.

Carpenter (1980), the reader uses the end of a sentence as occasion for resolving within-sentence ambiguities, for integrating it with prior text, and in recall situations, for rehearsing the current sentence.

Based on the results from the recall experiment, it is quite apparent that the combination of the recall task and the single-word procedure led the subjects to engage in special encoding operations which are not normally present in reading situations, but which are similar to those occurring in self-paced free recall studies using individual words (McFarland & Kellas, 1974). Consequently, two effects normally observed in reading situations, the frequency and repeated word effects, were not significant in this experiment. Similarly, the new-episode effect, which was observed in both single-sentence experiments and the question-answering experiment below was not present in the recall experiment. Instead the largest effects by any measure listed in the left panel of Table 8 were those associated with encoding for recall.

In the question-answering experiment all components included in Table 8 except for content words contributed significantly to the variance in word reading times. Several of these effects have been reported by previous investigators. Of special interest here were the serial position effect and the new-episode effect. Reading times of all word categories, whether first, last, or other words, of a sentence decreased significantly, although only by a small amount (see Figure 4). The coefficient (allw) was 1.2 milliseconds per word. With a mean of 8.3 words per node this amounts to about 10 milliseconds per node. Thus the last sentence of a story was read faster than the first of the first episode by about 120 milliseconds,

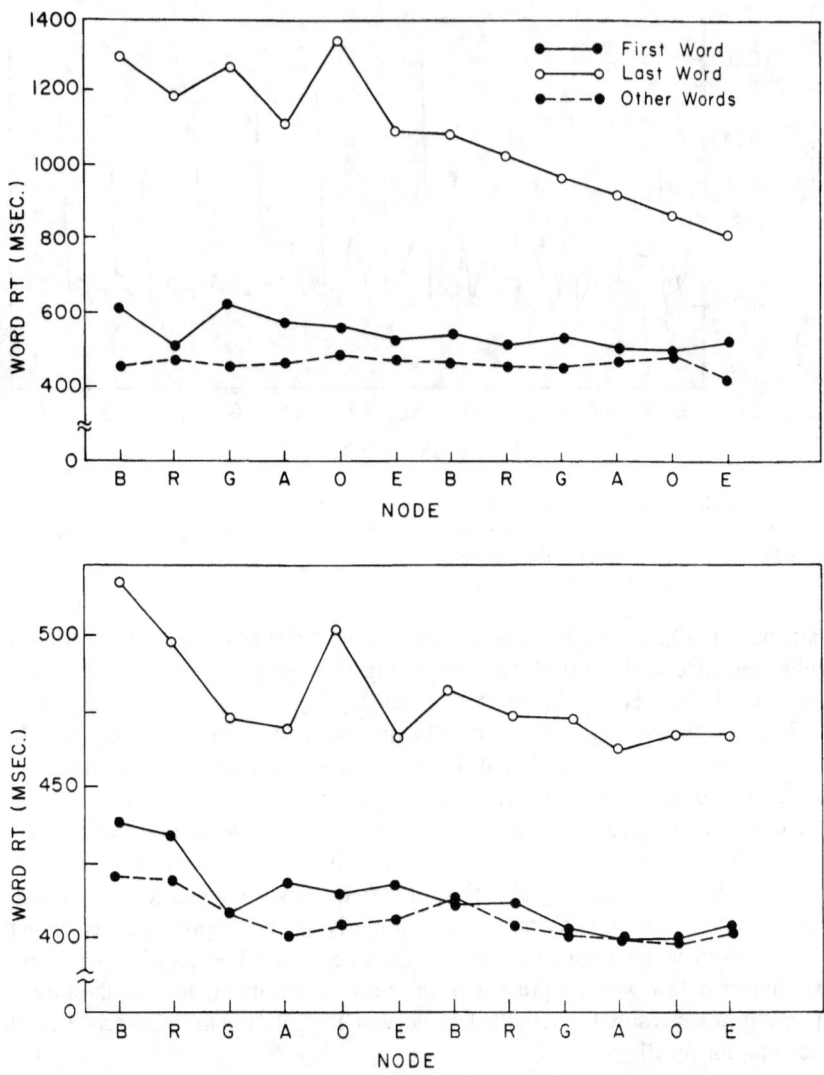

FIG. 4. Mean reading times of first words (solid circles, solid lines), last words (open circles, solid lines), and other words (solid circles, broken lines). The mean word reading times were averaged for each episode node across passages in the single-word condition recall experiment (top panel) and question-answering experiment (bottom panel).

partialing other factors. This serial position effect mirrored that observed in the single-sentence condition, and was probably also the result of facilitation between related arguments in successive sentences. In exploring the causes of the serial position effect it should be remembered, however, that the present passages were relatively short and that it would be unlikely to observe a linear serial position effect in longer passages.

TABLE 8
Regression Coefficients for
Single-Word Experiments

	Recall					Questions				
Variable	B	r^2	pr^2	sr^2	t	B	r^2	pr^2	sr^2	t
n of characters	17	.103	.043	.009	7.29	7	.154	.042	.029	7.19
frequency	- 8	.136	.002	.001	1.63N	- 6	.140	.008	.001	2.99
content word	- 10	.101	.001	.000	1.03N	-12	.083	.000	.000	<1
first word	92	.000	.073	.016	9.66	18	.000	.016	.011	4.45
last word (lw)	283	.702	.741	.594	57.97	31	.187	.164	.129	15.20
serial pos (allw)	- 1	.012	.008	.002	3.06	- 1	.035	.023	.015	5.25
serial pos (lw)	- 19	.050	.151	.037	14.44	- 2	.017	.006	.004	2.76
repeated word	- 3	.049	.001	.000	1.16N	- 4	.020	.010	.006	3.50
first five wds	9	.003	.001	.000	<1 N	10	.005	.004	.003	2.29

Note: N indicates t is not significant

In assessing the new-episode effect, it was assumed that the shift to a new episode is signalled to the reader primarily by the first few words of the first sentence of the episode. The first words include temporal phrases such as *One day*, *A month later*, and *One Saturday* followed by the name of the protagonist or the critical event posing the problem for the protagonist. Other phrases starting the first sentences of an episode were *While (actor) (was) (verbing)* and *When (actor) (verbed)*. In the present stories such temporal phrases and the critical event spanned about five words. During this span the new time frame, the new activity, and the new protagonist are typically introduced. Consequently, the word reading times of the first five words averaged across the Beginning nodes of all stories and those averaged across the remaining nodes were compared. Figure 5 exhibits these data for the recall and question-answering experiments. It illustrates that the word reading times were longer for the first five words of the Beginning than of the other nodes. Since word reading times were not "controlled" for a number of word characteristics such as length and frequency, this effect was evaluated in a multiple regression analysis which used the factors previously mentioned and an "episode shift" factor. This effect was coded by weighting the first five words of the Beginning node of each episode with 1 and all other words with 0. In the question-answering experiment the regression coefficient associated with this test was 10 milliseconds for each of the coded words ($p<.02$). This means that controlling for other factors, the first five words of Beginning nodes take 50 milliseconds longer to process than the remaining words of the passage. It should be remembered this value applies to first sentences of an episode, not to first sentences of the passage (see p. 231). In sum, excepting the recall experiment using the single-word procedure, there is evidence of additional processing occasioned by the shift to a new episode. This evidence is derived from multiple regression analysis which indicates that first sentences of an episode are processed more slowly than other sentences.

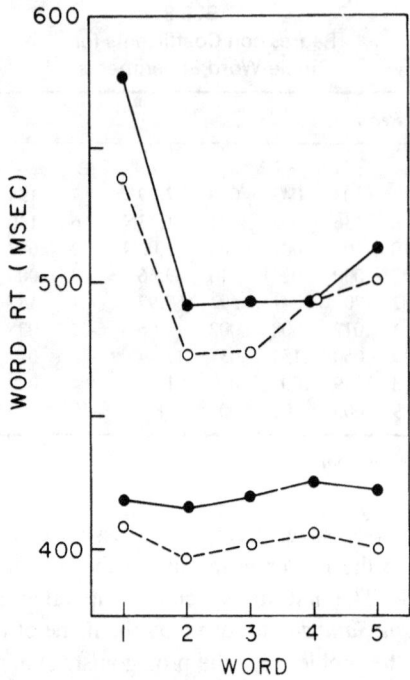

FIG. 5. Mean word reading times for the first five words for the Beginning node (solid lines) and for remaining nodes (broken lines). Means were derived by averaging across passages. The top curves are based on the recall experiment. The broken curves are based on the question-answering experiment.

The pattern of reading times at the Beginning node suggests the following scenario as a story shifts to a new episode. At that point there are the base-level processes including letter and word recognition, sentence parsing and integration, and additional shift processes. These include two or three sub-processes depending on whether or not a new agent is introduced. The two processes involve condensing of the previous text segment, transferring it to long-term memory, and establishing in working memory a set of anticipations of what might happen next. If a new agent is introduced, the reader is assumed to set up a working memory slot for the agent, because he or she is a potential protagonist. This slot is "privileged" compared to other slots because it is assumed to be resistant to decay. The additional processes at the Beginning are triggered by the co-occurrence of several cues including temporal phrases such as *One (point in time)*, a switch from a state or a habitually occurring event to an "acute" event, a change in perspective or content, and the introduction of a new agent.

While the present account has used a story grammar terminology, one could also have used the framework of story points and productions proposed by Schank & Wilensky (1978). Like proponents of story grammar these authors assume that stories have a standardized sequence of events beginning with a Problem Point, "which is essentially a problem that is posed for a character" (p. 423). The Problem Point (Beginning) is followed by a resolution path (Attempt), leading to a Solution Point, which is comparable to the Outcome. In Schank & Wilensky's terms the new-episode processes could be expressed as a production, a condition-action pair, such as (2)

(2) IF   there is a phrase such as *One (point in time)*, and there is a switch from a state to an acute event, and the event constitutes a potential problem, and there is a change in perspective or content, (and a new agent is introduced).
THEN   condense the previous text segment, and transfer it to long-term memory, and establish in working memory a set of anticipations, (and reserve a special memory slot for the new agent).

This production would be evoked during the Beginning by all or some of the cues listed in its condition-side in addition to a variety of productions dealing with letter recognition, word encoding, and sentence processing.

Comparison Across Stories. When text research first began, investigators used only a few passages, sometimes only one passage like the *War of the Ghosts* or the *Circle Island* passage. Bartlett (1932), Paul (1959), Dawes (1976), Frederiksen (1975) and other early researchers were able to gain much information from analyzing results of a single passage. Even if now more passages are used in an experiment, it is still important to go beyond the aggregate analysis and look at differences in responding to different stories.

Generally, when a researcher selects stimuli for a particular experiment, he or she expects that the effects obtained in the experiment generalize to new materials (see Clark, 1973) and that the aggregate results obtained in an experiment are more or less representative of individual cases. This is a general issue in psychology pertaining to any set of averaged data, whether to mean learning curves or to regression coefficients computed across different items. However, because a passage is a very rich stimulus compared to an individual sentence or an individual word it would be surprising if all passages used in a given experiment were processed in an identical fashion, even if they were equated for lexical, syntactic and structural aspects. Using mainly data from the single-sentence experiments, the present section will show that there were considerable differences among stories in my research, both in base-level reading times and in the pattern of the effects contributed by the predictor variables. These differences were partially due to the differences in story content, because the stories did not differ structurally, nor did they differ substantially in lexical or syntactic complexity.

Differences in base-level reading times in the recall experiment and question-answering experiment, both using the single-sentence condition, are illustrated by the data displayed in the columns 3 and 5 of Table 9. A systematic comparison of these differences was undertaken using a regression analysis on the aggregate data by coding individual stories with a unique pattern of indicator weights (for such "dummy coding" see Cohen & Cohen, 1975, Ch. 5; Pedhazur, 1977; a similar comparison could be achieved by residual analysis as suggested by Weisberg, 1980). In the single-sentence condition stories were coded by 11 vectors, each vector representing a dichotomy between a given story and the rest. Each of 11 stories was assigned one vector which was coded as 1 for the 12 sentences of the story and as 0 for the remaining 132 data points. The codes for the sentences of the twelfth story were 0 on all eleven vectors. Thus the twelfth story was the reference passage. Additionally, in the recall experiment the group factor was coded. Differences between stories in the base-level reading times partialing out other factors are reflected in the partial regression coefficients associated with each story. These are displayed in columns 4 and 6 of Table 9. Note that these values are relative to story 12, e.g., the coefficient of -347 for story 1 of the recall experiment indicates that the average sentence reading time *partialing other factors* was 347 milliseconds faster than that of story 12. Because of the partialing there was no one-to-one mapping between the observed mean sentence reading times and the regression coefficients of the stories. Note, for example, that the mean reading times of stories 1 and 12 were both 2611 milliseconds while the regression coefficients were -347 and 0, respectively. Including passages as a factor in the analysis of the aggregate data improved the overall fit of the regression somewhat. In the single-sentence and question-answering experiments the fit expressed by R^2 improved from .73 to .83 and from .69 to .73, respectively. The corresponding figures for the experiments using the single-word procedure were .79 and .80 and .33 and .54, respectively. Except for the single-word recall experiment these improvements were larger than those routinely observed by just adding more variables to the equation. Thus, in multi-passage experiments more of the variance in reading times is accounted for if passages are included as a factor in the multiple regression analysis.

The regression coefficients in Table 9 exhibit a wide range testifying to the base-line differences between the stories. From Graesser's (1981) work it is known that "narrativity" accounts for reading time differences between stories. However, because the range of narrativity was relatively small in the present stories, it was necessary to explore also other possibilities in order to explain the reading time difference.

I explored several factors distinguishing among the stories, for example, whether or not the protagonist was successful, whether there was a contest between a protagonist and an antagonist, and whether the emotional tone (Bartlett's "mood") of the story was "positive" or "negative". I also explored the number of new concepts in the the entire story, and the number of different agents in the story. Of these I found the number of different agents listed in column 2 of Table 9 to be correlated with reading times. In a multiple regression on the reading times from the recall and question-answering experiments the number of agents was entered as

TABLE 9
Mean Reading Times, Regression Coefficients, and
Number of Agents per Story in Single-Sentence Experiments

Story	N of Agents	Recall		Questions	
		Mean Reading Time	Regression Coefficients	Mean Reading Time	Regression Coefficients
1	1	2611	-347	2103	-279
2	3	3239	293	2303	-59
3	2	2777	0	2121	-129
4	2	2962	80	2122	-206
5	1	2857	-284	2293	-233
6	1	3045	-16	2475	3
7	2	2628	-335	2280	-273
8	3	2449	36	2173	-14
9	1	2528	-353	2323	-181
10	2	2912	-212	2549	-153
11	2	3074	34	2699	92
12	2	2611	0	2274	0

a predictor variable along with seven other variables but excluding the story factors. The multi-agent factor was reflected by regression coefficients of 228 milliseconds ($p < .001$) and 66 milliseconds ($p = .11$) in the recall and question-answering experiments, respectively. From the reader's point of view the multi-agent hypothesis appears plausible, especially when asked to recall the story. When reading sentence by sentence through a story, the reader does not know ahead of time who of the agents might become a protagonist later on. Therefore, it is a reasonable strategy for the reader to consider any agent encountered in the story as a potential protagonist and to monitor that agent's activities. It is as if the reader sets up and monitors for each character a separate causal or event chain (see Warren, Nicholas, & Trabasso, 1979, also Omanson 1982). Additionally, with more agents in a story it might be more difficult to recall who did what.

Graesser (1981) also found that differences in familiarity between stories contribute to reading time differences between them. This was also the case in the present stories as a comparison of stories 10 and 2 shows. Story 10 dealt with a familiar revenge theme and with familiar story characters. A bear steals honey from some bees and is being stung by them in return. Story 2 describes the kidnapping of some unknown politician and the failure of the police to find him. As the regression coefficients in Table 9 indicate story 10 was read faster than story 2 in both experiments using the single-sentence condition. Word reading times collected in the single-word condition also reflect these differences. Table 10 displays reading times for words common to both stories as a function of story and task. Words appearing first and last in a sentence were not included here.

TABLE 10
Reading Times of Words Common to Two Stories

Word	Recall Story		Questions Story	
	2	10	2	10
had	438	427	385	334
might	594	460	442	364
of	433	377	363	329
that	555	426	469	343
the	465	431	407	351
they	440	465	405	349
to	471	425	386	347
was	487	415	415	344

Most of these words have shorter reading times in story 10 than in story 2 although the two stories are comparable in terms of lexical and syntactic difficulty. However, the stories differ in the number of new arguments with story 10 containing only two new arguments and story 2 containing nine new arguments. The different number of new arguments, the different number of agents, different degrees of familiarity and other differences which are as yet unspecified , were substantial enough to affect the reading times of words including those words that happened to be common to the two stories. This observation is important because it suggests that the processes of word encoding and lexical access (cf. Just & Carpenter, 1980) are not only a function of the current word but also of their textual environment. It may well be that the content differences in the surrounding text globally slow down word encoding and lexical access (see Thibadeau, Just, & Carpenter, 1982, for a mechanism of such a slow-down). While the present experiments were not designed to address the effects of story differences on word-level processes, observations such as these call for further research into the problem of lexical processing during reading of natural texts. In such experiments one would embed a broader sample of identical words, clauses, and sentences in stories which differed in terms of global processing difficulty.

Let us now turn from base-line differences between stories to differences in individual components across different passages. These analyses were analogous to the aggregate analysis described on page 231 (see also Table 6 and 7) except that there was a separate analysis for each story. The dependent variable file for each story included the 12 node reading times of 32 subjects thus totalling 384 observations per story. The independent variable file included the same predictors as the aggregate analysis did, namely the number of words, propositions, and new arguments for each of the 12 nodes, and the serial position, the mean frequency of the content words, and the rated importance of each node. Finally, the episode shift effect was coded by weighting the two Beginning nodes with 1 and the other nodes with 0 (see page 232 and Table 7). The coefficients resulting from each one of these regressions occupy one row of Table 11. Thus the regression coefficients in Table 11

TABLE 11
Regression Coefficients for 12 Stories
Single-Sentence Recall

Story	Word	Position	Frequency	Propositions	New Arguments	Importance	Beginning
1	254	- 48	.10	-106	- 157	- 20	278
2	351	-103	-2.27	632	- 689	- 22	44
3	82	-100	-1.17	320	- 331	171	-642
4	- 8	- 57	.38	94	486	27	288
5	192	- 63	-1.35	137	- 13	- 58	101
6	232	- 3	- .41	149	- 112	50	506
7	115	- 35	.63	225	33	47	444
8	141	- 42	-1.62	246	157	5	44
9	169	- 18	.14	76	29	5	70
10	143	- 96	.43	- 55	1852	82	693
11	- 21	- 33	.16	94	165	- 20	-922
12	136	14	-1.30	- 7	92	28	672

resulted from 12 different analyses. While there is some variability in the absolute size of the coefficients across different stories, they exhibited the same direction for those factors that had a similar range across stories, e.g., serial position. The largest variability in the coefficients predictably occurred where the range of the independent variables differed most widely, namely in the new argument nouns with story 10 having only two new arguments and story 11 having 13.

Of particular interest was the finding that the new-episode effect was reflected by positive coefficients in 11 out of 12 stories. On the other hand, story 3 had a negative coefficient, indicating that the Beginning was read faster than the other sentences. Story 3 was written after the Helen Keller story used in the research by Sulin and Dooling (1974). The reason for failing to observe the new-episode effect in story 3 was that the Beginnings of both episodes were strongly implied by the preceding sentences. Texts (3) and (4) show the transition to the first and second episode of story 3, respectively.

(3) Setting: Sandy was a teacher of blind children.
Setting: She had been hired to tutor a spoiled little boy named Bill.
Beginning 1: One day, Bill began to scream and cry.

(4) Ending 1: Sandy could not stop the boy's screaming.
Beginning 2: One day, Bill behaved even worse than usual.

In both episodes, the information in the Beginning may be viewed as an instance of the more general statement made previously. On the other hand, in other stories the Beginning typically introduces a new topic or a new perspective. Interestingly, in the single-word experiments, word reading times for the Beginning of story 3 did not exceed those of remaining nodes as was the case in the other stories (see Figure 6).

The foregoing analysis of story differences is useful, because it points to content differences between stories. Three factors responsible for these differences were named here, familiarity, the number of different agents, and the degree to which the new episode introduces a new topic or a new perspective. From Graesser's et al. (1980) and from Kieras and Johnson's (1981) work it is known that the rate of processing is faster for relatively familiar passages. Graesser et al. (1980) noted that passages are familiar to the extent that a reader has a content-schema or a script for it. Thus, one must look to research on such content-schemata to account more fully for the story differences observed here.

CONCLUSION

The various on-line methods, including the single-sentence and word procedures described in the present chapter, are used in the service of understanding a reader's ongoing comprehension of texts. The judgment on these different methods will be based on whether or not they are fruitful in aiding the development of new insights into the reading process and whether the empirical observations they yield will lead to similar substantive conclusions. As I shall summarize below, there is empirical convergence for some effects at the word, sentence, and text levels, but not for others.

There are two basic word-level effects which are uniformly observed by different methods, the word frequency effect and the word length effect. The word frequency effect refers to the fact that more frequent words are read faster than less frequent words. It was observed measuring eye fixations (e.g., Just & Carpenter, 1980; Rayner, 1978), word reading times (Ferres & Aaronson, 1981), clause reading times (Mitchell & Green, 1978) and sentence reading times (Haberlandt et al., 1980). The word length effect indicates that longer words generally take longer to read than shorter words (for a remarkable exception see Rayner, 1978). There are some differences concerning the content word effect which was observed by Ferres and Aaronson (1981) who used the Stationary Window procedure but not in the present research which used the Moving Window condition. The content word effect means that content words take longer to read than function words. Of course, it is possible that the content word effect observed by Ferres and Aaronson is at least partially due to confounding with word frequency and length. Some other word-level effects, e.g., longer processing time for verbs than other words (Just & Carpenter, 1980; Rayner, 1977) have to date only been reported in eye fixation studies.

In a negative sense different labs have produced similar results on the effects of syntactic structure on sentence reading times in that such effects are not at all or only minimally present (Graesser et al., 1980; Kieras, 1981; see above). Of course, these negative findings may have been a result of the use of inappropriate metrics of sentence complexity and of the global nature of sentence reading times. With word reading times, however, certain sentence-level effects, e.g., at the end of clauses, and of sentences, have been observed (e.g., Aaronson & Scarborough, 1976).

Similarly Frazier & Rayner (1982) have observed syntactic effects when using an eye fixation method.

Turning from word- and sentence-level effects to text-level effects, the "convergence" picture begins to cloud over. While there are converging effects on certain text-level effects across labs and methods, the effects themselves are small and not as robust as one might wish. The small size and lack of robustness of these effects, however, may not be the fault of the methods used, but may well be attributable to the different approaches of theorists in describing and scaling texts and to individual differences among readers in processing text-level aspects of a passage. In the last decade many proposals of text description and text processing have been made. While many of them agree in their broad outline, e.g., on interactive processes in reading, they do differ in important details. Thus, there are differences on a description and taxonomy of texts (e.g., Brewer, 1980), on text representation (e.g., Kintsch & van Dijk, 1978; Schank & Abelson, 1977), and on the knowledge sources a reader uses, with some proposing structural schemata (e.g., Mandler & Johnson, 1977) and others opposing them while upholding instead content schemata such as scripts (Schank & Abelson, 1977; but see Schank, 1980). Furthermore, there are differences in the description and indexing of such attributes of text and text segments as importance, narrativity, "staticness", familiarity, interestingness, affect, and cohesiveness. To take but one of these, importance of a sentence has been scaled in numerous ways, with Cirilo & Foss (1980) using one of several story grammars, Haberlandt et al. (1980) using subject ratings, Black & Bower (1980) using distance of a surface event from a causal path, and Kintsch & van Dijk (1978) using first mentioning of a topic in a text and experimenter fiat in order to express importance of a sentence.

Even when these approaches will become more compatible as a result of further refinement in theory and of more research, the individual reader will remain the largest source of variability in text processing as reflected in reading times. It is quite plausible that readers should differ more in their processing of text-level than of word-level aspects of a passage (see Dee-Lucas et al., 1982). Word length is physically defined and every reader has to scan the characters of the word in order to form a word percept. Similarly, there is agreement between different readers on the relative frequency of words in English (see Tryk, 1968). On the other hand, at the text-level different reader capacities (Daneman & Carpenter, 1980), different reader motivations, and different degrees of knowledge can manifest themselves more readily. Thus, one reader may have a great deal of experience with simple schematic narratives, while another may not. It should also be remembered how redundant a text is in providing a reader with coherence, both through various surface cues and through the underlying content. As a result, different readers may select different strategies in extracting meaning from a text.

Considering the differences in theoretical approaches to text processing and those between individual readers, it is encouraging that there is at all agreement in observations of several text-level factors across methods and labs. Here are some of these convergent observations. Word reading times and eye fixations are faster for repeated than for new words (Just, Carpenter, & Woolley, 1982). Similarly, reading times of sentences are faster when the sentences contain repeated words (Graesser et al., 1980; Haberlandt et al., 1980; Kieras, 1981). Next, as one would expect, familiar passages are read faster than less familiar passages (Graesser et al., 1980; Kieras and Johnson, 1981). Finally, there is growing evidence of a variety of shift-effects, namely eye fixations and word reading times increase in the region of a sentence where a new local topic is introduced (Dee-Lucas et al., 1982), sentence reading times increase when a new point of view (Black et al., 1979) or a new focus (Yekovich et al., 1979) is presented, and word reading times and sentence reading times increase when a new global topic appears as is the case when a new narrative episode begins (Haberlandt et al., 1980; Olson, Duffy, & Mack, 1980). Thus, introduction of something new, whether it is a new word, a new local topic, or a new global topic increases the momentary processing load on the reader. Because the text-level effects account only for 1 to 5% of the variance in reading times, they are less robust than word-level effects, resulting in differences across labs. Thus, Cirilo & Foss (1980) observed an importance effect, while I did not (Haberlandt et al., 1980). Similarly, Graesser et al. (1980) and Haberlandt et al. (1980) observed that narratives were read faster than expository passages, while Just, Carpenter, & Masson (1982) did not find this difference using an expository passage from *Scientific American* and a narrative from *Reader's Digest*. Finally, we observed with our stories that story grammar category affects reading times, but Just et al. (1982) did not find such effects in their *Reader's Digest* story. I think that the resolution of these discrepancies will depend to a large extent on a refinement of text description, of theories of comprehension, and of our understanding and controlling differences between individual readers.

What is the verdict about multiple regression in the analysis of reading times? In spite of all the caveats about the relativity of the size of the coefficients, we found in our research that they varied relatively little as a function of the presence or absence of certain other factors. In general, I think that the multiple regression method is an indispensable tool when one uses stimulus materials where many independent variables covary as is necessarily the case with natural texts. Indeed Rubin (1980) and Cutler (1981) have argued that a multitude of variables covary even in the case of individual words and individual sentences. Furthermore, multiple regression offers the opportunity for controlling other factors in situations where experimental control by means of a factorial design is not feasible. For example, in order to evaluate the new-episode effect factorially one would need to construct passages with a target sentence placed in the Beginning of one condition and in some other node of a control condition. However, such control is problematic because the content of the Beginning is defined relative to that of the Reaction whose content is relative to that of the Goal in turn. Similarly, the content of the other nodes is relative to the neighboring nodes. Thus, it is not possible to simply exchange nodes without also affecting the neighboring nodes and without changing the style and the smoothness of the story.

An additional advantage of multiple regression is that it yields a variety of coefficients informing us about the relative contribution of sets of factors, of individual factors and of their levels of significance. At the very minimum, multiple regression analysis can be used as a "discovery procedure" leading to the formulation of experimental hypotheses. These can be evaluated in conventional experiments where the experimenter is able to manipulate the factors directly. Here are two illustrations of experimental hypotheses suggested by multiple regression analysis of reading times. One of the hypotheses was derived from the serial position effect observed in our research. The other deals with the differences between passages. The serial position effect reflected by significant regression coefficients in the present research was attributable, in part, to the possibility that concepts of a preceding sentence might facilitate processing of related concepts in a subsequent sentence. This possibility could be examined in a factorial experiment using pairs of sentences as stimulus materials with relatedness of concepts across sentences as the independent variable and reading times of the second sentence as the dependent variable. If related concepts "prime" each other, sentence and word reading times of second sentences should be a function of the level of relatedness between the sentences, where relatedness would express the degree to which the sentences may be subsumed under a common topic, frame, or script. Second, differences between passages, whether they are due to different levels of narrativity, to a different number of agents or some other factor, could be evaluated by constructing versions of a text of nearly equal content, one being "easy" the other "difficult". Each version would contain identical target sentences and paragraphs. Provided that difficulty has been properly formalized and measured, reading times of targets should be a function of the difficulty of the surrounding text. This design would also permit the evaluation of word-level processes as a function of the global discourse context as mentioned above.

The synopsis above suggests avenues for further improvements in research on the reading process. Reading research would benefit by a greater consistency in the characterization of reader knowledge sources and of texts including a fuller explication of dimensions that differentiate between texts such as cohesiveness, importance, familiarity, and narrativity. Similarly, differences between individual readers and different reading purposes need to be characterized and documented more fully. Finally, word- and sentence-level processing need to be explored in the context of different discourses. To accomplish these goals is a tall order and probably not feasible within a single conventional theory. It may well require the construction of simulation models to capture the different processes of reading and their interactions, an approach which is already emerging as several contributions to this Conference have shown.

ACKNOWLEDGMENTS

This research was supported by NFS grants BNS-8104958 and SPI-8165076. The single-word experiments and the data analysis were done while I was on sabbatical leave at

Carnegie-Mellon University. I am grateful to the Department of Psychology, especially to P. Carpenter, M. Just, and P. Lucas for their generous support of my work. I am also grateful to C. Berian, K. Brock, J. Maffiolini, R. Ravenscroft, J. Sandson and S. Phiansunthon who assisted with the research, and to D. Dee-Lucas, D. Kieras and R. Yekovich for their comments on earlier drafts. Please write to Karl Haberlandt, Department of Psychology, Trinity College, Hartford CT 06106, for reprint requests.

REFERENCES

Aaronson, D., & Scarborough, H. S. Performance theories for sentence coding: Some quantitative evidence. *Journal of Experimental Psychology: Human Perception and Performance*, 1976, *2*, 56-70.

Aaronson, D., & Scarborough, H. S. Performance theories for sentence coding: some quantitative models. *Journal of Verbal Learning and Verbal Behavior*, 1977, *16*, 277-304.

Bartlett, F. C. *Remembering*. Cambridge, Mass.: Cambridge University Press, 1932.

Black, J. B., & Bower, G. H. Story understanding as problem-solving. *Poetics*, 1980, *9*, 223-250.

Black, J. B., Turner, T. J., & Bower, G. H. Point of view in narrative comprehension, memory, and production. *Journal of Verbal Learning and Verbal Behavior*, 1979, *18*, 187-198.

Bower, G. H., Black, J. B., & Turner, T. J. Scripts in memory for text. *Cognitive Psychology*, 1979, *11*, 177-220.

Brewer, W. F. Literary theory, rhetoric and stylistics: implications for psychology. In R. S. Spiro, B. C. Bruce, & W. F. Brewer (Eds.) *Theoretical issues in reading comprehension*. Hillsdale, N.J.: Lawrence Erlbaum Associates, 1980.

Caramazza, A., Grober, E., Garvey, C., & Yates, J. Comprehension of anaphoric pronouns. *Journal of Verbal Learning and Verbal Behavior*, 1977, *5*, 601-610.

Carpenter, P. A., & Daneman, M. Lexical retrieval and error recovery in reading: A model based on eye fixations. *Journal of Verbal Learning and Verbal Behavior*, 1981, *20*, 137-160.

Carpenter, P. A., & Just, M. A. Reading comprehension as the eyes see it. In *Cognitive processes in comprehension*, M. A. Just, & P. A. Carpenter (Eds.). Hillsdale, N.J.: Lawrence Erlbaum Associates, 1977.

Cirilo, R. K., & Foss, D. J. Text structure and reading time for sentences. *Journal of Verbal Learning and Verbal Behavior*, 1980, *19*, 96-109.

Clark, H. H. The language-as-fixed-effect fallacy: A critique of language statistics in psychological research. *Journal of Verbal Learning and Verbal Behavior*, 1973, *12*, 335-359.

Cohen, J., & Cohen, P. *Applied multiple regression/correlation analysis for the behavioral sciences*. Hillsdale, N.J.: Lawrence Erlbaum Associates, 1975.

Cutler, A. Making up materials is a confounded nuisance or: Will we be able to run any psycholinguistic experiments at all in 1990? *Cognition*, 1981, *10*, 65-70.

Daneman, M., & Carpenter, P. A. Individual differences in working memory and reading. *Journal of Verbal Learning and Verbal Behavior*, 1980, *19*, 450-466.

Danks, J. H. *Some factors involved in the comprehension of deviant English sentences*. Ph.D. dissertation, Princeton University, 1968.

Dawes, R. M. Memory and the distortion of meaningful written material. *British Journal of Psychology*, 1976, *57*, 77-86.

Dee-Lucas, D., Just, M. A., Carpenter, P. A., & Daneman, M. What eye fixations tell us about the time course of text integration. In R. Groner & P. Fraisse (Eds.), *Cognition and eye movements*. Amsterdam: North Holland, and Berlin: Deutscher Verlag der Wissenschaften, in press.

Ferres, S., & Aaronson, D. A. *Word class encoding model for reading times.* Paper presented at the meeting of the Psychonomic Society, Philadelphia, November, 1981.

Frazier, L., & Rayner, K. Making and correcting errors during sentence comprehension: eye movements in the analysis of structurally ambiguous sentences. *Cognitive Psychology*, 1982, *14*, 178-210.

Frederiksen, C. H. Effects of context-induced processing operations on semantic information acquired from discourse. *Cognitive Psychology*, 1975, *7*, 139-166.

Graesser, A. C. *Prose comprehension beyond the word.* New York: Springer-Verlag, 1981.

Graesser, A. C., Hoffman, N. L., & Clark, L. F. Structural components of reading time. *Journal of Verbal Learning and Verbal Behavior*, 1980, *19*, 135-151.

Graesser, A. C., Robertson, S. P., & Anderson, P. A. Incorporating inferences in narrative representations: a study of how and why. *Cognitive Psychology*, 1981, *13*, 1-26.

Haberlandt, K. Story grammar and reading time of story constituents. *Poetics*, 1980, *9*, 99-118.

Haberlandt, K., Berian, C., & Sandson, J. The episode schema in story processing. *Journal of Verbal Learning and Verbal Behavior*, 1980, *19*, 635-650.

Haberlandt, K., & Bingham, G. Verbs contribute to the coherence of brief narratives: Reading related and unrelated sentence triples. *Journal of Verbal Learning and Verbal Behavior*, 1978, *17*, 419-426.

Haviland, S. E., & Clark, H. H. Whats new? Acquiring new information as a process in comprehension. *Journal of Verbal Learning and Verbal Behavior*, 1974, *13*, 512-521.

Hogaboam, T. W., & McConkie, G. W. *The rocky road from eye fixations to comprehension.* Technical Report, University of Illinois at Urbana-Champaign, 1981.

Just, M. A., & Carpenter, P. A. Comprehension of negation with quantification. *Journal of Verbal Learning and Verbal Behavior*, 1971, *10*, 219-225.

Just, M. A., & Carpenter, P. A. Inference processes during reading: reflections from eye fixations. In J. W. Senders, D. F. Fisher & R. A. Monty (Eds.), *Eye movement and the higher psychological functions.* Hillsdale, N.J.: Lawrence Erlbaum Associates, 1978.

Just, A. M., & Carpenter, P. A. A theory of reading: From eye fixations to comprehension. *Psychological Review*, 1980, *87*, 329-354.

Just, M. A., Carpenter, P. A., & Masson, M. *What eye fixations tell us about speed reading and skimming.* Technical Report, Carnegie-Mellon University, March 1982.

Just, M. A., Carpenter, P. A., & Woolley, J. D. Paradigms and processes in reading comprehension. *Journal of Experimental Psychology: General*, in press.

Keppel, G. *Design and analysis: A researcher's handbook.* Englewood Cliffs, N. J.: Prentice-Hall, 1973.

Kerlinger, F. N., & Pedhazur, E. J. *Multiple regression in behavioral research.* New York: Holt, Rinehart & Winston, 1973.

Kieras, D. E. *Analysis of the effects of word properties and limited reading time in a sentence comprehension and verification task.* Ph.D. dissertation, University of Michigan, 1974.

Kieras, D. E. Good and bad structure in simple paragraphs: Effects on apparent theme, reading time, and recall. *Journal of Verbal Learning and Verbal Behavior*, 1978, *17*, 13-28.

Kieras, D. E. Component processes in the comprehension of simple prose. *Journal of Verbal Learning and Verbal Behavior*, 1981, *20*, 1-23. (b)

Kieras, D. E., & Johnson, W. *Prior knowledge in comprehending technical prose.* Paper presented at the meeting of the Psychonomic Society, Philadelphia, November, 1981.

Kintsch, W. *The representation of meaning in memory.* Hillsdale, N. J.: Lawrence Erlbaum Associates, 1974.

Kintsch, W., & Keenan, J. Reading rate and retention as a function of the number of propositions in the base structure of sentences. *Cognitive Psychology*, 1973, *5*, 257-274.

Kintsch, W., Kozminsky, E., Streby, W. J., McKoon, G., & Keenan, J. M. Comprehension and recall of text as a function of a content variable. *Journal of Verbal Learning and Verbal Behavior*, 1975, *14*, 196-214.

Kintsch, W., & van Dijk, T. A. Toward a model of discourse comprehension and production. *Psychological Review*, 1978, *85*, 363-394.

Kleiman, G. M. Sentence frame contexts and lexical decisions: sentence acceptability and word-relatedness effects. *Memory and Cognition*, 1980, *8*, 336-344.

Lesgold, A. M., Roth, S. F., & Curtis, M. E. Foregrounding effects in discourse comprehension. *Journal of Verbal Learning and Verbal Behavior*, 1979, *18*, 291-308.

Mandler, J. M., & Johnson, N. S. Remembrance of things parsed: Story structure and recall. *Cognitive Psychology*, 1977, *9*, 111-151.

Manelis, L., & Yekovich, F. R. Repetitions of propositional arguments in sentences. *Journal of Verbal Learning and Verbal Behavior*, 1976, *15*, 301-312.

McConkie, G. W., Hogaboam, T. W., Wolverton, G. S., Zola, D., & Lucas, P. A. Toward the use of eye movements in the study of language processing. *Discourse Processes*, 1979, *2*, 157-178.

McFarland, C. E., & Kellas, G. Mode of input effects on subject-controlled processes. *Journal of Experimental Psychology*, 1974, *103*, 343-350.

McKoon, G., & Ratcliff, R. The comprehension processes and memory structures involved in anaphoric reference. *Journal of Verbal Learning and Verbal Behavior*, 1980, *19*, 668-682.

Miller, G. A., & McKean, K. O. A chronometric study of some relations between sentences. *Quarterly Journal of Experimental Psychology*, 1964, *16*, 297-308.

Mitchell, D. C., & Green, D. W. The effects of content on the immediate processing in reading. *Quarterly Journal of Experimental Psychology*, 1978, *30*, 609-636.

Olson, G. M., Duffy, S. A., & Mack, R. L. Knowledge of writing conventions in prose comprehension. In W. J. McKeachie, & K. Eble (Eds.), *New directions in learning and searching*. San Francisco: Jossey-Bass, 1980.

Omanson, R. C. An analysis of narratives: identifying central, supportive and distracting content. *Discourse Processes*, in press.

Paivio, A. *Imagery and verbal processes*. New York: Holt, Rinehart, & Winston, 1971.

Paul, I. H. Studies in remembering: the reproduction of connected and extended material. *Psychological Issues*, 1959, *1*.

Pedhazur, E. J. Coding subjects in repeated measures designs. *Psychological Bulletin*, 1977, *84*, 298-305.

Rayner, K. Visual attention in reading: eye movements reflect cognitive processes. *Memory and Cognition*, 1977, *5*, 443-448.

Rayner, K. Eye movements in reading and information processing. *Psychological Bulletin*, 1978, *85*, 618-660.

Rubin, D. C. 51 properties of 125 words: a unit analysis of verbal behavior. *Journal of Verbal Learning and Verbal Behavior*, 1980, *19*, 736-755.

Rumelhart, D. E. Notes on a schema for stories. In D. G. Bobrow and A. Collins (Eds.), *Representation and understanding: Studies in cognitive science*. New York: Academic Press, 1975.

Sanford, A. J., & Garrod, S. C. *Understanding written language*. New York: John Wiley & Sons, 1981.

Schank, R. C. Language and memory. *Cognitive Science*, 1980, *4*, 243-284.

Schank, R. C., & Abelson, R. P. *Scripts, plans, goals, and understanding: An inquiry into human knowledge structure*. Hillsdale, N. J.: Lawrence Erlbaum Associates, 1977.

Schank, R. C., & Wilensky, R. A. Goal-directed production system for story understanding. In D. Waterman, F. Hayes-Roth, (Eds.), *Pattern directed inference systems*. New York: Academic Press, 1978.

Stein, N. L., & Glenn, G. G. An analysis of story comprehension in elementary school children. In R. O. Freedle (Ed.), *New directions in discourse processing*, (Vol. 2) Norwood, N. J.: Ablex, 1979.

Sulin, R. A., & Dooling, D. J. Intrusion of a thematic idea in retention of prose. *Journal of Experimental Psychology*, 1974, *103*, 255-262.

Thibadeau, R., Just, M. A., & Carpenter, P. A. A model of the time course and content of reading. *Cognitive Science*, 1982, *6*, 157-203.

Thorndyke, P. W. Conceptual complexity and imagery in comprehension and memory. *Journal of Verbal Learning and Verbal Behavior*, 1975, *14*, 359-369.

Thorndyke, P. W. Cognitive structures in comprehension and memory of narrative discourse. *Cognitive Psychology*, 1977, *9*, 77-110.
Tryk, H. E. Subjective scaling and word frequency. *American Journal of Psychology*, 1968, *81*, 170-177.
Warren, W. H., Nicholas, D. W., & Trabasso, T. Event chains and inferences in understanding narratives. In R. O. Freedle (Ed.), *New directions in discourse processing*. (Vol. 2). Norwood, N. J.: Ablex, 1979.
Weisberg, S. *Applied linear regression*. New York: John Wiley & Sons, 1980.
Winer, B. J. *Statistical principles in experimental design*. (2nd ed.). New York: McGraw-Hill, 1971.
Wisher, R. A. The effects of syntactic expectations during reading. *Journal of Educational Psychology*, 1976, *68*, 597-602.
Yekovich, F. R., Walker, C. H., & Blackman, H. S. The role of presupposed and focal information in integrating sentences. *Journal of Verbal Learning and Verbal Behavior*, 1979, *18*, 535-548.

11
Thinking-Out-Loud as a Method for Studying Real-Time Comprehension Processes

Gary M. Olson
University of Michigan
Susan A. Duffy
University of Massachusetts
 and
Robert L. Mack
IBM Research Center

The analysis of cognitive processes in real time is one of the most methodologically difficult tasks in all of psychology. The events we wish to examine are internal to the mind, with only occasional observable correlates. Further, most cognitive tasks involve a host of hierarchically interrelated subcomponents, likely operating in parallel. Reading text in order to understand it is an excellent example of just such a task. And yet, there is increasing recognition of the fact that a deep understanding of how to assess the readability of text and how to remedy reading difficulties will require an analysis of the *process* of comprehension (e.g., Kintsch & van Dijk, 1977; Olson, Mack, & Duffy, 1981).

Though many psychological processes important to comprehension occur outside of awareness, any sophisticated reader is aware of much cognitive activity that occurs during reading. With this in mind, we felt that one simple strategy for obtaining information about the process of comprehension would be to have readers think out loud while reading. We were motivated by a belief that intelligent reading has many affinities with problem-solving, a domain in which thinking-out-loud (TOL) protocols have proved to be a useful research tool (e.g., Newell & Simon, 1972). Of course, to use TOL data to study cognitive processes, one must be aware of the limits and pitfalls of this method. As with any other method, it is useful for pursuing some goals and not others. The aim of this chapter is to discuss its usefulness as one technique for studying the comprehension of connected text.

This chapter is organized as follows. The general rationale for the use of the TOL method is described first. This includes a discussion of a general model of comprehension that has guided our research and our use of this method. The goals of the TOL method and the general assumptions made in using it are described.

Next, we list a variety of different types of TOL tasks that can be used, and briefly discuss their virtues. Then we illustrate the use of TOL data in the analysis of comprehension processes by discussing a series of studies conducted in our laboratories. We also describe a series of other applications of the TOL task to make comprehension activities explicit, though in some cases as a means to another goal. Since other investigators have used the TOL task with more mixed results than ours, we discuss some of the reasons why the TOL task may vary in its usefulness. In the concluding section, we summarize in a convenient form the advantages and the limitations of using TOL protocols for studying language comprehension.

THE USE OF THINKING-OUT-LOUD PROTOCOLS

What kind of information can we hope to obtain from TOL data? There has been much controversy in the history of psychology about verbal reports as data, focussing primarily upon their oft-reported unreliability (e.g., Nisbett & Wilson, 1977). In a detailed analysis of verbal reports as data, Ericsson and Simon (1980) clarified several points about their use that are important to keep in mind when thinking about TOL data. First, the focus of the TOL task should be to get subjects to report the content of their immediate awareness rather than to report explanations of their behavior. Further, subjects should be asked to report what they are thinking about right now, not what they remember thinking about some time ago. The TOL task should also have subjects talk about aspects of their immediate experience that they can talk about. Some processes are unavailable to introspection or are difficult to verbalize. In general, limits on what is available to be reported upon, what can be remembered, and on the human ability to offer explanations or justifications for one's own behavior should be respected.

Furthermore, TOL data should not be taken as *direct* reflections of thought processes but rather as data which are correlated with underlying thought processes. TOL data provide a sample of what's on the subject's mind during the task. But they will not necessarily reveal the strategies, knowledge sources, or representations actually used. These theoretical constructs must be inferred from the TOL data. The situation is quite analogous to the use of eye movements or reading times in studying comprehension. We are less interested in the statistical properties of eye movements or reading times than we are in the comprehension processes which generate these properties. These processes must be inferred from the data. TOL protocols are no different. They are unlikely to reveal in a direct fashion the underlying processes we are most interested in discovering.

These cautions are extremely important, for as Ericsson and Simon (1980) point out in some detail, many of the criticisms of verbal reports as data are based on faulty assumptions about the reasonable use of such data. As with any other form of data we collect in cognitive research, TOL data provide indicators of real-time processes that must be affirmed through the examination of as broad a range of different measures as possible. Of course, as with any other type of data, TOL data have a number of limitations which must be kept in mind. Ericsson and Simon (1980) present a clear discussion of the virtues and limits of TOL data in general, and this chapter will attempt to do the same for the specific case of text comprehension.

Reading involves a broad array of processes, from sensory and perceptual ones to higher level processes such as reasoning and inference. Table 1 presents a partial list of these. The perceptual, attentional, and memory processes involved in the recognition of letters and words for a skilled reader occur too rapidly and may not be available to consciousness. There are a variety of experimental procedures available for the analysis of these lower level processes. Such processes as the syntactic and semantic analysis of sentences may or may not be usefully analysed by TOL methods. But the TOL task is best used to study the higher level processes in reading: the inferences, predictions, schema elaborations, and other complex cognitions that occur as part of skilled reading. We assume these processes are most available to consciousness as the reader reads. The outputs of these processes are verbal, slow to arise, and samples of them are sufficient for the investigator to infer what must have transpired. In general, to the extent that one agrees with Neisser's (1967) characterization of reading as "externally guided thinking" (p. 136), the TOL method is specialized for the study of the thinking.

The investigation of reading processes can begin in many ways. Many have started with a formal analysis of the materials themselves. Those interested in letter or word recognition attend to the frequency and regularity of various items in typical text. Those interested in syntactic analysis turn to linguistic theories of sentence structure for hypotheses. Finally, those interested in text level variables look to linguistic analysis for descriptions of inter-sentence phenomena like anaphora or of the overall structure of texts. The information gleaned from such formal analyses of the properties of print and text is very important to the analysis

TABLE 1
Levels of Analysis in Reading

PERCEPTUAL ANALYSIS
   Perception of Features
   Perception of Letters
   Perception of Letter Patterns
DEVELOPMENT OF WITHIN-SENTENCE REPRESENTATION
   Recognition of Words
   Syntactic Analysis
   Semantic Analysis
   Pragmatic Analysis
DEVELOPMENT OF INTEGRATED REPRESENTATION ACROSS SENTENCES
   Inferences
   Elaboration
   Hypotheses

of reading, and in combination with assumptions about psychological processes provides a rich source of initial hypotheses about aspects of the reading process.

Formal analyses of the properties of print and text are much less useful in formulating hypotheses about the higher level processes—the thinking—that occurs as part of skilled reading. Further, although many of us are aware of the thoughts we have while reading, it is difficult to analyze these processes either on the basis of introspection or from other *a priori* considerations. The TOL task offers an opportunity to collect systematic observations about the thinking that occurs during reading, allowing the investigator to form hypotheses about this level of processing which can in turn be evaluated in a number of ways, including experimental tests. Thus, the optimal use of the TOL task is as a discovery procedure for studying these higher level processes.

In order to better appreciate what might be learned about the comprehension process from TOL data, we begin with a brief sketch of the nature of text comprehension. Figure 1 shows a schema for what is involved in reading, focussing on the higher level activities. The focus is on what the reader is doing at some particular point in the text. What controls the reader's thought processes at the point where sentence N in a text is being read? It is controlled by the structure of the text and sentence N's particular role in this structure. And it is controlled by the reader's knowledge of the world—both physical and social—that plays such an important part in language understanding in general. Further, it is quite clear that skilled readers possess knowledge about text conventions, about how texts are written in order to accomplish what they perceive to be the author's goals (see Olson, Duffy, & Mack, 1980; Olson, Mack, & Duffy, 1981).

To these general sources of constraints are added three types of knowledge constructed by the reader during comprehension. The first is a representation of what has been presented in the text so far. This is typically organized by a schema appropriate for the text type being read. Second, a workspace containing current lines of thought the reader is working on is constructed. In stories, the workspace might contain hypotheses about where the text is heading. For argumentative essays or journal articles, the workspace might contain criticisms of the author's arguments. The contents of the workspace can be more or less specific depending on a variety of reader and text variables (e.g., Olson et al., 1981), but they are an important part of what most skilled readers are doing in any text. Finally, although it has not yet been studied in much detail by cognitive psychologists, readers probably construct a model of the writer, the other participant in the social intercourse being mediated by the text. The reader's model of the writer may not be accurate, and may well be manipulated intentionally by the writer.

A reader facing sentence N in a text will use these various sources of knowledge along with a semantic representation of the sentence to modify each of the three representations being constructed during comprehension: the representation of what has been read, the representation of hypotheses, and the representation of the writer. For conceptual simplicity we imagine that a sentence that has already been given a semantic representation is passed on to those processes most directly

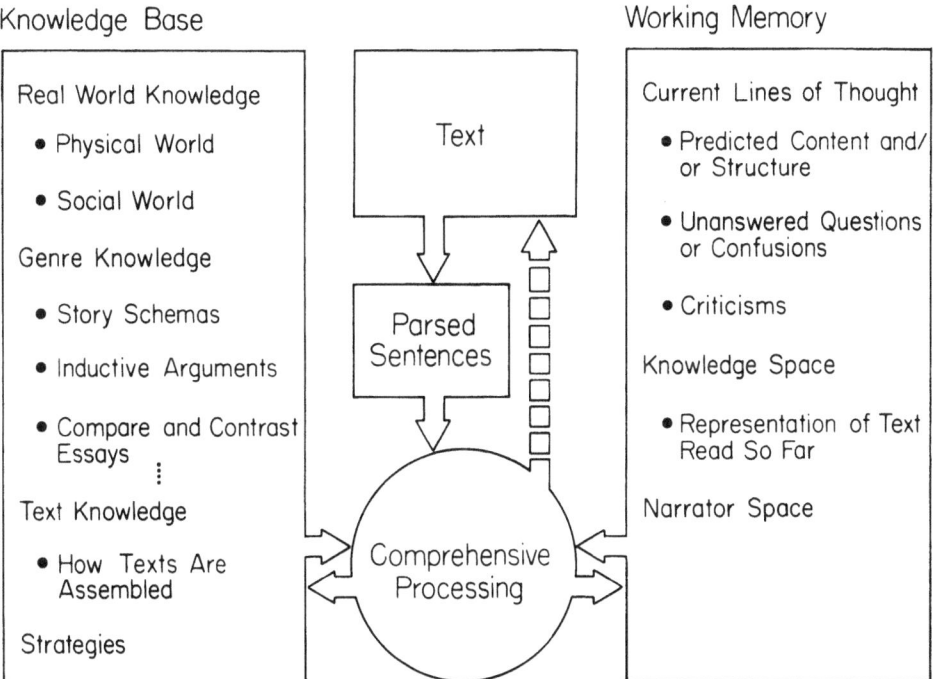

FIG. 1. Conceptual scheme for the reading process.

concerned with this updating (we ignore the undoubtedly important interactions between these updating processes and the lexical, syntactic, and semantic analyses of individual sentences). The major focus of the TOL data will be on the processes responsible for integrating the semantic representation of an individual sentence into the various cognitive structures being constructed during comprehension. These data should reveal the kinds of *strategies* used by readers in accomplishing these tasks, the kinds of *knowledge sources* employed, and the kinds of *representations* constructed. While memory measures like recall have provided useful information about the knowledge sources and representations used in text comprehension, they tell us very little about the strategies employed or about the sentence-by-sentence interactions among the knowledge sources and representations.

TYPES OF THINKING-OUT-LOUD TASKS

There are many kinds of TOL data that can be collected for studying text comprehension. In this section we will review several major types that have actually been used, and briefly discuss their virtues and limits.

Sentence-by-sentence Talking

In this version of the task, which could be considered its most basic form, the subject is asked to talk after each sentence in the text. The talking continues until the text is completed. Though in principle the text could be presented in almost any fashion, most investigators have presented it in such a way that the reader cannot look ahead. However, investigators have varied the extent to which the reader can look back at previous text. The most restrictive presentation makes only the current sentence available, while the least restrictive makes all the previous text available. Various windows of intermediate size could also be used. How exactly to organize the presentation of the text depends somewhat on the goals of the investigator. For instance, in much of our work we have been interested in explicating as fully as possible the role of the current sentence in comprehension. This has led us to use the single-sentence exposure most frequently, but other arrangements can be easily justified.

Another dimension of variation is what the readers are asked to talk about. We have used two types of instructions in our work:

General Instructions. In this version of the task, we encourage subjects to talk about a wide range of things. However, we typically give them a list of examples of the types of things we would like them to talk about. We feel it is inadequate to instruct them to "think out loud" without telling them what this means, at least in the context of studying comprehension.

We have done several studies in which we asked subjects to think out loud generally (e.g., Olson et al., 1981). Keep in mind that these subjects are talking after each sentence in the text. The kinds of things we asked them to talk about included any inferences or elaborations they felt compelled to draw on the basis of the current sentence, any connections they saw between the current sentence and any prior ones, any predictions they had about what might be coming up, and any comments they had about what they felt was the role of the current sentence in the overall organization of the text. These are obviously not the only things subjects could talk about. We included these because they were of theoretical interest to us. The important point vis-a-vis the use of the TOL task to study comprehension is that one be explicit with the subject about what to talk about. The exact list of suggestions should be motivated by theoretical ideas or by prior research.

Focussed Instructions. In this version of the TOL task, the subject is asked to talk about only one type of thing or to do one type of activity. Let us illustrate this with two examples from our own research. Because of our interest in predictive processing, we have collected TOL data in which all we asked subjects to do was to make predictions about what was coming up in the future in this text and to comment on the fate of earlier predictions if they felt this was warranted. Clearly, this task was motivated by a special theoretical concern for the importance of a particular type of activity. Earlier data from a general TOL task had indicated that predictions might be an especially informative kind of activity (Olson et al., 1981), so we wanted to collect a richer set of prediction data than we had obtained from the general task, where subjects talked about a number of different types of things which competed with predictions.

In a second example, we had subjects ask questions after reading each sentence. They were told to imagine that the text's author was present, and that the author was willing to answer any question the reader had about the text at that point, except for the obvious question of what comes next. Once again, we had a specific theoretical goal in using this task. As with the example of predictions, these kinds of questions occasionally appeared in the more general type of TOL task, but we wanted a richer set of data than we could get when a variety of different types of information were being collected.

Both of these examples share several important properties. First, the selection of the thing to be talked about was theoretically motivated. In both cases we had a background of general TOL data, reading time data, and theoretical models from which we arrived at the specific probes we used. Second, the main reason for using the focussed TOL task was to get richer data about this particular data type. TOL subjects will only say so much. When you have a variety of types of things for them to talk about, you will only get a modest amount of any one type. In order to get richer data of a specific type the focussed task is needed. But because it is focussed it provides a much narrower window into the process of comprehension. Later, when we discuss an example of this methodology in more detail, we will return to this issue.

Other Variants. Rumelhart (1982) and Graesser (1981) have both used a TOL task in which subjects answered specific questions after each sentence of a text. Rumelhart's subjects answered five WH-questions (who, what, why, when, where) after each sentence. The texts began ambiguously, with each successive sentence providing additional constraints on what was going on. Rumelhart used the TOL task to discover how subjects developed an interpretation of the texts and how the interpretation changed with each additional sentence. Graesser has used a variant of this task (subjects actually wrote down their answers) to investigate how readers construct a representation of the text, focussing on the contribution each sentence makes to the growing representation.

Selective Talking

Yet another variation on the TOL task is to have subjects talk at only particular points in a text. There are two broad classes of justifications for this. First, one may have a process theory that pinpoints certain places in a text as crucial tests of some aspect of the theory. Second, in designing materials for an experiment, there may be certain properties one wants to have at certain points in the experimental texts. A selective TOL task can be used to verify that the materials have in fact instantiated this property.

Except for the fact that it is selective rather than sentence-by-sentence for the whole text, the earlier discussions about what to have subjects talk about hold for this variation of the task too. We would especially like to underscore the use of this version of the TOL task for preparing stimulus materials for experiments. In most studies of text processing, the major independent variables are manipulations of the text. We have found through experience that what *seem* to be instantiations of a text variable are often not good examples of it. Using selective TOL to aid in developing the stimuli has been a major part of several studies we have done. The feedback from subjects who think out loud is extremely informative, so much so in fact that we have begun a whole line of research aimed at using TOL data as tools for providing feedback to writers. We will discuss this last example later.

In general, selective talking is used to study what processing is like at some particular point. However, to assess the role of local contributions to the talking versus global characteristics of the talking, the placement of control probes at points in the text different from those of specific interest is important. A variety of theoretical considerations would determine where to put such control probes, but they are a necessary part of the use of selective talking.

After the Fact Talking

Ericsson and Simon (1980) correctly stress that it is risky to ask subjects to talk about their cognitive experiences after the fact. Memory is too fallible to allow for accurate reporting of earlier mental states. However, if very short texts or text fragments were used, the memory problems are not as great, and useful TOL data could be collected after the fact.

Collins, Brown, and Larkin (1980) used just such a task to examine the general strategies used to comprehend short texts (3 and 4 sentences long). The texts were difficult to understand, and subjects were asked to talk about the hypotheses they had considered and rejected in trying to interpret the text. Because the texts were short, subjects could remember intermediate interpretations they had generated while reading. This method is less useful for exploring the processing of longer texts, especially if the investigator is concerned with evaluating the contribution each sentence makes in the comprehension process. Even with the short texts used by Collins et al., it is not clear how accurate subjects were in pinpointing exactly where a hypothesis was introduced or rejected.

Summary

Our descriptions of different TOL tasks in this section by no means exhaust all of the possibilities. Rather, these should be taken as suggestive of the kinds of ways in which TOL data can be collected to be used to explicate the nature of comprehension processing. One's specific theoretical and empirical goals will dictate which variant of the TOL task will be most useful.

EXAMPLES OF THINKING-OUT-LOUD DATA

In this section we present some examples of the use of TOL data from our own research. We present an example of both the general TOL sentence-by-sentence task and the focussed sentence-by-sentence question-asking task.

Sentence-by-sentence TOL for Simple Stories and Essays

These data, reported in more detail in Olson et al. (1981), illustrate the use of the general sentence-by-sentence TOL task. We had subjects think out loud while reading four different stories and four different essays. We used two well-formed simple stories, *Lentil* and *Stranger*, and two stories that violated certain conventions of story telling. These latter two stories were *Circle Island*, Dawes' (1966) story that was used by Thorndyke (1977) to study story processing, and *War of the Ghosts*, Bartlett's (1932) classic. We chose *Circle Island* and *War of the Ghosts* because we wanted to be able to contrast TOL data obtained from well-formed stories (*Lentil* and *Stranger*) with these two ill-formed stories. A different group of subjects talked out loud to two versions of each of four different essays. We present the story data in more detail here, so will not describe the essays or their data as completely (see Olson et al., 1981, for details).

It helps to have a sense of what TOL data are like. Thus, in Table 2, we present an excerpt from a subject thinking out loud to the first 17 sentences of *Lentil* (all of

TABLE 2
Sample Thinking-Out-Loud Protocol of a
Subject Reading *Lentil*

---

1. IN THE TOWN OF ALTO, OHIO, THERE LIVED A BOY NAMED LENTIL.

    In Alto, Ohio, is sort of ... I assume this is going to be a story ... something about music ... or vegetables because we have the boy named Lentil.

2. LENTIL HAD A HAPPY LIFE EXCEPT FOR ONE THING.

    Most of this story is going to be developed around this one exception. He is generally happy, except for this one thing.

3. HE WANTED TO SING — BUT HE COULD NOT.

    Ah hah. I'm remembering "Alto, Ohio", that it is going to be about music, and he wanted to sing is the one thing that was unhappy in his life. The story is going to be about how he learns to sing. He is either going to go out and find birds and learn from them, or he is going to have a trumpet like the trumpeter swan. The story is going to be about fixing the fact that he can't sing.

4. IT WAS MOST EMBARRASSING, BECAUSE WHEN HE OPENED HIS MOUTH TO TRY, ONLY STRANGE SOUNDS CAME OUT.

    I don't see what ... it's still talking about the fact that he can't sing (repeats) ... no, we are just elaborating on the fact that he can't sing.

5. AND HE COULD NOT EVEN WHISTLE BECAUSE HE COULDN'T PUCKER HIS LIPS.

More elaboration about his unhappiness ... he can't produce music at all ... "He couldn't even whistle". Now I'm beginning to think about how we are going to resolve this. Is it going to have anything to do with the fact that his name is Lentil? or vegetables? Is he going to do anything with vegetables?

6. BUT HE DID WANT TO MAKE MUSIC, SO HE SAVED UP ENOUGH PENNIES TO BUY A HARMONICA.

That seems reasonable. He is going to try different ways to make music. He wants to make music, not just sing.

7. LENTIL WAS PROUD OF HIS NEW HARMONICA, AND HE DECIDED TO BECOME AN EXPERT.

So now he's going to learn it from somebody else.

8. SO HE PLAYED A LOT, WHENEVER AND WHEREVER HE COULD.

Now I expect this to be generating a lot of annoyance from his mother ... having noisy children. (Repeats)

9. HIS FAVORITE PLACE TO PRACTICE WAS IN THE BATHTUB, BECAUSE THERE THE TONE WAS IMPROVED ONE HUNDRED PERCENT.

Like singing in the shower. (repeats) Now we are going to have developments about him turning into a prune or something ... a prune skin. (repeats)

10. HE USED TO PLAY ALMOST ALL THE WAY TO SCHOOL.

Now that's a place not in the bathtub. He "used to play" means he doesn't anymore. Maybe the children made fun of him, or something like that.

11. DOWN VINE STREET TO THE CORNER OF MAIN, PAST THE FINEST HOUSE IN ALTO, WHICH BELONGED TO THE GREAT COLONEL CARTER.

This isn't even a sentence. He is playing almost all the way to school. This is the route. Colonel Carter is just been introduced, and he is going to develop something with this little Lentil boy. "Used to play almost all the way to school". We haven't done anything with the bathtub. It might be ... this sounds like a children's story. So that's really reading about children making noise in the bathtub. Children love the sound of their own voices. Yell in parking structures and tunnels and stuff like that. That may develop, may not.

12. THEN PAST THE DRUG STORE, THE BARBER SHOP, AND THE ALTO LIBRARY, WHICH WAS A GIFT OF THE GREAT COLONEL CARTER, BY THE METHODIST CHURCH, THROUGH THE CARTER MEMORIAL PARK, AND AROUND THE SOLDIERS AND SAILORS MONUMENT THAT THE COLONEL HAD BUILT THERE.

So now we know Colonel Carter is rich ... not only famous but rich. "Then by the methodist church" ... Well, you could interpret this ... figure that the Alto library is a gift of the great Colonel Carter. We are describing more of his wealth. "He goes by the methodist church, through the memorial park". More of Carter's stuff ... very famous ... and "around the soldier's and sailor's monuments, which the Colonel had built there" ... sort of a central figure now. He is going to develop in some fashion.

13. THEN LENTIL WOULD STUFF HIS HARMONICA INTO HIS POCKET AND TAKE A SHORT CUT UP THE ALLEY BEHIND THE HARDWARE STORE SO HE WOULD NOT BE LATE FOR SCHOOL.

Why would he ... apparently all this stuff — playing — slows him down and he has to hurry up to get to school. "So he stuffs it in his pocket and takes a short cut up the alley behind the hardware store, so he wouldn't be late for school".

14. PEOPLE WOULD SMILE AND WAVE HELLO TO LENTIL AS HE WALKED DOWN THE STREET, BECAUSE EVERYONE IN ALTO LIKED LENTIL'S MUSIC — THAT IS, EVERYONE BUT OLD SNEEP.

   I'll bet you Old Sneep is Colonel Carter. That's got to be his nickname. He's going to be ... he is going to put an end to Lentil's playing. This is the story of a little boy against the giant ... David and Goliath. He is going to win over Old Sneep in the end.

15. OLD SNEEP DID NOT LIKE MUCH OF ANYTHING OR ANYBODY.

   Yep, we are developing Old Sneep, which I'm guessing is Colonel Carter.

16. HE JUST SAT ON A PARK BENCH AND WHITTLED AND GRUMBLED.

   Well, maybe it may not be. Can't imagine an old wealthy person sitting on a park bench, whittling and grumbling. But it could be all the same person.

17. ONE DAY THE NEWS GOT AROUND THAT THE GREAT COLONEL CARTER, WHO HAD BEEN AWAY FOR TWO YEARS, WAS COMING HOME.

   Well, now I'm deciding that Old Sneep is not the great Colonel Carter. So we have Old Sneep, little Lentil who is playing all the way to school, through, across, in front of Colonel Carter's house, and Colonel Carter, who is great, rich, and magnificent and all that. Haven't decided whether Colonel Carter is a good guy or a bad guy.

18. PEOPLE BEGAN TO PLAN A GRAND WELCOME.

   That's a welcome home for Colonel Carter. Oh, maybe we're going to have a parade and Lentil gets to be first in parade or something like that.

19. BUT WHEN OLD SNEEP HEARD THE NEWS HE SAID, "HUMPH. WE WUZ BOYS TOGETHER. HE AIN'T A MITE BETTER'N YOU OR ME AND HE NEEDS TAKIN' DOWN A PEG OR TWO".

   All right, now I know that Old Sneep is not Colonel Carter. Maybe not ... maybe ... maybe not ... probably not. So we have a humbug here, who is unhappy. So he is going to try to destroy the parade, or whatever we're going to do — the grand welcome.

TABLE 3
The Well-Formed Story *Lentil*

1. In the town of Alto, Ohio, there lived a boy named Lentil.
2. Lentil had a happy life except for one thing.
3. He wanted to sing — but he couldn't.
4. It was most embarrassing, because when he opened his mouth to try, only strange sounds came out.
5. And he couldn't even whistle because he couldn't pucker his lips.
6. But he did want to make music, so he saved up enough pennies to buy a harmonica.
7. Lentil was proud of his new harmonica, and he decided to become an expert.
8. So he played a lot, whenever and wherever he could.
9. His favorite place to practice was in the bathtub, because there the tone was improved one hundred percent.
10. He used to play almost all the way to school.
11. Down Vine Street to the corner of Main, past the finest house in Alto, which belonged to the great Colonel Carter.

12. Then past the drugstore, the barber shop, and the Alto Library, which was a gift of the great Colonel Carter, by the Methodist Church, through the Carter Memorial Park, and around the Soldiers and Sailors Monument that the Colonel had built there.
13. Then Lentil would stuff his harmonica into his pocket and take a shortcut up the alley behind the hardware store so he would not be late for school.
14. People would smile and wave hello to Lentil as he walked down the street, because everyone in Alto liked Lentil's music - that is, everybody but Old Sneep.
15. Old Sneep didn't like much of anything or anybody.
16. He just sat on a park bench and whittled and grumbled.
17. One day the news got around that the great Colonel Carter, who had been away for two years, was coming home.
18. People began to plan a grand welcome.
19. But when Old Sneep heard the news he said, "Humph! We wuz boys together - he ain't a mite better'n you or me and he needs takin' down a peg or two".
20. Sneep just kept right on whittling, but everybody else kept right on planning.
21. Colonel Carter was the town's most important citizen, so the people hung out flags and decorated the streets.
22. The mayor prepared a speech.
23. The Alto Brass Band put on their new uniforms.
24. And the printer, the grocer, the plumber, the minister, the barber, the druggist, the ice man, the school teachers, the housewives and their husbands and their children - yes, the whole town went to the station to welcome Colonel Carter.
25. The train pulled in.
26. The musicians in the band were waiting for the leader to signal them to play.
27. The leader was waiting for the mayor to nod to him to start the band.
28. And the mayor was waiting for Colonel Carter to step from his private car.
29. All the people held their breath and waited.
30. Then there was a wet sound from above.
31. Slurp! There was Old Sneep, sucking on a lemon.
32. Old Sneep knew that when the musicians looked at him their mouths would pucker up so they could not play their horns.
33. The whole band looked up at Old Sneep.
34. The mayor gave the signal to play, but the cornetist couldn't play his cornet, the piccolo player couldn't play his piccolo, the trombone player couldn't play his trombone, and the tuba player couldn't play his tuba, because their lips were all puckered up.
35. They couldn't play a single note!
36. The musicians just stood there holding their instruments and looking up at Sneep sucking on the lemon.
37. The leader looked helpless.
38. The people were too surprised to move or say a thing.
39. And the mayor wrung his hands and wore a look that said: "Can't somebody do something, please?"
40. As Colonel Carter stepped from his car, the only sound was the noise of Sneep's lemon.
41. Clouds began to gather on the colonel's brow and he said, "Humph!" in an indignant sort of way.
42. Of course Lentil's lips were not puckered and he knew something had to be done.
43. So he took out his harmonica and started to play "Comin' 'Round the Mountain When She Comes."
44. When Lentil began to play the second chorus, Colonel Carter smiled.
45. Then he let out a loud chuckle and began to sing, "...driving six white horses when she comes."
46. Then everybody sang and they all marched down Main Street behind the colonel's car.
47. Lentil rode with the colonel, who took a turn at the harmonica when Lentil's wind began to give out.

48. (He said he hadn't played one since he was a boy, but he did very well considering.)
49. They marched to the colonel's house and paraded through the gate and onto the front lawn.
50. The mayor's committee served ice cream cones to all the citizens and Colonel Carter made a speech saying how happy he was to be home again.
51. When he said that he was going to build a new hospital for the town of Alto, everybody was happy — even Old Sneep!
52. So, you never can tell what will happen when you learn to play the harmonica.

Lentil is shown in Table 3). These data are typical of what a skilled, educated adult reader talks about while reading a story of this type.

We have used protocol data of this type in two general ways. First, we have obtained qualitative impressions of the nature of comprehension processing for various types of texts. Second, we have related quantitative properties of the TOL data to other types of data, such as sentence-by-sentence reading times and recall data. We give examples of each type of analysis here to illustrate how TOL data can be used.

Qualitative Analyses. We focus on TOL data obtained for simple stories. What is a reader doing while reading such a text? The reader is confronted with the following task. A text embodying various aspects of the story is available as input. The text will be processed against a background of several types of knowledge that are relevant to it. The final product of understanding will be an interpreted representation of the essential elements of the story. However, with most stories, this representation must be constructed from incomplete information in the text. Much that is important to interpreting the elements of the text as a story is left implicit.

We can make this more concrete by describing some of the properties of TOL data for readers reading simple stories. Table 4 presents the relative frequencies of different types of things readers talked about during the four stories we described earlier. As is evident, most of their talking is devoted to making inferences, generating predictions, and commenting on connections to prior information. This follows from the stress we gave these three categories of information in our instructions to subjects. The relative frequencies of these activities are roughly the same across the four stories shown in Table 4, though there are some interesting exceptions that are discussed in Olson et al., (1981). Though comments about the story or about their own understanding are low in overall frequency, they are very diagnostic of aspects of stories that readers are sensitive to.

A portrait of story processing is revealed by readers reading a well-formed story, *Lentil* (see Table 3). This is a straightforward children's story whose organization is quite simple. The first 17 sentences introduce the three major characters and lay the seeds of later conflict among them. The detailed actions of the story begin at sentence 18, and the climax that distinguishes the complication in the plot from the resolution occurs during sentences 30 to 32. Our analysis of what readers are doing while reading *Lentil* is based on 12 subjects who thought out loud during it. We were especially concerned to identify aspects of their talking that

TABLE 4
Proportion of Thinking-Out-Loud
Productions in Each Category for Stories

Category	Lentil	Stranger	Ghosts	Circle Island
Predictions	.22	.23	.13	.26
Questions	.04	.02	.10	.01
Comments on structure	.09	.06	.08	.10
Comments on own behavior	.03	.03	.04	.02
Confirmation of predictions	.02	.03	.01	.02
References to antecedent information	.29	.36	.30	.27
Inferences	.30	.24	.30	.27
General knowledge and associations	.02	.04	.03	.06

were common across most of the group rather than idiosyncratic to individual subjects.

Throughout the first 17 sentences the subjects were clearly collecting information and formulating tentative hypotheses about what was likely to happen in the story. They all recognized that the three central characters yield a highly probable line of conflict and resolution. Two will be in direct conflict, and the third will produce the ultimate resolution. At sentences 18 and 19, where the detailed action of the story begins, the subjects brought together their tentative hypotheses and formulated general plans for the rest of the story. Table 5 shows some examples of what subjects said at this point. It was striking to us how regular this phenomenon was: virtually all subjects did the same thing at about the same place in the story.

TABLE 5
Examples of Reader Comments to Sentence 18 in "Lentil"

Subject	Comments
24	"I expect the plot will succeed in getting the Colonel to hear Lentil playing his harmonica. The Colonel will be impressed and Lentil will be rewarded somehow".
17	"Maybe a celebration is planned (parade, etc.) and Lentil will win the day with a rousing welcoming song".
07	"Expect to read that Colonel Carter now will have some kind of role in what's going on with Alto and his music and Old Sneep. Expect to hear something about Colonel Carter's reaction to Lentil".
23	"We expect to see some interaction between Colonel Carter, Old Sneep, and Lentil. Probably a great celebration. Suspect that Lentil will probably be asked to play for him".

Throughout the processing of the main part of the story, the hypotheses constructed by the subjects were much in evidence. Each event was incorporated into the general plan constructed at the end of the sentence 17. The impact of these hypotheses was most dramatically revealed at sentences 30 and 31, where the climax occurred. The readers were certain that something was about to happen, but were uncertain as to exactly what. Consistent with the expectation that a story contains novel elements, the readers expected to be surprised by the specific form of the complication, even though they knew it would involve two particular characters. The first sentence of the climax is totally surprising, yet subjects immediately knew that the climax must be at hand and that the third character is about to intervene to save the day. This is all the more interesting because the third character has not been mentioned for 16 sentences. Subjects are led to expect that people are mentioned in a story for a reason. When a character is not brought in for a while, expectations of an appearance grows. The readers are anticipating a place for the character to fit in. Because the story is well written, at least by the conventions for children's stories, the predictions subjects make in response to the climactic event are in fact right.

Once the climax is passed, the mode of processing changed quite drastically. The readers appeared to be operating in a confirmatory mode. No new surprises were expected. Over and over one finds in the protocols statements like "That's what I expected," or "Yup," indicating that predictions generated were now being found to be congruent with the emerging details of the post-climactic part of the story.

Lentil is a good example of a story where the writer and the reader are operating in harmony, and the TOL data give a clear picture of how this works. The early part of the story sets a background and leads to hypotheses which successfully guide the subsequent processing. The same expectations are derived by different readers at just about the same points in the story, and specific events tend to be interpreted in the same way. The climax is especially striking. Though it is unpredictable, it is immediately interpreted by all subjects and is integrated into the general representation being constructed by the reader.

In Olson et al. (1981) we discuss differences between the processing of *Lentil* and the ill-formed stories we investigated. These contrasts are especially informative in helping us construct the portrait of processing just presented. By seeing what subjects do when things are not working well, we obtain a clearer picture of the kinds of strategies subjects are trying to employ while reading.

Because they are written and read for different purposes, one would expect stories and argumentative essays to be read in somewhat different ways. An analysis of TOL data for stories and essays confirms this. Table 6 shows the relative frequencies of types of talking in the TOL data for two versions of two of the essays we used. The greater frequency of Comments on Structure is due to our instructions: we added this to the set of things we stressed to our TOL subjects.

The summary data in Table 6 do not reveal some important details regarding qualitative differences in the processing of stories and essays. Perhaps the most dramatic difference comes in the kinds of predictions made by readers. The typical predictions made by a reader of a story are specific. Subjects predicted events that might occur later in the story, involving specific characters. The examples in Table 5 are typical. The specificity of the predictions increased as the story developed, but even very early in the stories the predictions were remarkably specific. Those in Table 5 occurred less than a third of the way into *Lentil*. In marked contrast, the predictions given in the essays were much more general. They often consisted of comments to the effect that the reader expected to see another argument or another example. But the specific content of the argument or example was usually not predicted. This difference in the types of predictions generated by readers reflects some important differences in the way they approach the two text types. The reader of a story has a set of firm expectations about the type of substantive events that will constitute an acceptable continuation of the story. Given background information about the characters and their motives, much can be anticipated about how the conflict in the plot will arise and how it will be resolved. However, for a typical argument it is apparently more difficult to predict the specifics. Readers know that an inductive argument will have various elements of supporting evidence for the main point, and they know that a compare and contrast essay will make comparisons and draw contrasts. But their expectations do not readily translate into specific predictions. For example, Table 7 gives typical predictions generated by readers at the end of the first paragraph of the well-formed version of the *Carpeting* essay (the complete essay is in Table 8; the first paragraph ends at

TABLE 6
Proportion of Thinking-Out-Loud Productions
in Each Category for Essays

Category	Ice Ages Ill-formed	Ice Ages Well-formed	Carpet Ill-formed	Carpet Well-formed
Predictions	.24	.29	.18	.24
Questions	.12	.12	.06	.08
Comments on structure	.32	.24	.28	.32
Comments on own behavior	.03	.04	.03	.03
Confirmation of predictions	.01	.02	.01	.03
References to antecedent information	.18	.14	.28	.19
Inferences	.10	.12	.11	.10
General knowledge and associations	.01	.04	.04	.01

sentence 6). This paragraph presents some background information, introduces the thesis of the essay, and announces that there will be three arguments made in support of the thesis. In contrast to the predictions given at the end of the background section in *Lentil* (see Table 5), the essay readers do not seem to go beyond what the author has told them about the arguments to be presented.

While the predictions in the essay TOL data were not as rich as those for stories, the comments on essay structure were extremely informative. These comments revealed subjects' expectations about how an essay should be written. For example, our readers expected to find a topic or thesis sentence, and they expected to find it early. In one version of our essay on the coming ice age, we deliberately placed the topic sentence late in the essay. As a result, pieces of evidence for the coming ice age were presented before the author announced the main point. When reading this essay, many TOL subjects explicitly searched for the topic sentence and complained that the author took so long to come to the point (see Table 9). In the *Carpeting* essay, subjects revealed a sensitivity to surface signalling devices. For example, in response to a sentence that began with the phrase "In short", subjects predicted that the writer would now move on to the next point in the argument. When we presented subjects with a version of this essay with such signalling removed, we found evidence of confusion in the protocols.

In short, the reader of an essay has general expectations about the overall structure of the argument or thesis. The reader quickly recognizes the type of point being made, and at a general level is sensitive to the organizing devices in the surface structure of the essay. However, unlike the story reader, the reader of an essay does not appear to engage in rich hypothesis generation and testing. The reader seems to adopt a more passive strategy, waiting for each new item of information to be presented and trying to fit it into the overall scheme of the argument.

A capsule summary of the differences in strategies for the readers of stories and essays might go as follows. The basic orientation of the reader of a story is

TABLE 7
Examples of Reader Comments at the End of the
Introductory Paragraph of the Well-formed
Carpet Essay

Subject	Comments
02	"It's going to go on to describe what is good about carpeting. Before it just told how it came to be that they're using more carpeting. I think they're going to tell the reasons why".
03	"I expect to find out what the three central arguments in favor of carpeting are".
04	"Now you would expect him to go on and possibly list and possibly explain each of the arguments in favor of carpeting".
06	"Sounds like they are going to sell me carpeting now. They will go into all the good points of carpeting and try to sell me a roll".

TABLE 8
Well-formed Version of *Carpeting* Essay

1. I should start by admitting that as little as five years ago carpeted classrooms would rightly have seemed too fanciful and expensive.
2. The carpeting then available would have been costly, difficult to maintain, and would have required frequent replacement.
3. Now, however, because of improved materials the arguments in favor of extensive carpeting seem a great deal more plausible.
4. New indoor-outdoor synthetics are stain resistant, fade resistant, durable and inexpensive.
5. They have made carpeting seem much less a luxury than a reasonable, even desirable, alternative to tile floors.
6. Briefly, there seem to be three central arguments in favor of carpeting.
7. First, of course, carpeting is attractive.
8. Now, admittedly, modern technology offers a great variety of attractively colored tiles.
9. The days of drab, institutional grays, greens, and browns in tile are over.
10. But while tile may approach carpeting in terms of color it has a hard and unattractive texture.
11. Carpeting, on the other hand, is colorful, attractive to the touch, and comfortable to walk on.
12. It goes a long way toward creating a pleasant atmosphere all of us would like to work in, both in and out of class.
13. Richly colored carpeting, such as bold reds often used in banks and commercial offices, would make our facilities less institutional.
14. Bright carpeting can easily make attractive an area that would otherwise seem Spartan and sterile.
15. In short, carpeting seems desirable simply because it is more attractive to look at and walk on than tile.
16. The second argument in favor of carpeted classrooms is essentially that carpeting serves a useful acoustical function.
17. Of course, the flexible backing and rough texture of modern tiles make them far less noisy than those of just a few years ago.
18. Both tiles and carpets have improved significantly.
19. Carpeting, however, is a superior dampener of sound.
20. It cuts noise from crowded hallways, absorbs annoying background noise in classrooms and makes busy space less noisy, and therefore more practical.
21. In industry, if not in schools, one frequently finds carpeting in busy areas because it reduces noise.
22. A final argument in favor of carpeting is that over a period of time, carpeting is no more expensive than tile.
23. Certainly, carpeting costs more than tile and it does need eventual replacement.
24. But carpeting costs much less to maintain than tile, which needs frequent washing, waxing and dusting.
25. The new synthetic carpets resist stains and fading.
26. An ordinary vacuum cleaner will keep them in shape.
27. But the tile floor, unfortunately, needs frequent scrubbing and waxing, if it is not to look dull and yellow with accumulated wax.
28. This process is laborious and slow, and, in large institutions, it requires expensive scrubbing machines.
29. In short, tile costs less than carpeting to install.
30. But count in the maintenance, and carpeting becomes a legitimate economic alternative to tile.
31. Were it not for the advantages in appearance and acoustics of carpeting, one could perhaps argue in favor of conventional tile flooring.
32. After all, the costs over a very long period, say twenty or thirty years, are genuinely unpredictable.
33. We simply have not accumulated enough experience with the new synthetics.

34. Perhaps over a quarter of a century carpets will prove more expensive.
35. Perhaps we will discover that after a decade or so, the savings in maintaining carpets will evaporate.
36. To this point, however, our experience with the new synthetic materials is essentially affirmative.
37. And so, given the clear edge carpeting has over tile aesthetically and acoutically, and its economic justification, carpeting seems sensible.

TABLE 9
Comments from Thinking-Out-Loud Subjects
Reading Late-Thesis Version of Ice Age

Sentence	Subject 6
4.	With this sentence he is setting up what the subject will actually be. And the next sentence will almost certainly be what his essay is actually going to be about.
5.	Instead of telling right out what the problem is, the person is delaying it a little bit, and now you get a sense of unease—wondering what it is this person is talking about. I would expect though that the subject, the main subject of this essay will be coming up very shortly.
12.	Again there are more hints about ice ages here; even though the ice age — he has not really said anything about it. I now believe that the whole structure of the essay up to this point has been to keep the reader uneasy, just dropping little bits of information until finally he is aware that we should be expecting another ice age even though he has never said so yet.
13.	OK, finally he does say that we're on the verge of another ice age.

	Subject 8
4.	I expect the next sentence to tell us exactly what this serious problem is.
5	This is the beginning of a new paragraph, and I really don't know what they're going to be talking about yet. I think that perhaps the serious problem that the essay's going to discuss should have been mentioned in the first paragraph or somehow it's going to be tied in in the next couple of sentences.
6.	That's fine, but what does it have to do with a serious problem?
7.	It looks like they're giving us all the symptoms of a serious problem, but we don't know what it is.
8.	Wonderful, we still don't know why we're discussing this.
9.	Somehow I feel I missed the whole sentence tying this together. We still haven't been told exactly what the essay's going to be about, the main theme. All that's been done is examples after examples.
10.	All these examples are fine. However we're halfway done with the essay and we still don't know what we're talking about.
13.	This sounds like the theme of our essay, now that we're halfway through. I think the introduction was rather long.

	Subject 9
4.	I expect him now to give me what this more serious problem is.
11.	It has taken me 11 sentences to figure out where this essay is going to. It doesn't really seem that those 11 sentences have done a good job of telling me what the point of the essay is going to be.
13.	This sentence could have started the entire essay.

Note: Sentence 4 states: "But mankind may soon be facing a more serious problem than any of these".
Sentence 13 is the thesis statement: "It now seems probable, climatologists say, that the world is on the verge on another ice age".

prospective. The reader is looking ahead, trying to anticipate where the story is going. Except at the beginning, where an overall hypothesis is being developed, the story reader tends to relate each sentence to the general hypotheses and predictions that have been developed. In contrast, the reader of the essay adopts a *retrospective* orientation. Each new element in the essay is related to earlier elements. There is little anticipation of what is coming up, except at the most general level. See Olson et al. (1980) and Olson et al. (1981) for a more detailed discussion of these differences and their basis in the nature of the two genres.

Quantitative Analyses. An obvious question is whether the data obtained from a TOL task have anything to do at all with reading when not talking. There are certainly many peculiarities of the TOL situation that could distort the processes used by the reader, and thus give us a false impression of what is occurring during reading. There are many ways in which this could be assessed. In essence, one wants to see if properties of the TOL data in any way relate to properties of reading under other situations.

We have examined this by carrying out multiple regression analyses of TOL data, using properties of the TOL data as independent variables and sentence-by-sentence reading times as dependent variables. We measured reading times by having an independent group of subjects read each text at a computer terminal. Each time they pressed a key the next sentence of the text appeared. Only one sentence was shown at a time. Subjects were told to read the text as normally as possible. Those reading the stories were told that later we would explore how well they understood each story. Essay readers were told they would later have to write a one-sentence summary of each essay. The primary data from this task are the times subjects devote to reading each sentence of each text.

Figure 2 shows the reading rates for each sentence for a group of 12 subjects reading *Lentil*. The measure of reading rate on the ordinate takes into account differences in sentence length. Though there are interesting connections between the qualitative picture of story processing revealed by our general analysis of the TOL data and the profile of reading times in Figure 2, here we want to focus on the quantitative analyses.

A stepwise multiple regression was performed, using mean reading time per sentence as the dependent variable and a series of independent variables. We focus on the stories first. For each story, two analyses were done, one that included sentence serial position and one that did not. Table 10 shows the general results (see Olson et al., 1981, for the specific regression coefficients). This table lists the predictors selected by the stepwise regression and the cumulative variance accounted for for each of the two analyses for the four stories. Note that for both *Lentil* and *Stranger*, our two well-formed stories, the relative frequency of various TOL categories accounted for significant portions of variance in the reading times, when the effect of sentence length has been removed as a separate factor. Note also that serial position and predictions are independent variables that are correlated

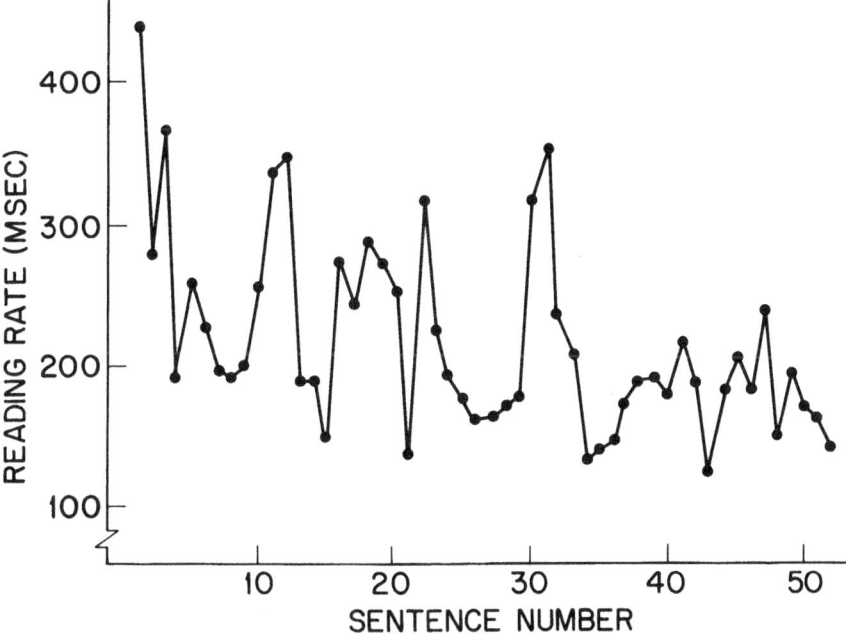

FIG. 2. Mean reading rate for each sentence in *Lentil*.

with each other. When serial position is excluded from the analysis, predictions takes its place as a predictor of reading times. The case is more mixed for the ill-formed stories. Only sentence length predicts reading times for *Circle Island*, while only one minor category of TOL productions accounts for any portion of the variance in reading times for *War of the Ghosts*. But the data for the well-formed stories are quite clear. Places where subjects in the TOL task generate more talking, especially predictions and inferences, are the same places where independent subjects slow down while reading silently. This supports the claim that the TOL data are related in an important way to what readers are doing during more ordinary types of reading.

A quite different picture emerged for the essays. Multiple regressions of reading time data for the essays revealed no relationships between the TOL data and mean reading times. The only variable to emerge as a significant predictor was sentence length. This is in marked contrast to the story data, where several indices of TOL behavior correlated with the reading times. This is yet another indication of the differences in the behavior of the two groups of subjects.

One other difference between story and essay processing emerges in the quantitative analyses. Serial position was a predictor of reading times for the well-formed stories, but it does not emerge as a predictor for the essays. We assume that serial position is a proxy for predictive processing. When subjects adopt a

TABLE 10
Significant Predictors of Sentence-by-Sentence
Reading Times for Simple Stories

	Lentil		Stranger		Ghosts		Circle Island	
Analysis with Serial Position	Syll.	.696	Syll.	.493	Syll.	.743	Syll.	.604
	Ser.Pos.	.748	Ser.Pos.	.588	Gen.Know.	.826		
	Inf.	.789	Gen.Know.	.659				
Analysis without Serial Position	Syll.	.696	Syll.	.493	Syll.	.743	Syll.	.604
	Inf.	.742	Imp.	.540	Gen.Know.	.826		
	Pred.	.762	Pred.	.603				
			Gen.Know.	.666				

Note: Syll. = number of syllables, Ser.Pos. = Serial position, Gen.Know. = general knowledge, Inf. = number of inferences, Pred. = number of predictions, Imp. = rated importance. Table entries are the cumulative variance accounted for by a stepwise multiple regression, listed in each cell in the order they were selected.

predictive mode they read more slowly at the beginning of a text as they generate hypotheses, and more quickly later in the text because they are confirming earlier predictions. As we argued earlier, the TOL data provide evidence that subjects adopt this strategy when reading stories but not when reading essays. The presence of a serial position effect in the reading times for stories but not for essays provides additional evidence for this strategy difference between stories and essays.

Question-Asking TOL for Simple Stories

One of the focussed TOL tasks we have used is one in which subjects ask questions following each sentence. We described the essence of this task earlier. In this section we present some data that show that the number of questions asked for each sentence correlates with sentence-by-sentence reading times.

Why use a question-asking task? We felt it tapped behavior relevant to what skilled readers do while reading. It seemed plausible to assume that each sentence encountered in a text raises certain questions in a reader's mind and answers other questions raised by earlier sentences. We wanted to explore this supposition in more detail by collecting rich data on the kinds of questions readers ask following each sentence in simple stories.

This study used *four* tasks. The primary task was one in which readers asked questions after reading each sentence in the story. In another task a different group of subjects read the same stories silently while we timed their reading. These same subjects performed the task of recalling the stories. Finally, another group of subjects rated the importance of the constituents of the story. Four simple short stories (maximum length was 41 sentences) were used as texts. They were all children's stories or simple folktales, and all were well-formed.

To better understand the results, a somewhat more detailed description of the four tasks is necessary:

Question-Asking. All four stories were presented to 9 subjects. Each sentence in the story was typed on a card, and the subject worked his or her way through the deck of cards, asking questions that were raised in his or her mind as a result of having read that particular sentence. The subject was told to imagine that the story's author was present, and that the author was willing to answer any questions the reader had about the story at that point, except for the obvious question of what happens next. The subject was allowed to spend as much time on any sentence as he or she desired, but was asked not to reread any previous sentences or to look ahead. The questions were tape recorded and later transcribed. The number of questions asked for each sentence was tallied and pooled over subjects. In addition, the questions were classified in various ways.

Reading Times. Sentence-by-sentence reading times were collected from 20 subjects. At the end of each story subjects wrote a brief (3 to 5 sentences) summary of the story.

Recall. The same 20 subjects were asked to recall the stories they had just read. They were presented with a brief descriptive title for each story, and were given unlimited time to try to recall as much as they could. They were asked to recall exact words, but were encouraged to guess if they could not remember exact words. Recall was scored by first doing a propositional analysis of each story and then matching the subject's recall against this, using a gist criterion.

Importance. Seventeen subjects read each story and crossed out the 50% of the words, phrases, or sentences in the story they felt was least important. For each sentence in each story the proportion of words left in averaged over subjects provided a measure of the relative importance of that sentence.

It is useful to have a better picture of what the question-asking data look like. Table 11 shows typical questions for the first sentence of one of the stories. These questions are grouped into those asked by two or more subjects and those that are idiosyncratic to one subject. Of course, we were also interested in the sentence-by-sentence variation in the questions asked. Figure 3 shows the total number of questions asked for each sentence in each of the four stories. With the possible exception of EMERALD, there is noteworthy variation in the number of questions asked from sentence to sentence. In EMERALD, there were a large number of questions at the beginning and then a fairly flat distribution of questions thereafter. Keep this difference in mind, because EMERALD will not follow the pattern of other stories in some of our later analyses.

TABLE 11
Sample Questions from *The Selling of the Cow*

Sentence 1: "Once there was a man named Cromer who lived on a farm that was way up on the side of a hill".

Questions asked by 2 or more subjects:	Subjects
1) Who is Cromer?	2
2) What is Cromer like?	3
3) Did Cromer live alone?	5
4) When did this story take place?	5
5) Where was the farm?	4
6) Where was the hill?	4
7) Why was the farm on a hill?	2
8) How far up the hill was the farm?	2
9) How high was the hill?	3
10) What kind of farm was it?	4
11) What will happen to Cromer?	2

Idiosyncratic questions asked by only 1 subject:
1) Does the fact that he lives on a farm have any significance?
2) Does he farm for a living?
3) Does he have another vocation?
4) Is Cromer married?
5) How old is Cromer?
6) How far away were Cromer's nearest neighbors?
7) Why did Cromer like to live on a farm?
8) Are they going to roll something down the hill?
9) Did a lot of the dirt wash off the side of the hill so that Cromer couldn't have his crops?
10) What was Cromer's first name?
11) Was that Cromer's first name?
12) Then what was Cromer's last name?
13) Did Cromer have more than one name?
14) What kind of name is Cromer?
15) What does Cromer mean?
16) What nationality is Cromer?

The first issue we addressed was whether the question-asking task is related to the reading times. We examined this by looking at the relationship between the total number of questions asked for each sentence in a story and the average reading time for each sentence for those subjects who were reading silently. The expectation was that sentences which elicited a lot of questions would be especially salient to real-time processing, and therefore would be read more slowly by subjects who were reading silently. This hypothesis was confirmed. We conducted a multiple regressions in which the average reading time per sentence was the dependent variable and several different predictor variables were explored. The predictor variables were sentence length, total number of questions, serial position, and importance. Only sentence length and number of questions emerged as

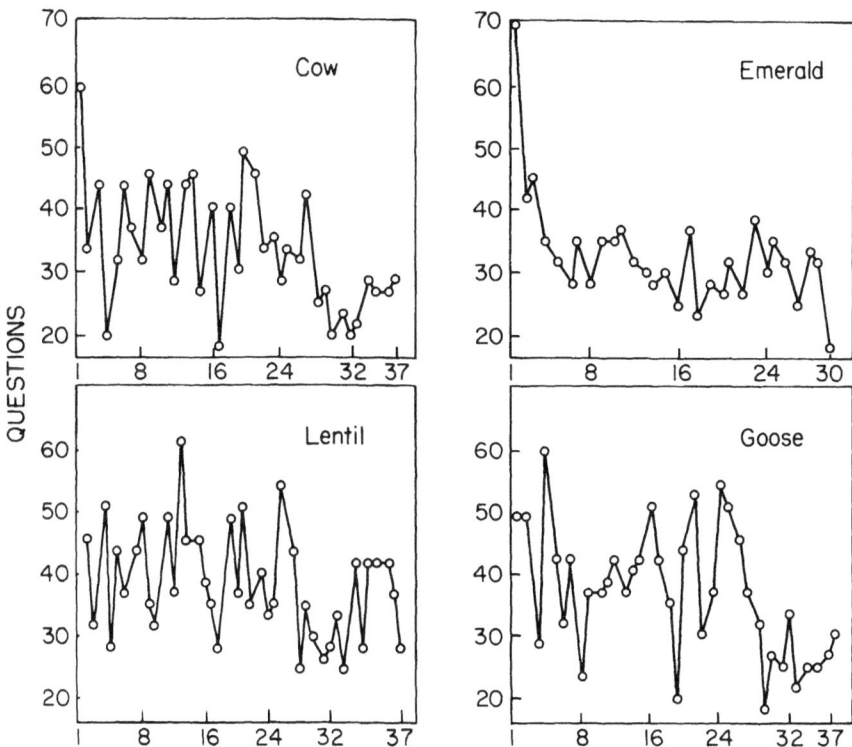

significant predictors of reading time. In this analysis all four stories were entered, with story as a variable. There are two types of questions that occur: those that are asked by several subjects, and those that are idiosyncratic. We next asked whether these two types of questions contributed differentially to this outcome. The answer is no. A multiple regression with number of questions asked by two or more persons and idiosyncratic questions entered separately showed that both emerged as significant predictors. Table 12 shows the details of these analyses.

So, number of questions asked accounts for a significant portion of the variance in sentence-by-sentence reading times. We next asked what relationship the question-asking task has with recall. And the answer was very simple: none. Table 13 shows the outcome of a multiple regression carried out on recall scores, and reveals that rated importance and serial position emerged as significant predictors of recall, while number of questions asked did not. This leads us to conclude that the information being revealed by the question-asking task is more closely associated with the activities that occur during comprehension than with the form of the final memory representation constructed as a result of comprehension.

TABLE 12
Multiple Regression Analyses of Reading Time in Question-Asking Experiment

	Coeff.	Sig.	Cum. R^2
Predictors selected:			
Sentence length	130.22	.0001	.589
Total number of questions asked	26.44	.0001	.640
Predictors not selected:			
Serial position of sentence			
Importance			
Predictors selected:			
Sentence length	130.81	.0001	.589
Idiosyncratic questions	40.27	.0004	.626
Number of questions asked by two or more subjects	87.42	.0015	.652
Predictors not selected:			
Serial position of sentence			
Importance			

Note: Forward stepwise regression, dependent variable = mean reading time per sentence.

This basic result confirms our initial supposition that the question-asking task would tap an aspect of what is going on in the skilled reader's mind while reading. The obvious question, of course, is what is it tapping? It is unlikely that a reader who is reading silently is actually asking questions while reading. Rather, we believe that the question-asking task taps the kinds of informational needs a reader encounters while proceeding through a text. As each sentence is understood and added to a growing representation of the story, the reader revises and elaborates the set of information still needed to have the developing story make sense. These

TABLE 13
Multiple Regression Analyses of Recall in Question-Asking Experiment

	Coeff.	Sig.	Cum. R^2
Predictors selected:			
Importance	341.12	.0001	.235
Serial position of sentence	-2.94	.0024	.283
Predictors not selected:			
Sentence length			
Total number of questions asked			

Note: Forward stepwise regressions, dependent variable = proportion propositions recalled per sentence.

informational needs interact with what is presented in the next sentence to generate a new set of information needs—or, if you will, a new set of questions—that guide the reader's comprehension through the succeeding parts of the text.

We have conducted a number of other analyses of these data that are discussed in Olson, Duffy, Eaton, Vincent, and Mack (in preparation). We have categorized the questions to see if certain types are more important than others. So far, the categories we have examined have not shown any differences. We have looked to see whether or not questions asked are later answered by the story, and there are interesting relationships here. Many questions *are* in fact answered, though it varies somewhat by type. However, the number of questions *answered* by a particular sentence does *not* predict reading time or recall. We have looked at the information tapped in the question, and find that questions which are derived from new information contained in the current sentence are especially important in predicting reading times. These and other details of these data are interesting and important, and will be reported on fully in Olson et al. (in preparation).

The main findings of this study strongly suggest that the question-asking task is a useful indicator of processes which may be an important part of comprehension. The number of questions asked by subjects as they read through a story correlates with the amount of time spent on that sentence by other readers reading silently. Keep in mind that this result is with the obvious effect of sentence length removed. But number of questions does not correlate with recall. Thus, question-asking seems more closely related to the real-time processes that occur during reading than to the final product of comprehension that remains when reading is completed.

This study is a nice example of the analytic usefulness of the focussed TOL task. No claim is made that the question-asking task taps *all* or even *many* relevant aspects of comprehension. Rather, one particular theoretically promising component of comprehension processing is singled out for detailed treatment. As with the general TOL task, the analysis of these data can proceed in both a qualitative and a quantitative fashion.

RELATED APPLICATIONS OF TOL

In this chapter we have focussed on the use of TOL to reveal comprehension processes. TOL techniques are useful in some closely related domains, and in this section we present a few examples. Each of these uses TOL during comprehension either in a special environment or for a special purpose.

Computer Text Editing

The TOL method has been used to investigate how new (computer naive) users learn text-processing procedures with self-study instructional materials (see Lewis

& Mack, 1982a, 1982b, 1982c; Mack, Lewis & Carroll, 1982). In this situation, the instructions were very general: new users were asked to talk about any aspect of their learning experience, including their interaction with the computer interface and the manual. They were asked to talk about any problems or questions they had, and any plans or decision they might be aware of. Except for occasional non-directive prompts for reticent talkers, users decided when to talk and what to say. TOL data were augmented by a video-taped record of the subject working at the computer terminal.

The TOL data revealed much qualitative information about the learning strategies and problems of new users. For example, self-study instructions were surprisingly "fragile" in that it was relatively easy for users to get side-tracked trying to follow them. This was due not only to simple oversights but also misunderstandings that reveal interesting reasoning strategies (see Lewis & Mack, 1982c; also Carroll & Mack, 1982a, 1982b). The new user's "innocence" about computers and their complexity made it surprisingly difficult for them to recover from these problems.

In this application of TOL Lewis et al. have not tried to relate qualitative observations to other more quantitative measures of immediate processing, although nothing would prevent doing so in principle. The qualitative data alone, however, have provided great insight into the problems of new users in a complex task domain. They have suggested a number of directions for more analytical investigation of learning, as well as practical applications in the design of interfaces and training methods. As such, it has already demonstrated the usefulness of TOL in research on an important genre of text: instructional materials in their real-world context of use.

TOL as Feedback to Writers

Recently, we have begun research that explores the usefulness of TOL data as feedback to writers. The rationale is quite simple. One of the difficulties that moderately skilled writers have is correctly discerning the state of mind of the reader. They, as writer, have the complete structure of their to-be-communicated ideas in mind. But it is difficult to imagine the state of mind of the reader, who does not know these ideas and who may have a somewhat different general state of knowledge than the writer.

We discovered, somewhat accidentally, that TOL data provided marvelous feedback to a writer. We had prepared materials for various text comprehension experiments, and in some of our early pilot work on the TOL task we gave these texts to TOL subjects. The information we received from these subjects about what parts of our texts were hard to understand, which parts miscommunicated what we intended, and which parts violated the conventions of writer-reader communication was incredibly valuable. This led us to develop and use the selected TOL task in the preparation of stimulus materials. In addition, it suggested to us that TOL behavior might in general be a useful form of feedback to writers.

We are currently conducting research that directly examines this. Writers generate texts of various types from content we provide them, and then a series of readers provide process feedback about the sentence-by-sentence comprehension of these texts either by thinking out loud or by combining talking with doing in the case of texts that give instructions for how to do something. The writers are given a chance to revise their texts in light of the process feedback they receive from readers. Though we have just begun this work, our initial impressions are that this is an effective form of feedback to the writer.

We as investigators as well as the writers of textual materials can use TOL data as a measuring instrument for the effectiveness of various texts. Indeed, since the effectiveness of particular texts is a joint function of text properties and reader properties, as Kintsch and his co-workers (Kintsch & Vipond, 1978; Kintsch & van Dijk, 1978) have so aptly demonstrated, studies using TOL tasks that varied both text properties and reader characteristics promise to provide especially informative data for developing theories of readers, writers, and textual transmission.

TOL and Metacognitive Awareness

Few people engage in TOL activities spontaneously. Does asking subjects to think out loud cause them to change their processing? The issue of whether or not such effects exist is central to the use of TOL methods (see Ericsson & Simon, 1980). Though such feedback effects from TOL are a methodological problem for the investigator interested in ordinary processing, they are a potential boon for the instructor who would like to improve the cognitive processing of a target population. Scardamalia and Bereiter (1983) have discussed this feature of TOL for children. There has been much research on the relationship between metacognitive awareness and comprehension with grade school children (see Brown, Bransford, Ferrara, & Campione, 1983). Scardamalia and Bereiter have found informally that TOL methods often increase the metacognitive awareness of children. Though they have not yet conducted any formal studies of this relationship, their extensive experience with TOL methods suggests to them that it may be a significant instructional device for reading and writing with children.

WHY DO TOL DATA PRODUCE VARYING RESULTS?

In our discussions with colleagues about our TOL research we have heard of several disappointing efforts to use TOL to study comprehension. In fact, in our own work, our results for the essay TOL task were somewhat disappointing. We reported earlier the substantial differences in both the richness of the TOL protocols and in the nature of their correlational relationship with sentence-by-sentence reading times for simple stories and essays. These mixed results are scarcely surprising. *Any* empirical technique will have successful and unsuccessful applications. When will TOL be useful? In considering some of the reports of disappointing outcomes and our own successful applications of the techniques, we have come up with several factors that can affect how useful the TOL technique will be.

Types of Instructions. We stressed earlier in this chapter the importance of being clear and explicit to subjects. The antecedent to this, of course, is understanding precisely what it is that one wants to get out of the task. Different instructions will produce quite different outcomes.

It is also important to make sure the instructions are appropriate to the texts being used. We have speculated that our essay TOL data were disappointing in part because of the instructions we gave subjects. Recall that our instructions for the essay TOL task were almost identical to those for stories. We used similar instructions so we could compare results across genres. The instructions, however, might have been inappropriate for essays. For example, we asked subjects to make predictions, yet the protocols revealed that making rich content predictions was an inappropriate task for reading essays. A more appropriate task might have been to ask subjects to evaluate how convincing an argument was. In fact some subjects spontaneously adopted a more critical mode of talking about the argumentative essays. In these protocols the talking seemed more natural.

Subjects. Even with clear instructions, not all subjects will talk equally informatively. We have found that some of the best subjects in our research have been faculty and graduate students in psychology, who have at least a passing acquaintance with TOL methods and therefore know the level of information we are seeking. Some subjects do not know this, even with explicit instructions. Where large pools of appropriate subjects are not available, training subjects to talk may be a way of ensuring reasonable quality data. The exact content of what subjects say has to be up to them, of course. But the amount and level of talking can be inappropriate and may be subject to training.

We have also found that large individual differences exist in how subjects read some texts. This seems especially true for the essay TOL task. Some subjects adopted a critical mode in reading the argumentative essays. Other subjects did not. Some subjects talked easily about aspects of essay structure (e.g., topic sentences, conclusions, pro and con arguments). Others did not. We assume these differences in talking reflect differences in strategies readers adopt when reading essays or differences in the knowledge readers have about the genre. While these individual differences might be interesting in themselves, they made it difficult to find common patterns in the TOL data for the essays. This heterogeneity was not so apparent in the story protocols where subjects seemed to have a common approach and knowledge base to use in reading the stories.

Type of Material. One major problem for the researcher in text comprehension is to find or construct appropriate texts. Too often investigators in this area have used "stories" that are not really stories, or paragraphs that are so artificial they do not resemble naturally occurring paragraphs. Our impression is that the richest protocols are elicited by texts that are natural and interesting. Our two well-formed stories were real children's stories. The plots were engaging enough to motivate the reader to read on to find out what happens. The TOL protocols were correspondingly rich. In contrast, the essays we used were, frankly, rather bland and boring. Subjects had no intrinsic reason to want to keep reading. The resulting TOL protocols were also rather boring. While the differences in our essay and story protocols may be in part due to genre differences, we do not believe that is the whole story. We suspect that essays with more controversial or interesting content might have elicited richer TOL data.

When TOL data are used in the context of discovery, it is especially useful to include a variety of text types in the set of stimuli. Our strategy of using well-formed and ill-formed texts, or of comparing different versions of texts (e.g., the essays) is a useful way of validating the quality of the data being obtained. If the TOL data are the same for well-formed and ill-formed texts, the investigator should be suspicious of what the subjects are doing.

What is Analyzed? There are many different ways to analyze data as rich as those obtained from TOL tasks. Whether one gets useful information or not will depend upon what one looks for. For instance, our essay TOL data yielded some general, useful information about the overall strategies used in reading the essays. But the multiple regressions exploring the ties between TOL behavior and reading times for essays did not yield much. We are currently carrying out a number of other more detailed analysis of our TOL data. For instance, we are in the midst of a detailed content analysis of our original story TOL protocols, coding the chains of hypotheses and other interconnections in the data as a possible clue to further aspects of the reading strategies of subjects. Similarly, we have conducted a number of other analyses of our question-asking data that also get at further aspects of the representation of comprehension processes in reading (Olson et al., in preparation). Not all analyses we have attempted have panned out. It will require broader experience with the use of TOL data to study comprehension before we will have a clearer picture of the types of analyses that are generally more useful.

SUMMARY AND CONCLUSIONS

We have used the TOL task as one window into the reader's mind. In this chapter we have described various versions of the tasks, discussed the overall rationale for the technique and discussed its application to various domains. We will now summarize by presenting in concise form a list of advantages and a list of limitations in using the TOL task to study the process of comprehension.

Advantages

1. The primary goal in using the TOL task is to explicate the higher level processes involved in comprehension. When used appropriately, it indeed seems to do this. In fact, it may be one of the few techniques available for getting at this level of comprehension activity.

2. TOL behavior, under at least some situations, appears to correlate with other forms of reading behavior, such as sentence-by-sentence reading times.

3. Though we have not done this yet in our research, TOL data in general have proven to be a useful means for studying individual differences in higher level cognitive processes (e.g., Newell & Simon, 1972). Studies of readers of varying levels of skill or varying degrees of background knowledge could profitably be pursued with this method, though there might be some difficulty in a confounding between level of reading skill and ability as a TOL subject (see below).

Limitations

1. The TOL task is sensitive to instructional variables. The instructions must be precise and must be carefully thought out in relation to one's research goals. Vague or very general instructions in general do not work well. Further, in light of Ericsson and Simon's (1980) analysis, it is important that the task focus on the reporting of current states of knowledge and not ask subjects to report on states of knowledge very far in the past or to offer explanations for their behavior.

2. The TOL task seems to work better for some text types than for others. In our research, we felt we obtained much better TOL data for stories than for essays. However, so far the task has not been used for a very wide range of text types. Further, as we suggested earlier, there are undoubtedly important interactions between text type and instruction that are not very well documented yet.

3. TOL data are difficult to analyze. Any form of data collection which monitors a continuous stream of behavior over long intervals of time produces data which can be difficult to analyze. The transcription, coding, and analysis of TOL protocols is extremely time-consuming, and little of it can be automated. Thus, the decision to use the TOL task must be thoughtful and must take into account cost-benefit ratios.

4. There appear to be big differences among subjects in their ability to provide informative TOL data. Some subjects are good talkers, some are not. The difficulty is one of getting talking at an appropriate level and in appropriate quantity to be useful to the investigator. This problem can be met by training subjects to talk, but that is time-consuming. There are probably limits in how young or how intelligent TOL subjects can be.

5. The TOL task may influence the nature of the comprehension processes used by subjects. The fact that we get correlations between properties of TOL data and silent reading times suggests that similar things may be going on in the two situations. But having subjects think out loud certainly has the possibility for

distorting their processing, and it is essential that TOL data always be used along with other converging evidence in order to determine what it is that readers are doing as they work their way through a text.

ACKNOWLEDGMENT

This research has been supported by a research grant from the National Institute of Education (NIE G-79-0133) and by a Research Career Development Award from NICHD (HD 00169) awarded to the first author. The authors are grateful for the comments of Mary Eaton, Mike Fehling, Judy Reitman, Lynn Roshwalb, and Mary Trahan on earlier drafts of this chapter. Communications about this work should be addressed to Gary M. Olson, Department of Psychology, University of Michigan, 330 Packard Road, Ann Arbor, Michigan 48104.

REFERENCES

Bartlett, F. C. *Remembering: An experimental and social study.* Cambridge: Cambridge University Press, 1932.
Brown, A. L., Bransford, J. D., Ferrara, R. A., & Campione, J. C. Learning, remembering, and understanding. In J. H. Flavell & E. M. Markman (Eds.), *Handbook of child psychology* (Vol. 2). *Cognitive Development.* New York: Wiley, 1983.
Carroll, J. M., & Mack, R. Learning to use a word processor: By doing, thinking and knowing. In J. Thomas & M. Schneider (Eds.), *Human factors in computer systems.* Norwood, N. J.: Ablex, in press. (a)
Carroll, J. M., & Mack, R. Actively learning to use a word processor. In W. Cooper (Ed.), *Cognitive aspects of skilled typewriting.* New York: Springer-Verlag, in press. (b)
Collins, A., Brown, J. S., & Larkin, K. M. Inference in text understanding. In R. J. Spiro, B. C. Bruce, & W. F. Brewer (Eds.), *Theoretical issues in reading comprehension.* Hillsdale, N. J.: Lawrence Erlbaum Associates, 1980.
Dawes, R. Memory and the distortion of meaningful written material. *British Journal of Psychology,* 1966, *57,* 77-86.
Ericsson, K. A., & Simon, H. A. Verbal reports as data. *Psychological Review,* 1980, *87,* 215-251.
Graesser, A. C. *Prose comprehension beyond the word.* New York: Springer-Verlag, 1981.
Kintsch, W., & van Dijk, T. A. Toward a model of text comprehension and production. *Psychological Review,* 1978, *85,* 363-394.
Kintsch, W., & Vipond, D. Reading comprehension and readability in educational practice and psychological theory. In L. W. Nilsson (Ed.), *Memory: Processes and problems.* Hillsdale, N. J.: Lawrence Erlbaum Associates, 1978.
Lewis, C. Using thinking aloud protocols to study the "cognitive interface". Research Report RC 9265, IBM Thomas Watson Research Center, Yorktown Heights, New York, 1982.
Lewis, C., & Mack, R. The role of abduction in learning to use text-processing systems. Paper presented at the annual meeting of the American Educational Research Association, New York, March 1982. (a)
Lewis, C., & Mack, R. Learning to use a text processing system: Evidence from "thinking aloud" protocols. Paper presented at the Conference on Human Factors in Computer Systems, Gaithersburg, MD., March 1982. (b)

Lewis, C., & Mack, R. Why is it hard to write a good instruction manual? Ms., 1982. (c)
Mack, R., Lewis, C., & Carroll, J. Learning to use word processors: Problems and prospects. Research Report RC 9712, IBM Thomas Watson Research Center, Yorktown Heights, New York, 1982.
Neisser, U. *Cognitive psychology*. New York: Appleton-Century-Crofts, 1967.
Newell, A., & Simon, H. A. *Human problem solving*. Englewood Cliffs, N. J.: Prentice-Hall, 1972.
Nisbett, R. E., & Wilson, T. D. Telling more than we can know: Verbal reports on mental processes. *Psychological Review*, 1977, *84*, 231-259.
Olson, G. M., Duffy, S. A., Eaton, M. E., Vincent, P., & Mack, R. L. On-line question-asking as a component of story comprehension. Manuscript in preparation.
Olson, G. M., Duffy, S. A., & Mack, R. L. Applying knowledge of writing conventions to prose comprehension and composition. In W. E. McKeachie (Ed.), *Learning, cognition, and college teaching*. San Francisco: Jossey-Bass, 1980.
Olson, G. M., Mack, R. L., & Duffy, S. A. Cognitive aspects of genre. *Poetics*, 1981, *10*, 283-315.
Rumelhart, D. E. Understanding understanding. Center for Human Information Processing Report No. 100, University of California at San Diego, January 1981.
Scardamalia, M., & Bereiter, C. Child as coinvestigator: Helping children gain insight into their own mental processes. In S.G. Paris, G. M. Olson, & H. W. Stevenson (Eds.), *Learning and motivation in the classroom*. Hillsdale, N. J.: Lawrence Erlbaum Associates, 1983.
Thorndyke, P. W. Cognitive structures in the comprehension and memory of narrative discourse. *Cognitive Psychology*, 1977, *9*, 77-110.

12 Coordinating Discovery and Verification Research

John B. Black, James A. Galambos and Brian J. Reiser
Yale University

Cognitive psychologists are masters of hypothesis testing, but rank amateurs at discovering new hypotheses. If a group of capable cognitive psychologists were asked to devise a series of experiments relating to a topic with an established research history, then the group could quickly devise a sequence of well-designed studies. For example, most cognitive psychologists could easily design studies to determine whether a certain kind of inference were made when people read a particular kind of text and whether that kind of inference became part of the memory for the text. In contrast, this same group of psychologists would probably not know how to proceed if asked to determine what kinds of inferences might be necessary for a reader to understand a particular kind of text (that nobody has analyzed this way before). Thus once given an hypothesis (in this case that a certain kind of inference is made) the cognitive psychologists can use their professional skills to design experiments that will verify or disconfirm the hypothesis; but if asked to discover a new hypothesis (in this case about what inferences are made), the psychologists have no skills to apply. It would be even worse if the topic under investigation were something radically new; for example, visualize a group of cognitive psychologists confronted with the problem of determining how experts give advice about situations within their area of expertise. This lack of discovery skills puts cognitive psychologists at a disadvantage in the modern world where new topics for investigation appear at an alarming rate. Moreover, it puts the field at a disadvantage when compared to more discovery-oriented fields like artificial intelligence and linguistics.

The problem here is that cognitive psychologists (and experimental psychologists in general) have devoted much effort to devising and refining research methods for verifying or disconfirming hypotheses. In contrast, virtually no thought has been given to methodologies for discovering hypotheses. In fact, hypothesis discovery seems to be somewhat disreputable: any study that creates more hypotheses than it eliminates is considered to be a bad study. One side-effect of this situation is that frequently when investigators in other fields (e.g., linguistics and artificial intelligence) examine psychological research for ideas, they find to their astonishment that the studies they find most valuable are considered by psychologists to be poor studies. In fact, some outspoken researchers in artificial intelligence have claimed that they "only like poor psychology research". Of course, the hypotheses to be verified must come from somewhere, so they are devised informally, under the table, behind closed doors and are not discussed in polite society. The unfortunate effect of this is that no thought is given to devising effective methodologies for discovering hypotheses.

Thus we maintain that experimental psychologists have ignored half of the research process (the discovery half), while devoting all of their attention to the other half (verification). We think that this imbalance needs to be eliminated by the development of discovery methodologies. What might such methods be? We are not sure, but clearly they will not be developed if the issue is ignored. In this paper we call attention to the issue and describe a few studies that we think provide some initial clues. Specifically, in the following sections we describe studies employing naturalistic observation, systematic questioning, verbal protocols, and a new method of sorting we call "augmented clustering". Our purpose in describing these studies is twofold. First we want to indicate that discovery research is possible, interesting, and not (as some people have called it) a mere undirected fishing expedition. Secondly we hope to show, by these examples, some possible criteria relevant to developing a methodology of discovery research.

NATURALISTIC OBSERVATION

One discovery method is to gather observations of naturalistic behavior, then analyze and categorize these observations to yield verifiable hypotheses. Three recent studies in cognitive psychology that have employed this method are Schank (1982), Norman (1981) and Neisser (1981). Schank asked people to report instances of one experience reminding them of another, then he classified these remindings according to the commonalities between the experiences. Similarly, Norman collected and categorized reports of errors that people made when performing actions (e.g., saying "come in" rather than "hello" when answering the telephone). Neisser took advantage of a fortuitous opportunity to compare a person's actual recall of a series of naturally occurring conversations with secret recordings of those conversations. In particular, he compared John Dean's recall in testimony before Congress of meetings concerning Watergate with actual tape recordings of those meetings.

However, simply collecting and categorizing observations is not enough to make a study good discovery research; it must lead to valuable new hypotheses that can be tested using verification methods. We cite the Schank, Norman and Neisser studies because we think that they fulfill this criterion of generating verification followups which will prove valuable. We use Schank (1982) as an example since we have conducted verification experiments related to his original discovery study.

When analyzing the reminding observations, Schank noticed that most of them seemed to involve failures of expectations about what normally happens in situations. For example, one subject reported that hearing about a wife not making a steak as rare as her husband liked, reminded the subject of not being able to get a barber to cut his hair as short as he wanted. Since one normally expects a person performing a service to conform to the wishes of the person being served, both of these experiences represented an expectation-failure of the same type. Schank hypothesized from analyses such as these that various kinds of expectation failures serve as indices under which experiences are classified and stored in memory. An implication of this hypothesis is that expectation-failure cues should allow people to retrieve experiences from their memories faster than expectation-success cues. Reiser, Black and Abelson (1982) tested this implication in a verification experiment and found the reverse — namely, that expectation-success cues were the fastest. The important point here is that Schank did not merely collect and classify reminding experiences, but analyzed them in a way that generated useful verification research. In fact, Schank's analysis also provided numerous other hypotheses that could usefully be tested using verification methods.

AUGMENTED CLUSTERING

The Schank and Neisser studies just described represent rather unconstrained production tasks in which the subjects produce verbal answers to questions asked by the researcher. Production tasks in general seem appropriate for discovery research but it is often possible to constrain the types of responses and thus obtain a rich but more focused set of data than that obtained by these naturalistic studies. One type of production task that we have used is an augmented clustering task. Clustering analyses, and sorting tasks in general, have been used to suggest and examine hypotheses about subjects' mental categories. Typically subjects are asked to group various stimulus items together to form clusers which they find meaningful. Clustering is a production task in that the subjects' data is analyzed to discover specific relationships between the target items, based on the subjects' responses. These relationships are used to construct or examine a theory of the categories the subjects use in the task. Reiser, Lehnert, and Black (1981) have developed an augmented clustering task that incorporates an additional production component. The method was originally developed to use judgments of thematic similarity of stories to investigate thematic knowledge in comprehension (Reiser,

Lehnert, & Black, 1981; Reiser, Black, & Lehnert, 1982). The augmenting clustering procedure has two phases. The first involves the standard clustering instructions, where subjects sort the items into groups according to similarity, placing as many items in each group as desired. After the sorting, subjects are asked to label each group with a phrase that describes what the members of that group have in common. Standard clustering analyses depend on the experimenter's intuitions to decide the meaning of the clustering patterns produced by the subjects. The goal of the second part of the augmented clustering procedure is to reveal what *the subject* considers to be the salient aspects of the items by analyzing the subjects' labels. Thus, clustering itself is a good discovery task, since it allows the subject a wide range of responses but is constrained by the type of stimulus items presented. The responses generated may be used to suggest hypotheses about mental categories. In addition, augmenting the standard procedure with a labelling task allows a content analysis that could reveal what the subjects find similar about the items. This content analysis may suggest hypotheses that were not anticipated when the experiment was designed. We now consider an example to illustrate how the subjects' labels are analyzed, and used to augment the standard hierarchical clustering analysis.

Reiser, Lehnert, and Black (1981) had subjects sort stories into groups with "similar plots". This part of the task simply applies the standard clustering paradigm to stories instead of words or sentences. In the second phase, the subjects were instructed to label each of their groups with a phrase that described what the stories in that group had in common. The subjects' groups were analyzed using the standard hierarchical clustering algorithms (Johnson, 1967) to produce a hierarchical clustering diagram. The subjects' labels were then used to label each cluster in the graph as follows: the labels (produced by at least 10 of the subjects) were categorized into synonymous classes, with synonymy judgments made by the experimenters such that labels conveying essentially the same gist were classed together, then the frequency of each label class was computed for each story and each cluster of the graph was associated with the labels that were common to all the stories in that cluster. Thus, each label represented the intersection of the most frequent labels for the stories in the cluster.

Reiser et al. were investigating the thematic knowledge structures proposed by Lehnert (1981). According to Lehnert, a story is mentally represented as a graph of overlapping *plot units*. Each of these plot units is composed of a pattern of goals, plans and events that represents a unique pattern of interaction and resolution for one or more characters. Some example plot units are *competition, reneged promise*, and *success born of adversity*. Reiser et al presented subjects with 36 three-sentence stories, (six stories each constructed from six plot unit configurations). The stories constructed from a plot unit configuration varied in content; that is, they involved different problems, goals, and events while keeping the plot unit structure constant. As expected, a hierarchical clustering analysis of the subjects' groups revealed six clusters of stories that correspond to the six different plot unit configurations. The plot unit structures of the stories were successful in predicting which stories tended to be sorted together, and thus accounted for subjects' thematic judgments about stories. Furthermore, the gist of the appropriate plot units was generally what the subjects used as labels for their groups of stories. Thus, the labels were additional evidence that the thematic similarities detected by the subjects were those that were embodied in the plot units, and not some other salient features of the stories that might have been correlated with the particular plot unit patterns chosen to construct the stories.

However, analysis of two aspects of the subjects' labels revealed some unexpected results that generated new hypotheses. First, some labels were more abstract than the level of plot units, and represented a more general pattern than those embodied in the plot units. These general labels (e.g., "cheating," "malicious responses" and "rational behavior") seemed to be evaluations of how justifiable the subjects considered the protagonist's plan. Secondly, the subjects' labels did not refer equally often to all the plot units in a particular configuration. Instead, the labels tended to focus on the plans of the protagonist, rather than on the circumstances that created the problem situation. Thus, the subjects considered the plans of the protagonist to be more important than the type of problem situation in the story. This observation was supported by the higher level connections between the six clusters of stories. The six clusters were grouped into higher level custers, based on evaluations of the justifiability of the protagonist's plan to resolve the problem. Indeed, although two of the sets of stories contained a reaction to the same problem situation (a competition), the stories were not clustered together. Instead, the competition retaliation stories were clustered with reneged promise stories, while the competition alternate plans stories were clustered with the overcoming threat stories. The first of these two higher-level clusters contains stories with malicious plans, while the other stories contained stories with justifiable plans.

The tendency of readers to focus on the protagonist's plans rather than the problem situation was examined in further experiments with the same materials. Reiser, Black, and Lehnert (1982) gave subjects three stories from each of the six sets based on different plot units. Subjects were asked to write a new story for each set that had the "same type of plot", but not the same events as the other stories in the set. Approximately three fourths of the plot units in the prototype stories were present in the subjects' stories. However, the plans of the protagonist to resolve a problem were more likely to be preserved in the subjects' stories than the situation that created the problem. In addition, when the stories written by these subjects were given to another group of subjects in a clustering task, the results of the first clustering study were replicated; that is, the stories were clustered by the plot unit configurations, with the labels and higher level clusters suggesting a focus on the protagonist's plan rather than on the problem situation.

These exploratory studies were designed as initial investigations of thematic knowledge, but because they were discovery-oriented they revealed an interesting and unexpected finding — namely, the central importance of the nature of the protagonist's plan in people's conceptualization of stories. Thus the experimenters were enlightened by the pattern of results obtained, in that unexpected but informative organizations of the plot units emerged. A more narrowly focused experiment that tried merely to verify the hypothesized plot units would have missed the more abstract organization the subjects were employing. Thus the moral here is that it is best to explore a new topic with a few general discovery-oriented studies before conducting more specific verification experiments.

SYSTEMATIC QUESTIONING

In this section we discuss another study which examines subjects' productions in a constrained situation. In particular, this study examined the representation of plan and goal information in people's knowledge about common activities. These structures organize information pertaining to the performance of the activity represented and this includes both information about what actions are part of the activity and about how those actions fit into the plans to accomplish the activity. In this study, subjects were presented with an activity phrase (e.g., changing a flat) and a phrase describing one of the component actions in the activity (e.g., take off the hubcap). They were asked to produce the reasons they knew for doing this action in the context of the general activity. The stimuli for this task had been developed for a series of verification experiments (Galambos, 1981 and Galambos and Rips, 1982) and had been investigated in a series of normative studies specifying values on potentially important dimensions. The idea of using questions about reasons to indicate mental structure was suggested by Graesser (1981).

The original motivation was to examine the knowledge of activities in terms of how the actions organize into the plans and subplans to accomplish a given activity. The intention was that analysis of the reasons given by subjects would provide insight into which actions were superordinate in the sense that they were given as reasons for other actions and how the actions clustered in the sense that they had a common reason. There was also an interest in the relevance of these plan patterns to the representation of the sequentiality of actions in an activity. These are typical of the type of "hypotheses" found in discovery research. They differ from verification hypotheses in that they do not specifically predict a certain pattern and they do not typically have matching counter-hypotheses against which they are tested. Rather these discovery hypotheses provide a framework that guides the observational methods employed. In fact, one major function of discovery research is to convert general frameworks into specific hypotheses that can be verified. Of course, if a general framework does not exist, then that also must be discovered.

Two specific features of the results in this study have turned out to be very useful. One of these features is the clustering of the actions into subactivities or "scenes", and the other is when there was a direct reason link between two actions (i.e., when one was given as the reason for the other). It was possible to look at the scenes of the activities in two ways. The first involved comparing the structures

12. DISCOVERY AND VERIFICATION   293

built from the reasons results with those indicated by an augmented clustering study which used the same stimuli. In the augmented clustering study, subjects sorted actions in an activity into groups and labeled these groups. These labels corresponded to the major subgoals that need to be accomplished when doing the activity and the groups corresponded to the actions that need to be done for each subgoal. Thus the groupings given by the augmented clustering results were essentially the same as the groups of actions that had common reasons. The second way of defining a scene is by using the content of the subjects' responses from the questioning study to map out the scenes. For example, the most frequent type of reason was "action-enablement" where the reason for one action was a second action that followed the first in the performance of the activity. It was possible to trace a chain of enablements only so far and the endpoints were typically the important subgoals of the activity. Also a given action could receive a reason that jumped some of the subsequent actions in between it and the subgoal. The units that were formed in these two ways corresponded to the scenes of the activity. Typically there were three to six of these scenes that could be extracted from the reasons answers for each activity. There were also different types of scenes. Some of the scenes were very linear in that the enablement reasons formed a fairly strict chain with each action getting the next subsequent action as its reason. Other scenes involved less linearity in that there was more use of the main subgoal as the reason for all of the actions in the scene.

There were other ways to categorize scenes. One of these was by the scene's role in the performance of the activity. There were preparatory scenes, main scenes and closing scenes. Preparatory scenes and closing scenes tended to be non-linear and often the reason given for actions in these scenes included phrases like "to get ready for ..." or "to finish ...". The main scenes of the activities were much more linear. This distinction is relevant to how sequential order was represented in memory for these activities. In an earlier study subjects sorted the actions into their temporal order in an activity. When the means and standard deviations of the action positions in the sequence were calculated, the standard deviations were greater for the actions in the scenes that did not show a linear pattern of enablement reasons — namely, the preparatory and closing scenes. This result is consistent with the interpretation of the nonlinear scenes as subsidiary to the linear ones, because the actions of the subsidiary scenes need to be done before (to prepare for) or after (to close out) the actions in the main scenes but these subsidiary actions have little necessary order amongst themselves.

Another reanalysis using the reasons results was performed on data from a reaction time (RT) experiment. In the original RT experiment two actions of varying temporal separation were presented to subjects who then indicated whether the two actions were from the same activity. This temporal-separation factor had no effect on the time to respond: i.e., pairs separated in the activity were verified as fast as pairs that were close together. However, when these RT data were reanalyzed in light of the reasons results, a difference emerged. In particular, pairs of actions linked by a reason were much easier to report as being members of the same activity. Thus the discovery-oriented reasons results allowed new hypotheses to be uncovered from existing data (and this has spawned a new line of verification research that is now in progress examining the effects of reason links on activity comembership RT).

The data from the reasons study were also examined in terms of their relations to other previously developed factors (i.e., the centrality and the distinctiveness of the action to the activity). These comparisons have been discussed elsewhere (Galambos and Black, 1981 and Galambos, 1982a), but it is worth emphasizing here that the reasons results have provided much useful insight into the nature of those factors and hence allowed us to better understand the mental representation of knowledge about activities. Thus the usefulness of new discovery-oriented data is increased when there are results on hand from a series of other studies in the same domain. In the current case, the new discovery study helped to reconceptualize the earlier results in addition to generating new verification research. The results of this discovery study were not easily analyzed, but conducting the study moved this line of research from a hunch to the design of a controlled experiment in relatively less time than would have a series of pilot verification studies. Furthermore, it provided insight into the topic that generated potentially interesting hypotheses for examination in experiments other than one that might have been piloted — e.g., hypotheses about how subjects answer why-questions in general.

This study using why-questions illustrates how systematic questioning can be used to discover hypotheses about a new topic, but it also illustrates another useful function of discovery research — namely, that discovery research can provide new insight into existing results. Thus discovery research can be valuable for finding new hypotheses in both old and new data.

VERBAL PROTOCOLS

When doing discovery research, one must strive to minimize the likelihood that the new hypotheses discovered are misleading. We will discuss this issue in terms of a study that used verbal protocols. There has been much contention over whether collecting verbal protocols (i.e., verbal reports of mental processes) is appropriate for verification research (Nisbett and Wilson, 1977; Ericsson and Simon, 1980), but protocols are a rich source of hypotheses and therefore appropriate for discovery research. However, good discovery research does not merely generate hypotheses, it provides hypotheses that lead to useful verification research. Thus, for example, if the protocol is a report of what the subject believes he should have been thinking rather than what he was thinking or if the act of giving the protocol distorts the mental processes being investigated, then the hypotheses derived are not likely to foster useful verification research. Ericsson and Simon (1980) provide guidelines for maximizing the likelihood that subjects are reporting their actual mental processes. For example, they stress that concurrent protocols (i.e., ones collected while the subjects are performing a task) are better than retrospective verbal reports.

To insure that giving protocols is not distorting subjects' thinking, protocol studies should include a no-protocol control group. For example, Black and Wilkes-Gibbs (1982) utilized a no-protocol control in a study that investigated how subjects utilized different kinds of information while writing a story. In particular, the subjects in this study each wrote a brief story set in a fantasy forest where animals talk and behave like people. The subjects were instructed to utilize in their stories some portion of the information on 60 cards arrayed on a table in front of them. They were also instructed that they were to pick up a card when they considered using the information on it (and these card considerations were recorded). The kinds of information on the cards were animal characters (e.g., a bear), character names (e.g., Raymond), enjoyment goals (e.g., relax in the sun), satisfaction goals (e.g., eat), time of year (e.g., April), day of week (e.g., Monday), personality traits (e.g., generous) and relationship factors (e.g., trust). Half the subjects gave verbal protocols while writing and picking up cards, but half did not. Thus the record of the cards considered provided a trace of each subject's thoughts in addition to the protocol, so comparing the cards considered in the protocol and no-protocol groups provided a test of whether giving the protocols distorted the mental processes of the subjects.

The results showed that the protocol and no-protocol subjects did indeed differ on the information they considered for inclusion in their stories. In particular, the protocol subjects considered personality trait, relationship factor, character and name information more than the no-protocol subjects, while the no-protocol subjects considered more goal (both satisfaction and enjoyment), day, and month information. In addition, the protocol and no-protocol subjects differed in the kinds of information actually used in the stories written. Specifically, the protocol subjects used more character and name information, while the no-protocol group used more goal (both satisfaction and enjoyment), day and month information.

These results indicate that the writers in this study used quite different processes when giving a verbal report on their mental processes in addition to writing than when they were writing normally. Hence hypotheses about writing processes drawn from these verbal protocols are suspect and thus not useful for verification followup research. It remains to be seen whether a variation in the protocol procedure used in this study will eliminate these distortions. However, the important point is that this study shows the importance of using a no-protocol control group when collecting protocols, regardless of whether the protocols are to be used for verification or discovery purposes. Thus mere collection of subjects' protocols as a discovery methodology must be done with care if the results are to be interpreted as relevant to the generation of hypotheses to be tested in a verification setting.

CONCLUSIONS

Cognitive psychologists need to develop methodologies for discovery research to supplement the available verification methodologies. We claim that research is best conducted by doing discovery-oriented studies to generate useful hypotheses and generally explore the topic under investigation, before doing more tightly focused studies to verify hypotheses. This discovery-then-verification procedure should remove the inhibitions to investigating new topics that currently plague the field. In addition, by encouraging general exploration before detailed but narrow investigations, this procedure will help insure that the research results are more "ecologically valid" (Neisser, 1976) — that is, generalizable to issues of concern in the real world.

Our advocacy of discovery research should not be mistaken as a plea for sloppy research; rather it is a call for cognitive psychologists to develop methodologies appropriate to discovery research. Discovery research must be as well designed as verification research, but the design principles are different. We are not sure what these new methodologies and design principles are, so we have described some example studies that we think represent good discovery research.

These examples illustrate some characteristics of good discovery research. In particular, the naturalistic observation studies illustrate how researchers can develop general frameworks for major topics (e.g., errors and remindings) as a prelude to more formal studies of specific aspects of the topics. Exploring a general framework first will provide a better perspective on the specific studies than would a premature dive into the specifics. The augmented clustering and systematic questioning studies illustrated methods that are more constrained than naturalistic observation, but are still unconstrained enough to allow discovery of new and unexpected hypotheses. Frequently this level of constraint may be necessary to obtain enough observations of interest to allow conclusions to be made.

Both the augmented clustering study and the systematic questioning study demonstrate how new and unexpected hypotheses can be generated. In particular, the augmented clustering study uncovered two new abstract ways that people conceptualize stories, while the systematic questioning study uncovered a crucial unanticipated factor — namely, whether actions were directly related by a reasons link. In addition, the systematic questioning study showed that discovery research can provide new perspectives on old data (in this case, action order judgments and activity comembership reaction times) in addition to guiding the collection of new data.

Collecting verbal protocols is another useful discovery research method, although the example study we used here illustrated a potential pitfall. In particular, the study showed that we must try to insure the discovery research method used does not distort the phenomenon being investigated. In the example, collecting verbal protocols changed the kinds of information that the subjects considered when writing a story. However, the study also illustrated how we can guard against this problem by including control groups that catch any effect of observation-method.

While it is unfortunate that cognitive psychologists have not developed discovery methodologies, this lack represents an exciting opportunity for enterprising researchers. Discovery research represents half of the research process and how to do it is a ripe area for investigation. In fact, we suspect that discovery research is the most important half of research, so contributions to discovery design should have a large impact on the productivity of psychological research.

REFERENCES

Black, J. B. & Wilkes-Gibbs, D. Distortions of the writing process by verbal reports of mental processes. Paper presented at the Annual Meeting of the American Education Research Association, New York, 1982.

Ericsson, K. A. & Simon, H. A. Verbal reports as data. *Psychological Review*, 1980, *87*, 215-251.

Galambos, J. A. *The mental representation of common events*. Doctoral Dissertation, University of Chicago, 1981.

Galambos, J. A. Question answering and the plan structure of routine activities. Paper presented at the Annual Meeting of the American Education Research Association, New York, 1982. (a)

Galambos, J. A. Reason generation and the structure of activities. Paper presented at the Convention of the American Psychological Association, Washington, DC, 1982. (b)

Galambos, J. A. & Rips, L. J. Memory for routines: Just one thing after another? *Journal of Verbal Learning and Verbal Behavior*, in press.

Graesser, A. C. *Prose comprehension beyond the word*. New York: Springer-Verlag, 1981.

Johnson, S. C. Hierarchical Clustering schemes. *Psychometrika*, 1967, *37*, 241-254.

Lehnert, W. G. Plot units and narrative summarization. *Cognitive Science*, 1981, *5*, 293-336.

Neisser, U. *Cognition and reality*. San Francisco: Freeman, 1976.

Neisser, U. John Dean's memory: A case study. *Cognition*, 1981, *9*, 1-22.

Nisbett, R. E. & Wilson, T. D. Telling more than we know: Verbal reports on mental processes. *Psychological Review*, 1972, *84*, 231-259.

Norman, D. A. Categorization of action slips. *Psychological Review*, 1981, *88*, 1-15.

Reiser, B. J., Black, J. B. & Abelson, R. P. The retrieval of memories for personal experiences. *Proceedings of the Fourth Conference of the Cognitive Science Society*, Ann Arbor, Michigan, 1982.

Reiser, B. J., Black, J. B. & Lehnert, W. G. Thematic units in the writing of stories. Paper presented at the Annual Meeting of the American Education Research Association, New York, 1982.

Reiser, B. J., Lehnert, W. G. & Black, J.B. Recognizing thematic units in narratives. *Proceedings of the Third Conference of the Cognitive Science Society*, Berkeley, CA, 1981.

Schank, R.C. *Dynamic memory*. New York: Cambridge University Press, 1982.

13 A Method for Comparing a Simulation to Reading Time Data

David E. Kieras
University of Arizona

An increasingly popular measure in the study of reading comprehension is that of *reading time*, or *inspection time*, the time a reader takes to process a piece of verbal input. In constrast to the more commonly used recall measure, which assesses the *results* of comprehension, the reading time measure taps an aspect of the comprehension process as it occurs. For this reason, the study of reading times can contribute uniquely to our growing understanding of comprehension processes.

The logic of using a reading time measure is that differences in the amount or type of processing should show up as differences in the amount of time required. However, this is not a necessary relationship (see Kieras, in press-a). The current approach in much comprehension research is to use these time data to construct process models for the comprehension process. This process is believed to be extremely complex, consisting of several subprocesses such as word perception, syntactic analysis, memory search, integration, memory storage, and other processes, such as schema-using strategies. The problem, then, in devising models based on reading time is how to assign differences in reading times to the comprehension subprocesses, and so decompose the total reading time into theoretical components, as was done in the classical applications of reaction time methodology (e.g. Sternberg, 1969). But this is not a straightforward matter for comprehension processes. For example, in the data in Kieras (1978), the longer reading times for unintegrable sentences could be due to differences in memory search, integration, topic maintenance, or storage processes. Also, the differences in reading time between sentences of different types, such as between the simple one-noun sentences like *The ants were hungry* and the more complicated two-noun sentences like *The ants ate the jelly*, can not be interpreted at all since they differ not only with regard to these same processes, but also in the amount of syntactic analysis and the amount of content information as well.

The empirical approach generally taken to ensure that reading times can be interpreted in a theoretically useful way is to use careful manipulations that hopefully affect only the process of interest; but Kieras (1981) and Rubin (1978) have argued that a set of true orthogonal manipulations of prose variables is usually impossible. Likewise, the theoretical approach has been to use either general models that make only directional predictions, for example, Kintsch (1974, 1977), or highly specific mathematical models tailored to particular experiments, such as Carpenter and Just (1977). These approaches are required because traditional empirically-based theories of comprehension are not able to describe comprehension processes at a level of detail that would enable the theorist to completely divide up the total reading time for a sentence among the subprocesses. Because of this, the field has been faced with an impasse in that computerized laboratory technology and the systems of content and structure analysis of verbal materials now available make it possible to collect extremely detailed data about reading times, but conventional methods of theorizing can not be depended on to fully exploit this empirical detail.

SIMULATION MODELS OF COMPREHENSION

In contrast to conventional theories of comprehension, the computer simulation models of comprehension and the allied efforts in artificial intelligence are committed to describing at a general level and in great detail exactly what must be done in comprehension. Because of this feature, it is possible to use computer simulation as a theoretical tool, to try out different ideas about comprehension to see if they actually work. This has enabled theorists about comprehension to account for a wide variety of comprehension processes, ranging from the basic level of sentence integration (e.g., Kieras, 1977a, in press-b), to high-level schema-directed comprehension (e.g., Schank, 1978).

Limitations of the Simulation Approach

In spite of the recognized importance of simulation models, in fact very little simulation work is going on in cognitive psychology. So, a very important theoretical tool is not being fully exploited. Some possible reasons for this can be listed (see also Bower & Hilgard, 1981; Smith, 1978):

First, at present, the programming involved in simulation modelling is very difficult. Few people trained as experimental psychologists have the necessary programming expertise. Thus, for most psychologists, getting started in simulation work requires a very large investment of time and effort. The academic system

13. COMPARING A SIMULATION TO READING TIME DATA   301

offers few opportunities for this investment; post-doctoral fellowships or sabbaticals are almost the only ones. Very few graduate training programs make it possible.

Second, serious simulation work requires the use of a high-capacity interactive computer such as a DEC-10, and advanced programming languages such as one of the sophisticated LISP systems such as INTERLISP or UCI LISP. It may come as a surprise, but very few university psychology departments have access to suitable computers and software. Furthermore, the work is likely to be expensive. Funds to support simulation work, especially to *learn* simulation techniques, have never been readily available.

Third, even if one has the time, expertise, computer, and money, it is difficult to publish the results of simulation work that stands alone, due to the traditional (and wise) bias of academic psychology in favor of empirical data collection as opposed to theoretical speculation. Simulation work that relates very clearly to data is publishable. However, few simulation projects have actually related that closely to data, meaning that a paper focused primarily on a simulation is unlikely to make it into the usual empirically-oriented journals. Consequently, a disproportionate number of treatments of simulation work have appeared in the less-referenced publications, such as chapters in edited books, or whole books. It is possible that new journals like *Cognitive Science* may provide a place, but this is not yet clear.

These are the major reasons why simulation work, despite its recognized importance, is not being pursued heavily in cognitive psychology. This is unfortunate because there is available in the current simulation models a wealth of theoretical ideas that have proven their worth in the simulation work, and can then be evaluated empirically. An example of where this has already happened in another experimental domain is the semantic network memory model and the concept of spreading activation as a general memory search process. Similar success could be expected in the domain of comprehension process.

THE GENERAL PROBLEM OF EVALUATING SIMULATIONS

Before a simulation model can provide a solid basis for experimental work there has to be some way to connect the simulation model with empirical data. The lack of techniques for doing a goodness-of-fit test of a simulation model to data has long been a sore point. For example, it is discussed extensively in the 1966 edition of Hilgard and Bower (1966). The problem was still the focus of discussion in 1975 at a national conference on the evaluation of computer simulations in psychology held in Ann Arbor, and continues to be cited as a problem in Hilgard and Bower (1981). There is simply no set of comparison techniques comparable to the simple, elegant, and rigorous techniques familiar in the older mathematical models. Thus, while simulation models of comprehension have been very influential, the actual use of them as explanations for comprehension data has mostly consisted of only informal claims and demonstrations. This situation means that the field is getting a poor scientific return for the amount of work put into developing simulation models. Fortunately, as reflected in several papers in this volume, the situation is beginning to change.

Some modellers have, in effect, disclaimed trying to account for experimental data, apparently feeling that the theoretical return on devising a simulation is worth the ambiguity in its empirical status. But other simulation modelers have attempted to cope with the evaluation problem in several ways.

A useful way to look at this issue is in terms of a four-fold classification of whether the simulation model is *deterministic* or *stochastic*, and whether the data consist of a *single-observation* sample of behavior, or a *multiple-observation* sample. Note that the combination in which a stochastic model is used on single-observation data has apparently never appeared anywhere in the literature.

Simulation models show a strong split between being stochastic or deterministic. Stochastic simulations explicitly include a random process that ensures that the behavior of the model is variable. In order to see what the model does, it is necessary to run it repeatedly to obtain a sample of its behavior. On the other hand, deterministic simulations do not have an explicit random process, and thus are committed to explaining any variability in behavior in terms of differences in the exact details of the prior or current conditions. Generally, behavioral data represents a sample of subjects, or a sample of behavior from each individual subject. However, if only one subject is used, or only one protocol, this single-observation data has no variability, making its treatment basically different from multiple-observation data that is collected from a sample of at least several subjects, or several observations of the same subject under the same conditions. Such data has variability, and variability is what usually makes comparing a simulation to data difficult.

The combination of *single-observation* data and *deterministic* simulation represents much of the "classic" simulation work. For example, Newell and Simon (1972, p. 469) have reported comparisons of models with individual subject's protocols. This approach essentially finesses the difficult problem of variability in the data, as well as reflecting a scientific committment to understanding mental processes at the level of the individual, rather than at the level of group data. However, it does implicitly assume that a single protocol is a representative example of the individual's behavior; given the usual variability of behavior, this assumption is perilous. A further difficulty is the custom in experimental psychology that results must be generalizable to a large population of subjects; it is hard to see how this condition is satisfied if only one subject's protocol is used. There is also another problem in this approach, namely the metatheoretical problem of whether mental processes are in fact basically deterministic. This is shared by the other approaches described below.

13. COMPARING A SIMULATION TO READING TIME DATA   303

The most common type of comparison between simulations and data appearing in the literature are those in which the data is multiple-observation, having been collected over a sample of at least several subjects. The comparisons seem to have been split almost evenly between ones in which the simulation is stochastic, and ones in which the simulation is deterministic.

The basic strategy for comparing a *stochastic* simulation to *multiple-observation* data is to have the simulation produce the behavior of a single simulated subject at a time. Then in multiple runs of the simulation, the result is a multiple-observation sample of behavior that corresponds conceptually to having run several subjects in an ordinary experiment. Then the sample of behavior from the simulation can be compared to the sample of behavior from the subjects by ordinary statistical techniques. To some extent the older mathematical modelling techniques were a special case of this type of approach. One of the oldest examples of this approach is Hintzman's (1968) stochastic discrimination net model, which was compared to typical verbal learning data. More recent examples are Anderson's FRAN (1972) and ACT simulations (1976).

While this approach is straightforward, it has an important practical problem in that collecting the simulated data from the model can be extremely expensive. The artificial intelligence programming technology used in most simulation work involves considerable computation, and thus is expensive to run; by the time one has simulated several subjects, further tests may not be possible. If there are free parameters to be fitted by simulation runs, it may be impractical to evaluate the accuracy of the model except in qualitative terms.

The remaining combination is using a *deterministic* simulation to account for *multiple-observation* data. At first glance, the comparison seems logically bound to fail. A deterministic model does everything with certainty; it will do a certain thing under certain conditions with a probability of 1, but this is rarely reasonable with subjects. For example, only 90% of them might do the same thing as the simulation. How is this result interpreted? The assumption in this approach is that the data have a stochastic component imposed on an underlying deterministic component, in the same sense that the models commonly used in statistics have a component that represents a "true" score, and a stochastic component that represents random deviations from the true score. Thus the comparison includes specifying (perhaps implicitly) a *statistical model* that bridges between the simulation and the data. The statistical model represents the stochastic component present in the data, while the simulation model represents the deterministic component.

The major advantages of this approach are that deterministic simulation models are relatively easy and cheap to construct, debug, and evaluate, and the comparison to data can be done using standard statistical or mathematical modelling techniques. Three versions of this approach have appeared in the literature:

The first version of the approach is to assume that each subject on each response either follows the underlying deterministic model, or else responds at random. If the simulation and subjects agree on the response most of the time, then the simulation appears to successfully represent the underlying process. Such logic underlies most comparisons that are an agreement-counting technique, such as in Newell and Simon (1972, p. 499). This approach works well when the responses can be classified as a small set of discrete qualitative responses.

In the second version of the approach, the simulation model specifies probabilities, or probability distributions, of response events in terms of free parameters. The simulation specifies what all of the relevant response event probabilities are as a function of the stimulus condition, and then the free parameters are estimated in the usual ways, and the goodness-of-fit between the predicted values and the observed results are assessed in the usual ways. Perhaps the best example of this approach is the Kintsch and van Dijk (1978) model in which a deterministic simulation specifies the contents of short-term memory at each point during comprehension of passage sentences, which in turn specifies the probability of recall of individual propositions in terms of certain parameters. These parameters were estimated from the data, and the resulting complex model fits the data quite well. Thus, this methodology represents a nearly direct application of the earlier mathematical modelling techniques to deterministic simulation models.

The third version of the approach, which is the focus of this chapter, can be used where the response variable is a temporal variable such as verification latency or reading time. The basic approach is that the simulation specifies which processes and how many steps in these processes must be performed on every stimulus item; the response time then should be related to this process specification. Thus the simulation provides predictor variables which can be used in a linear model to predict the observed time data. The most suitable statistical technique to fit the model to the data is multiple regression.

In this method, the simulation again represents the deterministic aspect of the data and the regression model is used as the bridge to the statistically noisy reading time data. The assumption is made that in the population of subjects, the simulation's deterministic processes are the "true" representation of their reading times, in exactly the same sense as the fixed-effects terms in a linear model in an analysis of variance or multiple regression is taken to represent the true characteristics of the population. Then every individual subject, or every sample of a subject's behavior, is assumed to depart from this true characterization by some random error component. Thus the variation between subjects, and within subjects as well, is represented by the error component assumptions in the multiple regression analysis, while the simulation represents the "true" model of the processes involved.

The precursor of this approach appeared fairly early in the context of traditional process models for comprehension times. For example, Carpenter and Just (1975), in their constituent testing models for sentence verification, used simple bivariate regression to fit the process model predictions to their verification time data, and evaluate the resulting goodness-of-fit. Their models contained a variable consisting of the number of constituents to be matched. Under the assumption that each constituent match takes a constant amount of time, the predicted verification time is thus a linear function of the number of constituents. An ordinary regression line is fitted to the data; the slope of the line is the coefficient of the variable, the time per match, and the intercept is the time to perform the other, remaining, components of the task. Finally, the square of the correlation coefficient provides a measure of the goodness-of-fit of the model in terms of the percent of variance among the observed mean times accounted for.

The method described here is essentially the same, but in a multivariate case. The reading time on each sentence in a passage is the dependent variable. The independent, or predictor, variables are variables whose values are supplied by the simulation model. That is, the simulation model has many different internal processes, each of which consists of a series of steps. The number of steps in the individual processes may vary, depending on exactly what the simulation must do in order to understand an individual sentence in the context of the preceding sentences. The number of steps in each kind of process for each input sentence is a set of values for predictor variables in a multiple regression analysis. The results of the regression analysis are a set of coefficients, one for each variable. If the processes combine additively (Sternberg, 1969), these coefficients can be interpreted as the number of seconds required for each step in the corresponding process. As in the simple case, the intercept of the regression line is the amount of time taken for all other processes. And also as before, the square of the correlation coefficient gives the proportion of variance accounted for by the regression equation, and is thus a measure of the accuracy of the model. By examining where reading times predicted from the regression equation match and mismatch the observed reading times, this overall measure of goodness-of-fit can be augmented by the detailed conditions under which the model is a good fit or a bad fit.

This technique was apparently first applied to a simulation model by Kieras (1977b, 1979), using a subset of the data from Kieras (1978). Two sets of reading times for individual sentences in simple passages were used, one from a coherent presentation order, the other from an incoherent order. The reading time profiles were rather different for the two presentation orders. Applying this method to fit a simulation model (basically that of Kieras, 1977a) to this small set of data showed that substantively different versions of the simulation could be distinguished by their goodness-of-fit to the data. The worst fitting version could account for only 62% of the variance among mean reading times, the best for 83%.

Recently, several researchers have reported using this type of comparison technique with other simulation models (Kieras, 1982; Miller & Kintsch, 1980; Thibadeau, Just, & Carpenter 1982). Due to the fact that this approach takes advantage both of the convenience of deterministic simulation models, and the power of multiple regression analysis, the method appears to be very promising. This paper provides a detailed treatment of the method.

THE METHOD

The Paradigm

The data are reading times for single sentences in passages, collected in a self-paced procedure. The subject sits at a video terminal driven by a lab computer. The subject taps the space bar, and a sentence appears on the screen. When the subject is finished reading the sentence, he or she taps again. The sentence disappears and the next sentence appears, and so on through the whole passage. The reading time is defined as the time each sentence is left on the screen. The data resulting from this paradigm consists of the reading time *profile* for each passage in each experimental condition, which is the pattern of reading times on each sentence. For passages of any length and complexity, the profile is very complex, and is hard to make sense of with standard analyses, except at a very global or gross level.

Procedure

Multiple regression is the heart of the method. A brief summary of this statistical technique will be given here; see Knight (this volume) and Haberlandt (this volume) for more detail. Multiple regression is based on a linear model for a set of data. The dependent variable, or predicted variable, is the reading time on the individual sentences, and is predicted by a linear combination of independent variables, or predictor variables, each of which has a coefficient that relate each predictor variable to the predicted. The multiple regression process is given a set of values for the predicted variable and each predictor variable, and computes the values of the coefficients that gives the best least-squares fit to the predicted variable. The resulting equation can then be used to predict the reading times from the predictor variable values. The equation is usually constructed in a stepwise fashion, by adding predictor variables one at a time, to arrive at an equation that gives a satisfactory fit with the fewest variables. I use the forward stepwise method, in which variables are added in decreasing order of their ability to improve the fit. This process stops when a new variable no longer makes a significant contribution.

In my application of the method, the predictor variables come from two sources. One of these is the simulation model, the other is the *auxiliary model*, which will be described more below. The method can be described step-by-step:

1. Give the passages to subjects and obtain a set of reading times for each sentence.

2. Give the same passages to the simulation model, and have it process each sentence.
3. Have the simulation report how many steps of each type of process it must perform in order to process the sentence. For example, suppose that to process a sentence, the simulation must perform a certain number of parsing steps, a certain number of representation-building steps, and a certain number of memory-searching steps. These are the values of the predictor variables for that sentence.
4. These predictor values for each sentence, and the observed reading times for each sentence, are the input to the multiple regression program. The output of the program includes a measure of the overall goodness-of-fit, R^2, the proportion of variance in the predicted variable accounted for by the equation. This provides a single summary statistic of the quality of the model as an account of the data. The coefficient values in the equation correspond directly to the amount of time one step of each process takes, under the assumption, discussed more below, that the processes are additive. The significance of each variable in the equation allows one to determine which aspects of the model have empirical content. The predicted reading time for each sentence can be compared to the observed values to obtain detailed information on where the model fits the data and where it does not.
5. Examine the fit and determine where there are important discrepancies. There are two choices for how to handle them. The simulation can be modified in some appropriate way, and a new comparison made, or else new predictor variables can be defined that represent theoretical mechanisms that are not represented in the model. The definition of these variables make up the auxiliary model. If they significantly improve the fit, then conclusions can be drawn about the phenomena involved and the adequacy of the simulation model.

Issues in Using the Method

There are several important issues involved in the method. The first concerns the overall philosophy of the method. The use of the linear model involves two assumptions: One is that the linear combination of processing steps is a satisfactory characterization of the total processing time; a model which contains parallel processes may not characterize well this way (but see Just & Thibadeau, this volume; Thibadeau, Just, & Carpenter, 1982). The major consequence of using this method on such a model is that the regression coefficients will not have a straightforward interpretation. However, if other variables can be chosen that do combine additively, the method can still be applied. The other assumption is that the simulation model is deterministic, and the only stochastic element is in the regression model's error component. This makes the method fit well with the usual simulation techniques imported from artificial intelligence, since these are most naturally applied with deterministic mechanisms. However, this is not necessarily a good characterization of cognitive processes.

A second issue concerns the experimental materials and design. In order to use this method, the simulation must be able to process the very same passages that the subjects are given. This can be very difficult to accomplish, and so constitutes a major disadvantage of the approach. The way to handle the problem is to use materials that have been selected beforehand so that the simulation can process them.

Potentially, the method can allow one to account for any material that the model can process. This encourages the use of very natural materials in the experiment, since the model can supposedly handle a wide variety of sentence lengths, structure, content, and so forth. This suggests that one of the rules of thumb in psycholinguistic research, that the materials be equated as fully as possible on all irrelevant variables, can be relaxed. This opens the way to studying much more natural experimental materials than has been customary, since the model provides a theoretically justified method for statistically controlling the nuisance variables.

However, I have found that haphazard selection of materials does not ensure that the model processes can be distinguished with the method. The simple passage work in Kieras (1981) involved taking the very same sentences, with only a small range of different sentence structures, and manipulating their order. This strongly varied some of the processing variables from the simulation, but left some of the others, such as parsing, almost intact. In contrast, in some of my technical passage work, I have been unable to distinguish syntactic-level processing from even the macrostructure-level processing (Kieras & Bovair, 1981). So, while the use of this method with a simulation model can potentially allow us to deal with a far more natural set of materials and manipulations, it is still important to be very careful in the choice of materials and manipulations.

A third set of issues concerns the use of multiple regression. Multiple regression is not a cut-and-dried method; there are many tricky problems and pitfalls, and statisticians do not all agree on the best ways they should be handled. The most serious problem is that many of the variables provided by the simulation can be correlated with each other. For example, the amount of parsing can be highly confounded with the amount of memory structure needed to represent sentence content. One standard solution to such *collinearity* problems is to choose, on theoretical grounds, one of the correlated variables, and discard the other. In the work described in Kieras (1981), I decided that the amount of structure built was the most important variable, based on the previous work in the field, and so the role of other variables was evaluated only with that variable already in the regression equation. Other approaches are discussed by Knight (this volume).

A second technical problem concerns *suppression* between predictor variables. Under certain conditions, variables can enter the regression equation with negative coefficients, even though their simple correlation with the reading time is positive. Since these coefficients represent the time required per step, this situation implies negative time in one of the processes, rendering the equation meaningless.

My policy is to stop the stepwise process when the next variable entering would acquire a negative coefficient, regardless of the significance levels involved.

Another issue concerns treatment of the dependent variable. Many comprehension workers, myself included, have been in the habit of basing our analysis of such data on the mean reading times for each sentence, collapsed across subjects. The advantage of doing this is that it greatly reduces the number of data points that have to be analyzed. It also suppresses a great deal of between-subject variability. This, it would seem, should result in higher R^2's and greater significance for individual predictor variables. The suppression of the between-subjects variability is perhaps often justifiable on the basis that the model does not specify anything about individual differences, and thus there is no point in having this variation present. However, as Richard Anderson (1982) and Kliegl, Olson, & Davidson (1982) have pointed out recently, this collapsing of the data can be misleading.

Consider instead the approach of just using the raw data consisting of the individual reading times from each subject on each sentence. A simple conservative analysis would consist of using this mass of data as is, without attempting to account for or remove any of the between-subject variability. But there are ways to remove this variability; see Pedhazur (1977) or Knight (this volume). Despite the greater variance in this mass of data, the sample size is also considerably larger. Apparently, depending on just how large the sample and the between-subject variability are, there is a trade-off between the error variance and the sample size in these two situations. In several cases in which I have computed the regression equations for both the collapsed and the raw data, it seems that if there are a large number of sentences, on the order of 60-80, then the equations constructed for the collapsed and uncollapsed data are very similar. However, if the number of sentences is smaller, such as 30 or fewer, then there can be substantial differences between the two analyses. Variables may be *insignificant* in the collapsed data analysis, and *significant* in the full data. So, compared to the collapsed data, sometimes the larger sample size in the raw data more than makes up for the greater noise. My conclusion, unfortunately not arrived at soon enough for all of the results reported here, is that it is best to use either the raw data, or to perform the analysis both ways.

A final statistical matter is the relative amounts of between-subjects and within-subjects variation. The problem just described suggests that the between-subjects variation is not overwhelmingly large compared to the size of the effects that might be under consideration. In Johnson & Kieras (in press) we put all of the subjects on the same scale of reading time by z-transforming the reading times for each subject. That is, an individual subject's reading times were transformed using the mean and standard deviation for that subject. The regression analysis using these transformed reading times generally produced the same results in terms of standardized coefficients, with the overall R^2 being increased, of course. However, the increase is not dramatic. A typical result is an R^2 of .2 increasing to .4. This suggests that a considerable portion of the variance that is not accounted for in these analyses lies in within-subject sources, rather than between-subject sources.

EXAMPLES OF USING THE METHOD

A Prose Integration Simulation

The method can be thoroughly illustrated with a summary of the work reported in Kieras (1979, 1981). The experimental data consisted of sentence reading times for simple passages, such as the one in Table 1. The passages were presented one at a time in a self-paced procedure. Two aspects of the passages were manipulated by altering the order of the sentences in the passages. First, the sentence-to-sentence coherence was either high, medium or low, depending on the patterns of whether the sentences contained a *given* referent, in the sense of Haviland and Clark (1974), or contained only *new* referents, and was thus not integratable with the previous sentences until an appropriate later sentence appeared. Thus, the different orders varied in the number of chunks, or integrated units, being maintained during reading; the incoherent orders involve high peaks of number of chunks. Kieras (1978, 1981) argued that such orders present high processing load due to the need to store an excessive number of *topic pointers*, which refer to the individual chunks, in short-term memory (Kieras, 1977a). A second aspect that was varied was whether the passage began with a good "topic sentence". In these passages, the sentence labelled *A* in Table 1, which is in the center of the propositional structure, is usually perceived as the main idea of the passage (Kieras, 1978). This sentence appeared either first or last in the passage. While this manipulation unavoidability affects the passage coherence, the issue was whether first appearance of the main idea had a unique effect beyond coherence changes.

Three different tasks were used, which should differ in the components of the reading process involved. These were a Free Reading Task, similar to the Haviland & Clark (1974) approach; a Topic Choice Task, in which the subject has to supply a title after reading the passage; and a standard gist Recall Task. There were 11 sentences in each passage, so the data consisted of a total of 66 mean reading times in each task, or 198 points in all. In Figures 1, 2, and 3 are shown the observed

TABLE 1
Example of Simple Passages

A. The ants were eating the jelly.
B. The ants were hungry.
C. The jelly was grape.
D. The ants were in the kitchen.
E. The jelly was on the table.
F. The kitchen was spotless.
G. The table was wooden.
H. The kitchen was equipped with the blender.
I. The table was against the stove.
J. The blender was white.
K. The stove was hot.

---

mean reading time profiles for the 6 orders in the three tasks. Overall, the Recall Task by far produced the longest and most variable reading times. As would be expected, the Free Reading Task produced the smallest and least variable reading times. The Topic Choice Task reading times were only slightly slower and more variable than the Free Reading times. Hence in terms of overall reading time, the Free Reading and Topic Choice Tasks are very similar, with the Recall Task being markedly different. However, trying to understand in detail the differences appearing in these profiles is very difficult. By applying the simulation model, a clear picture emerges.

A detailed presentation of this model can be found in Kieras (in press-b). The original goal in developing the simulation model was to explore in some detail the referential and integrative processes involved in prose comprehension (see Kieras, 1977a, in press-b). The model would have to understand given and new references correctly, so that, after a series of sentences were read in, the model would have in memory an integrated representation of the passage content. In order to devise the model, theoretical ideas had to be developed on the function of noun phrases, the

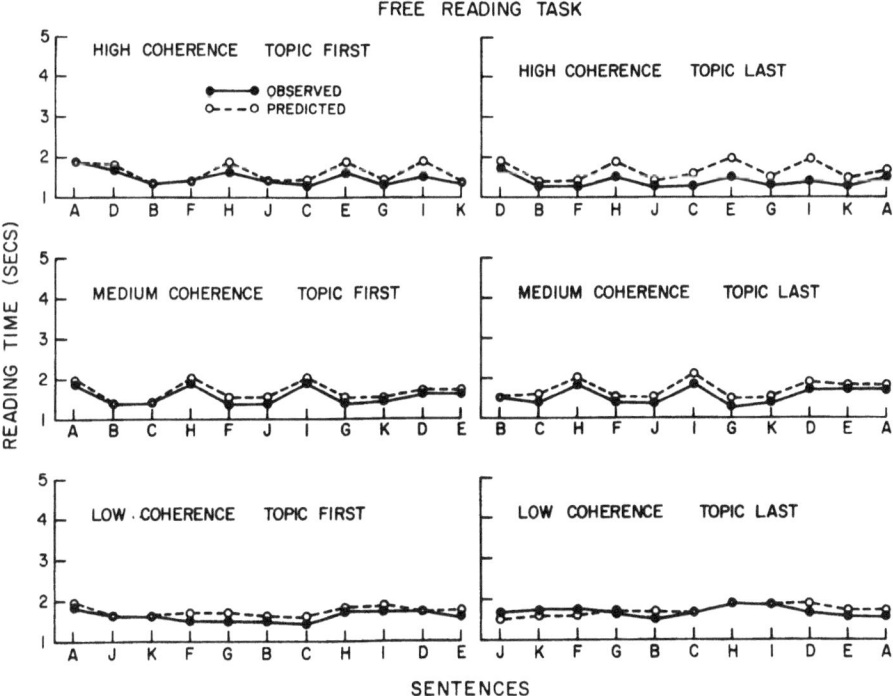

FIG. 1. Observed and predicted reading time profiles for simple passages in the Free Reading Task for the six different presentation orders, using the Table 5 analysis.

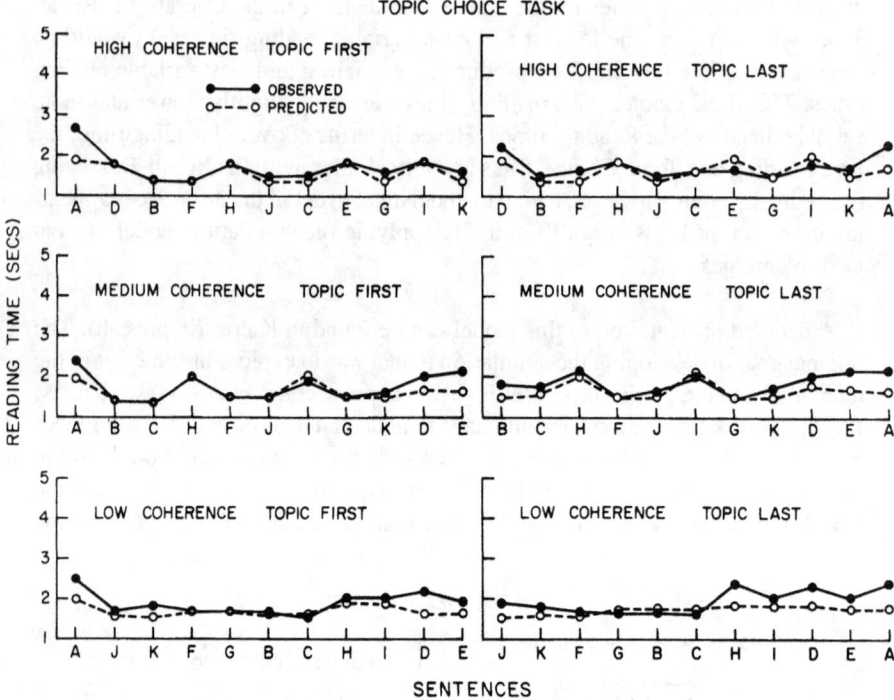

FIG. 2. Observed and predicted reading time profiles for the Topic Choice Task, using the Table 5 analysis.

use of long-term memory information during integration, and how the processing of each sentence should take into account the context supplied by the previous sentences. Throughout the simulation, certain popular pre-existing ideas about language processing were used, such as current notions about memory representations, memory search, and sentence parsing. This means that what is being tested empirically in this work are some of the commonly held notions about how language might be processed.

The simulation model was not originally intended to be used to model experimental data at the quantitative level. Rather it was developed to meet the informal, loose criteria for accuracy and plausibility commonly used in simulation work. That is, the model had to behave in an apparently realistic manner by understanding a variety of sentence and text forms, and operate using psychologically plausible mechanisms. Although this criterion is only loosely stated, in practice it is very hard to meet because the model is required to behave appropriately for a very wide range of linguistic inputs, a much wider range than is usually addressed by conventional psychological theories of language processing. Hence, although the model was not originally intended to be subjected to the formal quantitative test

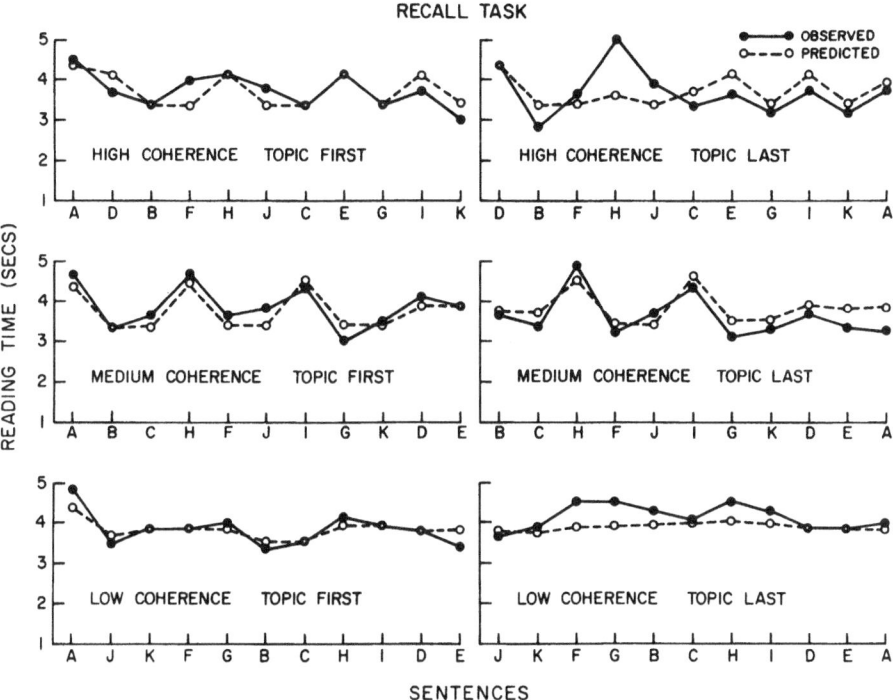

FIG. 3. Observed and predicted reading time profiles for the Recall Task, using the Table 5 analysis.

that is the subject of this paper, it nonetheless had to give the appearance of realism by meeting many of the requirements involved in actually processing prose. In general, the strictness of this constraint on the process of constructing a simulation is often underestimated by researchers who are not actually familiar with simulation modelling (see Kieras, in press-b for more discussion).

The simulation uses an augmented transition network (ATN) parser that was generalized to simple text structures, and uses ACT (Anderson, 1976) semantic network memory representations to represent the sentence content. For each sentence, the simulation identifies the given and new content, and then searches memory for the representations of the given referents, and then builds the representation for the new information onto them. It uses a spreading activation memory search, in which the passage topic serves as one of the activation sources, and thus acts to provide contextual guidance for the memory search. Incoherent passages result in multiple topics being defined and maintained, which compete for the limited activation capacity, and thus slow down memory search and reading. The model does not contain any processes that are distinctive to the Recall or Topic Choice Tasks; all it does is parse, represent, and integrate the sentence content. A key point is that although the model did not have any task-specific mechanisms in it, it was still useful in understanding how the tasks were different. Part of this process was to define some auxiliary variables.

The simulation processed the passages in the 6 different orders, and reported values for the variables shown in Table 2 for each sentence. TRANSITS is the number of ATN links crossed while parsing the sentence. LINKS is the number of one-way links of semantic network structure built to represent the sentence content. TOPICS is the number of topics being maintained and serving as activation sources. TAGGED is the number of nodes activated during the memory searches done for the sentence processing. These were used as the predictor variables, and the collapsed data, mean reading time on each sentence, was used as the dependent variable.

The first step was to conduct a separate regression analysis of each task separately; the results are shown in Table 3. In these analyses, the parsing variable TRANSITS did not enter the equations once LINKS was present, due to their high correlation. The percent of variance accounted for is 75% in the Free Reading Task, 62% in the Topic Choice Task, and 55% in the Recall Task. Notice that the constant is much larger in the Recall Task compared to the other two. This means that the Recall Task took longer on each sentence in a way that did not vary with any of the simulation processes, a puzzling result (see Kieras, 1981). More interesting, however, is the fact that the coefficient for LINKS, the amount of memory structure built, is quite a bit bigger in the Recall Task than in the other tasks. This shows that more time was being used for each unit of content in the Recall Task. This makes sense, if we consider that the reader would have to build the representation for a sentence in all three tasks, but in the recall task, the representation would have to be memorized, or encoded into long-term memory. While the simulation does not represent the memorization process, the amount of work involved should be proportional to the amount of structure built, which the simulation does represent.

To capture these task differences, I defined some auxiliary variables, and computed an analysis on the combined data for the three tasks. The auxiliary variables are shown in Table 4. RTASK is 1 for sentences in the Recall Task, and zero otherwise, and so represents the constant difference. RLINKS is an interac-

TABLE 2
Predictor Variables Supplied by the Simulation Model

TRANSITS	Number of ATN links crossed in parsing the sentence.
LINKS	Number of one-way semantic network links built to represent the sentence content.
TOPICS	Number of topic pointers being maintained and used for activation sources in all memory searches done while processing the sentence.
TAGGED	Number of memory nodes tagged, or activated, during all memory searches required to process the sentence.

TABLE 3
Results of Single Task Regression Analysis

Task	Step	Variable	R^2	Final Coefficient
Free Reading Task				
	1.	LINKS	.59**	.035
	2.	TAGGED	.71**	.030
	3.	TOPICS	.75**	.002
		CONSTANT		1.116
Topic Choice Task				
	1.	TRANSITS	.51**	.007
	2.	LINKS	.60**	.036
	3.	TAGGED	.62*	.003
		CONSTANT		1.210
Recall Task				
	1.	LINKS	.51**	.082
	2.	TOPICS	.55*	.068
		CONSTANT		2.950

*F-ratio significant at .05, ** at .01

tion variable, the product of RTASK and LINKS, and it represents the additional time per link of memory structure that would be involved only in the Recall Task. Using these predictors on the data for all three tasks gave the analysis shown in Table 5, which accounts for 94% of the variance. The structure variable LINKS can be assigned a coefficient for all three tasks, and in the Recall Task, each unit of structure requires some additional time, given by the RLINKS coefficient. The plots of the predicted reading times from this equation are shown together with the observed times in Figures 1, 2, and 3. So the simulation model, together with an auxiliary model, provides a fairly good account of this detailed data.

Another example of the use of an auxiliary variable shows how the simulation can be used as an analytic tool, as well as a theoretical statement. Notice in Figure 2 that in the Topic Choice Task the time on the first sentence, or the type A sentence at the end, is consistently underpredicted. This does not appear in the other tasks. This pattern suggests that there is another process that is not represented in the

TABLE 4
Predictor Variables Used in the Combined Task Models

TTASK	The constant effect of being in the Topic Choice Task.
RTASK	The constant effect of being in the Recall Task.
RLINKS	The number of one-way semantic network links being encoded while processing the sentence for later recall in the Recall Task.
FIRSTA	The constant effect of processing a highly thematic sentence in the Topic Choice Task.

TABLE 5
Overall Task Fit using RTASK and RLINKS

Step	Variable	R^2		Final Coefficient
1.	RTASK	.89	**	1.794
2.	LINKS	.93	**	.033
3.	RLINKS	.94	**	.040
4.	TOPICS	.94	**	.038
5.	TRANSITS	.94	*	1.130

* R-ratio significant at .05, ** at .01.

model, namely one that processes highly thematic sentences in a task that requires specifically thematic processing. To see if this was a reliable misprediction, I defined an auxiliary variable, FIRSTA, that is 1 only for initial or type A sentences in the Topic Choice Task, and 0 otherwise. I also defined another 0-1 variable, TTASK, to represent the slightly different constant in the Topic Choice Task.

In the new analysis, shown in Table 6, the FIRSTA variable accounted for a significant amount of variance, and about .447 seconds longer are spent on the highy thematic sentences in the Topic Choice Task. In Figures 4 and 5 are shown the predicted times from this new equation for the Free Reading and Topic Choice Tasks; the new plot for the Recall Task is indistinguishable from Figure 3. Notice that not only is the overall fit somewhat better, but the fit on the highly thematic first and type A sentences in the Topic Choice Task is very good. Given that the model represents the processes of parsing, memory search, basic sentence integration, and representation-building, we can conclude that something is happening on the first sentence that is not simply one of these processes working in the way that they do on the other sentences. Rather, there is a unique thematic process present. Thus the method and the simulation have revealed a process that would be otherwise obscured.

TABLE 6
Overall Task Fit using TTASK and FIRSTA

Step	Variable	R^2	F	Final Coefficient
	CONSTANT			1.010
1.	RTASK	.8850	1507. **	1.887
2.	LINKS	.9289	120.7**	.029
3.	TTASK	.9414	41.4**	.232
4.	RLINKS	.9476	22.7**	.046
5.	TOPICS	.9520	17.7**	.051
6.	FIRSTA	.9584	29.6**	.447
7.	TRANSITS	.9599	6.7*	.006

*F-ratio significant at .05, ** at .01.

13. COMPARING A SIMULATION TO READING TIME DATA   317

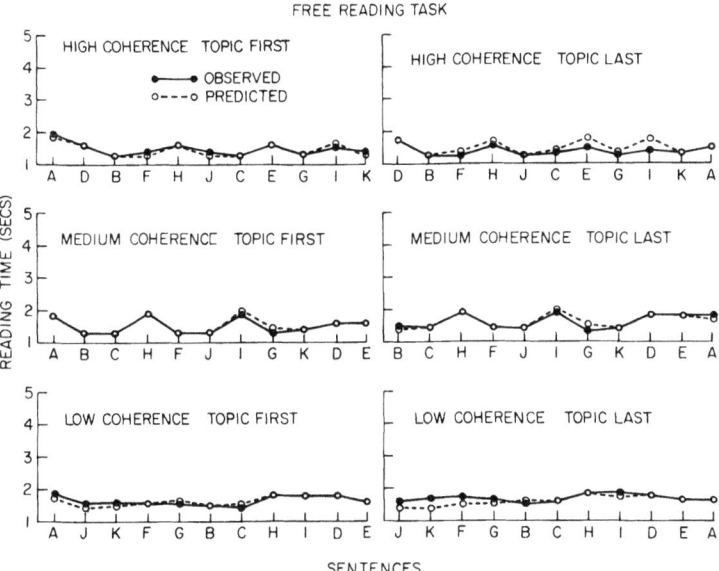

FIG. 4. Observed and predicted reading time profiles for the Free Reading Task, using the Table 6 analysis.

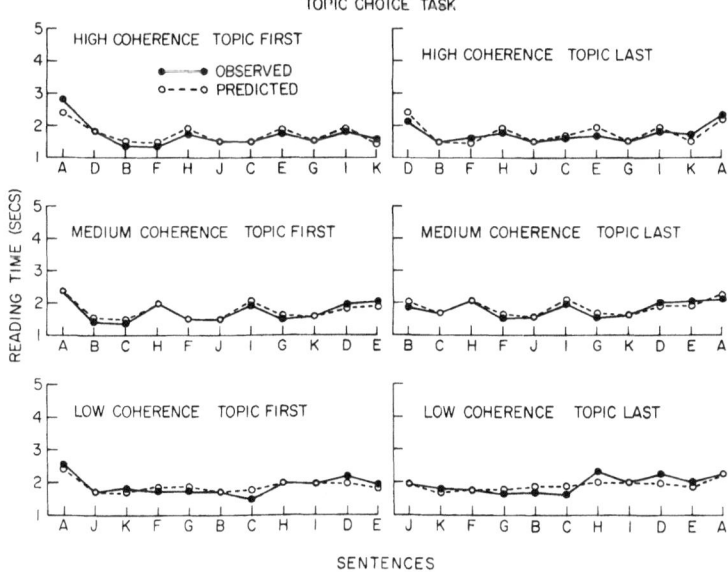

FIG. 5. Observed and predicted reading time profiles for the Topic Choice Task, using the Table 6 analysis.

Simulation of Prior Knowledge Effects

Another example of the use of the method is some work on the role of prior knowledge on the comprehension of simple technical prose, which is reported in more detail in Johnson and Kieras (in press). The question is whether readers who know some of the factual content of a passage will read it faster and recall it better than readers who lack prior knowledge, and whether these effects can be predicted by a specific mechanism in a simulation model. The effects on recall of prior knowledge are highly task specific; here the concern will be only with the study time effects, and modelling these effects with a simulation.

Table 7 shows an example of the passages that we studied. Using four such passages, we collected study times and recall in the self-paced one-sentence-at-a-time paradigm. After reading all of the sentences, the subject goes on to the next passage. Finally, after reading all of the passages, the subject does cued recall of the passage content.

The empirical question is how long the individual sentences are read as a function of the prior knowledge that the subject has about the sentence content. Rather than having subjects acquire prior knowledge in the course of the experiment, we measured the amount of true, pre-experimental, prior knowledge that the subjects possessed. The subjects took a multiple choice test of prior knowledge of individual propositions and rated the content of each sentence for prior familiarity before they studied the passages for recall. Thus we obtained a familiarity rating and a study time at the level of individual subjects and individual sentences. A comparison of the ratings with scores on the multiple choice test showed that the rating scale measure is valid (see Johnson & Kieras, in press).

In summary, prior knowledge did indeed have facilitative effects on study time and recall, and these effects can be accounted for both in terms of the empirical variables and a simulation model. The effects are ones that everyone would expect, but they have not been systematically demonstrated before. The effect of prior knowledge on study time is shown in Table 8, which summarizes a regression analysis that predicts study time from several empirical variables, including the familiarity rating, which was a significant predictor of study time. Each additional

TABLE 7
The METALS Passage

1. Throughout history, man has used metals for many purposes.
2. The ancient Hellenes used bronze swords.
3. The Hellenes invaded ancient Greece before the Trojan war.
4. The Incas lived in South America.
5. The Incas used gold in religious ceremonies.
6. The Spaniards conquered the Incas for their gold.
7. Aluminum is used in camping equipment.
8. Titanium is the brilliant white pigment in oil paints that are used by some artists.

point on the familiarity scale resulted in about a .377 seconds decrease in study time.

Two popular mechanisms that could be used to explain prior knowledge effects in comprehension are schemas and elaboration (see Johnson & Kieras, in press). However, there is another explanation, which we term the "representation saving" idea. The basic idea is that in order to remember a piece of material, the first step one has to do is build a representation for the material, and then tag it to indicate that it has appeared in a certain experimental context. Then at recall time one searches memory based on these tags, and then produces the recall using the representation for the presented material. So the encoding process consists of two basic steps: First, construct the representation for the sentence propositions, and then second, tag these representations for later recall. If the subject already knows one of the propositions expressed in a sentence, then the representation for it need not be constructed; rather this pre-existing representation only has to be tagged. Prior familiarity with the material would mean that less representation-building work has to be done to encode the sentences, and thus less time would be required to perform the encoding.

If an important role of prior knowledge is to simply save on the amount of representation that is to be built, then a simulation model that works on this principle should show a pattern of savings on processing effort that agrees with the data that we collected. The simulation model will be briefly described, and then the method applied to show how its use of prior knowledge seems to correspond to the study time data.

The simulation model used in this work is an extension of the one described above (see Kieras in press-b, for details). The parser had to be expanded to handle the simple technical passages used in the experiment. The model also needed to have prior knowledge in its long-term memory, and mechanisms for making use of that prior knowledge in constructing representations. These mechanisms identify any portions of memory structure for the input sentence that are already present in the system's long-term memory, and will then reuse these pre-existing representations to reduce the amount of new structure that has to be built.

TABLE 8
Regression Analysis on Self-Paced Task Study Times (N = 960)

Variable	Step	Final Coeff.	Final Std. Coeff	R^2	F	
CONSTANT		6.552				
WORDS	1	.355	.317	.1231	51.2	**
FAMILIARITY	2	-.377	-.227	.1739	94.4	**
CONFRQ	3	-.098	-.108	.1812	11.4	**
MEANIMP	4	.382	.099	.1905	10.9	**

** $p < .01$

Rather than working with the collapsed data and the average amount of prior knowledge on each sentence, we wanted to account for prior knowledge effects at the level of individual subjects. One approach to obtaining the appropriate predictor variable values would be to give the model a set of facts in long-term memory corresponding to the knowledge possessed by an individual subject. Then the model could process each sentence in the passage, and report how much parsing work and how much structure-building work it had to perform. This expensive process could then be repeated for each subject.

Instead, we used a short-cut. The parsing work done on each sentence is independent of the amount of prior knowledge, so a single processing of each sentence in the passages provided a measure of the amount of parsing work required. By setting up the simulation with no prior knowledge, we were able to determine how much structure had to be built when no savings from prior knowledge could be accomplished. We went through the multiple choice test scores for each individual subject, which showed which propositions that person did and did not know. We could use these scores to determine the amount of structure already known by each individual subject on each sentence.

Thus, for each sentence and each subject we had a score corresponding to the number of memory structure links already known by that subject. We also used the total number of structure links for the sentence as a predictor, and the amount of parsing work for that sentence, which did not vary between subjects. Table 9 shows the results of the regression analysis. As you can see, we can predict almost as well using the simulation variables as we could with the purely empirical variables (Table 8). Notice that the coefficient for the structure is roughly similar in size to that of coefficient for the already known structure, but the known structure coefficient is negative. Hence in predicting study time from the amount of memory structure, the relevant information is the difference between the total amount of structure and the amount of known structure. A link of unknown structure takes about 68 ms to construct, while a link of known structure takes about 19 ms.

Because the model's representation of prior knowledge can be used to account for some of the variance in study time, it can be concluded that the representation-

TABLE 9
Regression Analysis on Self-Paced Task Study Times Using Simulation Variables (N = 960)

Variable	Step	Final Coeff.	Final Std. Coeff	R^2	F	
CONSTANT		7.382				
TRANSITS	1	.028	.212	.0812	15.5	**
KNOWN-LINKS	2	-.049	-.206	.1083	36.8	**
TOTAL-LINKS	3	.068	.235	.1312	17.9	**
CONFREQ	4	-.140	-.154	.1464	20.0	**
MEANIMP	5	.290	.075	.1513	5.5	*

* $p<.05$; ** $p<.01$

saving idea is a reasonable explanation for at least part of the effect of prior knowledge on comprehension. The method made it possible to compare a detailed simulation model to what is actually a small and subtle effect (see Johnson & Kieras, in press, for more discussion).

Simulation of Macrostructure Building

A final example of the use of the method involves a rather different simulation, one that uses production rules to extract passage macrostructure from the propositional representation of the passage sentences. More detail can be found in Kieras and Bovair (1981), and Kieras (1982).

The experimental question is how people abstract the main idea from a piece of simple technical prose, such as the passage shown in Table 10. The subject reads the passage one sentence at a time, and then provides a statement of the main idea of the passage in the form of a single brief sentence. The passage is based on a generalization, which appears in the first sentence, and appears in two versions, which differ in whether the first sentence that states the main idea is present or not. The reading time profiles for the two versions of the Table 10 passage appear in Figures 6 and 7; the "bad" version, which is missing the main idea sentence, takes longer to process at various points.

The simulation model is a fairly complex production-system model based on van Dijk's (1977, 1980) rules for abstracting the macrostructure of a passage. The model starts with the propositional form of the passage sentences, and generates a simple generalization main idea from the passage content. It revises its hypothesis about the main idea as it goes through the passage one sentence at a time. Depending on whether the first sentence is present or not, the model will execute a different set of macrostructure-building rules. Usually, if the first sentence is a good statement of the main idea, the model will simply adopt the content of this

TABLE 10
The METALS Passage

1. Different cultures have used metals for different purposes.
2. The ancient Hellenes used bronze swords.
3. The ancient Greeks used copper shields.
4. The Hellenes invaded ancient Greece before the Trojan War.
5. The bronze weapons that were used by the Hellenes could cut through the copper shields that were used by the Greeks.
6. Because the color of gold is beautiful, the Incas used gold in religious ceremonies.
7. The Incas lived in South America.
8. However, the Spaniards craved the monetary value of gold.
9. Therefore, the Spaniards conquered the Incas.
10. Because aluminum does not rust and is light, modern Western culture values aluminum.
11. Aluminum is used in camping equipment.
12. Titanium is used in warplanes and is essential for spacecraft.
13. Warplanes are extremely expensive.
14. Titanium is the brilliant white pigment in oil paints that are used by artists.

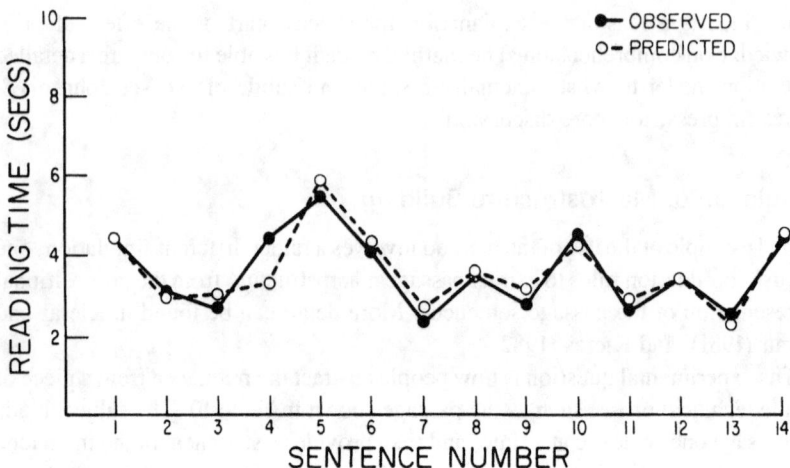

FIG. 6. Observed and predicted reading time profiles for the METALS passage, good version, in a main idea task.

sentence as the main idea, and confirm this choice with the remainder of the passage. If the first sentence is not a good main idea, the model must "change its mind" and infer a new choice of main idea.

The reading time data was modelled with an analysis that included as predictor variables the number of words in each sentence, the content familiarity rating of the sentence, a FIRST variable to capture the longer time spent on the initial sentence, and a single variable from the simulation. This variable was the total number of operations on propositions done in the macrostructure processing for the sentence, that is, the number of propositions built, deleted, or moved from one working

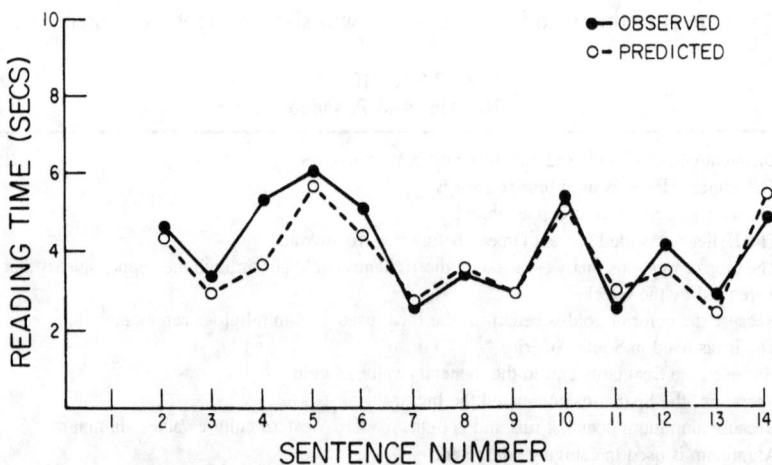

FIG. 7. Observed and predicted reading time profiles for the METALS passage, bad version.

memory list to another. The choice of this variable was based on the widely-held idea that the execution time of a production system is a function of the mental actions involved, not a function of the number of rules, or of the complexity of the conditions of the rules. The predicted reading times for the good and the bad versions of the Table 10 passage are shown in Figures 6 and 7. The variance among the mean reading times accounted for is about 80%. The conclusion is that the model accounts for some of the extra processing on some of the sentences entailed by the bad version. Thus, some empirical support was obtained for the processing time predictions of an extremely complex model.

CONCLUSION

Since this method is a very strongly theory-driven approach, the results of applying it are highly conditional on the acceptability of the simulation model being used. Likewise, a positive outcome of a comparison is a strong argument in favor of the model. But the simulations that I have used are based on some fairly old notions, that are in some sense "standard," and may in fact be obsolete from an artificial intelligence perspective. However, their success at accounting for reading time data indicates that they actually have some definite empirical value. So these older notions can serve as a benchmark for some of the newer and more sophisticated ideas about comprehension and memory. If they are good ideas, they should be able to do at least as good an empirical job as the older ideas. Aside from this global contribution, there are some important small-scale results from applying the method, which are described in Kieras (1981, 1982) and Kieras and Bovair (1981), such as the special status of the first sentence of a passage, the specific effects of incoherence in recall tasks, and the value of representation-saving as an explanation for prior knowledge effects.

But, the most intriguing contribution of the method is the quantitative interpretation of the model processes. Table 11 shows the coefficient values for the simple passage work described above. For example, it takes 6 ms to do an ATN transition step, and 29 ms to construct one link of semantic network structure, and an additional 46 ms to convert that link into long-term structure for the purposes of recall. These numbers can not be taken very seriously without a lot more cross-validation. Notice that in Table 9 the coefficient for LINKS is about twice as large, and the coefficient for TRANSITS is about four times larger, than in Table 11. Since the materials were so different, it is not clear at this time how to interpret this difference. But being able to decompose reading times into this level of theoretical detail is very exciting.

To conclude: This method seems to work well, and it is suited for routine use with different simulations. The method can distinguish between good and bad models, allows a quantitative interpretation of the model, and most importantly, also allows a detailed criticism of the model. Finally, even if the simulation is

TABLE 11
Summary of Component Processing Times
From the Regression Analyses

Process	Time per step, item, or sentence
Parsing	.006 secs/ATN transition
Memory activation	.003 secs/node
WM structure building	.029 secs/one-way link
LTM encoding	.046 secs/one-way link
Topic list processing	.051 secs/topic entry
Perceptual, response, and other processes	1.010 secs/sentence
Topic identification on each sentence in a topic choice task	.232 secs/sentence
Processing a highly thematic sentence in a topic choice task	.447 secs/sentence
Rehearsal processing during each sentence in a recall task	1.887 secs/sentence

incomplete as an account of the phenomena, the method allows the simulation to be used as an analytic tool to show where the missing process is occurring. Thus, this method allows us to take simulation models of comprehension a lot more seriously than we have in the past.

ACKNOWLEDGMENT

This work was supported by the Personnel and Training Research programs, Office of Naval Research under Contract Numbers N00014-78-C-0509 and N00014-81-C-0699, Contract Authority Identification Numbers NR 157-423 and NR 157-473.

REFERENCES

Anderson, J. R. FRAN: A simulation model of free recall. In G. H. Bower (Ed.), *The psychology of learning and motivation*. Vol. 5. New York: Academic Press, 1972.
Anderson, J. R. *Language, memory, and thought*. Hillsdale, N. J.: Lawrence Erlbaum Associates, 1976.
Anderson, R. C. Allocation of attention during reading. In A. Flammer & W. Kintsch (Eds.), *Discourse Processing*. Amsterdam, North Holland Publishing Company, 1982.
Carpenter, P. A., & Just, M. A. Sentence comprehension: A psycholinguistic processing model of verification. *Psychological Review*, 1975, *82*, 45-73.
Carpenter, P. A., & Just, M. A. Integrative processes in comprehension. In D. LaBerge & S. J. Samuels (Eds.), *Basic processes in reading: Perception and comprehension*. Hillsdale, N. J.: Lawrence Erlbaum Associates, 1977, 217-241.
Haviland, S. E., & Clark, H. H. What's new? Acquiring new information as a process in comprehension. *Journal of Verbal Learning and Verbal Behavior*, 1974, *13*, 512-521.
Hilgard, E. R. & Bower, G. H. *Theories of Learning*. (3rd ed.). New York, N. Y.: Appleton-Century-Crofts, Division of Meredith Publishing Company, 1966.

Hilgard, E. R., & Bower, G. H. *Theories of learning* (5th ed.). Englewood Cliffs, N. J.: Prentice-Hall, 1981.

Hintzman, D. L. Explorations with a discrimination net model for paired-associate learning. *Journal of Mathematical Psychology*, 1968, *5*, 123-162.

Johnson, W., & Kieras, D. E. Representation-saving effects of prior knowledge in memory for simple technical prose. *Memory & Cognition*, in press.

Kieras, D. E. Problems of reference in text comprehension. In M. Just & P. Carpenter (Eds.), *Cognitive processes in comprehension*. Hillsdale, N. J.: Lawrence Erlbaum Associates, 1977. (a)

Kieras, D. E. Comparing a simulation to data using multiple regression. Presented at the Tenth Annual Mathematical Psychology Meetings, University of California, Los Angeles, August, 1977. (b)

Kieras, D. E. Good and bad structure in simple paragraphs: Effects on apparent theme, reading time, and recall. *Journal of Verbal Learning and Verbal Behavior*, 1978, *17*, 13-28.

Kieras, D. E. Modelling reading times in different reading tasks with a simulation model of comprehension. Technical Report No. 2, University of Arizona, March, 1979.

Kieras, D. E. Component processes in the comprehension of simple prose. *Journal of Verbal Learning and Verbal Behavior*, 1981, *20*, 1-23.

Kieras, D. E. A model of reader strategy for abstracting main ideas from simple technical prose. *Text*, 1982, *2*, 47-81.

Kieras, D. E. Thematic processes in the comprehension of technical prose. In B. Britton & J. Black (Eds.), *Understanding expository text*. Hillsdale, N. J.: Lawrence Erlbaum Associates, in press. (a)

Kieras, D. E. A simulation model for the comprehension of technical prose. In G. H. Bower (Ed.), *The Psychology of Learning and Motivation*, Vol. 17, in press. (b)

Kieras, D., & Bovair, S. Strategies for abstracting main ideas from simple technical prose. Technical Report No. 9 (UARZ/DP/TR-81/9), University of Arizona, November, 1981.

Kintsch, W. *The representation of meaning in memory*. Hillsdale, N. J.: Lawrence Erlbaum Associates, 1974.

Kintsch, W. On recalling stories. In M. Just & P. Carpenter (Eds.), *Cognitive processes in comprehension*. Hillsdale, N. J.: Lawrence Erlbaum Associates, 1977.

Kliegl, R., Olson, R. K., & Davidson, B. J. Regression analyses as a tool for studying reading processes: comment on Just and Carpenter's eye fixation theory. *Memory & Cognition*, 1982, *10*, 287-296.

Miller, J. R., & Kintsch, W. Readability and recall of short prose passages: A theoretical analysis. *Journal of Experimental Psychology: Human Learning and Memory*, 1980, *6*, 335-354.

Newell, A., & Simon, H. A. *Human problem solving*. Englewood Cliffs, New Jersey: Prentice-Hall, 1972.

Pedhazur, E. J. Coding subjects in repeated measures designs. *Psychological Bulletin*, 1977, *84*, *2*, 298-305.

Rubin, D. C. A unit analysis of prose memory. *Journal of Verbal Learning and Verbal Behavior*, 1978, *17*, 599-620.

Schank, R. C. Computer understanding of natural language. *Behavior Research Methods and Instrumentation*, 1978, *10*, 132-138.

Smith, E. E. Theories of semantic memory. In W. K. Estes (Ed.) *Handbook of learning and cognitive processes, 6, Linguistic functions in cognitive theory*. Hillsdale, N.J.: Lawrence Erlbaum Associates, 1978.

Sternberg, S. Memory-scanning: Mental processes revealed by reaction-time experiments. *American Scientist*, 1969, *57*, 421-457.

Thibadeau, R., Just, M. A., & Carpenter, P. A. A model of the time course and content of reading. *Cognitive Science*, 1982, *6*, 157-203.

van Dijk, T. A. *Text and context*. London: Longman, 1977.

van Dijk, T. A. *Macrostructures*. Hillsdale, N. J.: Lawrence Erlbaum Associates, 1980.

14 Prose Comprehension and the Management of Working Memory

James R. Miller
Computer ∗ Thought Corporation

While the concept of short-term memory is one of cognitive psychology's oldest traditions, with roots in the beginnings of experimental psychology (James, 1890) and modern cognitivism (G. Miller, 1957), its theoretical status has become clouded in recent years. While short-term memory was one of the primary concerns of traditional learning theorists, many of the researchers who have studied such domains as prose comprehension and problem solving have placed a lesser emphasis on the nature of short-term memory, concentrating instead upon how the meaning of a text or the solution to a problem might be represented in memory and upon the processes that construct these representations. The terminologies of these domains have reflected this divergence: the term "short-term memory" is generally used in discussions of such phenomena as list learning, while "working memory" is more often used in discussions of tasks — such as comprehension and problem solving — that require the construction and maintenance of often elaborate mental structure.

However, the studies of these more complex processes have rarely addressed, in a principled way, how working memory differs from long-term memory and what processes are responsible for the management of these systems, issues that were the focal points of early research on learning and memory. In view of the progress that has been made in recent years in these complex domains, it seems appropriate to reconsider these aspects of the cognitive system. Correspondingly, this chapter will discuss prose comprehension from the reference point of working memory, paying special attention to the ways in which the various kinds of information needed for comprehension are combined in a memory system of limited capacity.

These recent shifts toward the study of more complex cognitive structures and processes have been accompanied by changes in the methodological tools used to study these phenomena. The study of learning and memory has long been associated with the development of quantitative models. However, as psychology began to study questions for which domain knowledge was relevant to the phenomena being studied, statistically-oriented mathematical models became less able to characterize the relevant cognitive processes. These models now have been all but replaced by simulation models based in the techniques of artificial intelligence, a field in which the representation and manipulation of knowledge is of primary concern.

In contrast, many of the experimental procedures used to gather data that address the validity of these newer models differ little from those used throughout the history of cognitive psychology. Recognition and recall, for instance, are still widely used. The goal of all these procedures has remained the same — to determine the contents of memory structures at various points in an experimental procedure, and thereby infer the characteristics of these structures and the processes that control them. It has, of course, been necessary to adapt these existing procedures to the new domains, and this task has not always been straightforward. In addition, new procedures have been developed as a result of the requirements imposed and the opportunities offered by these new domains of study. These new procedures often suffer from the usual growing pains of adolescence: their promise is great, but their powers and limitations are still being discovered.

The newness of these domains and of these methodological tools means that the potential for methodological confusion is great. Consequently, this chapter is also meant to be a guide to the use of these theoretical and experimental tools. Special emphasis will be placed on comparing two rather different models of prose comprehension, particularly in terms of what must be known and what must be done to build these kinds of models. Similarly, the experiments presented here should be considered not only from the perspective of what they say about comprehension or a particular comprehension model, but also what their relative strengths and weaknesses are, and what each technique is capable of revealing about the phenomenon it is designed to study.

WORKING MEMORY AS PROPOSITIONAL GRAPH STRUCTURES

A beginning model of working memory in prose comprehension was proposed by Walter Kintsch and myself (Miller & Kintsch, 1980). This model was a partial implementation of the Kintsch and van Dijk (1978) comprehension theory, and was tested by comparing the model's processing of a number of texts to empirical data obtained from subjects reading those texts.

The model simulates only the micropropositional processes described by Kintsch and van Dijk — those actions of the model that require macropropositional processes are based on the intuition of the experimenter using the model. In addition, it does not work directly with the natural language of a text. Rather, a text is first parsed into a propositional representation of predicates and arguments by the experimenter, and the resulting propositions are made available to the model for processing. The process of deriving propositions from text has been discussed by Kintsch (1974), Turner and Greene (1978), and Bovair and Kieras (1981).

The model processes a text in chunks of propositions that correspond to a single sentence or phrase, and builds a graph structure that represents the coherence relations among such a group of propositions. To do this, the model begins with one particularly important proposition[1], and connects to this proposition other propositions that share arguments with it, recursively, until all the propositions in working memory are organized into a single graph structure. A text, the SAINT text discussed by Miller and Kintsch (1980), the propositions derived from the first sentence of this text, and the graph structure built from these propositions are shown in Figure 1.

The complete propositional coherence obtained in this example may not always be present: a new topic might be introduced by the text, or the coherence of a set of propositions may rely upon a proposition that had been removed from the coherence graph by the leading edge strategy on a previous cycle. In such cases, the model searches its long-term memory representation of the text for a proposition that can tie the unrelated parts of the text together. If no such proposition can be found, the model assumes that a bridging inference must be generated to maintain coherence (although it does not generate that needed inference).

This coherence graph is presumed to be built in a limited capacity working memory that does not have room for all the propositions in a paragraph, much less an entire text. Correspondingly, the model uses the factors of hierarchical position in the graph structure and temporal recency to select a subset of the coherence graph's propositions that will be retained in working memory for the purpose of linking this chunk to the rest of the text — this is the *leading edge* strategy described in Kintsch and van Dijk (1978).

What are the implications of this model, particularly with respect to the relations between the model and empirical data? Three validations of the model have been carried out in two projects. In the first (Miller & Kintsch, 1980), subjects read and free recalled several texts of differing difficulty, producing two kinds of data: the probabilities of recall of individual propositions, and whole-text reading time. The predictions of the model were derived and fit to the data as follows:

Propositional Recall. The frequency of recall of a proposition was predicted to be a function of the number of times that the proposition was processed in working memory. Each proposition received at least one cycle of processing when it was first read; others received additional cycles when they were held over from one cycle to the next by the leading edge strategy, or when they were retrieved from long-term memory and reinstated in working memory. These processing frequen-

---

[1] This selection is a macro-level process, and, as such, is carried out by the experimenter.

In the request to canonize John Newman, the "frontier priest, bishop of Philadelphia in the 19th century, two miracles were attributed to him in this century. In 1923, Eva Benassi, dying of peritonitis, dramatically recovered after her nurse prayed to the bishop. In 1949, Kent Lenahan, hospitalized with two skull fractures, smashed bones, and a pierced lung after a traffic accident, rose from his deathbed and resumed a normal life after his mother had prayed ardently to Newman.

```
P1: (REQUEST P2 P8)
P2: (CANONIZE P3)
P3: (ISA JOHN-NEWMAN FRONTIER-PRIEST)
P4: (ISA JOHN-NEWMAN BISHOP)
P5: (LOCATION P4 PHILADELPHIA)
P6: (TIME-OF P4 19TH-CENTURY)
P7: (TWO MIRACLES)
P8: (ATTRIBUTE P7 JOHN-NEWMAN)
P9: (TIME-OF P8 THIS-CENTURY)
```

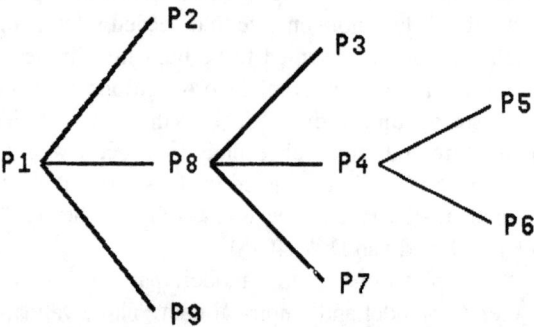

FIG. 1. The SAINT text (Miller & Kintsch, 1980), the propositions derived from this text's first sentence, and the coherence graph formed by this set of propositions.

cies were then fit to the propositions' observed frequencies of recall (summed across subjects) by a hill-climbing chi-square procedure (STEPIT: Chandler, 1965).

This procedure resulted in good chi-square fits for 15 of the 20 texts. However, the procedure is less than straightforward in several ways. First, like all the analyses to be discussed here, the analysis of propositional recall is fundamentally dependent upon an accurate propositionalization of the text, which is itself a difficult task. Some accuracy can be obtained by following a fixed set of rules (cf. Turner & Green, 1978; Bovair & Kieras, 1981) and by comparing the results of several judges' independent analyses, but it cannot be denied that this is a complex and sometimes unavoidably subjective process.

A second, related problem centers around the scoring of subjects' recall data. Since texts are simply not recalled in verbatim form, most analyses of recall consider whether the "gist" of the proposition is present in a subject's recall. Like the propositionalization of texts, comparing what a subject has recalled from a text to a list of propositions derived from that text is difficult and often subjective, even (or perhaps *especially*) when a non-exact criterion is used. Again, a rigorous set of rules for determining what constitutes gist recall and the cross-validation of multiple judges' scoring on at least part of an experiment's data are desirable steps in the analysis of text recall data.

Third, this technique bases its recall predictions solely upon the encoding of individual propositions; retrieval strategies that might select certain propositions for special treatment do not enter into these predictions. For instance, Miller and Kintsch (1980) noted that some propositions were recalled with extremely low probabilities, suggesting that subjects intentionally omitted these propositions from subjects' recall because of their redundancy with other parts of the texts. These low levels of recall disrupted the fitting of the model's predictions to the data, and, in the absence of theoretical interpretations of these omissions and ways of incorporating hypothesized omissions into the model's predictions, statistical techniques unrelated to the model's theoretical content were required to make interpretable analyses possible.

These are all serious problems, and they make the interpretation of recall experiments difficult. However, it would be an overreaction to abandon the use of recall experiments — they are a rich source of data that has been instrumental in developing current theories of comprehension. Perhaps the best strategy for the use of this powerful but flawed technique is to use it in as rigorous a way as possible, and to corroborate findings derived from recall procedures with analyses based on other sources of data.

Text Reading Time. Predictions for the reading times for each of the studied texts were generated by collecting a number of variables derived from the texts themselves (such as the number of words or propositions per text) and from the model's analyses of these texts (such as number of reinstatement searches), and using these variables in a multiple regression as predictors of the texts' reading times; regressions predicting probability of proposition recall and text readability[2] were also carried out. These analyses found that about 85% of the variance in these measures could be accounted for by some set of these variables, and that the variables that

---

[2]Readability was computed as reading time per proposition recalled: a "readable" text is one that can be read quickly with high recall.

accounted for the most variance were those derived from the model's processing of the texts — in particular, the numbers of propositional reinstatements and inferences, which indicate failures in the local coherence of the text.

Two major classes of problems surround these analyses. The first is the type of data that is being analyzed. The reading time for an entire text is a rather coarse measure of comprehension; measurements of reading times for individual sentences or words would be more valuable (presuming that the theoretical machinery existed to support the analysis of these data). However, some controversy exists as to which text units are most appropriate for depicting the comprehension process (cf. Haberlandt's (this volume) comparison of the benefits of syllables versus words). The second class of problems revolves around the proper use of multiple regression. This is not a simple procedure; selecting the right analysis from the many that make up the family of multiple regression techniques is difficult and often controversial (Just & Carpenter, 1980; Kliegl, Olson, & Davidson, 1982). One must also be wary of analyses involving intercorrelated variables, and take the appropriate steps to avoid confounding these analyses. Many of the variables that are commonly studied in prose comprehension research because of their known influence on comprehension are correlated (for instance, word frequency and word length); these correlations can make the use of multiple regression problematic. However, as with recall data, there is much to be gained if this technique can be used appropriately.

Propositional Access. Through its construction and manipulation of coherence graphs, this model makes strong predictions of the propositions that are present in working memory at any time during the processing of a text. These predictions have been tested by Fletcher (1981). Subjects reading the texts that had been analyzed by the coherence graph model were interrupted during their reading and asked to verify sentences that corresponded to three classes of propositions distinguished by the model's analyses: propositions that were predicted by the model to be in working memory at the time of the test, those that had appeared in the text but that had since been removed from working memory by the leading edge rule, and foil propositions that had not appeared in the text.

By the definitions of working memory as a store that allows rapid access to its contents and long-term memory as a static repository in which information can be stored or retrieved but not actively processed, those propositions predicted to be in working memory at the time of the test should be verified faster than those propositions that had been read, but that needed to be located in long-term memory before a response could be made. The model's predictions were confirmed − the verification times for the propositions were functions of whether or not a proposition was predicted to have been present in working memory at the time of the test.

Given these findings, what can be said about the model? In its favor is the fact that it is a straightforward, formal system: it will produce the statistics described above for any set of propositions provided to it. However, the model has no knowledge about any of the events described by the texts, and, as a result, none of the knowledge-based macroprocesses that are central to comprehension can be represented in its analyses. This makes the application of the model to longer, more knowledge-rich texts problematic, if not altogether inappropriate. Similarly, the model's recall predictions were based solely on the frequency with which propositions were processed, without concern for the knowledge structures that interact to determine the meanings of the propositions. Including such knowledge-based structures and processes in the model should improve all of its predictions.

The model's reading time predictions were good, but the data being predicted — whole text reading times — were rather coarse. As noted earlier, a more powerful test for a model would be to predict the reading times of individual sentences, phrases, or words. Finally, although Fletcher's propositional access experiments support the working memory management decisions made by the leading edge strategy, they should not be taken to mean that there is no need for the inclusion of knowledge-driven processes in a model of prose comprehension. The leading edge strategy was always meant to be an approximation to the kinds of knowledge-driven processes that people use to identify the important points in a text; Fletcher's technique can succeed to the extent that the products of the leading edge strategy coincide with the "conceptual focus" of the text. Formalistic simplications aside, tracking the focus of a text is ultimately a macro-level concern, and is an issue central to a sound model of working memory in prose comprehension.

WORKING MEMORY AS INTEGRATED TEXT-KNOWLEDGE STRUCTURES

The insufficiencies of the coherence graph system have led this research toward a model that attempts to examine the reading process with a finer grain than that of the previous work, and that explicitly represents knowledge about important topics discussed in the text. This model is described in detail in Miller (1982); a brief description here is meant to illustrate the issues with which the model is concerned, particularly those that have been addressed by subsequent experiments.

The intent of this model is to describe how text and knowledge structures are manipulated in working memory during prose comprehension. There are other aspects of the reading process that have been left unstudied — in particular, the decoding of words from a physical text and the parsing of natural language into the propositional structures with which this model works. The comprehension of a text results from the interaction of all of these processes (Schank, Lebowitz, & Birnbaum, 1980; Lehnert, 1981; McClelland & Rumelhart, 1981); studying any one of them in isolation is risky, as important phenomena may be observable only in the context of the other processes. However, the benefits of a more complete comprehension model must be weighed against the burden of having to deal with those parts of word decoding and parsing systems that are ancillary to the topics under study here. While this model could, in principle, be extended to include decoding and parsing mechanisms, its current domain is restricted to the integration of text and knowledge structures, and it is hoped that these processes comprise a nearly decomposable part of the comprehension system (Simon, 1969), one whose components interact to a much greater extent with each other than with components outside this system.

In the absence of explicit parsing strategies, but in view of the desire to simulate the word-by-word aspect of reading, this model works with *text elements* - structures similar to propositions, but that specify smaller, case frame-like pieces of information that might be obtained from a parser. For the "SAINT" text (Figure 1), these elements describe concepts and relations such as (REQUEST OBJECT CANONIZE) — that the OBJECT of a REQUEST was a CANONIZation — or (CANONIZE RECIP NEWMAN) — that the RECIPient of the CANONIZation was NEWMAN. Also associated with the text elements are pieces of syntactic information derived from the parse, such as whether this element describes a part of the text that appeared in subject position, or that was expressed with passive focusing. Here, the (REQUEST OBJECT CANONIZE) element has a syntax marker — (SYNTAX (REQUEST SUBJECT-POSITION)) — noting that REQUEST appears in the sentence's subject position. The model will then combine these elements to produce the same propositions that were processed by the coherence graph model; this representation is also augmented by the identification of the cases of the propositions' arguments. In addition, it becomes possible to examine the comprehension process with a much finer grain, at the level of the small groups of words that correspond to these text elements.

A schematic illustration of the model's architecture is shown in Figure 2. In this model, the structures built during comprehension are organized into a number of different levels (indicated by the points and horizontal lines in this figure), which are divided into two sections, corresponding to working memory and long-term memory. Both of these sections are hierarchical, moving from the low-level processing associated with text elements and propositions through the integration of these elements with knowledge structures. Further, this hierarchy is present at both propositional and macropropositional levels in both working and long-term memory. Finally, an explicitly defined set of knowledge structures is present, which can provide a wide range of conceptual information to all levels of the model.

The processing of this model falls roughly into two categories: *construction* and *interpretation*, which can best be illustrated by an example from the SAINT text. When the first text element — (REQUEST OBJECT CANONIZE) — is processed, a proposition is constructed around REQUEST, and an argument is added to this proposition denoting that CANONIZation is the OBJECT of this REQUEST. This propositional structure is then matched against the model's knowledge structures, which requires that a piece of knowledge capable of providing a meaningful interpretation of this textual information be found. The first concept that should be considered in this search is REQUEST — simply the predicate of the

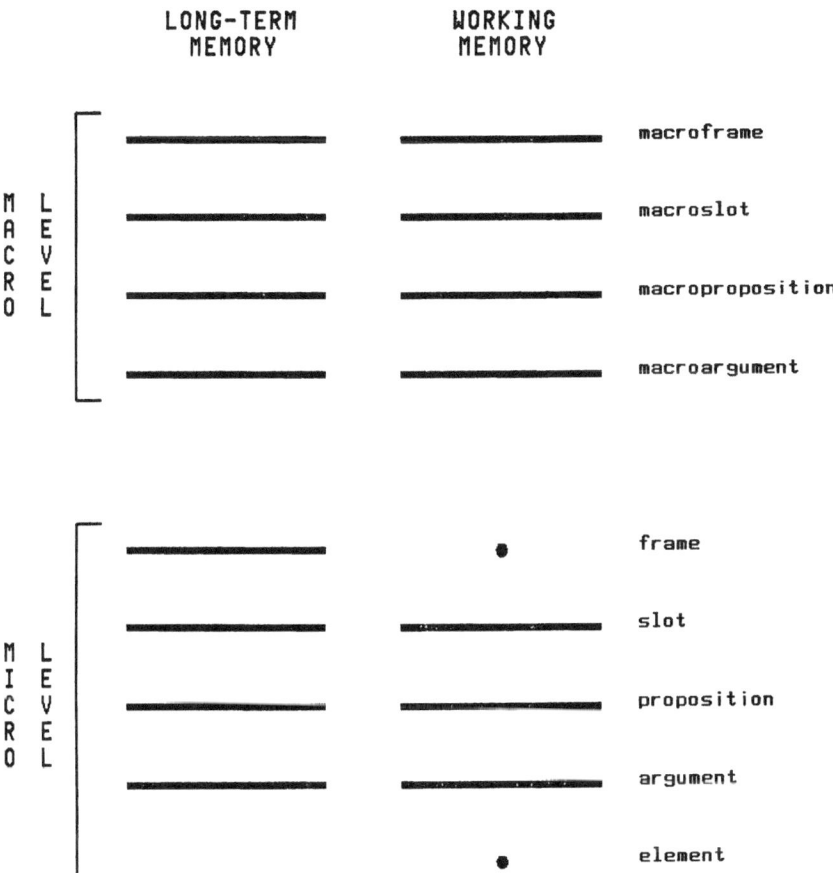

FIG. 2. A schematic view of the text-knowledge integration model. The lines and points represent the different levels of information represented in this model

proposition. As is usually the case, this predicate works well: the REQUEST knowledge structure states that ACTIONS and EVENTS can be requested, and CANONIZE is defined in the knowledge base as an action. This matching serves to link the propositional structure to a knowledge structure, and thus to the reader's long-term semantic memory system as a whole. The model now moves on to the next text element — (CANONIZE RECIP NEWMAN) — and continues this alternation between proposition construction and interpretation until a phrase or sentence boundary is found — here, this is the phrase break after the reference in the text to the "frontier priest".

At this point, the model will try to summarize the gist of this phrase — more specifically, the gist of the propositions currently in working memory — into a single macroproposition. This project is at an early stage in specifying the strategies responsible for building macropropositions; the model's current strategy is to evaluate those propositions in working memory by several criteria: whether or not the proposition's predicate is an action, the centrality of a proposition (how many other propositions it is connected to), any intrinsic interest in the proposition's concepts (handled by lists of concepts the model is presumed to be interested in), and whether any of the text elements that were involved in building this proposition were marked as being syntactically important (as noted earlier, Element 1 contains a "syntax note" indicating that REQUEST appeared in subject position in the sentence). The proposition that receives the highest rating by this method is instantiated as a macroproposition.

Here, Proposition 2 — (CANONIZE (RECIP NEWMAN)) is selected[3] and instantiated as a macroproposition. The resulting macroproposition serves the goal of building the text's macrostructure, and also supports a macrolevel strategy for working memory management — only the proposition instantiated as a macroproposition and those that directly reference that proposition are retained in working memory for the next cycle of processing. The macroproposition also offers top-down guidance for the comprehension of the rest of the text, by helping to focus the model's attention on topics that are particularly likely to be discussed. Here, it has focused on the fact that Newman was canonized, and the text continues by further specifying the nature of this canonization: that it took place because two miracles were attributed to Newman.

There are several important differences between this system and the coherence graph model, and several benefits that result from these differences. First, the application of explicit knowledge structures to comprehension makes the model more realistic in its interpretation and processing of the semantic content of text, replacing a strictly formal set of rules for proposition interrelation and selection with rules more sensitive to the conceptual content of the text. These knowledge structures will also support a realistic model of recall, one that can describe the search for a set of propositions embedded in the reader's semantic memory. Perhaps most importantly, these structures provide the building blocks for the construction of the text's macrostructure.

An important technique for evaluating this model will again be to use multiple regression techniques to predict reading times. However, the greater detail of this model will permit analyses involving individual text elements, which, in turn, allow the evaluation of the processes that operate on the text at the text element level: the processes executed in the course of building propositional structures, accessing world knowledge, and integrating these two structures can be fit to the time required to read that text element, producing estimates of the duration of each of the model's processes. If such analyses are successful, they would be useful in comparing the reading strategies of good and poor readers, indicating how these readers distribute their processing capacity among the various stages of com-

---

[3] See Miller (1982) for the details of this selection.

prehension, and what components of the comprehension process act as bottlenecks in poor readers' comprehension systems.

Finally, the model's predictions of the contents of working memory can again be tested with Fletcher's "interrupt and verify" method. Here, again, the finer grain of this model's analysis allows more detailed predictions: not only can predictions be made about the contents of working memory after the processing of each text element, but these predictions can refer to information contained in any of the model's levels of processing, from text elements to the knowledge structures associated with the macrostructure of the text.

As this model is still being developed, a detailed evaluation of quantitative predictions derived from its performance on a set of texts — like that conducted by Miller and Kintsch and by Fletcher — is not now possible, although such projects are planned for the future. In the absence of such explicit predictions, however, it is appropriate to use experimental techniques to study the phenomena that the model is meant to address, so that necessary structures and processes can be identified and incorporated into the model, and so that proposed model components can be studied and refined. The following sections of this chapter describe two such studies.

SYNTACTIC CONSTRAINTS ON CONCEPTUAL FOCUS IN WORKING MEMORY

An important part of the comprehension process is to accurately identify the conceptual focus of a text. This task is difficult because of the frequent shifts in focus that occur in most texts: a text may begin by talking about a trip to a restaurant, but may later only use the restaurant as a setting for some completely different event, such as a business deal. Most work in this area has emphasized the knowledge-driven component of focus identification, in which the failure of a once-selected knowledge structure to adequately describe a text's content is taken as a signal that the text's focus has shifted, and that a new and more appropriate knowledge structure (one that corresponds to the text's new focus) should be identified and activated. However, it is also possible that the linguistic structure of the text can, in a bottom-up manner, offer cues to the text's rhetorical structure and help select knowledge structures that match the text's shifting focus.

Researchers in functional linguistics (Bates & MacWhinney, 1978; Givon, 1979) have discussed how the structure of a sentence can affect the apparent focus of that sentence. The word that appears in *subject position* is commonly viewed as being central: the sentence

"John kicked the cat".

seems to be primarily about John, while

"The cat was kicked by John".

seems to be more about the cat (see also Haviland and Clark, 1974). Effects of "punchline" position have also been discussed — one might say

"John used the knife to slice the roast".

to emphasize that it was the roast, and not the bread, that was sliced (Bates & MacWhinney, 1978). The ability of these forms to bias what the sentence seems to "be about" implies that the syntactic forms of the sentences affect the activation of knowledge structures in working memory. Two studies were therefore carried out to study the effects of syntactic structure on the perceived focus of a text.

In the first of these experiments, subjects were given brief texts such as the following:

1 A big robbery had just taken place.
2 A detective and a reporter rushed to the scene of the crime.
3 The detective found the jewel in the basement.

These texts were meant to manipulate the conceptual focus following Sentence 3, which was done in two ways. First, through the syntax of Sentence 3 — whether the agent, the object, or some other component (such as the basement *location*) of this sentence was in subject position; second, through the semantic content of the second sentence, which mentioned one of the components of the third sentence. These effects were manipulated orthogonally — subjects also saw such texts as:

1 A big robbery had taken place.
2 A jewel and necklace were reported missing.
3 The jewel was found in the basement by the detective.

Here, the object of the sentence — the *jewel* — not only was in subject position, but also received semantic focus by its mention in the second sentence. The question of interest in this experiment was the extent to which these manipulations of text syntax and semantics affect the texts' focus.

For each of these texts, subjects were instructed to read the text carefully and to then write a sentence that described how they thought that text would continue. The continuations generated in this paradigm should depend upon and be consistent with the contents of the reader's working memory, making it possible to work backward from the continuations to infer what was present in working memory when a continuation was generated. The data of interest here were then those parts of the sentences that received focus in the subjects' continuations, where focus was operationally defined as the first content word that appeared in the continuation.

Three of the effects in this experiment are of particular interest. The semantic focus manipulation had its expected effect: each of the three sentence components was particularly likely to be chosen as the focus of the generated sentence when that component received semantic focus in the text. In addition, subjects tended to focus on the initial component of the syntactic focus sentence — the agent of active sentences, and the object of passive sentences — and tended *not* to focus on the parts of the sentences that appeared in final, "punchline" position. These results indicate that both the manipulations of semantic content and syntactic structure influenced the perceived focus of these texts.

This experiment was concerned with questions of text generation; one might also ask whether similar semantic and syntactic effects occur during comprehension. If text propositions can be integrated with knowledge structures only within the limited capacity of working memory, the knowledge structure capable of providing the most meaningful interpretation for a given proposition may not be present in working memory and available for processing at the time that the proposition is encountered. The necessary knowledge structure must then be retrieved from long-term memory, which will take a certain amount of time. Shorter reading times would then be expected for sentences that correspond to the currently held focus (since those sentences can be incorporated into the existing knowledge structure), while sentences that are inconsistent with the current focus should be read more slowly, due to the additional time required to retrieve an appropriate knowledge structure from long-term memory.

These hypotheses were tested in a second experiment, in which subjects read texts like the following:

1 A big robbery had just taken place.
2 A detective and a reporter rushed to the scene of the crime.
3 The detective found the jewel in the basement.
4 The detective went to look for the thief.
5 The detective called his station for more information.

This text is the same as that presented in the description of the continuation experiment, but with an additional *test* sentence (Sentence 4) whose subject was the agent or the object of the syntactic focus sentence, and an optional *trailer* sentence (Sentence 5) that appeared half the time to keep the lengths of the texts unpredictable. Subjects read these texts, one line at a time under computer control, permitting the recording of the reading times for the texts' sentences. After the subjects read a block of eight texts, they answered true-false questions about the text's test sentences.

The data ultimately analyzed were the reading times for the test sentences whose corresponding questions were answered correctly. These data revealed the same effects as in the generation experiment: the reading time for a test sentence depended upon the agreement of that sentence's focus with the focus created by the semantic and syntactic manipulations. The test sentence was read faster when there was agreement of either kind, and fastest of all when all three sentences agreed in focus.

The effects observed in this experiment can be accounted for in a straightforward way by the text-knowledge integration model described earlier. One of the contributing factors in the model's selection and specification of macropropositions is whether a proposition was created from a text element that had been marked as having particular syntactic importance. This factor does not completely determine macroproposition selection — nor should it, given the demonstrated power of semantic factors in these experiments — but it describes a way in which the syntactic form of the text can affect the selection of macropropositions. By affecting this part of the comprehension process, the concepts that receive focus in working memory are also affected.

This is an example of how experiments can be used to evaluate a partially developed model. If the model did not permit text and sentence syntax to affect the selection of macropropositions and knowledge structures for working memory processing, modifications would be required to accommodate these findings — without, of course, disturbing the model's performance in other areas. However, the results of these experiments should not be overstated: they support the hypothesis that syntax can affect working memory management, but they do not support the specific collection of techniques that this model used to produce these effects. These structures and processes must be confirmed by other, more powerful techniques before it can be said that the mechanisms by which syntax affects a text's focus have been identified. Experiments like those described here are not the end, but only the beginning of a cycle of verification studies.

SEMANTIC CONSTRAINTS ON CONCEPTUAL FOCUS IN WORKING MEMORY

The syntactic effects studied in the previous experiments will often be overshadowed by more powerful constraints derived from the semantics of a text's sentences and the text itself. Consider the following text:

> "John was in a big hurry to get to work because of an important meeting with his boss. As he was about to leave the house, he slipped on his son's roller skate, fell down two flights of stairs, and...."

How might this text continue? The phrase

> "... and broke his leg."

is a reasonable conclusion to this text, as the result of the interpretation of three pieces of knowledge:

- the world knowledge that falling down a flight of stairs can lead to an injury,

- the knowledge about text structure indicating that the statement of an action is typically followed by the result of that action, and

- the interaction of these pieces of knowledge, which confirms that an injury to John is a plausible result of his fall.

The heart of this acceptability issue lies in the ways that text and world knowledge interact to constrain the possible development of the text. The continuation,

"...*and made some coffee.*"

is inappropriate, even though it is syntactically correct and, by itself, does not contradict any aspect of a typical reader's knowledge — John is probably perfectly capable of making coffee. The problem is that this latter continuation does not fall within the semantic space defined by the interaction of these two sources of knowledge: making coffee cannot be interpreted as the result of John's fall.

Recall that one of the major parts of the text-knowledge integration model described earlier brings knowledge structures into working memory and compares them to text propositions. These processes have the side effect of establishing knowledge-based text constraints at virtually no additional cost. As suggested by the above discussion, these constraints are the result of the interaction of text and world knowledge.

A set of experiments was carried out to investigate under what conditions constraints of various types are established. The methodology used in these experiments was to divide a number of texts — longer versions of those studied by Miller and Kintsch (1980) — into phrase- or sentence-sized chunks, and to show these texts to subjects, one segment at a time. A sample segmentation of part of one such text — a discussion of the Tournament of Roses parade — is presented in Table 1. The subjects were told to read the segment and to write a sentence that described how they thought the text would continue. After this continuation was generated, the subjects were shown the text's actual continuation, and were then to describe how they thought the text would continue from *that* point. Both empirically easy and hard texts were studied, as determined by the reading time and recall data for the parts of the texts studied by Miller and Kintsch (and as ultimately confirmed by these experiments). In the results described below, the subjects' continuations were scored against the text's actual continuation at a gist criterion.

TABLE 1
A Sample (Partial) Text Segmentation
from the Continuation Experiment.

1: It may be the greatest show on earth
2: A fantastic fireworks of music and color.
3: of snappy marching bands and stately floral floats.
4: of beautiful girls and brightly outfitted horses.
5: It's the annual Tournament of Roses in Pasadena, California,
6: which begins with a 5 1/2 mile parade
7: and ends with the spirited competition
8: of the Rose Bowl football game. (end of paragraph)
9: Although the Tournament of Roses opens and closes in one day,
10: it is one of the country's longest running spectacles.
11: Since it began, there have been 86 parades.
12: And while the parade itself lasts only two hours,
13: a whole year goes into its planning. (end of paragraph)

Note that the use of this criterion raises problems similar to those encountered in the scoring of text recall; as in those analyses, a rigorous set of rules for guiding judgments of "gist-ness" and cross-validation of subjects' continuations by multiple judges will help in obtaining accurate data.

There were two effects in this experiment that are relevant to the current discussion. First, subjects' continuations became increasingly accurate as they progressed through a paragraph. This suggests that the rhetorical structure of a paragraph becomes increasingly constrained as the paragraph develops, and that, in this experiment, subjects were able to use these constraints to refine their selection of world knowledge relevant to the comprehension of the text and the anticipation of the text's continuation.

Second, subjects' continuations were more accurate in easy than in hard texts: a constraint established in an easy text was likely to correspond to the actual continuation of the text. The inter-subject agreement on the expected continuation of individual segments indicated that there were two causes for the inaccurate continuation of difficult texts. Hard texts can establish and then explicitly violate a constraint; they can also establish vague constraints, so that the chance that the continuation generated by a subject will match this constraint is low.

These effects could be artifacts of interrupting subjects and asking them to generate continuations, revealing nothing about the comprehension process itself. Therefore, in a second experiment, subjects were tested in a reading time paradigm in which they read these texts on computer terminals, one segment at a time, under instructions to read the texts carefully so as to be able to recall them later. Subjects in this experiment did not generate continuations for the text segments. As in the syntax study, the reading times for these segments were collected.

There are three particularly relevant trends in these data. First, subjects read the easy texts faster than the hard texts; this was essentially a confirmation of the way that the experimental materials were constructed, as the readability metric used by Miller and Kintsch (1980) — reading time per proposition recalled — was used to classify this experiment's texts as easy or hard. Second, the segments at the ends of paragraphs, which had been shown to be highly constrained in the previous experiment, were read faster than the other segments. Third, in a cross-experiment analysis, subjects in the reading time experiment were found to have read quickly those segments that had been accurately predicted by the subjects in the continuation experiment.

These experiments indicate that effects of text constraints do appear in more typical comprehension paradigms: text and world knowledge are actively manipulated during comprehension, and successful comprehension depends, among other things, upon the reader's ability to accurately process this information. As in the syntax experiments, processes have been identified that have significant effects upon comprehension, and, as such, should be represented in an accurate model of the comprehension process.

Processes that exploit the constraint of a text's development can be observed by describing how the proposed model would process those segments from the continuation experiments that subjects were able to read quickly and predict accurately. Such a segment in the "Roses" text was:

"Despite the precise planning of the Tournament of Roses...
things still go wrong"

The facilitated processing of *things still go wrong* following the reading of *Despite the precise planning of the Tournament of Roses* depends upon both the knowledge structures that are activated during the comprehension of this sentence and the processes that manipulate these structures. First, consider the basic structures for DESPITE and PLAN (Figure 3a): the DESPITE knowledge structure states that some action with a particular goal occurs, but that the goal of this event is not achieved. A PLAN is an action that has as its goal the orderly achievement of the thing being planned.

The model begins the processing of the sentence *Despite the precise planning...* by accepting the propositional representation of this phrase, activating the DESPITE knowledge structure, and trying to match the propositional information to this structure. The success of this match allows the model to replace the general information in DESPITE's definition (Figure 3a) with the information found in the text — that the action being described here is the "precise planning of the Tournament of Roses". Similar changes can be made in the PLAN knowledge structure; the states of these knowledge structures following the comprehension of the first segment of this sentence are shown in Figure 3b.

The manipulation of these knowledge structures in working memory establishes the constraints on the text's development described previously; the effects of these constraints can be observed in two ways. First, a subject's continuation of a sentence should depend upon the contents of his working memory at the time the continuation is written. In the example above, when the active text and knowledge structures interact to constrain each other, the DESPITE knowledge structure, as modified by the comprehension of the text, will dominate the continuation generation process. Correspondingly, subjects should — and did — generate continuations that reflect the new value of DESPITE's RESULT, either matching the text's continuation or overspecifying the idea of things going wrong, perhaps by saying "the weather has not always been good". When the development of a text is unconstrained — when a large number of candidate knowledge structures exist or when the contents of these structures have not been filled with text information — continuations that match that of the text cannot be assured. Second, the process that is responsible for matching propositional structures to knowledge structures should run more quickly when the relevant knowledge structure is present in working memory and when the match between these two structures is good. The faster segment reading times found at the ends of sentences and paragraphs, where the texts were highly constrained, supports this proposal.

PLAN: an *ACTION* with:

   object: an *ACTION* or an *EVENT*

   goal: efficient execution of *OBJECT* of *PLAN*

DESPITE: an *ACTION* with:

   event: an *ACTION* with:
      goal: X
   result: X is not achieved

(a)

PLAN: an *ACTION* with:

   object: TOURNAMENT-OF-ROSES

   goal: efficient execution of
             TOURNAMENT-OF-ROSES

DESPITE: an *ACTION* with:

   event: (PLAN TOURNAMENT-OF-ROSES)

   result: (efficient execution of
             TOURNAMENT-OF-ROSES)
             is not achieved

Text: "Despite the precise planning of the Tournament of Roses..."

FIG. 3. The knowledge structures for DESPITE and PLAN, (a) before and (b) after the integration of the text information, *Despite the precise planning of the Tournament of Roses.*

SUMMARY

The two sets of experiments discussed above were meant not only to describe some of the properties of the text-knowledge integration model, but also to illustrate some of the advantages of this style of research. These advantages primarily surround the explicit nature of computer simulation models: the ability to describe the structures and processes underlying comprehension is an extremely powerful tool in model construction and verification. Needless to say, the simulation approach is not without its problems. Some of these are well-known — the time and resources needed to build simulation models, or the difficulty in understanding other peoples' models — while others are somewhat more theoretical in nature, and need the backdrop of a concrete example — like the model described here — to be fully appreciated:

Generality. The formality of the coherence graph system has one clear-cut advantage over the knowledge-based system: it can be applied to any text from which a list of propositions had been derived. In contrast, before a knowledge-based model can analyze a text, a large number of concepts that are explicitly and implicitly relevant to that text must be defined in considerable detail. This complicates the process of building a general model, since a large set of knowledge structures must be accumulated for all of the texts to which this model might be applied, and since all of the members of this set must be internally consistent. While different models have been applied to domains as diverse as international terrorism (Schank et al, 1980) and gardening (Lehnert & Bain, 1980), a model should ideally be applied to several different domains, to insure that its processes have not inadvertently been "fine tuned" to any one domain.

Knowledge Structure Specification. The specification of these knowledge structures is itself a problem, with two horns: which knowledge structures must be defined to enable the model to comprehend the text, and how should these structures be defined? The question of whether words have independently specifiable meanings is a difficult one that has troubled artificial intelligence for some time (Dreyfus, 1979). It is unclear whether there is any principled way to define these structures other than by recourse to the experimenter's intuition and by trying not to define the structures in ways that guarantee the (apparent) success of the model.

Processing Strategy Specification. Needless to say, the first formulation of a model is rarely perfect. How, then, should a model that is acknowledged to be imperfect be corrected — should the model be presumed to be "nearly correct", so that only relatively minor adjustments are made to the model's structure, or should entire segments be declared totally incorrect, and replaced by a completely new design? Few, if any, principles exist to guide these decisions; simulation models are typically so large and complex that it is difficult to identify one of a set of highly interrelated processes as the one at fault. It is equally difficult to make modifications (of either kind) without having the effects of these repairs propagate throughout the system and cause a variety of new and unexpected problems.

Who is Being Modelled Here? These problems regarding the desired specificity of structures and processes raise a final question: who, if anyone, is this system meant to model? Under ideal circumstances, the predictions of the model would be compared to subjects with exactly the structures and processes possessed by the model. This illustrates one of the advantages of simulation models — the ability to describe a certain class of subjects, perhaps experts or novices in some domain, and simulate their comprehension of a text. However, it would be naive to think that all members of even such a specifiable class of subjects would have identical structures and processes, yet the comparison of a model's performance to group data requires that the differences in these structures and processes be ignored. The effect is almost one of "averaging" over structures and processes, and the validity — if not the simple meaning — of this action is very unclear.

This discussion should emphasize that there are nontrivial problems with the computer simulation approach, and that solutions will not be easy to find. However, the advantages that this methodology provide almost certainly outweigh the problems. The ability to specify the comprehension process in such detail is available in virtually no other way, and workers in this area are finding not only new answers to old questions, but also new questions that weren't even recognized before. If we want the power that simulation models have to offer, we will have to face up to these very challenging questions.

REFERENCES

Bates, E., & MacWhinney, B. The functionalist approach to the acquisition of grammar. In E. Keenan. *Developmental pragmatics.* New York: Academic Press, 1978.

Bovair, S., & Kieras, D. E. A guide to propositional analysis for research on technical prose. Technical Report No. 8, Department of Psychology, University of Arizona, July 1981.

Chandler, P. J. *Subroutine STEPIT: An algorithm that finds the values of the parameters which minimize a given continuous function.* Bloomington: Indiana University, Quantum Chemistry Program Exchange, 1965.

Dreyfus, H. L. *What computers can't do.* New York: Harper and Row, 1979.

Fletcher, C. R. Short-term memory processes in text comprehension. *Journal of Verbal Learning and Verbal Behavior,* 1981, *20,* 564-574.

Givon, T. *On understanding grammar.* New York: Academic Press, 1979.

Haviland, S. E., & Clark, H. H. What's new? Acquiring new information as a process in comprehension. *Journal of Verbal Learning and Verbal Behavior,* 1974, *13,* 515-521.

James, W. *The principles of psychology.* New York: Dover, 1950 (originally published in 1890).

Kintsch, W. *The representation of meaning in memory.* Hillsdale, N.J.: Lawrence Erlbaum Associates, 1974.

Kintsch, W., & van Dijk, T. A. Toward a model of text comprehension and production. *Psychological Review,* 1978, *85,* 363-394.

Kliegl, R., Olson, R. K., & Davidson, B. J. Regression analyses as a tool for studying reading processes: Comment on Just and Carpenter's eye fixation theory. *Memory and Cognition,* 1982, *10,* 287-296.

Lehnert, W. Plot units and narrative summarization. *Cognitive Science,* 1981, *5,* 293-332.

Lehnert, W. G., & Bain, W. M. VEGE: Variable processing in a natural language query system. Technical Report No. 183, Department of Computer Science, Yale University, April, 1980.

McClelland, J. L., & Rumelhart, D. E. An interactive activation model of context effects in letter perception: Part I. An account of basic findings. *Psychological Review*, 1981, *88*, 375-407.

Miller, G. A. The magical number seven, plus or minus two: Some limits on our capacity for processing information. *Psychological Review*, 1956, *63*, 81-97.

Miller, J. R. A knowledge-based model of prose comprehension: Applications to expository texts. In B. K. Britton and J. B. Black (Eds.), *Understanding expository text*. Hillsdale, N.J.: Lawrence Erlbaum Associates, in press.

Miller, J. R., & Kintsch, W. Readability and recall of short prose passages: A theoretical analysis. *Journal of Experimental Psychology: Human Learning and Memory*, 1980, *6*, 335-354.

Schank, R. C., Lebowitz, M., & Birnbaum, L. A. An integrated understander. *American Journal of Computational Linguistics*, 1980, *6*, 13-30.

Simon, H. A. *The sciences of the artificial*. Cambridge: MIT Press, 1969.

Turner, A., & Greene, E. The construction of a propositional text base. *JSAS Catalog of Selected Documents in Psychology*, August, 1978.

15 Developing a Computer Model of Reading Times

Marcel A. Just and Robert H. Thibadeau
Carnegie-Mellon University

This chapter describes a method of modeling human reading with a computer simulation that reads the text word by word, and whose processing time or effort on each word corresponds to the human gaze duration on that word. The simulation program, called READER, required the development of a system architecture that permitted the mapping between the humans' and the simulation's processing effort. This architecture, called CAPS, provides an unusual sort of operating system within which simulation programs can be written (Thibadeau, Just, & Carpenter, 1982). (CAPS is an acronym for *Collaborative, Activation-based, Production System*. The significance of these terms will be clarified below). CAPS is particularly useful for modeling the time course of the processing. The methodological content of the chapter consists of the issues and problems raised at various points in the model's development, and some of the tentative solutions. We will describe the chronology of the modeling work, and the ways the data constrained that work.

This chapter will focus on the methodological problems that were specific to our project, rather than problems common to all computer simulations of a human cognitive process. Many simulations are first motivated by their designers' intuitions, and then later experiments are designed to test various aspects of the simulation. What distinguishes our simulation project is that it was strongly motivated by a rich new source of empirical results, namely the measurement of human performance provided by the gaze duration on each word of a text.

CONSTRAINTS ON THE MODEL

Several factors constrained the modeling. The most obvious is that the simulation's processing effort on each word of the text should have some correspondence to the human gaze duration. Some of the main empirical findings are reported in another chapter of this volume by Just and Carpenter. Specifically, there were large and clear effects of word length and word frequency. The gaze duration increased linearly with the length of a word and decreased linearly with the logarithm of its normative frequency, and the two effects were additive. By contrast the effects of higher level processes were small or unsystematic. For example, there were few manifestations of syntactic processing except at points where a clear syntactic difficulty existed. The effects of semantic analysis and text-level integration were specific to lexical items and semantic relations and topic domains. Another constraint from the data was that the simulation had to use the strategy of immediate interpretation, trying to process each word as far as possible, at all levels of processing (e.g. lexical, syntactic, semantic), before proceeding to the next word. The empirical result that imposes this constraint is that a processing difficulty introduced by a given word is manifested as an increase in gaze duration on that word, and little increase on words that follow (see Just & Carpenter, this volume, for a more detailed discussion of immediacy of processing).

There were other constraints that did not directly emanate from the gaze duration data. The model would have to "understand" the text, which refers to extracting information from a text and being able to use it appropriately, in this case by recalling the passage approximately the way the human subjects did. Second, the organization of the information processing had to conform to a more general theory of human cognition and reading in particular. There had to be several levels of processing that could be coordinated appropriately, with potential for mutual influence between levels. Third, the specific processing mechanisms had to conform to performance characteristics of such mechanisms as indicated not only by our data, but by relevant data from other experiments. These general constraints would seem to be desirable for most simulations of cognitive processes.

DECIDING TO USE A PRODUCTION SYSTEM ARCHITECTURE

In this section, we describe our reasons for choosing production systems as the formalism for the computer model. The term "production system" has a very unfortunate ambiguity, in that it refers both to an operating environment, like a TOPS operating system, and a particular program that runs within that environment. Our simulation work involved a development of both levels of production systems, CAPS at the higher level and READER at the lower level. Production systems were first proposed as a model of the human system by Newell and Simon

(1972), and continuously developed and refined by Newell and his colleagues (e.g. Newell, 1980).

A production system program (in the lower level sense of the word) is a formalism in which procedural knowledge is embodied in a set of condition - action rules called productions. The condition part specifies what elements should be present in working memory to enable the action. An illustration of a production that might be used in parsing is [If you encounter the word *the*, then as an action, postulate that a noun phrase is being read]. The flow of control in a production system is distributed among its productions and is governed by its dynamically changing knowledge state. The sequence of processing is self-organizing, so that a grand plan for performing a task does not have to be constructed or executed. Local chunks of procedural knowledge take the system from one state (that it knows how to deal with) to another. This somewhat resembles human mental and physical actions that are embarked on when only the first step is evident, but many of the intermediate steps are not explicitly planned beforehand. A production system embodies the strategy of "I'll do what I know how to now, and hope I can deal with what happens next".

We do not universally advocate the use of production systems, but point out why it seemed the appropriate choice for our project (see Newell, 1973; 1980 for general advocacy of production systems). Most simulations of cognitive processes choose not to make any commitment to the processing architecture, preferring to use arbitrary LISP programs structured in conventional ways. Production systems have certain characteristics that seem to resemble aspects of the human processing system, such as the self-organization without the need for an executive, as mentioned above. This particular feature allows a production system model of comprehension processes to be guided jointly by the text, by the program's previous relevant knowledge of the content, and by its current goals. As any of these factors changed, the nature of the comprehension might be different. Another production system feature that satisfied an important constraint is that immediacy of processing is a naturally emergent property of a production system. As soon as the enabling information is available in working memory, the enabled process begins to operate, rather than waiting for control signals to enable the process. Such control signals can be included in a production's condition elements of course, but the default is to let a production fire as soon as the enabling information is present. Still another desirable production system feature is that the outputs (partial and final results) of all processes are continuously available in a common forum, the working memory, where they can be used by other processes. For example, the partial result of a syntactic analysis could influence the assignment of a referent, or vice versa.

An advantage of production systems at a more general level is that a theoretically motivated architecture imposes some useful constraint on the modeling. For example, using a single architecture for modeling different tasks holds some promise for unifying those models and allowing cross-task commonalities and differences to emerge. We have developed models within CAPS not only for reading, but also for solving visual analogies and for performing some mental rotation tasks. Production systems have other virtues (and drawbacks), but the outstanding virtue is that there is no existing alternative theory of the human processing system, so we accepted the basic concepts of a production system architecture.

DESIGNING AN APPROPRIATE PRODUCTION SYSTEM ARCHITECTURE

The decision to use a production system architecture did not immediately enable us to begin development of the model. All the existing production system architectures were incompatible with the goal of modeling the time course of comprehension. The main problems were to account for similar processes taking different amounts of time depending on the text input, and to permit several levels of analysis (e.g. syntactic and referential) to be concurrent, with the potential for mutual influence.

The Growth of Knowledge Over Time

Within a conventional production system, it is difficult to explain why a given production should take different amounts of time on different occasions. For example, consider a production that does lexical access, such that when it is given the encoding of a printed word, it retrieves the associated word meaning to working memory. We know from our data and from other studies that the time for the access depends on the word's properties, such as its frequency. But what is there in a production system that would make the access of *SABLE* take longer than the access of *TABLE*? In both cases, a single production would simply take an action. In a conventional production system, an action generally inserts or deletes an element of knowledge (say a proposition) from working memory. And typically a production performs its function by firing once for each time its operation is called for. A single firing of such a production would accomplish the lexical access function in this illustration. It is difficult to explain why lexical access should take longer for *SABLE* than for *TABLE* within this scheme.

One part of our solution was to modify the way that knowledge was represented, and the way that productions modified that knowledge. Unlike conventional production systems, knowledge elements in CAPS (propositions) are not just present or absent from working memory, but can vary in their strength or activation level. CAPS productions modify the strength of propositions, which includes insertion and deletion in the extreme case. Moreover, if a given proposition were the condition of a production, it would not satisfy the condition unless its strength were above a conventional threshold level. In this scheme, a production could sensibly fire repeatedly, each time incrementing the activation level of a knowledge element. Thus there can be a growth of knowledge over time. We could relate human processing time to the number of iterations it required one or more productions to raise the activation of some proposition to the threshold level. By designing appropriate productions, we could try to make the number of iterations in the growth process correspond to the human processing time. The growth can be contributed to by several different productions which can collaborate to bring the activation level of a given proposition to threshold. This is a form of linear integration whose time course can be systematically manipulated, embedded in a production system framework.

Stratification of Processing

The second major modification to conventional production systems was designed to permit a stratification of processing, by permitting concurrent execution of various processes. The processing of language has often been construed as several levels or strata of processing, operating at the levels of features, words, syntax, and so forth (cf. Lamb, 1966). The problem of stratifying processes in a theory of reading or in a simulation is to specify the temporal relations between strata (e.g. which ones wait for particular other ones to be completed), and to specify how and when they communicate with each other.

The arrangement that most naturally arises in a conventional production system architecture is a strictly sequential operation of various levels, but this scheme does not match what is known about human reading. In one particular version of this incorrect scheme, the level dealing with the lowest features (say letters) operates first, while all other levels wait. Then the letter level would transmit its results to the next highest level, and that level would operate, while all higher ones waited, etc. The reason that this scheme is incorrect is that higher levels of analysis of a unit like a word can influence lower levels of analysis, like recognizing a particular word. One example of such a phenomenon is called the word superiority effect, the higher ability to recognize a letter when it is embedded in a word than when it is isolated. This effect shows that higher levels do not necessarily wait for lower levels to send information upwards, and that in fact the higher levels might send information downwards. It is likely that similar influences exist between other levels. A suitable processing architecture must permit this form of interaction among levels.

The CAPS solution to the stratification problem was to allow any number of productions to fire at one time, so long as their conditions were satisfied. Allowing several productions to fire at the same time (i.e. during the same cycle) means that several levels of computation can occur concurrently. For example, having encoded *HAMMER* and accessed the corresponding word concept, the program can simultaneously compute that it is used as a noun, that it is an instrument, and that it may be coreferential with a previously mentioned hammer. Each level of analysis may involve a sequence of productions successively enabling each other over successive cycles, so that there could be several concurrent streams of processing.

Although this architecture allows concurrence among levels, it just as easily permits sequentiality, if it is desired. A later level will follow an earlier one if the productions in the later level have as their condition that the earlier level has completed its operation. Thus there can be functional parallelism between some levels, and sequentiality between others. Moreover, the relation can vary as a function of the strength of some information.

The Metric: CAPS Cycles

The metric of processing effort of the simulation is provided by its cycles of processing. A CAPS cycle is defined as a single iteration in which the working memory is scanned and all the satisfied productions are fired. All cycles are assumed to consume the same amount of time, regardless of the contents of working memory or the number of productions that are satisfied. The number of CAPS cycles spent on each word of a text provide the metric of processing time in the simulation that can be related to the human gaze duration.

The communication among levels of processing occurs in the working memory, where all productions perform their actions. Once something is in the working memory, it becomes available on the very next cycle as input to productions from all levels and hence becomes a potential source of influence. Thus the intermediate and final products of each level of analysis are deposited in working memory on each cycle, and so they are continuously available.

A BRIEF OVERVIEW OF READER'S PROPERTIES

The development of CAPS and READER was not completely sequential, but involved a number of versions of CAPS-like systems, followed by attempts to develop the READER model. The final version of CAPS was selected when it seemed likely that a reading model could be written to account for the specific results obtained in the gaze durations. From that time, all further development was done only on READER.

Each traditional "level" of reading such as word encoding, lexical access, syntactic parsing, and so on, is realized as a set of productions. READER identifies and accesses individual word concepts. It determines how word meanings combine to produce the meaning representation of a sentence by doing a conceptual dependency analysis (Schank, 1972). It identifies referents of described objects, constructs a model of the referential world that is described in the passage, and uses it to interrelate the information presented in different sentences. The conceptual dependency analysis is accompanied by a syntactic analysis that searches for surface syntactic relations, such as subject, verb, object, and prepositional phrase, and checks for noun-verb agreement, and so on. In addition, READER possesses a schema of a scientific text that specifies the general categories of information to expect, such as the mechanism's name, purpose, operating principles, applications, examples, and so on. The schema guides the inference processes during reading and organizes the subsequent recall.

READER's knowledge base consists of propositions in the form of concept-relation-concept triples, constituting a semantic network. The propositions have activation levels that can vary over a range of values, indicating the extent to which the proposition has supporting evidence. Activation is typically directed by the productions from known propositions to other as yet uncertain propositions. It is possible for several different productions to collaboratively increase READER's certainty of a particular piece of information to some threshold level, where one production alone would have failed to do so. If there are two or more alternative interpretations of some aspect of the text, each interpretation may accumulate supporting evidence until one of their activation levels reaches threshold and becomes the accepted interpretation.

READER operates from left-to-right on the text, processing it one word at a time. The processing of each word continues for cycle after cycle, so long as successive productions are enabled. Each word is processed as far as possible at all levels before proceeding to the next word. This corresponds to the immediacy strategy. READER does not buffer information unless it is unavoidable; a production will execute as soon as working memory contains sufficient information to initiate it.

Like most other natural language understanding systems, READER understands only a small subset of English text, a 140 word scientific passage on the topic of *Flywheels*. To understand other types of passages would have required the ability to choose among schemas, and while this is an important problem it was not one that we wanted to deal with. But READER could easily be extended to understand most of the other 14 scientific passages that the subjects in the experiment actually read, because almost all of them fit the same schema. To understand the remaining 14 passages would have required much more lexical and general knowledge and more complete parser, but no fundamental change in the model. As of November, 1980, CAPS was a running system, written in MACLISP, on the PDP-10a in the Computer Science department at Carnegie-Mellon University. READER has 225 productions, with about 20 of them designed for handling word recognition and lexical access, 30 for surface syntactic analysis, 15 for agreement and other forms of consistency checking, 85 for conceptualizations or case relations, and 75 for schema-level processes. This classification is somewhat arbitrary because some productions are multi-faceted.

THE MECHANISMS OF READING

Word Encoding

The main empirical result to be accounted for is that the gaze duration increased linearly with word length. The proposed mechanism to account for the effect is that the word encoding process operates iteratively on successive parts of a word. READER generates the word length effect because it encodes a word letter by letter, forming chunks and looking for subword units and then for word units to lexically access. A word with more letters will require more encoding cycles, so the time READER spends on a word increases with the length of the word.

It has often been argued that the letters of a word are not encoded sequentially (e.g. Brewer, 1972), but this argument is flawed. The main evidence cited in favor of this argument is that the letters of a word are processed faster than would be predicted by the sum of the processing times for isolated letters (e.g. the word superiority effect). The flaw in the argument is that if there are several ways to recognize letters, then it is fallacious to conclude that the fastest way must necessarily involve parallel recognition of the letters. It is logically possible that letters in words (or perhaps even in pseudowords) are encoded faster than unrelated strings of letters, but still the encoding process can be sequential. Our data and several other studies show an increase in word encoding time with word length that is best accounted for by an iterative encoding process.

The Lexical Access Mechanism

The main empirical constraint on the lexical access mechanism was the word frequency effect, namely that gaze durations decreased linearly with the logarithm of the word's normative frequency. The mechanism READER uses is a combination of a logogen's linear integration and a cell assembly's reverbatory loop. The lexical access process is initiated by the encoded form of a word-percept, which directs activation to the underlying word concept; the concept then starts activating itself (i.e. is both the source and the destination of the directed activation) over successive cycles, such that the added activation on each cycle is proportional to the immediately preceding level of activation. So, if the base level activation were .3, after one cycle of self-activation the level would be $(.3 + .3k)$, where k is some constant. This continues until the concept reaches a fixed threshold that is the same for all words. Each concept in READER's lexicon has a base level of activation that is linearly related to the normative frequency of the corresponding word. Consequently, the number of cycles of self-activation necessary to reach threshold will be a logarithmic function of a word's normative frequency. Thus a mechanism was devised that fits the observed data and makes sense as a psychological process.

Two additional points increase the plausibility of the lexical access mechanism. First, the assumption that the base activation level of a word concept is proportional to its normative frequency is partly motivated by the fact that subjects' ratings of normative frequency are linearly related to objective frequency counts (Tryk, 1968). Thus, subjects seem to possess the information we are inserting in the base activation levels. Also, it is not difficult to imagine how such information could be acquired with experience. Some sort of counting mechanism could keep track of the number of occurrences of a word, and the activation level could reflect that count. The second aspect of the lexical access plausibility is that it chooses between multiple meanings of a word similarly to human subjects (Swinney, 1979). READER initially activates all meanings to a degree, but then chooses the one whose activation level reaches threshold first, and discards (deactivates) the others. The factors that determine which meaning's activation level will reach threshold first are the prior context and relative frequencies of the various meanings. For example, the more frequent meaning of *does* meaning "he does things" would have a higher base activation level than the less frequent "female deer" meaning.

Fitting the Model to Word Length and Frequency Effects

We knew before starting the simulation project that word length and word frequency alone accounted for a large proportion of the variance among the mean gaze durations on each of the words. Since the number of cycles used by READER's word encoding and lexical access mechanisms was linearly related to the corresponding independent variables in the regression equation, READER obviously would provide at least that good a fit. Specifically, the gaze duration increased by 32 msec for each additional letter in a word, and decreased by 31 msec with each log unit increase in frequency, and the READER cycles match this result quantitatively. Evaluating the fit is not a problem for variables or mechanisms treated in this way. First, we look for a mathematical relation between some theoretically motivated independent variable, and then we design a plausible processing mechanism whose performance (i.e. number of CAPS cycles to completion) is described by the mathematical function. We will describe the fitting procedure in slightly greater detail in the later section on multiple regression.

Note also that word length and word frequency have additive effects on gaze duration (Just & Carpenter, this volume). This result suggests that the two processes generally operate sequentially, presumably with lexical access generally following word encoding. Of course other experiments suggest that lexical access might influence word encoding, but the overall additivity of the effects indicates that such top down influence is small or rare or is detrimental as often as it is helpful. READER has the capability of having lexical access affect word encoding, but the top down productions have a high enabling threshold, such that the upper level evidence would have to be very strong before it exercised the downward influence. Although word length and word frequency are correlated (as Zipf, 1965, and others have pointed out), their collinearity does not present a statistical problem. There should be no attempt to determine which variable to keep and which to discard, since they each have their own effect.

READER also spends extra cycles on entirely novel words, scientific terms that most of the subjects had probably never seen before. If the word is not in its lexicon, READER tries first to identify the word by segmenting out subwords, prefixes, and affixes. Thus, READER can identify the plural of a noun or the past tense of a verb even if it never saw that particular variant before. But if these processes fail, READER creates a new word-concept, taking considerable additional cycles. Similarly, the gaze duration of human readers is 686 msec longer on average on novel words, but this effect is particularly variable across the small number of instances and the 14 subjects. Here the fit to the data is simply qualitative, and no serious attempt is made to quantitatively match the number of cycles to the gaze durations.

If the additional time on a novel word results because the reader is creating a new lexical entry, then the next time the reader sees this word the time should be less. The human reading data support this. Processing a novel word the second time is much faster. We also found a more general repetition effect; certain other words were also fixated for less time on the second and subsequent occurrences (Thibadeau et al., 1982). Interestingly, the repetition effect was limited to topical words, like *red fire ant, fluorocarbons, radioisotopes, vitreous humor, Pteranodon, glial cells*. Non-topical words did not show repetition effects. This suggests that the repetition effect is not due entirely to faster encoding, but in part may be due to relating topical words to a schema.

Parsing Processes

A central aspect of comprehension is the parsing process — determining the syntactic and semantic roles and boundaries of sentence constituents. One major approach to parsing both in psychology and in artificial intelligence has been a syntactically oriented one, in which determining the syntactic roles of the words in a sentence constituted the core of comprehension (see Fodor, Bever, & Garrett, 1974; Kimball, 1973; Marcus, 1980). In English, this approach often focuses on word order, particularly function words, suggesting that these words narrow the range of possible roles that an upcoming content word may play. At the other extreme is the semantic approach which emphasizes how the semantic properties of the major constituents plus schematic and pragmatic knowledge will often determine the roles of the constituents in a sentence (e.g. Schank, 1972). For example, a reader can infer the roles of *boy*, *apple*, and *eat* without the benefit of the syntactic information provided by word order. However, neither the syntactic nor the semantic approach alone is entirely satisfactory, and countless studies have shown that all information sources play a role at least some of the time.

It is unfortunately the case that neither the gaze duration data nor any other performance data tell us very much about the nature of human parsing processes. Parsing processes have a clear effect on human performance only if they are extremely difficult, as they are in doubly center-embedded sentences like *The boy the girl the man liked saw cried* or in garden path sentences like *The horse raced past the barn fell*. However, the parsing effects in naturally-occurring texts are generally small, and account for much less of the variance than do the variables that affect encoding and lexical access. This suggests that parsing processes are concurrent with other processes that are longer or more variable in duration, so that parsing effects are not visible under most circumstances. While this is not a large constraint, READER's parsing processes were developed to be consistent with this aspect of the gaze duration data. The number of cycles used by the semantic and syntactic analyses were relatively invariant, compared to the lexical access and word encoding processes. Consequently, they seldom extended the number of cycles needed on a word, and in this sense mimicked the lack of syntactic effects in the gaze duration data. Of course, when a large parsing difficulty is encountered, many cycles can be consumed, but on this particular text, this seldom happens in the gaze durations nor in READER's performance.

READER's syntactic, semantic, and referential analyses collaborate by sharing partial or final analyses. Moreover, a sentence can often be interpreted even if one of the levels of analysis fails. For example, human readers have less difficulty with a syntactically devastating sentence if the conceptual relations among the individual words provide cues to interpretation e.g. *The cow the farmer the dog bit milked mooed* is easier to comprehend than *The boy the girl the man liked saw laughed* (Stolz, 1967). Similarly READER functions without total dependence on any one analysis. The analyses attempt to operate on each new word as soon as it is lexically accessed, so that READER attempts to parse constituents, interpret them, and assign them to referents as soon as possible. It has about 130 productions that constitute the parsing routines for the passage. About 30 of these productions are a "core parser" that is robust over passages. The semantic productions do a conceptual dependency analysis (Schank, 1972), while the syntactic productions analyze the sequential aspects of the surface structure. While READER does not have a complete parser for English, we see no inherent obstacles to expanding READER, while maintaining the qualitative features of its design.

One parsing effect that we did find in the gaze durations on the scientific texts was that readers spent less time on nouns that contained multiple modifiers, such as *red fire ant*. On the first occurrence, readers spent a relatively long time on *ant*; however, on subsequent occurrences, the average gaze duration was considerably shortened. One explanation is that the reader could begin constructing a referent for the noun phrase as soon as one or two modifiers were read, such as the words *red fire*, and it was not necessary to wait for the entire phrase. This strategy differentiates human parsing schemes from those proposed by ATNs. As an ATN grammar processes a constituent, it puts the components on a push-down stack until the end of the constituent is reached, at which point it "pops" the stack and processes the entire constituent. The ATN model would suggest that, if anything, nouns that are modified would take longer, since the reader would process the noun and its modifiers after encountering the noun. However, the reading time data suggest that this hypothesis is incorrect. The simulation and the human readers attempt to process constituents of a noun phrase as soon as possible, sometimes before the head noun is read.

Schemas and Inferential Processes

Comprehension depends only in part on the information provided by the text itself; the reader also uses his or her knowledge of the topic. READER makes use of a schema, a frame and slot structure, to organize the information from the scientific texts. Since READER has been developed to comprehend a scientific exposition, READER's schema is specific to this domain. Nevertheless, the general principles of what kind of information is stored and how it is used may be more widely applicable.

To read a passage, READER uses a schema called Mechanism schema, which specifies the kinds of information a reader expects to find about man-made devices and biological mechanisms as they are used by human or animal agents. The schema consists of slots that specify the general types of information to be expected, and the slots are filled in the course of comprehension. For example, one slot is that of the mechanism's *Name*. Another slot is its *Goals*, which specify the end state that the mechanism is used to achieve. A third slot is for the *Principles* that relate the mechanism's physical properties and actions to its goals. Another slot is the *Exemplar* slot, which contains specific instances of the mechanism. READER attempts to match what it is reading with the schema slots. One way this is done is by making inferences on the basis of the sentence-level representations. For example, if a sentence describes something as a purpose or goal, READER can relate this information to its *Goals* slot. In other cases, READER must make inferences based on probable categories of information and specific cues in the text. Finally, some slots may be filled with default values; if the text does not specify some particular piece of information, READER will assume a likely filler.

Human readers tend to spend different amounts of time on different kinds of information in a schema. For example, we found that readers spend extra time on relatively important pieces of information, like *Names* and *Goals*, relative to *Exemplars*. This is time above and beyond that accounted for by the word-level variables (Just & Carpenter, 1980). The explanation is that readers use this additional time to ensure that such information is correctly encoded and will be accessible in memory for later recall. READER similarly reads more carefully (i.e. with higher thresholds) those segments recognized as *Names* and *Goals* slot fillers. The higher thresholds produce slower reading (i.e. more cycles per word are required for the knowledge growth to reach a higher threshold) and better recall.

As successive words of a text are encountered, they are evaluated as a potential basis for action by all the productions, including those that attempt to fit the new information into schema slots. The schema-level integration actions are evoked as soon as enough of the sentence has been processed to indicate how it fits into the schema. The place where the schema production will be evoked depends on the sentence wording and structure. Sometimes, an entire clause or sentence must be read to determine its relation to the schema. At other times, a word in the middle of a clause will evoke the production. This is consistent with the results that integrative processes sometimes occur at the end of the sentence and at other times within the sentence itself (Carpenter & Just, 1977; Dee-Lucas, Just, Carpenter, & Daneman, in press). There is no attempt to explicitly fit this aspect of the data to the gaze duration data. We assume that the text level analysis is concurrent with a number of other levels, and would extend the processing time on the word only if it required more cycles than any of the other levels. Since any point in the sentence at which text level processing occurs (other than at the end) is idiosyncratic to each sentence, we simply let the total cycle count reflect on the processes, among them text level integration. Generally, READER's text integration processes (at the schema level) extend the number of cycles on the last word of a sentence, matching the human gaze durations in this respect.

In summary, the general characteristics of human reading are compatible with the overall theory of the processing architecture embodied in CAPS, and the specific results we have obtained can be accounted for by the READER model. The immediate, collaborative nature of the processes in READER captures important features of human reading. The scope of the model, from perceptual to schema-level processes is sufficiently broad to accommodate many other temporal properties of human reading. The specific mechanisms of encoding, lexical access, parsing, and integration are compatible with a variety of detailed empirical results obtained in our eye fixation experiments as well as in other types of studies.

THE USE OF MULTIPLE REGRESSION IN THIS APPROACH

One straightforward application of multiple regression is the analysis that compared the number of CAPS cycles on a word to the observed gaze duration. A regression analysis on only the 140 words of the *Flywheels* passage, in which the independent variable is the number of CAPS processing cycles, and the dependent variable is human gaze duration, accounts for 67% of the variance. Much of this fit is attributable to the word encoding and lexical access processes. In the absence of alternative models of this fine grain, it is difficult to evaluate the importance of the 67%. It does provide a benchmark against which other models can be compared, but it is not a very high benchmark, attainable by any model that accounts for word length and word frequency effects. READER does account for these effects, as well as accomplishing the task of understanding, all in an internally consistent and plausible manner.

READER's fit to the data might be improved in a number of ways. First, one simple way is to give READER the ability to sometimes encode a short function word (like *the*, *of*, and *and*) to the right of the current word without fixating it, thereby approximating the frequent (60%) human skipping (non-fixation) of short function words. This probably occurs when the last fixation on the preceding word is close enough to the right boundary of the word to permit parafoveal or peripheral encoding of a short word with a very familiar shape. READER already skips the word *of* sometimes, but not on the basis of peripheral vision.

READER has several free parameters that can be tuned to bring the number of cycles and the gaze duration into closer correspondence. These parameters are the initial activation levels of propositions, the activation weights of productions, (the amount by which a production multiplies the source activation before adding it to the destination activation) and various threshold levels. To the extent that these parameters might correspond to human characteristics that could be independently estimated, such a tuning exercise might be fruitful. However, since we currently have no such independent estimates, the tuning exercise would consist of a search of a large parameter space, with little psychological motivation.

To make the fit a great deal better, we believe it will be necessary to know more about individual readers' prior knowledge of the content area and their reading style, and then to fit a model to their individual data. The READER cycles currently account for 22-46% of the variance in the gaze durations of the individual human subjects. This account would be greatly improved by the ability to process short function words without fixating them, as mentioned above.

Another way of using multiple regression analysis to relate the simulation to the gaze duration data is to develop a regression model whose independent variables can be loosely associated with some of READER's processes. Some of these independent variables have long been known to affect human processing time. For example, it is well known that people take longer to recognize less familiar words, although the exact function relating word frequency and reading time was previously unknown. Other variables came to light when READER's performance suggested particular loci of processing ease or difficulty. For example, READER's performance suggested that the length of a noun phrase might affect the time spent on a head noun, and indeed the regression analysis showed that the gaze duration on the head noun decreased by 10 msec with each additional modifier. Similarly, READER's performance led to the finding that there is extra time spent on the first occurrence of the word that designates the passage topic.

The interpretation of the regression results must take into account the postulated concurrent execution of certain processes. READER performs some processes in sequence (e.g. word encoding followed by lexical access) and in those cases the interpretation of the regression results is straightforward. The regression weight indicates the amount of extra processing time per stimulus unit, such as the time to encode another letter. For concurrent processes, a reliable regression weight means that when that process occurs, the gaze duration is longer (or shorter), but the magnitude of the regression weight does not directly correspond to the duration of the process. For example, the regression analysis shows that the first mention of a topic is gazed at for an extra 183 msec, but we cannot conclude that the extra processes associated with such words take 183 msec to be executed. If they are concurrent, they could take much more time to be executed, but only the last 183 msec might extend beyond the execution of other processes.

The regression analysis that incorporates the independent variables suggested by READER's performance provides a somewhat better fit (an increase of 7% in R-squared) than the original regression equation (see Thibadeau et al. 1982, for a detailed comparison). Moreover, the improved regression equation provides a better fit not only to the data from the *Flywheels* passage READER processed, but to the entire set of mean gaze durations on the 1936 words in all 15 passages. But the main appeal of the current regression equation is that the independent variables are grounded in processing characteristics existing in an explicit process model.

SUMMARY

This chapter describes some of our attempts at relating a complex simulation model to detailed human performance data. Conventional questions about goodness of fit seem inappropriate because the model was constructed to fit these data, using plausible mechanisms sufficient to perform the task. An example of this is READER's lexical access mechanism, whose number of cycles to reach threshold is a logarithmic function of a word's frequency. Of course the model fits the data in this regard. In other cases, a qualitative property of the processing was inferred from the eye fixation data using conventional statistical techniques, and then that property was made an inherent part of the model. For example, the results reported by Just and Carpenter in this volume indicate that interpretation is immediate, and so immediacy was a design feature of the model, with no further necessity for model fitting with regard to this property. With this approach to constructing a simulation, the question is not so much "How well does the model fit the data?" but "Given that the theory-building was considerably constrained by the data, what kind of model emerged?"

ACKNOWLEDGMENT

This research was partially supported by Grant MH-29617 from the National Institute of Mental Health and Grant N-00014-82-C-0027 from the Office of Naval Research. The chapter was written while the first author was a Fellow at the Netherlands Institute for Advanced Study.

REFERENCES

Brewer, W. F. Is reading a letter-by-letter process? In J. F. Kavanaugh & I. G. Mattingly (Eds.), *Language by eye and ear*. Cambridge, MA: MIT Press, 1972.

Carpenter, P. A., & Just, M. A. Reading comprehension as eyes see it. In M. A. Just & P. A. Carpenter (Eds.), *Cognitive processes in comprehension*. Hillsdale, N. J.: Lawrence Erlbaum Associates, 1977.

Dee-Lucas, D., Just, M. A., Carpenter, P. A., & Daneman, M. What eye fixations tell us about the time course of text integration. In R. Groner & P. Fraisse (Eds.), *Cognition and eye movements*. Amsterdam: North Holland, and Berlin: Deutscher Verlag der Wissenschaften, in press.

Fodor, J. T., Bever, T., & Garrett, M. *The psychology of language*. New York: McGraw-Hill, 1974.

Just, M. A., & Carpenter, P. A. A theory of reading: From eye fixations to comprehension. *Psychological Review*, 1980, *87*, 329-354.

Kimball, J. P. Seven principles of surface structure parsing in natural language. *Cognition*, 1973, *2*, 15-47.

Lamb, S. *An outline of stratificational grammar*. Washington, D. C.: Georgetown University Press, 1966.

Marcus, M. *Theory of syntactic recognition for natural language*. Cambridge, MA: MIT Press, 1980.

Newell, A. Harpy, production systems and human cognition. In R. Cole (Ed.), *Perception and production of fluent speech*. Hillsdale, N. J.: Lawrence Erlbaum Associates, 1980.

Newell, A. Production systems: Models of control structures. In W. G. Chase (Ed.), *Visual information processing*. New York: Academic Press, 1973.

Newell, A., & Simon, H. A. *Human problem solving*. Englewood Cliffs, N. J.: Prentice-Hall, Inc., 1972.

Schank, R. C. Conceptual dependency: A theory of natural understanding. *Cognitive Psychology*, 1972, *3*, 552-631.

Stolz, W. A. A study of the ability to decode grammatically novel sentences. *Journal of Verbal Learning and Verbal Behavior*, 1967, *6*, 867-873.

Swinney, D. A. Lexical access during sentence comprehension: (Re)consideration of context effects. *Journal of Verbal Learning and Verbal Behavior*, 1979, *18*, 645-659.

Thibadeau, R. H., Just, M. A., & Carpenter, P. A. A model of the time course and content of reading. *Cognitive Science*, 1982, *6*, 157-203.

Tryk, H. E. Subjective scaling and word frequency. *American Journal of Psychology*, 1968, *81*, 170-177.

Zipf, G. K. *The psycho-biology of language*. Cambridge, MA: MIT Press, 1965.

AUTHOR INDEX

Numbers in *italics* indicate pages with bibliographic information.

A

Aaronson, D. A., 9, 33, 38, 40, 42, 43, 45, 50, 58, 64, 65, *66*, *67*, 74, *87*, 98, 99, 109, *116*, 164, *179*, 212, *215*, 220, 221, 233, 234, 244, *248*, *249*
Abelson, R. P., 84, *88*, 191, *218*, 245, *250*, 289, *297*
Ainsfeld, M., 55, *66*
Anderson, J. R., 55, *66*, 313, *324*
Anderson, P. A., 191, *216*, *249*
Anderson, R. C., 184, 189, *217*, 309, *324*
Anglin, J. M., 40, *66*
Anisfeld, M., *66*
Arwas, R., 111, *116*
Asher, S. R., 189, *215*

B

Baddeley, A. D., 110, 113, *116*, 178, *179*
Bain, W. M., 345, *347*
Balota, D. A., 101, *116*
Baron, J., 49, *66*
Bartlett, F. C., 40, *66*, 239, 240, *248*, 261, *285*
Bates, E., 337, 338, *346*
Begg, I., 40, *66*

Bent, D. H., 14, *29*, 193, *217*
Bentler, P. M., 193, 214, *215*
Bereiter, C., 281, *286*
Berian, C., 40, 41, 42, *67*, 193, 205, *216*, 226, 232, 244, 245, 246, *249*
Bertera, J. H., 100, 101, *118*
Bever, T. G., 51, 55, *66*, 144, 145, *149*, 167, *180*, 358, *364*
Bingham, G., 221, *225*, *249*
Birnbaum, L. A., 333, 345, *347*
Bisanz, G. L., 190, 191, *215*
Black, J. B., 189, *215*, 221, 224, 225, 245, 246, *248*, 289, 290, 291, 294, 295, *297*
Blackman, H. S., 225, 246, *251*
Blalock, H. M., 24, *29*
Blanchard, H. F., 101, *117*, 158, *180*
Bloom, P. A., 80, 81, *87*, 94, 96, 108, *116*
Blumenthal, A. L., 147, *149*
Bobrow, D., 210, *217*
Bouma, H., 47, *66*, 71, *87*, 131, *149*, 158, 168, *180*
Bovair, S., 189, *215*, 308, 321, 323, *325*, 329, 331, *346*
Bower, G. H., 55, *66*, 221, 224, *248*, 300, 301, *325*
Bransford, J. D., 85, *87*, 102, *116*, 281, *285*
Brauth, S., 38, *66*

365

Brehmer, B., 28, *29*
Brewer, W. F., 245, *248*, 356, *363*
Britton, B. K., 190, *215*
Brooks, R. J., 113, *117*
Brown, A. L., 281, *285*
Brown, E., 98, *117*
Brown J. S., 260, *285*
Brown, M. B., 14, *29*
Bush, R. R., 64, *66*

C

Campione, J. C., 281, *285*
Caramazza, A., 225, *248*
Carey, P., 144, 145, *149*
Carlson, M., 132, 146, *150*
Carmines, E. G., *29*
Carpenter, E., 94, 108, *117*
Carpenter, P. A., 9, 38, 39, 40, 42, 46, 47, 50, 67, 71, 79, 80, 86, *87*, *88*, 93, 98, 99, 105, 106, 109, *117*, 132, 134, 142, *149*, 154, 155, 157, 162, 163, 165, 166, 169, 170, 171, 173, 174, 177, 178, 179, *180*, 188, 189, 191, 210, 211, 212, 214, *215*, *216*, 220, 221, 223, 225, 233, 234-235, 242, 244, 245, 246, *248*, *249*, *250*, 300, 304, 305, 307, *324*, *325*, 332, 349, 350, 357, 358, 360, 361, 363, *363*, *364*,
Carr, T. H., 97, *116*
Carroll, J., 35, *66*, 280, *286*
Carroll, J. M., 280, *285*
Carroll, P. J., 132, 140-142, *149*
Carter, D. S., 25, *29*
Carter, L. F., 24, *29*
Chandler, J. P., 50, *66*
Chandler, P. J., 330, *346*
Chen, H. C., 92, 93, 94, 95, 100, 104, 106, 111, 114, *116*
Chiesi, H. L., 192, *218*
Cirilo, R. K., 225, 232, 245, 246, *248*
Clark, E. V., 45, 49, *67*
Clark, H. H., 45, 49, 55, *66*, *67*, 189, 191, *215*, 220, 239, *248*, *249*, 310, *325*, 337, *346*
Clark, L. F., 143, *149*, 185, 191, 211, *216*, 225, 226, 230, 232, 233, 244, 246, *249*
Cocklin, T., 92, 93, 94, 100, *116*
Cohen, A. D., 185, 187, 210, 211, *216*
Cohen, J., 13, 14, 16, 23, *29*, 226, 227-228, 240, *248*
Cohen, P., 13, 14, 16, 23, *29*, 226, 227-228, 240, *248*

Collins, A., 260, *285*
Curry, C., 190, *215*
Curtis, M. E., 210, 211, *216*, *217*, 225, *250*
Cutler, A., 246, *248*

D

Dagenbach, D., 97, *116*
Daneman, M., 154, 171, 177, 178, *180*, 245, *248*, 361, *364*
Danks, J. H., 220, 225, 230, *248*
Darlington, R. B., 16, *29*
Davidson, B. J., 148, *149*, 309, *325*, 332, *346*
Davies, P., 35, *66*
Dawes, R., 261, *285*
Dawes, R. M., 239, *248*
Dee-Lucas, D., 169, 177, *180*, 223, 225, 245, 246, *248*, 361, *364*
Dell, G., 120, 127, *127*
deVoogd, A. H., 47, *66*, 71, *87*, 131, 149, 168, *180*
Dixon, W. J., 14, *29*
Dommergues, J. Y., 95, 106, 108, *116*, *118*
Dooling, D. J., 243, *250*
Drewnowski, A., 213, *216*
Dreyfus, H. L., 345, *346*
Duffy, S. A., 191, *217*, 246, *250*, 253, 256, 258, 259, 261, 265, 267, 272, 279, 283, *286*
Dumais, S. T., 210, 211, *218*
Dwyer, J. H., 6, *11*

E

Eaton, M. E., 279, *286*
Eddy, J. K., 190, *216*
Ehrlich, K., 80, *87*, 132, 134, 136-140, 142, *149*
Ehrlich, S. F., 107, *116*, *149*
Eimas, P. D., 83, *89*
Engelman, L., 14, *29*
Ericsson, K. A., 254, 260, 281, 284, *285*, 294, *297*
Eriksen, C. W., 97, *116*

F

Ferrara, R. A., 281, *285*
Ferres, S., 40, 42, 43, 45, 50, 55, 64, 65, *66*, *67*, 74, *87*, 244, *249*

Fischler, I., 80, 81, *87*, 94, 96, 108, *116*
Fletcher, C. R., 332, 333, 337, *346*
Foder, J. A., 167, *180*
Foder, J. T., 358, *364*
Forster, K. I., 69, 70, 80, 84, *87*, 92, 93, 94, 95, 96, 97, 98, 106, 107, 110, 111, *116*
Forsyth, D., 38
Foss, D. J., 136, *149*, 188, *216*, 225, 232, 245, 246, *248*
Francis, W. N., 35, 44, *67*, 188, *216*
Frane, J. W., 14, *29*
Frauenfelder, U., 95, 107, 108, *116*, *118*
Frazier, L., 132, 144, 145, 146, *149*, 245, *249*
Frederiksen, C. H., 239, *249*
Frederiksen, J. R., 49, *67*
French, P., 94, 107, 111, *116*

G

Galambos, J. A., 292, 294, *297*
Galanter, E., 64, *66*
Garrett, M. F., 111, *116*, 167, *180*, 358, *364*
Garrod, S. C., 190, *218*, 225, *250*
Garvey, C., 225, *248*
Gibson, E. J., 46, 52, *67*
Givon, T., 337, *346*
Glanzer, M., 40, *67*
Glass, A. L., 190, *216*
Glenn, G. G., 193, *218*, 221-222, *250*
Gold, C., 82, *89*
Goldman, S. R., 83, *88*
Goldstein, S., 31*n*
Goodman, K. S., 84, *88*
Goodman, S. M., 191, *216*
Gordon, R. A., 16, *29*
Gough, P. B., 212, *216*
Gowie, C. J., 51, *67*
Graesser, A. C., 10, 41, 42, 51, *67*, 99, 143, *149*, 185, 187, 189, 191, 196, 205, 210, 211, *216*, 220, 221, 225, 226, 230, 232, 233, 240, 241, 244, 246, *249*, 259, *285*, 292, *297*
Granaas, M., 92, 93, 94, 100, *116*
Grant, D. A., 8, *11*
Green, D. W., 42, *67*, 69, 70, 71, 74, 75, 83, 84, 85, 86, *88*, 106, *117*, 188, 205, *217*, 221, 225, 234, 244, *250*
Greene, E., 329, 331, *347*
Grober, E., 225, *248*

H

Haberlandt, K., 9, 40, 41, 42, *67*, 99, 193, 205, *216*, 221, 224, 225, 226, 232, 244, 245, 246, *249*
Hammond, E. J., 85, *88*
Hammond, K. R., 28, *29*
Harris, C., 70, 79, *88*, 94, 95, 97, 98, 100, 102, 106, 110, 114, *118*, 213, *217*
Harris, R. J., 25, *29*
Hauft-Smith, K., 185, 187, 210, 211, *216*
Haviland, S. E., 220, *249*, 310, *325*, 337, *346*
Hays, W. L., 6, *11*
Healy, A. F., 213, *216*
Hilgard, E. R., 300, 301, *325*
Hill, M. A., 14, *29*
Hintzman, D. L., 303, *325*
Hitch, G., 178, *179*
Hochberg, J., 45, *67*
Hoffman, N. L., 143, *149*, 185, 191, 211, *216*, 220, 225, 226, 230, 232, 233, 244, 246, *249*
Hogaboam, T. W., 45, 46, 47, *67*, 83, *88*, 130, 148, *149*, 220, 221, *249*, *250*
Holdredge, T. S., 190, *215*
Holmes, V. M., 94, 111, *116*, 132, 143, 144, *149*, 190, *216*
Hornak, R., 48, *68*
Huang, D. S., 16, *29*
Huey, E. B., 52, *67*, 129, *149*
Hull, C. H., 14, *29*, 193, *217*
Hunt, E., 178, *180*, 212, *216*

I

Inhoff, A. W., 100, *118*, 134-136, *149*

J

James, W., 327, *346*
Jarvella, R. J., 179, *180*
Jenkins, J. G., 14, *29*, 193, *217*
Jennrich, R. I., 14, *29*
Johnson, M. K., 85, *87*, 102, *116*
Johnson, N. S., 193, *217*, 221, 222, *250*
Johnson, S. C., 290, *297*
Johnson, W., 190, *216*, 244, 246, *249*, 309, 318, 319, 321, *325*
Johnson-Laird, P. N., 40, *67*
Joreskog, K. G., 193, 214, *216*
Juola, J. F., 92, 93, 94, 96, 100, 104, 107, 109, 114, *116*, *118*

Just, M. A., 9, 38, 39, 40, 42, 46, 47, 49, *67*, 71, 79, 80, 86, *87*, *88*, 93, 98, 99, 105, 106, 109, *117*, 132, 134, 142, *149*, 154, 155, 157, 162, 163, 165, 166, 169, 170, 174, 177, 178, *180*, 188, 189, 191, 205, 210, 211, 212, 213, 214, *215*, *216*, 220, 221, 223, 225, 234-235, 242, 244, 245, 246, *248*, *249*, *250*, 300, 304, 305, 307, *324*, *325*, 332, 349, 350, 357, 358, 360, 361, 363, *364*

K

Kahneman, D., 210, *216*
Kanwisher, 94, 95
Keenan, J., 98, *117*, *216*, 220, 225, *249*
Keenan, J. M., 187, 190, *216*, 225, 230, *249*
Kellas, G., 234, *250*
Kennedy, R. A., 40, *68*
Kenny, D. A., 193, 214, *216*
Keppel, G., 228, *249*
Kerlinger, F. N., 13, 16, 20, 25, *29*, 228, *249*
Kieras, D. E., 9, 41, 99, 189, 190, 192, 205, 210, 214, *215*, *216*, 220, 221, 225, 226, 244, 246, 249, 299, 300, 305, 308, 309, 310, 311, 313, 314, 318, 319, 321, 323, *325*, 329, 331
Kimball, J. P., 167, *180*, 358, *364*
Kintsch, W., 98, *117*, 187, 189, 190, 192, 210, *216*, *217*, 220, 225, 226, 230, 245, *249*, 253, 281, *285*, 300, 304, 305, *325*, 328, 329, 331, 337, 341, 342, *346*, *347*
Klein, G. A., 144, *149*
Klein, L. R., 17, *29*
Kleinman, G. M., 49, *67*, 83, *88*, 225, *250*
Klenbort, I., 55, *66*
Kliegel, R., 148, *149*, 309, *325*, 332, *346*
Knight, G. P., 183, 308, 309
Kolers, P. A., 131, *149*
Koury, G., 98, *118*
Kozminsky, E., 98, *117*, 187, 190, *216*, 225, 230, *249*
Kroll, J. F., 49, *67*, 70, 79, *88*, 94, 95, 97, 98, 100, 101, 102, 105, 106, 107, 110, 112, 113, 114, *117*, *118*, 213, *217*
Kucera, H., 35, 44, *67*, 188, *216*
Kurkowski, F., 144, *149*

L

LaBerge, D., 210, 212, *216*, *218*
Lamb, S., 353, *364*
Landauer, T. K., 113, *117*

Langford, J., 190, *216*
Larkin, K. M., 260, *285*
Lawrence, D. H., 96, *117*
Lebowitz, M., 333, 345, *347*
Lehnert, W. G., 189, *215*, 289-290, 291, *297*, 333, 345, *346*, *347*
Lesgold, A. M., 45, *67*, 210, 211, 213, *216*, *217*, 225, *250*
Levin, H., 46, 52, *67*
Levy, B. A., 49, *67*, 213, *217*
Levy, E. I., 101, *118*
Lewis, C., 279-280, *285*, *286*
Lewis, J., 212, *216*
Lewis V. J., 110, 113, *116*
Li, C .C., 20, *29*
Lovelace, E. A., 101, 113, *117*
Lucas, P. A., 45, *67*, 130, *149*, 221, *250*
Luce, R. D., 64, *66*
Lunneborg, C., 212, *216*

M

Mack, R. L., 191, *217*, 246, *250*, 253, 258, 259, 261, 265, 267, 272, 279-280, 283, *285*, *286*
MacWhinney, B., 337, 338, *346*
Macworth, N. H., 158, *180*
Mandler, G., 51, *67*
Mandler, J. M., 193, *217*, 221, 222, *250*
Manelis, L., 220, 230, *250*
Marcel, T., 97, *117*
Marcus, M., 358, *364*
Marcus, M. P., 110, *117*, 167, *180*
Markowitz, N., 109, *116*
Marslen-Wilson, W. D., 213, *217*
Masson, M., *180*, 246, *249*
Masson, M. E. J., 94, 95, 96, 98, 104, 114, *117*
McClelland, J. L., 212, 214, *217*, *218*, 333, *347*
McConkie, G. W., 45, 46, 47, *67*, *68*, 79, 83n, *88*, 101, *117*, 130, 136, 137, *149*, *150*, 158, 161, *180*, 220, 221, *249*, *250*
McDonald, J. L., 154, 169, 173, *180*
McFarland, C. E., 234, *250*
McKean, K. O., 220, *250*
McKeen, O. K., 40, *67*
McKillop, B. J., 49, *66*
McKoon, G., 98, *117*, 120, 123, 126, *127*, *128*, 187, 190, *216*, 220, 225, 230, *249*, *250*
McNamara, T., 92, 93, 94, 96, 100, 104, 107, 114, *116*
Mehler, J., 95, 108, 106, *116*, *118*, 144, 145, *149*
Merikle, P. M., 97, *117*

AUTHOR INDEX 369

Miller, G. A., 40, 45, 66, 67, 220, 250, 327, 347
Miller, J. R., 192, 217, 305, 325, 328, 329, 331, 333, 336n, 337, 341, 342, 347
Miron, M., 98, 117
Mitchell, D. C., 9, 31n, 39, 42, 67, 69, 70, 71, 73, 74, 75, 77, 78, 79, 80, 83, 84, 85, 86, 88, 98, 99, 100, 104, 106, 108, 109, 117, 188, 205, 217, 221, 225, 234, 244, 250
Mood, A. M., 20, 29
Morrison, R. E., 100, 118
Morton, J., 82, 88, 188, 217

N

Neisser, U., 255, 286, 288, 289, 296, 297
Newell, A., 212, 217, 253, 284, 286, 302, 304, 325, 350, 351, 364
Nicholas, D. W., 241, 251
Nie, N. H., 14, 29, 193, 217
Nisbett, R. E., 254, 286, 294, 297
Norman, D. A., 189, 210, 217, 288, 297
Nunnally, J. C., 23, 24, 29

O

Olbrei, I., 111, 116
Olkin, I., 25, 29
Olson, G. M., 9, 10, 191, 217, 245, 250, 253, 256, 258, 259, 261, 265, 267, 272, 279, 283, 286
Olson, R. K., 148, 149, 309, 325, 332, 346
Omanson, R. C., 241, 250
O'Regan, J. K., 132, 143, 144, 145, 149

P

Paivio, A., 40, 66, 225, 250
Patkau, J. E., 40, 68
Paul, I. H., 239, 250
Pedhazur, E. J., 13, 14, 16, 20, 24, 25, 26, 29, 228, 240, 249, 250, 309, 325
Perfetti, C. A., 83, 88, 210, 211, 213, 217
Petrick, M. S., 94, 95, 96, 108, 110, 114, 117
Pfafflin, S. M., 94, 98, 107, 117
Pollatsek, A., 80, 88, 96, 101, 118, 132, 150
Posner, M. I., 123, 127, 210, 211, 217
Potter, M. C., 9, 70, 79, 88, 94, 95, 96, 97, 98, 100, 101, 102, 105, 106, 107, 108, 109, 110, 111, 112, 113, 114, 117, 118, 213

Powell, C. M., 113, 117
Powers, J. W., 51, 67
Pratt, J. W., 25, 29
Purcell, D. G., 97, 118
Pyles, L. D., 185, 187, 210, 211, 216

R

Ratcliff, R., 120, 123, 126, 127, 127, 128, 220, 250
Rayner, K., 9, 42, 45, 46, 67, 68, 79, 80, 87, 88, 96, 100, 101, 107, 116, 118, 130, 131, 132, 134, 136-140, 137, 142, 144, 145, 146, 149, 150, 158, 161, 170, 180, 181, 220, 225, 244, 245, 249, 250,
Razel, M., 40, 67
Reddy, R., 212, 213, 214, 217
Reiser, B. J., 289, 290, 291, 297
Reynolds, R. E., 184, 217
Richman, B., 35, 66
Riha, J. R., 99
Rips, L. J., 292, 297
Robertson, S. P., 191, 216, 249
Rosch, E., 140, 150
Roth, S., 211, 213, 217
Roth, S. F., 210, 217, 225, 250
Rubin, D. C., 246, 250, 300, 325
Rucci, A. J., 4, 5, 11
Rumelhart, D. E., 84, 88, 188, 189, 193, 210, 212, 213, 214, 217, 218, 221, 250, 259, 286, 333, 347
Ryder, L. A., 94, 97, 111, 116

S

Samuels, S. L., 210, 212, 216
Sanders, E., 48, 68
Sandson, J., 40, 41, 42, 67, 193, 205, 216, 226, 232, 244, 245, 246, 249
Sanford, A. J., 190, 218, 225, 250
Sapir, E., 49, 68
Scarborough, D. L., 109, 118
Scarborough, H. S., 42, 58, 66, 164, 179, 212, 215, 220, 221, 233, 234, 248, 249
Scardamalia, M., 281, 286
Schank, R. C., 84, 88, 191, 218, 238-239, 245, 250, 288, 289, 297, 300, 325, 333, 345, 347, 354, 358, 359, 364
Schneider, W., 122, 128, 210, 211, 218
Schuberth, R. E., 83, 89

AUTHOR INDEX

Schwartz, S. P., 189, *215*
Sechrest, L., 176, *181*
Segui, J., 95, 106, 108, *116, 118*
Selfridge, O. G., 212, *218*
Shaffer, W. O., 210, *218*
Shapiro, H., 109, *116*
Sharkey, N. E., 71, 74, 81, *88*
Sherak, R., 31*n*, 39
Sherman, J., 94, 98, 100, 101, 105, *118*
Shiffrin, R. M., 210, 211, *218*
Shiffrin, R., 122, *128*
Shulman, H. G., 6, 48, *68*
Simon, H. A., 253, 254, 260, 281, 284, *285, 286*, 294, *297*, 302, 304, *325*, 334, *347*, 350, *364*
Simpson, G. B., 172, *181*
Slowiaczek, M. L., 100, *118*
Smith, E. E., 212, *218*, 300, *325*
Smith, F., 49, *68*
Snodgrass, G. S., 49, *68*
Snyder, S., 123
Sorbom, D., 193, 214, *216*
Southall, S. D., 101, *117*
Spilich, G. J., 192, *218*
Spoehr, K. T., 49, *68*, 212, *218*
Stanovich, K. E., 83, *89*, 97, *118*, 126, *128*
Stein, N. L., 193, *218*, 221-222, *250*
Steinbrenner, K., 14, *29*, 193, *217*
Steinmann, D. O., 28, *29*
Sternberg, S., 5, *11*, 53, *68*, 84, *89*, 109, *118*, 299, 305, *325*
Stevens, A., 188, 189, *218*
Stewart, A. L., 97, *118*
Stewart, T. R., 28, *29*
Sticht, T. G., 98, *118*
Stolz, W. A., 359, *364*
Streby, W. J., 98, *117*, 187, 190, *216*, 225, 230, *249*
Sulin, R. A., 243, *250*
Swinney, D. A., 96, *118*, 126, *128*, 172, *181*, 357, *364*
Synder, C. R., 210, *217*
Synder, S., 123, *127*

T

Taft, M., 49, *68*
Thibadeau, R. H., 210, 213, 214, 221, 225, 242, *250*, 305, 307, *325*, 349, 358, 363, *364*

Thorndyke, P. W., 193, *218*, 222, 225, *250, 251*, 261, *286*
Tinker, M., 154, *181*
Toporek, J. D., 14, *29*
Townsend, J. T., 49, *68*
Trabasso, T., 241, *251*
Tryk, H. E., 245, *251*, 356, *364*
Tulving, E., 40, *68*, 82, *89*
Turner, A., 329, 331, *347*
Turner, T. J., 221, 224, *248*
Tweney, R. D., 4, 5, *11*

V

Vanacek, E., 134, *150*
van Dijk, T. A., 192, 193, 210, *216, 218*, 245, *249*, 253, 281, *285*, 304, 321, *325*, 328, 329, *346*
Vesonder, G. T., 192, *218*
Vincent, P., 279, *286*
Vipond, D., 192, *218*, 281, *285*
Voss, J. F., 190, 191, 192, *215, 218*

W

Walker, C. H., 225, 246, *251*
Wallace, W. P., 98, *118*
Wanat, S., 143, 144, *150*
Ward, N. J., 92, 93, 94, 96, 100, 104, 107, 109, 114, *116, 118*
Warren, R. E., 211, *217*
Warren, W. H., 241, *251*
Weinberg, E., *117*
Weisberg, S., 228, 240, *251*
Well, A. D., 101, *118*
Wells, C. S., 24, *29*
Welsh, A., 213, *217*
West, R. F., 126, *128*
Westbrook, R. D., 190, *215*
Wherry, R. J., 25, *29*
Whorf, B., 3
Wilensky, R. A., 238-239, *250*
Wilkes, A. L., 40, *68*
Wilkes-Gibbs, D., 295, *297*
Wilson T. D., 254, *286*, 294, *297*
Winer, B. J., 228, *251*
Wisher, R. A., 225, *251*
Wolverton, G. S., 45, *67*, 101, *117*, 130, *149*, 158, *180*, 221, *250*
Woods, W., 188, *218*

Woolley, J., 39, 40, *67*
Woolley, J. D., 98, *117, 180,* 220, 221, 225, 233, 246, *249*
Wright, S., 20, *29*

Y

Yachzel, B., 94, 98, 100, 101, 105, 106, 107, 113, *118*
Yarbus, A. L., 166, *181*

Yates, J., 225, *248*
Yeaton, W. E., 176, *181*
Yekovich, F. R., 220, 225, 230, 246, *250, 251*

Z

Zeller, R. A., 24, *29*
Zipf, G. K., 357, *364*
Zola, D., 45, *67,* 83n, *88,* 101, *117,* 130, 132, 136, 137, *149, 150,* 158, *180,* 221, *250*

SUBJECT INDEX

A

Action-enablement, 293
Activation, 119–127
Active verbs, 55
Additivity, 50, 53, 62–63, 305, 307
Adjusted squared multiple correlation, 25
Age, 33–34, 44, 50, 56
Aggregate, 155
Ambiguous sentences, 144–146
Ambiguous word, 111–112
Analysis of variance, 4–6
Anomalous material, 74
Anomaly effects, 84
Anaphoric reference, 120–122, 142
Artificial intelligence, 300, 303, 307, 323
Assumptions, 219–222, 228, 233
Attenuation, 23
Augmented clustering, 288–290, 293, 296
Augmented transition network (ATN), 188, 192, 313–314, 323, 359
Automatic processes, 122–125, 210–211, 213

B

Beta weights, 15, 200–202, 213
Between-subject variability, 304, 309
Blackboard, 212
Bottom-up models, 212
Boundary effect, 226, 231–232
Boundary hypothesis, 222–223, 226, 231
Buffer, in reading, 93, 105–107, 109–110
Buffer control hypothesis, 71–72, 74, 77–80
Button-pressing experiments, 81

C

Canonical correlation, 28
CAPS, 349–350, 352–355, 361
Casual hypotheses, 20
Casual modeling, 22, 193, 214
Child reading, 33, 35, 40, 44, 49–61, 64–65, 233, 240
Chronometric paradigms, 9–10
Cluster analysis, 28
Code, 234, 237, 240, 242
Coding, 50–54, 56, 60–61, 63, 65
Cognitive lag hypothesis, 132
Cognitive psychology, 300–301
Coherence, 310, 329, 332
Coherence graph, 329, 332–334, 336, 345
Collapsed data, 309, 314, 320
Collinearity, 14, 16–17, 193, 195–197, 308
Commonality, 19–20, 196
Components, 210–214
Components of processing, 125
Comprehension, 33, 37, 43, 50–57, 65, 94–95, 98, 100, 102–104, 106, 109–111, 113, 130, 134, 147, 183–184, 186, 190–192, 206–210, 214–215

373

374 SUBJECT INDEX

Comprehension problems, 184
Comprehension process, 259, 265, 279, 283–284
Comprehension task, 54, 64
Compressed speech, 98
Computers, 31–32, 38, 41, 61, 301, 306
Computer simulation, 300–301, 346
Computer text editing, 279
Conceptual focus, 337–338, 340
Content analysis, 245, 290, 293
Content words, 43, 46, 54, 57, 64
Context effects, 134, 137, 140
Contextual information, 82
Consolidation, 110–111, 114
Criterion scaling, 26
Cross-validation, 18, 25
Cue deletion hypotheses, 85–86

D

Deterministic simulation models, 302–304, 306–308
Differences between stories, 219, 239, 240, 242–243
Direct control, 71–74, 77–80
Discovering hypotheses, 288–289
Discovery, 287–292, 294–297
Discovery methodology, 288, 297
Discovery-then-verification, 296
Discriminant function analysis, 15, 28
Distinctiveness, 294
Double cross-validation, 25–26
Dummy variable, 14–15, 26–27

E

Ecological validity, 72, 296
Effect, 227–228, 235, 237, 239
Effect size, 176–177, 228
Effect-size question, 6
Enablement, 293
Encoding, 361
End-of-sentence effects, 85–87, 177–179, 234, 244
Error detection, 151, 171, 176
Error recovery, 160, 170–173, 176–177
Essays, 256, 261, 267–269, 272–274, 281–284
Evaluating simulations, 301
Expectations, 188, 190–191, 289

Exponential transformations, 201
Expository prose, 185, 190–191, 193, 202, 209
Eye fixations, 130–135, 137–140, 142–146, 148, 151–156, 159, 162–164, 171–174, 179
Eye-mind assumption, 47, 71, 131–132, 169–170
Eye-monitoring, 71, 79, 81
Eye movements, 91, 99–101, 107, 115, 129–138, 140, 142–148, 205
Eye movement recording systems, 129, 133
Eye movement time, 125
Eye-voice span, 171

F

Factor analysis, 17, 193
Familiarity, 186, 190, 195, 197, 200, 204–205, 207, 209, 211, 214, 241–242, 244–245, 247
Fast readers, 31, 34, 40, 50, 59–60
Focussed instructions, 258
Frequency, 35, 44, 210, 226, 235, 237, 242
Function words, 43, 64
Functional linguistics, 337

G

Gaze duration, 80, 93, 154–156, 158–164, 166, 168–170, 174, 176
General instructions, 258
Gist, 331, 335, 341–342
Given references, 310–311, 313
Goals, 211, 290, 292, 295
Goodness-of-fit, 301, 304–305, 307

H

Hierarchy, 212

I

Idea units, 94, 100
Imagery, 186, 190, 195, 197, 200–202, 204–205, 207, 209
Immediacy, 46, 132, 151, 164, 166–171, 173, 177
Importance, 258, 275–277
Independence, 63–65

SUBJECT INDEX   375

Independent variables, 224–231, 233–234, 242–243, 246–247
Individual differences, 151, 178
Individual reader, 245–247
Inference, 190–191, 287
Information processing models, 47
Instructions, 282, 284
Integration, 59–63, 85, 299–300, 310–313, 316
Interaction, 201–202, 212, 214
Interactive models, 212–214
Interestingness, 186, 189–191, 195, 197, 200–201, 204–205, 207–208

K

Knowledge structures, 333–341, 343, 345

L

Latent variables, 193, 195, 214
Leading edge strategy, 329, 332–333
Letters, 186–187, 193, 195–196, 210–212
Level of aggregation, 155
Lexical access, 242, 352, 354–357, 359, 361–363
Lexical decision, 71, 81–84, 96, 108, 119, 126
Lexical processing, 31–37, 42, 48, 50, 52, 61, 65
Linear assumptions, 201
Linear model, 304, 306–307
Linearity, 61
Linguistic attributes, 40, 49
Linguistic influences on picture scanning, 165
Linguistic variables, 32, 34, 36, 63
LISP, 301
Listening, 91, 95, 98, 101, 103, 115
Logarithmic transformation, 201
Long-term memory, 327, 329, 332, 334–335, 339

M

Macroprocesses, 328, 333–336, 339–340
Macrostructure, 192, 308, 321–322, 336
Main idea, 310, 321–322
Mask, 93–94
Masking, 91, 97, 100
Mathematical models, 328

Mean gaze duration, 159, 161, 169, 174–175
Mean reading times, 240, 309, 314, 323
Meaning processing, 49, 51–53, 55–56, 60–64
Measurement error, 22–24
Memory, 95–96, 102, 109–111, 287, 289, 293, 335
Memory load, 192
Memory search, 299, 301, 307, 312–314, 316, 319
Message center, 212–213
Metacognitive awareness, 281
Methodologies, 288, 295–296
Methods, 287–288, 292, 296
Micropropositional processes, 328
Microstructure, 192
Model, 47–50, 52–56, 59–64, 212, 256
Model fitting, 8
Moving window paradigm, 162–164, 174, 177
Multi-agent hypothesis, 241
Multicollinearity, 16–17, 197–198, 226
Multiple correlation, 15–16, 23–26
Multiple-observation data, 302–303
Multiple regression, 5–6, 13–17, 20, 22, 24, 26–28, 161–162, 169, 183–184, 188, 193, 195–199, 201–202, 205, 209, 211–215, 219, 223–226, 228–231, 237, 240, 246–247, 304–306

N

Naming, 96, 108
Naming latency, 126
Narrative, 185, 190, 193, 209
Narrative passages, 202
Narrativity, 190–191, 193, 195–197, 200–202, 204–205, 207, 211, 240, 245, 247
Natural, 37–42, 63
Naturalistic observation, 288, 296
New argument nouns, 187–188, 195, 197, 200–202, 204–205, 207, 211
New episode, 223, 234, 237–238, 244
New references, 310–311
No-protocol control, 295
Nonautomatic, 210–211
Number of words, 200
Nuisance variables, 308

O

On-line measurement, 36, 63, 130, 133, 137, 143

376 SUBJECT INDEX

On-line methods, 219–220, 244
On-line processing, 105, 108–109
Operations, 213
Organization, 59–63
Organizational words, 43
Organization in memory, 121–122

P

Parabolic transformations, 201
Paragraphs, 94–96, 98, 100–104, 106, 108–110
Parallel, 211, 213
Parsing, 82, 85, 173, 329, 333–334, 351, 355, 358–359, 361
Part correlation, 16
Partial correlation, 23
Partial regression coefficient, 15–16, 18, 23–24, 28
Partialing, 236, 240
Passive verbs, 55
Path analysis, 20–22, 193
Perceptual span, 130–131, 145
Phrase boundary, 37, 39, 47, 55, 58–59, 64
Phrase breaks, 37, 40–41, 44, 53, 58–59, 61
Pictures, 94–96, 101, 107, 112–113
Plans, 290–292
Plausibility, 94–95, 99, 101–102, 105–107, 110–112
Plot units, 290–292
Practice, 34, 40–41, 50, 52–53, 57
Prediction, 255, 258–259, 265, 267–269, 272–274, 282
Priming, 20, 69, 82, 119–127
Principal components, 17
Prior knowledge, 318–321, 323
Probability manipulations, 123
Problem solving schema, 221–223
Process monitoring hypothesis, 132
Processing load, 39, 45, 47, 63
Processing operations, 192
Processing resources, 189–190, 206, 209–210, 214
Production rules, 321
Production systems, 349–353
Production tasks, 289
Pronouns, 35, 43, 45–47, 51, 64
Propositions, 186, 189, 191–192, 195, 197, 200–202, 204–205, 207, 209–210, 212, 328–329, 330–336, 339, 343–345
Proposition recall, 329, 330–331

Prose comprehension, 327–328, 332–333
Protocols, 294–295, 302

Q

Question-asking, 259, 261, 274–280, 283
Queuing model, 77

R

Rapid sequential visual presentation (RSVP), 69–70, 76–80, 91–102, 104, 106–115
Reading rate, 91, 93, 97, 103, 108, 110
Reading for retention, 32, 40, 58, 65
Reading tasks, 310
Reading time, 125, 184, 186, 189, 190–193, 195–197, 199–210, 214–215, 219, 221, 223–224, 226, 228–230, 232–234, 238, 240, 242, 244–247, 254, 259, 272–277, 279, 283–284
Reading time profile, 305–306, 311, 321
Reading units, 39, 42, 44, 63
Reasons, 292–294, 296
Recall, 33, 37, 43, 50–58, 60–61, 63–64, 95, 97–98, 100, 102–103, 105, 107–109, 112, 257, 265, 275, 277, 279, 328–329, 330–333, 341–342
Recognition, 95, 109, 119–127
Regression equation, 184, 195, 197–199
Regressive eye movements, 134, 139–140, 142, 144, 146, 161, 331
Relative clauses, 54
Reliability, 16, 18, 22–24, 37, 63
Reminding, 288–289, 296
Repeated measures design, 26–27
Retention, 31
Residuals, 228–229
Resource allocation, 184, 209–210

S

Saccade, 130, 132–134, 139, 143
Scenes, 292
Schemas, 354–355, 358, 360–361
Scrambled sentences, 94, 101, 107–108
Script theory, 84
Search, 95–96
Self-paced procedure, 69–70, 73, 76, 81, 85–87, 99–100, 106, 115, 306, 310, 318

SUBJECT INDEX 377

Semantic network, 301, 313–314, 323
Semantic processing, 31, 34–35, 49, 51, 54–55, 61, 134
Semipartial correlation, 16, 20, 23–24, 196–197, 200, 202–204, 228, 234
Sentences, 316
Sentence complexity, 244
Sentence reading time, 183–184, 186–187, 193, 195, 197, 199–202, 204–206, 209–211, 214, 219–221, 223–226, 228–230, 232–233, 240, 244, 246–247
Sentence structure, 143
Sentence verification, 95, 305
Serial position, 225–226, 230, 232–234, 235, 236, 242–243, 247
Serial processing, 211
Short-term memory, 191, 192, 210, 327
Shrinkage, 22, 24–25
Simulation models, 300–308, 312, 316, 318–319, 321, 323–324, 328, 344, 345, 346
Single-observation data, 302
Single-sentence procedure, 219–220, 223, 226, 229–230, 233–236, 239–241, 244
Single-word procedures, 220–221, 229, 233–235, 237, 240–241, 243–244
Skimming, 98, 104, 114
Slope coefficient, 184, 188, 197, 199–200, 202–209, 211, 213–214
Slow readers, 31, 34, 40, 48, 50, 57, 59–61, 65
Span of apprehension, 158
Spillover, 46, 71–74, 76, 79–81, 87, 162, 221
Spreading activation, 301, 313
Squared multiple correlation, 16
Standardized partial regression coefficient, 15, 20–22
Staticness, 189, 191, 193, 195–197, 200, 203
Statistical model, 303
Step-wise regression, 18, 23
Stochastic simulations, 302–303, 307
Stories, 256, 261, 265–269, 272–279, 281–284
Strategic processes, 122–125
Structural processing, 31, 48–55, 60–64
Study time, 318–320
Subgoals, 293
Subliminal processing, 97
Suppression, 308–309
Syllable, 35, 40, 42, 44, 48, 64, 186–187, 193, 195–198, 200–201, 204–205, 207, 209–212, 214
Syntactic analysis, 299, 300

Syntactic attributes, 31, 34–35, 49, 51, 61
Syntactic complexity, 54, 94, 111–112, 232
Syntactic variables, 37
Syntax, 49, 186, 188–189, 192, 195, 197, 200, 203, 210–212, 334, 336–342
Systematic questioning, 288, 294, 296

T

Technical prose, 318, 321
Telegraphic prose, 94, 107, 111–112
Text genre, 185
Text grammar, 193
Thematic processes, 289–291, 316
Thinking-out-loud, 253–261, 265, 267, 269, 272–274, 279–285
Top-down processing, 82–83, 87
Topic familiarity, 185, 187
Topic sentence, 310
Transposition data, 77

V

Variability, 37, 302, 309
Verbs, 35, 42–44, 49, 53, 64
Verb complexity hypothesis, 85
Verbal protocols, 288, 294–296
Verification, 288–289, 292, 294–296
Visual clarity, 93–94
Visual masking, 97–98

W

Within-subjects design, 26
Within-subjects variation, 304, 309
Words, 32–33, 35–37, 39, 40–48, 50, 53–54, 57–61, 63–65, 186–188, 195, 197, 201–202, 204–205, 207, 209–212, 214
Word as the stimulus unit, 155–156
Word-by-word reading, 120–121
Word encoding, 361–362, 364–367, 369
Word frequency, 40, 42, 64, 74, 162, 174–177, 188, 195, 197, 200–201, 204–205, 207, 219, 225, 230, 244
Word length, 162–163, 174–177
Word order, 112

Word reading times, 233–235, 237, 241, 243, 246
Word recognition, 82–85
Working memory, 327–329, 332–341, 343
World knowledge, 191
Wrap-up, 151, 166, 177–179
Writing, 280–281, 295, 297

Y

Y-axis intercept, 15

Z

Z-transform, 309

For Product Safety Concerns and Information please contact our EU
representative GPSR@taylorandfrancis.com
Taylor & Francis Verlag GmbH, Kaufingerstraße 24, 80331 München, Germany

www.ingramcontent.com/pod-product-compliance
Lightning Source LLC
Chambersburg PA
CBHW071142300426
44113CB00009B/1056